American Sensations

AMERICAN CROSSROADS

Edited by Earl Lewis, George Lipsitz, Peggy Pascoe,
George Sánchez, and Dana Takagi

American Sensations

Class, Empire, and the
Production of Popular Culture

Shelley Streeby

UNIVERSITY OF CALIFORNIA PRESS
Berkeley · *Los Angeles* · *London*

University of California Press
Berkeley and Los Angeles, California

University of California Press, Ltd.
London, England

© 2002 by
The Regents of the University of California

Library of Congress Cataloging-in-Publication Data

Streeby, Shelley, 1963–
   American sensations : class, empire, and the production of popular culture / Shelley Streeby.
      p. cm.—(American crossroads ; 9)
   Includes bibliographical references and index.
   ISBN 0-520-22314-4 (alk. paper)—ISBN 0-520-
22945-2 (Pbk. : alk. paper)
      1. American fiction—19th century—History and
criticism. 2. Popular literature—United States—
History and criticism. 3. Literature and society—
United States—History—19th century. 4. Social
classes in literature. 5. Sensationalism in literature.
6. Ethnic groups in literature. 7. Imperialism in
literature. 8. Nativism in literature. 9. Race in
literature.   I. Title. II. Series.
   PS374.P63 S77 2002
   813'.309355—dc21

2001006437

Manufactured in the United States of America

10 09 08 07 06 05 04 03 02
10 9 8 7 6 5 4 3 2 1

The paper used in this publication is both acid-free
and totally chlorine-free (TCF). It meets the
minimum requirements of ANSI / NISO Z39 0.48-
1992 (R 1997) (Permanence of Paper). ♾

In loving memory of Kathryn Claire Gage Traul
(1908–1996);
and for my parents,
Joyce Kay and James Alan Streeby

Contents

PART 4: BEYOND 1848

Illustrations

Preface

The argument of this book is that an understanding of the U.S.-Mexican War (1846–1848) and mid-nineteenth-century empire building is required in order to understand the histories of race, nativism, labor, politics, and popular and mass culture in the United States. The popular literature that I examine in *American Sensations* both responded to and helped to define the shifting parameters of nineteenth-century U.S. racial formations, which were powerfully affected by the Gold Rush, the U.S.-Mexican War, the Treaty of Guadalupe Hidalgo, and imperial projects in the Caribbean. The sensational literature of empire also brings into focus the long history of anti-immigrant, nativist movements, which have continued to be an important force in the United States, especially during periods of economic crisis. In addition, this literature makes it clear that working-class institutions, cultures, and movements have responded in diverse ways to debates about U.S. expansion, immigration, and, more generally, the relationship between the United States and the other Americas. Finally, I have tried to show that all of these issues are central to the popular and mass cultures that emerged in the mid–nineteenth century in the wake of the print and transportation revolutions; these forms of popular and mass culture, moreover, importantly influenced later forms of popular entertainment, particularly twentieth-century films. In all of these ways, the U.S.-Mexican War, which some have called a "forgotten war," as well as various imperial ventures throughout the Americas, have crucially shaped U.S. politics and culture.

My earlier efforts to formulate some of these ideas have been incorporated into this study, although often with significant alterations. Parts of chapters 1 and 2 were published as "American Sensations: Empire, Amnesia, and the U.S.-Mexican War," in *American Literary History* (spring 2001). Much earlier versions of parts of chapter 2 were published as "Haunted Houses: George Lippard, Nathaniel Hawthorne, and Middle-Class America," in *Criticism: A Quarterly for Literature and the Arts* (summer 1996): 443–72; and as "Opening Up the Story Paper: George Lippard and the Construction of Class," in *boundary* 2 (spring 1997): 177–203. An earlier version of chapter 9 appeared as "Joaquín Murrieta and the American 1848," in *Post-Nationalist American Studies,* ed. John Carlos Rowe (Berkeley: University of California Press, 2000). I thank all of the publishers for permission to reprint, as well as all of the editors and readers for their helpful suggestions.

I am also grateful for the financial support that allowed me to complete the research for this book and that gave me the much-needed time to write it. A Humanities Research Grant that I received while a graduate student at the University of California, Berkeley, was especially important, for it made it possible for me to visit the American Antiquarian Society in Worcester, Massachusetts, and the Historical Society of Pennsylvania in Philadelphia—and to come away with enough ideas to write a dissertation. Then, in the summer before I started my job at the University of California, San Diego, a fellowship at the Huntington Library allowed me to deepen my knowledge of nineteenth-century popular literature and culture. In the years that followed, generous annual support from the Academic Senate at the University of California, San Diego, as well as two UCSD Chancellor's Summer Faculty Fellowships and two Hellman Fellowships, enabled me to visit the New York Historical Society; the New York Public Library; the Library of Congress; the Bancroft Library at the University of California, Berkeley; Special Collections at Stanford University; and the American Antiquarian Society (again!). I thank all of the librarians at those institutions, and also, for their help with the illustrations, Mary Elings at the Bancroft Library, Jennifer Hanson at the University of Minnesota Libraries, Edward Skipworth at Rutgers University Libraries, Ngadi Kponou at the Beinecke Rare Book and Manuscript Library at Yale University, Lynne Farrington at the Annenberg Rare Book and Manuscript Library at the University of Pennsylvania, and Georgia Barnhill at the American Antiquarian Society. Without the financial support for my research and the help of individuals at all of these institutions, this book could not have been written. I also appreciated the time off from teaching that was provided by a Mellon Dissertation Year Fellowship, two UCSD Faculty Career Development Grants, and a University of California Humanities Research Institute Fellowship.

I wish to thank a number of people at the University of California, Berkeley, where I first began to develop some of the ideas that served as a starting point for this book. The members of my dissertation writing group, especially Steve Rubio, Sandra Gustafson, Kristina Brooks, Kim Drake, Simone Davis, and Arthur Riis, provided careful readings and crucial feedback at an early stage in the project. Bruce Burgett was a particularly important interlocutor; I have benefited from my many conversations with him as well as from reading his work. In addition, I appreciated the insights of Cindy Franklin, Carol Hamilton, Lori Merish, Lauren Muller, Cindy Schraeger, and John Wilkins. The members of my dissertation committee, Mitch Breitweiser, Carolyn Porter, David Lloyd, and Michael Rogin, were also helpful. The support of my dissertation director, Mitch Breitweiser, was particularly valuable, as were Michael Rogin's thought-provoking comments about this project. I also learned a lot from conversations with others in the larger Bay Area community, especially Evan Shively, Karen Adelman, and Greg Greenway.

My contact with students and colleagues at the University of California, San Diego, has contributed immeasurably to *American Sensations*. I have been lucky to have had the freedom to teach the kinds of classes I think are important, and I have enjoyed participating in the Cultural Studies section as well as the English section of the Literature Department. Special thanks go out to all of the graduate students who participated in the "Class Formation and Sensational Popular Cultures," "Natives and Aliens," "The American Renaissance and Empire," and "American Studies and the Politics of Location" seminars. I have benefited from dialogue with, and from reading the work of, my colleagues Rosaura Sánchez, Beatrice Pita, Lisa Lowe, Kathryn Shevelow, Judith Halberstam, Lisa Yoneyama, Rosemary Marangoly George, Michael Davidson, Nicole Tonkovich, Marta Sánchez, Daphne Brooks, and David Gutiérrez. George Mariscal provided a detailed reading of chapter 2, and George Lipsitz generously gave me extensive feedback at an earlier stage in the project, advice that helped me to finish the book. Special thanks to Beatrice Pita, Lisa Yoneyama, Rosaura Sánchez, and Nicole Tonkovich for their participation on conference panels that allowed me to learn from their work as I was producing my own.

I have also benefited from the contributions of colleagues at other institutions. John Carlos Rowe provided a helpful reading of earlier ver-

sions of chapters 2 and 9. And I want to thank Amy Kaplan for her detailed suggestions as well as for encouraging me to write a book that focused centrally on popular and mass culture rather than a more traditional literary study. Kaplan's excellent work on the cultures of U.S.
imperialism has always inspired me. I am grateful to the audiences at the
many conferences where I have delivered early versions of my work, as
well as to everyone who organized or participated on those panels, especially Kathryne V. Lindberg, Susan Gillman, Lauren Berlant, the late
Lora Romero, Kirsten Silva Gruesz, Dana D. Nelson, Frances Smith Foster, Jesse Aleman, and José David Saldívar. My friendship with Kathryne
V. Lindberg has also been important to me during the many years that I
have worked on this project.

My work with the "Post-Nationalist American Studies" group at the
Humanities Research Institute at the University of California, Irvine, in
the fall of 1996 came at a critical time for me, and I want to thank everyone at the HRI, especially the members of my group: Katherine Kinney,
Barbara Brinson Curiel, David Kazanjian, George Sánchez, Henry Yu,
Jay Mechling, and Steve Mailloux. John Carlos Rowe deserves the credit
for convening that group and for gently encouraging us to stay on sched-
ule as we completed our various contributions to the volume that
emerged from the project. I've learned so much from George Sánchez's
own work, from his generous responses to various versions of this manuscript, and from his remarks during our weekly discussions. Katherine
Kinney's suggestions were also a great help, and I want to thank Katherine and Geoff Cohen for their friendship and for their participation on an
ASA panel that we organized on war, memory, and postnationalist American Studies; I first articulated many of the ideas that appear in Part 2 as
we worked together on that panel. Thanks to Barbara Brinson Curiel for
all of our talks and for suggesting that I bring Richard Rodriguez into
chapter 9. David Kazanjian offered a rigorous and helpful reading of an
early version of that chapter. Finally, I'd like to thank everyone in my
group and at UCSD who attended a forum on postnationalist American
Studies that we held in La Jolla, California, in the spring of 1997.

Linda Norton of the University of California Press was a very supportive editor. Senior editor Suzanne Knott and copy editor Martin
Hanft also helped to make this a better book. All three deserve thanks
for their patience and hard work.

Through the years, my family has always been a steady source of emotional support and inspiration. I was lucky enough to have had close relationships with all four of my grandparents—Marie, Jim, Joe, and

Kathryn—as I grew up; I learned a lot from all of them about some of the things that I write about here, and a great deal more. My grandmother Kathryn Claire Gage Traul would have loved to read this book, and it is dedicated to her because of her luminous intelligence, generosity, and keen sense of humor, because of the example that she provided for me, and because of her insistence on the importance of the struggles of working-class people. This book is also dedicated to my mother, Joyce Kay Streeby, and my father, James Alan Streeby, for all of their love, courage, know-how, tenacity, and support. I also continue to greatly enjoy and learn from my conversations with my brothers Patrick, Eric, Victor, Tony, and Jim.

I owe a special thanks to Chris Cunningham, most of all for two decades of intense and sustaining friendship and marathon discussions of movies, books, and politics, but also for letting me use his computer during the summer that I began writing my dissertation in West Hollywood and for letting me stay with him in Jersey City while I was completing the research for the final chapters of this book. I miss running around Los Angeles and San Diego with him more than he knows.

Finally, Curtis Marezø has read innumerable drafts of this book; my ongoing conversations with him as well as the insights I have gained from his own work have shaped it in more ways than I can possibly name. I could never say how much our life together means to me.

ONE

Introduction

City and Empire in the American 1848

Ned Buntline (E. Z. C. Judson), one of the most prolific and successful producers of popular sensational literature throughout the second half of the nineteenth century, is probably best known today for his role in creating the legend of Buffalo Bill. In 1869, Buntline took a train from California, where he had been lecturing on the virtues of temperance, to Nebraska, where he fell in with a group of men who had recently participated in a battle against Sioux and Cheyenne Indians. One of these men was William Cody, an army scout and hunter who had, among other things, made a living by supplying buffalo meat to railroad crews. Soon after Buntline returned East, he published a story for Street and Smith's *New York Weekly* that was nominally based on Cody's adventures, though it was in fact almost entirely invented by Buntline.[1] This novel, *Buffalo Bill, the King of Border Men,* was hugely successful, so much so that it generated more than a hundred sequels by Buntline, Prentiss Ingraham, and many others from the 1870s through the early part of the twentieth century. Buntline's novel also helped to inspire the traveling Wild West show that Richard Slotkin has called "the most important commercial vehicle for the fabrication and transmission of the Myth of the Frontier" in the late nineteenth century.[2] In 1899, Buffalo Bill's Wild West show replaced a performance of "Custer's Last Fight" with a re-creation of the battle of San Juan Hill and thereby, according to Slotkin, marked "the Wild West's evolution from a memorialization of the past to a celebration of the imperial future." The substitution, he says, dramatized "the imperial frontier as the logical extension of the continental frontier."[3]

If this genealogy identifies Buntline with the trans-Mississippi West, the Western as a popular genre, and the imperial frontier of the late nineteenth and early twentieth centuries, however, another influential narrative about Buntline and popular culture turns eastward, especially to New York City, focusing particularly on Buntline's participation in the Astor Place theater riot, his role in shaping white working-class culture through various forms of sensational literature such as journalism and the urban melodrama, and his significance in the story of the emerging split between high and low culture. In 1848, Buntline moved from Boston to New York, where he began to write massive, muckraking urban-gothic novels such as *The Mysteries and Miseries of New York* (1848), *The B'hoys of New York* (1850), *Three Years After* (1849), and *The G'hals of New York* (1850). In these novels, he helped to develop the white working-class characters of Mose and Lize, the Bowery B'hoy and G'hal who were also the stars of incredibly popular New York theatrical melodramas written by Benjamin Baker.[4] During this time and intermittently for many years afterward, Buntline edited his own newspaper, *Ned Buntline's Own,* for which he claimed thirty thousand readers, who were drawn to his sensational stories as well as, presumably, the notices for meetings of nativist organizations such as the Order of United Americans and the Order of United American Mechanics that appeared in its columns.

Buntline was also jailed for inciting the Astor Place theater riot, the event that Lawrence Levine claims dramatically marked a "growing chasm between 'serious' and 'popular' culture" in the mid–nineteenth century.[5] On May 10, 1849, U.S. militiamen killed at least 22 and wounded more than 150 people who were part of a rowdy crowd gathered outside the theater, where the British Shakespearean actor William Charles Macready was pelted by lemons and chairs hurled by Bowery B'hoys, among others. If, as Eric Lott argues, the Astor Place riot indicates a "class-defined, often class-conscious, cultural sphere," Buntline was one of the most important figures and producers within that sphere; indeed, Lott calls him "a direct link between the new culture of amusements and growing social fissures."[6]

Although both of these accounts—one that focuses on public culture and class formations in Northeastern cities, the other on the West and the imperial frontier of the late nineteenth century—testify to Buntline's considerable significance in the production of nineteenth-century popular culture, neither traces the connections between city and empire in his work or examines in any detail the imperial adventure fiction that he wrote for the publishers of mass-produced story papers and pamphlet novels. Throughout his career, but especially in the 1840s and early 1850s, however, Buntline produced a considerable number of adventure novels with foreign settings, including two U.S.–Mexican War romances: *The Volunteer: or, The Maid of Monterey* (1847), a hundred-dollar-prize story that was serialized in the popular Boston-based story paper *Flag of Our Union* and then reprinted as a pamphlet novel, and *Magdalena, the Beautiful Mexican Maid* (1846). He also wrote several novels set in Panama, Cuba, Florida, and Peru. These sensational adventure novels, as well as many others that Buntline produced throughout the century, suggest that his role in developing a popular culture that transmitted the myth of an imperial frontier need not be isolated at the end of the nineteenth century, for his fiction was closely imbricated with empire in an earlier period as well, encompassing the Seminole War and other U.S. conflicts with indigenous peoples; the U.S.-Mexican War; imperial rivalries with Spain, Britain, and other European powers in the Americas; and filibustering expeditions to Cuba.[7]

The multiple connections between city and empire that can be traced in Buntline's life and literature are certainly not unique to his sensational body of work, for many mid-nineteenth-century producers of popular culture returned to this double axis of city and empire. In his groundbreaking study *Mechanic Accents: Dime Novels and Working-Class Culture in America* (1987), Michael Denning suggests that an "emphasis on the early westerns, tales of the frontier and of Indian fighting, as the dominant, most characteristic, and most interesting genre" of popular sensational literature has made it difficult to comprehend the significance of other genres, such as the "mysteries of the city," which he argues was the "first genre to achieve massive success and to dominate cheap fiction."[8] But many producers of cheap sensational literature worked with both of these genres—as well as others, such as the international romance and imperial adventure, which foregrounded issues of empire—to explore the mysteries of the capitalist city and to address issues of U.S. empire-building.[9] The sensational literature of this period responds, in other words, to a double vision of Northeastern cities divided by battles over class, race, national origin, and religion, on the one hand, and on the other to scenes of U.S. nation- and empire-building in Mexico, Cuba, and throughout the Americas. To understand this important early form of popular culture, then, we need to attend to and bring together discussions of empire and the American 1848 as well as studies of urbanization and class formation during this period.

1848 AND EMPIRE

Although *American Sensations* addresses several different instances of U.S. empire-building, the U.S.-Mexican War is central to this study of popular and mass culture, class, and racial formations in the American 1848. Sometimes called a forgotten war, this conflict nonetheless had formative effects on constructions of race, class, and nation in the mid–nineteenth century and on the Civil War itself. Indeed, some of the most influential American Studies work on the significance of 1848 has focused on the U.S.-Mexican War as a cause of the Civil War. In *The Impending Crisis: 1848–1861* (1976), historian David Potter argued for the importance of the events of 1848 by suggesting that the "victory over Mexico" had "sealed the triumph of national expansion, but it had also triggered the release of forces of sectional dissension" that culminated in the Civil War. Although a precarious "national harmony" had previously depended upon "the existence of a kind of balance between the northern and southern parts of the United States," he suggested, the war "disturbed this balance, and the acquisition of a new empire which each section desired to dominate endangered the balance further."[10] In his 1983 study of Herman Melville, Michael Rogin drew on Potter's analysis when he coined the periodizing phrase "the American 1848" to explain how in "the wake of the Mexican War," slavery "threatened to destroy the Union."[11] Comparing the events in the United States to the European revolutions of 1848, Rogin claimed that while "the Europe of 1848 disintegrated in class war" (102), in the United States the "internal stresses" that threatened the "external triumph" of nationalism "revolved around slavery" (103). Both Potter and Rogin thereby called attention to the connections between the U.S.-Mexican War and the Civil War, between foreign conflict and domestic discord, and between the acquisition of a new empire and the increasingly divisive debate over slavery.

Although these (re)periodizing narratives of the American 1848 had important implications for the fields of U.S. history and literature, where the antebellum period marker often effectively meant that the Civil War displaced other nineteenth-century conflicts, they still implicitly constructed the United States-as-America and stopped short of addressing the broader hemispheric significance of the year 1848. But for scholars working in the fields of Chicano and Latino Studies, 1848 had long been considered a crucial year in the history of inter-American power relations.[12] Building on the premises of this body of work, in *Border Matters,* José David Saldívar asked, "What might happen if we viewed 1848 not merely as an episode in the violent history of the borderlands of Nuestra América? What if U.S. imperialism were displaced from its location in a national imaginary to its protoempire role in the Américas and the rest of the world?"[13] The present study addresses these questions by examining how the popular sensational literature of 1848 and thereafter both reveals and struggles to conceal the role of U.S. imperialism in the Americas in the mid–nineteenth century. The adjective "American" in *American Sensations* indicates both the hemispheric dimensions of this imperial activity and the process whereby U.S. Americans appropriated the term "America" for themselves, a process that was both bolstered and complicated by what I call the "culture of sensation."

To understand the hemispheric dimensions of U.S. imperial activity in the American 1848, it is important to place the U.S.-Mexican War in the context of other inter-American encounters and conflicts. While the end of the war in 1848 led to the remapping of U.S. national boundaries and the addition of vast new lands, the discovery of gold in California early that spring drew miners and other workers to the area from all over the world.[14] After the war ended, many disbanded U.S. soldiers hurried to the gold fields, where some became nativists and sought to exclude so-called foreigners from the mines.[15] Other war veterans signed up to fight in behalf of the "white" race against the Maya Indians in Yucatán, where a bloody and prolonged "Caste War" had broken out; or followed the filibuster William Walker to Sonora, Mexico, and Nicaragua; or joined filibustering expeditions to take over Cuba.[16] Meanwhile, in 1848, Polk thought about annexing Yucatán before unsuccessfully trying to purchase Cuba from Spain, and U.S. designs on Cuba were made manifest again and again during the 1850s as several attempts were made to purchase the island. After 1848, the United States became more aggressive in the Caribbean, striving for commercial domination of the Dominican Republic as well as Cuba. Central and South America also became objects of imperial interest during the debates over the meaning of the Monroe Doctrine that took place between the United States and various European powers. All of this suggests that, far from being an isolated moment or an aberration, 1848 was a "watershed year" in the history of U.S. empire, a year when the boost to U.S. power in the world system provided by the U.S.-Mexican War, combined with the distracting social upheavals in Europe, made the United States a major player in the battles for influence in and control of the Americas.[17]

The year 1848 must also be placed within a longer history of U.S. empire-building at the expense of North American Indians. During the congressional debates about whether the United States should intervene in the Caste War in Yucatán in 1848, which I address in chapter 6, politicians raised questions about the political relationship between Mexican Indians and creoles that also had important implications for the relationships between U.S. Indians and white U.S. Americans. Some criticized the creoles there for not getting rid of "their" Indians as effectively as the U.S. Americans had, while others suggested that Indians were citizens in Mexico and thus were a part of the "people." For both sides, however, debates about imperial intervention abroad recalled the ongoing history of "Indian Wars" and the dispossession of indigenous peoples in North America. Notable recent moments in that nineteenth-century history include the removal of the Cherokees and other tribes to lands west of the Mississippi in the 1830s; the Black Hawk War of 1832, fought against the Sauk and Fox; the wars against the Seminole Indians in Florida in the 1830s and early 1840s; as well as genocidal attacks on California Indians.[18] After the signing of the Treaty of Guadalupe Hidalgo in 1848, the increasing westward movement of white U.S. settlers provoked conflicts in the newly acquired lands of the Great Plains, the Southwest, and the Northwest, as well as in older possessions such as Minnesota; a war there erupted in 1862 between Dakota Indians and white settlers that resulted in the deaths of hundreds of settlers and Indians, the defeat of the Dakotas, and the hanging of thirty-eight Dakota men, the largest mass execution in U.S. history.[19] The resistance of Indians to the encroachments of white settlers in lands acquired by the rapidly expanding United States during the long, imperial nineteenth century is another important part of the story of the American 1848.

It has become conventional to distinguish, as Slotkin does, between the continental expansionism of 1848 and the overseas empire-building, often identified with imperialism as such, of the 1890s. Along with William Appleman Williams, Walter LaFeber has been one of the most influential theorists of a late nineteenth-century New Empire that depended on the pursuit of the strategic control of widely dispersed foreign markets, military bases, and transportation routes rather than "continental" expansion, the acquisition of large amounts of land, and direct political control.[20] Although LaFeber called this formation a New Empire, he also insisted that it represented a continuation rather than an

PART I

American Sensations

absolute break. In his 1963 study *The New Empire: An Interpretation of American Expansion, 1860–1898,* he began by asserting that "the climactic decade of the 1890's can be properly understood only when placed in the context of the last half of the century."[21] But although his title indicated that 1860 was the beginning date of his study, LaFeber repeatedly returned to even earlier moments as he searched for the origins of this empire. He claimed at the outset, for instance, that "[m]odern American diplomatic history began in the 1850s and 1860s" (1); he noted that it was during the late 1840s that U.S. exports, which he considered a key stimulus of the New Empire insofar as they provoked a search for even more foreign markets, "began their rapid climb to the dizzying heights of the twentieth century" (1); he cited the long nineteenth-century history of the Monroe Doctrine and U.S. interest in expansion into the Pacific and the Caribbean in the 1840s and 1850s; and he even argued, contra his title, that the "roots of this empire date back at least to the 1843–1860 period, which climaxed in the taking off of the economy" (7). Even though he kept returning to the period roughly marked by the American 1848 in his account of the roots of the New Empire, he ultimately suggested that "the dynamic and characteristics" of this empire indicated a "new departure" (60) that was best marked by the 1890s, "the watershed period of American history" (101).

Building on the analysis of LaFeber and others, *American Sensations* draws upon this conception of a New Empire but also seeks to trouble the distinction between the "continental frontier" of 1848 and the "imperial frontier" of 1898 in a number of ways—first, by arguing for the importance in the earlier period of the idea of a commercial empire that would not involve the incorporation of vast territories or large populations, especially of nonwhite peoples. As chapter 4 suggests, this conception of empire was often endorsed by those who opposed the annexation of any densely inhabited parts, or all, of Mexico in 1848; it was also championed by those who did not favor the acquisition of Cuba but who hoped to profit from the neocolonial commercial domination of that Caribbean island. Second, especially in chapters 5 and 8, I complicate the identification of the post-1848 period with "continentalism" by recalling the strong interest in overseas or noncontiguous empire-building, especially in Cuba but also in Nicaragua, the Dominican Republic, and other sites even during these years. Finally, this study suggests that to describe the earlier moment of expansion as continental and the second as imperial is to risk naturalizing the post-1848 boundaries of the nation as well as the violent expansionism that made possible the reconstruction of those boundaries. As one historian has argued, advocates of U.S. "continentalism" often opposed U.S. expansion to European practices by asserting that the United States "was engaged in a domestic and thereby inevitable policy of territorial extension across the continent"; the United States thereby "redefined the conventional terms of foreign relations by domesticating its foreign policy."[22] In other words, by claiming that contiguous lands were part of the continental "domestic" space rather than foreign territory, U.S. continentalists promoted an exceptionalist understanding of the United States as a nonimperial nation.

Although the western boundary of the "continent" was marked by the Pacific Ocean, its southern and northern boundaries were by no means self-evident to those with designs on Mexico and Canada; and to many Mexicans, for instance, U.S. expansionism southward certainly registered as "imperial." While it is important to understand the specificities of the imperialisms of 1848 and 1898, to reserve the term "imperialism" for the 1890s is to reproduce that tenuous and certainly ideological distinction and to marginalize or even dismiss a much longer history of U.S. imperialism in the Americas. It contributes to that historical amnesia that subtends what Amy Kaplan has called "the simple chronology that plots the U.S. empire emerging full blown at various stages of the twentieth century to step into the shoes of dying European empires."[23] Marking the 1890s as the originary moment for periodizations of U.S. imperialism also makes it difficult to connect the anti-imperial struggles of the twentieth century with those that took place before that decade.

On the other hand, I do not mean to suggest that 1848 marked the "true" origin of U.S. imperialism. Such a claim would ignore the longer history of U.S. empire-building that antedated 1848. Furthermore, attention to 1848 as an important moment in the history of U.S. empire must not elide the Spanish and Mexican oppression of indigenous peoples in the Americas or the struggles of indigenous peoples against U.S. empire-builders. Without taking 1848 as an origin point for U.S. imperialism, then, *American Sensations* insists not only on the differences but also on the many connections between 1848 and 1898, between "continental" imperialism and the New Empire, and between U.S. empire-building and class and racial formations in the metropolis.

1848 AND THE CITY

The American 1848 also marks a crucial period in the transformation of urban white working-class cultures. As Richard Stott suggests, massive immigration during this period remade the white working class in the late 1840s and early 1850s.[24] From 1845 through the early 1850s, the repeated failures of the potato crop in Ireland culminated in the Great Famine, which provoked the departure of one and a half million Irish to the United States.[25] These immigrants were joined by large numbers of German speakers from central Europe, many of whom were fleeing agrarian, economic, and political turmoil.[26] By 1855, the majority of New York City's population was foreign-born, and about 85 percent of those immigrants were from Ireland or central Europe.[27] In Philadelphia, foreign-born workers constituted 40 percent of the male labor force by the end of the 1840s: two-thirds of those were Irish and about 20 percent were German.[28] And in Boston, Irish workers arrived in large numbers, also in the late 1840s.[29] During the 1840s and the 1850s these new immigrants, along with native-born whites who moved from the country to the city during those years, contributed to the two highest rates of urbanization, measured by decade, ever recorded in U.S. history.[30] In other words, U.S. cities grew more quickly than ever before, more dramatically than they ever would again, and this population surge further divided the Northeastern urban working classes along lines of religion and national origin as well as ethnicity and race.

These dramatic changes in urban life were accompanied by many others. Innovations in print technology included the development of stereotyping and electrotyping; the invention of Napier's cylinder press and then, in 1846, Hoe's ten-cylinder press with revolving type, which produced up to twenty thousand sheets per hour; as well as Fourdrinier's paper-making machine, which was first introduced in the 1820s and which by 1860 had cut paper costs in half.[31] These technological innovations supported the emergence in the mid-1830s of the first mass-circulation daily newspapers such as Benjamin Day's New York *Sun* and James Gordon Bennett's New York *Herald*.[32] By 1840, more newspapers were published in the United States than in any other nation; in 1850, there were 2,526 newspapers being published throughout the country.[33] The 1840s also witnessed the proliferation of other kinds of periodicals, from elite journals such as the *North American Review;* to sentimental publications such as *Godey's Lady's Book* and *Graham's Magazine;* to cheap, sensational story papers such as the *Flag of Our Union* and the *Star Spangled Banner;* as well as a host of other, smaller publications. Improvements in transportation and communications facilitated the ever more rapid circulation of information and print. With the opening of the Erie Canal in 1825, which provided crucial linkages to Western markets,

New York adopted the nickname "The Empire State," and the construction of other canals soon followed.[34] Transportation by steamboat in the first half of the mid–nineteenth century was another significant innovation, but the most important development in transportation was undoubtedly the completion of extensive railroad networks in the 1840s and 1850s.[35] The rise of the railroad not only increased the circulation of newspapers and other periodicals, but it also changed reading practices. Ronald Zboray suggests that as "the future belonged to the railroad, so the book and periodical inevitably took their place on the passenger's lap as part of the package of modernity."[36] The invention of another important marker of modernity, the telegraph, took place in 1844, and in 1848 the Associated Press was formed to "harness" its "technological advantages."[37]

These demographic patterns and technological and cultural innovations in the American 1848 both resulted from and contributed to larger urban economic shifts in this period. Manufacturing, spurred by the arrival of large numbers of new immigrants, became more and more important to the national economy from the 1840s through the 1860s.[38] According to Sean Wilentz, at the end of the 1840s, the "manufacturing complex" that was organized around the "metropolitan center" of New York was "probably the fastest-growing large industrial area in the world."[39] Early industrialization did not mean, however, that most workers toiled in large, heavily capitalized factories; instead, industrialized labor took place in a variety of settings, including small mechanized workshops, machineless manufactories, where tasks were subdivided, and outwork manufactories, where skilled labor took place on site but unskilled work was "put out" to contractors or outworkers.[40] Wilentz suggests that by the late 1840s, "New York's position as the nation's leading manufacturing site was secure and the split labor market and the fragmentation of the artisan system were complete."[41] During this period, Philadelphia, too, Laurie argues, was transformed "from a commercial port with a broad but shallow industrial base to a major center of commodity production, whose industrial output reached $140 million and was second only to [that of] New York on the eve of the Civil War."[42] Uneven industrialization in Philadelphia slowly broke up the artisan system, with native-born whites holding on to most of the better jobs; two-thirds of the German immigrants took on skilled work; about 40 percent of Irish immigrants were employed as unskilled laborers; and another 40 percent toiled as hand loom weavers or worked in trades that were being transformed by industrialization.[43] And the influx of new immigrants and the availability of cheap labor in the late 1840s made Boston the fourth most prominent U.S. manufacturing city in the decades that followed.[44] In all of these cities and elsewhere, too, shifting demographics along with the changing organization of production, the decline of the artisan system, and the spread of wage labor significantly altered urban working-class life.

The heterogeneous labor cultures that arose in Northeastern cities during this period have been documented by a number of historians. Some scholars have emphasized working-class political and economic institutions; others have focused on popular culture, examining cheap literature, blackface minstrelsy, the firemen's company, and the world of the Bowery B'hoy and G'hal as indices of the transformation of working-class cultures in the middle of the nineteenth century. Although that work has provided important insights into class formations during those years, much of it has marginalized issues of race. On the other hand, David Roediger, Eric Lott, and Noel Ignatiev, among others, have offered important revisions of these earlier models. In *The Wages of Whiteness* (1991), Roediger made a significant breakthrough in exploring the absence of a compelling analysis of race in many classical Marxist theories of class and in works of new labor history. Drawing on the work of W. E. B. Du Bois and others, Roediger examined how working-class whiteness and conceptions of free labor were constructed in the antebellum period in opposition to blackness and to slavery. In *Love and Theft* (1993), Eric Lott similarly argued for the centrality of race in working-class culture and insisted that working-class whiteness was defined in relation to blackness in the antebellum minstrel show, but he emphasized "how precariously nineteenth-century white working people lived their whiteness" and suggested that blackface was a "peculiarly unstable form."[45] Finally, in *How the Irish Became White* (1995), Noel Ignatiev focused on antebellum Irish immigrants and investigated how "the Catholic Irish, an oppressed race in Ireland, became part of an oppressing race in America."[46] A key to this transformation, he concluded, was "a society polarized between white and black" that rewarded the Irish for seeking "refuge" in "whiteness" and for subordinating "county, religious, or national animosities" to "a new solidarity based on color."[47] Each of these important studies relies primarily upon a binary, black/white model of race to understand the reformation of working-class whiteness in the decades before the Civil War, and all three for the most part marginalize issues of empire and inter-American conflict as they examine the centrality of race in reshaping Northeastern urban working-class communities.

Because U.S. labor historians often separate their accounts of economic and social unrest from the story of U.S. empire, the linkages between mid-nineteenth-century class and racial formations, empire, and international conflict have rarely been examined.[48] Alexander Saxton's *The Rise and Fall of the White Republic* (1990) is, however, an especially insightful effort to explore some of these linkages. In this dazzling study of nineteenth-century class politics and mass culture, Saxton reads story papers and dime novels, mass-circulation newspapers and the labor press, blackface minstrelsy, and Westerns, as well as other cultural forms, against the broad canvas of the transformation of party politics and class and racial formations during the century. Saxton begins with the claim that in the nineteenth-century United States, "a theory of white racial superiority originated from rationalizations and justifications of the slave trade, slavery and expropriation of land from non-white populations."[49] These concerns require him to engage issues of national expansion and empire-building along with issues of slavery and black/white race relations. Two of Saxton's conclusions are particularly important for my analysis of class, race, empire, and mass culture in the American 1848. First, he demonstrates that in the wake of the emergence of mass culture and the extension of white male suffrage in the early nineteenth century, the Democrats, the Whigs, and later, the Republicans all had to engage mass cultural forms and develop distinct positions on empire-building and slavery as they struggled to construct cross-class coalitions of white male voters. Saxton's research thereby shows how early forms of mass culture were implicated in these attempts by the political parties to construct cross-class alliances among whites. Second, Saxton suggests that different varieties of white egalitarianism were the glue that held these coalitions together. White egalitarianism involves a leveling of distinctions among whites at the expense of nonwhites. The United States, Saxton argues, "sought to provide equal opportunities for the pursuit of happiness by its white citizens through the enslavement of African Americans, extermination of Indians, and territorial expansion at the expense of Indians and Mexicans."[50] Saxton associates white egalitarianism especially with the Democrats, but he shows how the Whigs had to develop their own version of this appeal to different classes of whites even though they struggled to reconcile egalitarianism with older hierarchies of class and status. The Whig version of racism was also "softer" than that of the Democrats, which meant that the Whigs still adhered to racial hierarchies but were more likely to favor the demise of slavery and to oppose expansion, although Saxton insists that they tended toward soft racial policies for a variety of class-based reasons. By bringing together a discussion of mass culture and class politics with an analysis of debates over slavery, Indian removal, Indian genocide, and national expansion, Saxton made a significant contribution to discussions of class and race in the American 1848 and throughout the nineteenth century.

In other studies as well, Saxton has been one of the most important contributors to the scholarly literature on class and race, particularly because of his ability to compare multiple racial formations.[51] In an essay entitled "Race and the House of Labor" (1970), Saxton analyzed "white America's three great racial confrontations" with Indians, African slaves, and Asian contract laborers in order to explore the ways in which class consciousness "cut at right angles to racial identification," leaving a legacy of racism that has haunted the house of labor.[52] But although in this essay and in *The Rise and Fall of the White Republic* Saxton made an analysis of national expansion and the expropriation of Western lands central to his account, he had little to say about white U.S. America's racial confrontations with Latinos or cultural production that focuses on Mexico and the Americas. And although in the last three decades a significant body of work has emerged that extends Saxton's insights about the overlapping histories of class and racial formation, few have considered the significance for U.S. class formations and popular culture of inter-American imperial encounters in 1848 and beyond. One of the theses of *American Sensations,* however, is that class and racial formations and popular and mass culture in Northeastern U.S. cities are inextricable from scenes of empire-building in the U.S. West, Mexico, and the Americas. The present study builds on the framework developed by Saxton, drawing particularly on his accounts of white egalitarianism and the transformation of the political parties. But it also seeks to make the U.S.-Mexican War and the mid-nineteenth-century U.S. history of imperial encounters in the Americas central to an analysis of class, race, and popular and mass culture in the American 1848, for during this period, languages of labor and race were shaped in significant ways by inter-American contact and conflict.

Debates about the whiteness of working-class immigrants, for example, were importantly affected by the participation of immigrant soldiers in the U.S.-Mexican War. By 1847, the majority of soldiers in the U.S. Army were foreign-born, and about a quarter of them were Irish.[53] During the late 1840s, as I argue in chapter 2 and throughout Part 2, representations of Irish soldiers, which recurred in much of the war literature, condensed an array of anxieties about the Irish as weak links in the united front of whiteness and about the boundary between the foreign and the domestic. These anxieties were compounded by the fact that the desertion rate was higher in this war than in any other foreign war and that a significant number of immigrant soldiers switched sides and fought for the Mexicans.[54] Although the much greater numbers of Irish soldiers who continued to fight for the United States suggest that war service, like blackface minstrelsy, helped to facilitate the incorporation of the Irish into the white working class and into the expansionist and anti-nativist Democratic Party, the literature on the San Patricios, a brigade of foreign soldiers who fought for Mexico, and the many representations of the Irish as traitors to the white nationalist cause also register what seemed to some to be startling resemblances between the United States as an imperial Protestant "Anglo-Saxon" power invading and despoiling Catholic Mexico and Protestant England as the oppressor of Catholic Ireland. The anti-Catholic riots that took place in several U.S. cities during this period must have also made many immigrant and Catholic U.S. soldiers wonder just what they were fighting for.[55] According to historian Robert Ryal Miller, an 1847 broadside issued by Santa Anna that invited Catholic U.S. soldiers to desert to the Mexican side included the question: "Can you fight by the side of those who put fire to your temples in Boston and Philadelphia?"[56]

Nativism in general and white working-class nativism in particular are also illuminated by the history of mid-nineteenth-century imperial expansion. During the 1840s and 1850s, nativist political parties, secret societies, and other organizations flourished, and white workers, especially those involved in crafts that had not yet been transformed by industrialization, developed their own nativist institutions (such as the Order of United American Mechanics) that flourished in Philadelphia and New York City.[57] Rather than erasing class, nativism often "conveyed a strong sense of class identity," as Bruce Laurie argues, but it also registered the split between the old, largely native-born working class and the new immigrants.[58] And if nativist anti-Catholic battles took place at the polls, in the work of public associations and secret societies, and on the streets of U.S. cities, they also erupted in Mexico during the war as churches were destroyed, sacked, or deliberately desecrated and as U.S. soldiers and journalists disparaged Mexican Catholics.[59] What is more, as we shall see in the chapters that follow, debates about whether all or part of Mexico could or should be incorporated into the United States frequently turned on both questions of race and fears about what it would mean to add large numbers of Catholics to the union. Many nativists and anti-imperialists viewed both Mexicans and Irish Catholics as slaves to priestly and papal authority and as insufficiently independent to make good republican citizens. On the other hand, expansionist sentiment was often driven by fears—which were fanned by nativist tracts such as Lyman Beecher's *Plea for the West* (1835) and Samuel F. B. Morse's *Foreign Conspiracy against the Liberties of the United States* (1844–46)—of an imperial Catholic conspiracy to take over the West.[60] For both sides, however, questions of nativism, anti-Catholicism, and white national unity were all framed by imperial and inter-American conflicts.

In *Whiteness of a Different Color,* Matthew Frye Jacobson suggests that U.S. expansion and conquest "pulled for a unified collectivity" of whites even as "nativism and the immigrant question fractured that whiteness into its component—'superior' and 'inferior'—parts."[61] In the American 1848, imperial expansion both fortified and undermined working-class whiteness, for immigrant soldiers were incorporated into the white U.S. military forces to fight a Mexican army that was widely viewed as made up largely of nonwhites, even as nativist and anti-Catholic sentiments were reanimated during the war in ways that fractured whiteness along lines of religion and national origin. This complicated dynamic nonetheless reinforces Jacobson's claims about "the influence of empire in the racial formation of 'white' Europeans" in the United States.[62]

If issues of empire-building influenced debates about nativism and immigrant whiteness, however, they also both shaped and were in turn affected by ideas about land reform promoted by many urban working-class advocates in the 1840s and 1850s. Thomas Hietala suggests that for the Democrats, expansionism became the "antidote to the toxins of modernization"; in other words, Democrats "hoped that new territory and additional markets" could ward off the evils of "industrialization and its inevitable concomitants such as urban congestion, uncertainty of employment, class stratification, labor agitation and domestic strife."[63] But this theory of new Western lands as a "safety valve" that might mitigate urban class tensions has been identified most closely with the National Reform Association, a popular mid-nineteenth-century land reform movement that was led by the radical George Henry Evans and that had significant ties to working-class organizations and the labor press. Saxton, for instance, contends that the National Reform position that "western land offered the solution for social and economic problems of eastern cities" underpinned the project of territorial expansion.[64] In

Part 3, especially in chapter 6, I argue that although some land reformers, such as New York City politician Mike Walsh, championed imperial
expansion, others, such as Evans himself, criticized the U.S.-Mexican
War and the acquisition of vast new territories. But although such opposition resulted from many different motives, the antiwar positions of
these land reformers and working-class advocates often reveal a privileging of white labor and white forms of property, even as they participate in fierce public debates about the meaning and significance of these
concepts. By placing land reform within the context of the U.S.-Mexican
War, discussions of the annexation of all or part of Mexico, and responses to the Maya Indian uprisings in Yucatán, *American Sensations*
insists that emerging theories of free land and free labor in the American
1848 were shaped by arguments about the war and imperial expansion.

While Roediger and others have discussed the role of race in the making of the U.S. working class by examining comparisons made by white
workers between chattel slavery and the competing concepts of free labor
and wage or white slavery, one of the premises of Part 3 of this study is
that ideas about Mexican labor and land arrangements as well as the
complex array of racializations that were identified with Mexico also
played a significant part in such comparisons.[65] In *Racial Fault Lines,*
Tomás Almaguer suggests that mid-nineteenth-century proponents of
free labor ideology "believed that social mobility and economic independence were only achievable in a capitalist society unthreatened by
nonwhite populations and the degrading labor systems associated with
them."[66] By citing other forms of "unfree labor" associated with nonwhite populations, such as Mexican peonage and Asian contract labor,
Almaguer demonstrates that a nonbinary model of race is required in
order to understand the emergent racialized ideal of free labor. Chapter
7 of *American Sensations* builds on Almaguer's insight by exploring comparisons of chattel slavery, free labor, and Mexican labor arrangements
in the American 1848. One important key to these comparisons was the
Wilmot Proviso, an amendment that was passed by the House but not
by the Senate; it would have required that slavery and other forms of involuntary servitude be banned in any territory acquired from Mexico
after the war. While scholarly discussions of the Wilmot Proviso rarely
consider forms of unfree labor other than slavery, Part 3 suggests that
debates about Mexican labor and land systems figured significantly in
the construction of free labor ideology and in the intensifying division
between North and South. Finally, Part 4 examines how inter-American
conflict and imperial expansion affected the racialization of people of

Mexican origin and other Spanish speakers in the wake of the American 1848. Instead of providing a safety valve for the pressures of urbanization and class stratification, the newly acquired Western lands became battlefronts where class conflicts colored by race and nationalism erupted in the gold fields of California and elsewhere. Chapter 9 concludes that an investigation that isolates the nation-state as a unit of analysis cannot adequately track the changes in these post-1848 class and racial formations, for both were powerfully shaped by international migrations, inter-American contact, and global transformations.

THE "MECHANIC ACCENTS" OF EMPIRE

At the outset, I claimed that the career and literary corpus of the sensationalist Ned Buntline reveal many of the multiple connections between city and empire in the American 1848. Not only Buntline, however, but also George Lippard and A. J. H. Duganne—two of the other writers that Denning discusses in the part of *Mechanic Accents* that focuses on this period—wrote both the mysteries-of-the-city fiction that Denning calls "the genre of 1848" and sensational stories set in Mexico. Many mysteries-of-the-city novels, moreover, open up onto questions of empire. George Lippard's *New York: Its Upper Ten and Lower Million* (1853), for instance, begins by deploring the monstrous growth of capitalism and the inflation of property values in New York City, but this urban gothic plot is entwined with another that involves an international Catholic conspiracy to take over the West and a virtuous mechanic's dream of establishing a worker's utopia on the Pacific coast. And although Buntline's *The B'hoys of New York* opens with a typical scene of a miserable prostitute making her way down Broadway late at night, his story of urban crime crucially involves a Spanish pirate who simultaneously schemes to seduce the virtuous heroine and to foment a revolution in Cuba. Another of Buntline's urban gothic novels, *The Mysteries and Miseries of New Orleans* (1851), starts off as an urban cautionary tale of seduction and revenge, but about halfway through it turns into a story of imperial adventure in Cuba, when Buntline's protagonist joins a filibustering expedition. In all of these novels, the mysteries-of-the-city are entangled with questions of empire, and this entanglement suggests that "the paradoxical union of sensational fiction and radical politics" that Denning identifies with this moment in the history of cheap literature must be assessed in relation to a politics of empire-building as well as a politics of class.[67]

But the politics of empire in early sensational fiction, like the politics of class, are far from uncomplicated, and the fears and contradictions that shadowed contemporaneous political and literary debates about the U.S.-Mexican War, as well as other imperial encounters, also haunt many of these sensational visions of imperial expansion. Despite the widespread support for the troops in Mexico and the appeal of exceptionalist ideas about the nation's future, the war was extremely controversial, even during the 1840s. In New England it was especially unpopular, because of pacifist and religious beliefs, as well as fears that it was being fought to extend slavery, that it would increase the power of Southern interests, and that it might mean incorporating large numbers of Catholics and nonwhites into the republic.[68] Ironically, many Southeasterners, notably John C. Calhoun, also opposed it, because they thought that slavery could not thrive in Mexico, where it had been abolished; that it might therefore increase the power of Northern antislavery interests; and that contact with, or incorporation of, foreigners and nonwhites might threaten what Calhoun called the government "of the white race."[69] Support for the war and for expansion was strongest in the West, in the mid-Atlantic region, and in New York City.[70] In general, many Democrats defended Polk's expansionist policies, though there were exceptions, such as Calhoun, and although fears of the extension of slavery provoked Pennsylvania Democrat David Wilmot's famously divisive proviso.[71] Many Whigs, on the other hand, denounced Polk for invading Mexico and argued for a "No Territory" position, though some supported the acquisition of California and other more sparsely settled portions of northern Mexico and almost all of them continued to vote to send more supplies and troops to Mexico.[72] But although most Democrats favored the acquisition of at least some territory, many who supported Polk and the war still argued, like the Whigs, against the annexation of densely populated Mexican areas.[73] The New York–based *Democratic Review,* for instance, where John O'Sullivan famously coined the term "Manifest Destiny," defended Polk and welcomed the acquisition of California and New Mexico, but it argued that the "annexation of the country to the United States would be a calamity. Five million ignorant and indolent half-civilized Indians, with 1,500,000 free negroes and mulattoes, the remnants of the British slave trade, would scarcely be a desirable incumbrance, even with the great natural wealth of Mexico."[74] The war and national expansion, in other words, brought to the fore contradictions in the concept of Manifest Destiny and disagreements about its meaning even among those who promoted it.[75]

Although Buntline, Lippard, and other early sensationalists frequently criticized party politics and declared that their commitments were irreducible to the platforms of either the Whigs or the Democrats, these debates about the war, expansion, and Manifest Destiny resound throughout the pages of sensational war literature. And that literature is especially revelatory of the ways that debates about empire shaped and organized the working-class subcultures and social movements that Denning aligns with some of the authors of mysteries-of-the-city literature. Buntline's two U.S.–Mexican War novels, for instance, anticipate the Westerns that he produced late in his career as well as the nativist forms of white working-class protest that he elaborated in his urban reform literature. Both *The Volunteer* and *Magdalena*, like most of the other war novels published in story papers such as the *Flag of Our Union* and the *Star Spangled Banner*, are international romances. In these novels, relationships between U.S. soldiers and Mexican women, especially, are used to figure possible postwar relationships between nations. But although one might expect these novels to celebrate U.S. intervention and promote the annexation of all or part of Mexico, many raise questions about the justice of the war and express various fears about the incorporation of Mexico and Mexicans into the union. Even as Buntline celebrates the U.S. citizen-soldier in *The Volunteer*, for instance, his hero calls the conflict a "war of invasion," and in *Magdalena*, the romance between a U.S. soldier and a Mexican woman ends tragically when the heroine discovers the hero's corpse on the battlefield at Buena Vista. Although Buntline supported the U.S. troops and glorified U.S. military leaders, his proslavery, nativist, and white egalitarian beliefs made him wary of unequivocally endorsing a policy of U.S. empire-building in Mexico, and those same beliefs would play a significant role in the working-class nativism that he later promoted in his newspapers, in his novels, and on the streets of New York City.[76]

Nativism and white egalitarianism also shaped representations of Mexico and the war by poet, novelist, and reformer A. J. H. Duganne. Duganne was born in Boston, and the combination of nativism, antislavery beliefs, and anti-imperialism that characterizes much of his work was not uncommon in New England during the period. In the 1840s, when he lived in Philadelphia, Duganne produced mysteries-of-the-city novels such as *The Knights of the Seal; or, The Mysteries of the Three Cities* (1845) and *The Daguerreotype Miniature; or, Life in the Empire City* (1846). He also became involved in George Henry Evans's land reform movement, so much so that historian Jamie Bronstein has called

him the "poet" of "National Reform."[77] Duganne's poetry, which championed the laborer's right to the soil and included titles such as "The
Landless," "Homes for the Homeless," and "The Unsold Lands," appeared in such reform newspapers as the *Voice of Industry* and Evans's
Young America. Despite his advocacy of utopian reforms that might
enable large numbers of small freeholders to settle in the West, however, Duganne denounced U.S. imperialism in the long poem "Manifest
Destiny" (1855), in which he argued against war in general and sati-
rized the rhetoric of Manifest Destiny in particular. But he also saw the
war as an unfair contest between the "Yankee Nation" and the "Mexic
mongrel," and his anti-imperialism derived from nativist beliefs about
the importance of keeping foreigners and Catholics out of the republic
as well as from pacifist, radical republican, and antislavery convictions.
After moving to New York around 1850, he was elected to one term as
a representative of the nativist Know-Nothing Party in the state assem-
bly and later served as lieutenant colonel of a company of New York Volunteers during the Civil War.[78]

In the early 1860s, Duganne also contributed several stories to the
first series of Beadle's famous dime novels, including *The Peon Prince; or,
The Yankee Knight-Errant. A Tale of Modern Mexico* (1861) and its sequel, *Putnam Pomfret's Ward; or, A Vermonter's Adventures in Mexico*
(1861). These novels, which take place in the 1840s, register the contradictions of anti-imperialism, white egalitarianism, and the emerging
ideal of free labor during the antebellum period. Duganne's dime novels
neither rehearse nor champion U.S. military victories in Mexico; he is
much more interested in imagining how a coalition composed of creoles
and Indians might remake Mexico in the image of the United States by
ending the system of debt peonage and enacting other liberal reforms.
But Duganne's representation of Mexico as a space of anarchy, lawlessness, and race-mixing; his emphasis on peonage as a system of degradation that destroys republican independence; and his Yankee's racist invective against "greasers" and "ingens" all suggest some of the limits of
his anti-imperialist position. Duganne's stories are but two of the scores
of dime novels that were written about Mexico and the Mexico-U.S. borderlands, and they should remind us that the West in the dime novel
Western is a hemispheric and global, and not only a national, space. And
Duganne's poetry and fiction as well as his involvement in the cultures
of labor and land reform also suggest how intimately questions of land,
labor, and nativism in Northeastern cities were connected to issues of
empire.

George Lippard's sensational literature and advocacy of the working class also revolved around this double axis of city and empire. The work of David Reynolds, Denning, and others has put Lippard back on the literary map as one of the most popular writers of his age and as the author of sensational, quasi-pornographic mysteries-of-the-city literature such as *The Quaker City; or, The Monks of Monk Hall* (1845), *The Empire City* (1850), *The Killers* (1850), and *New York*.[79] But Lippard's urban novels often include scenes of empire; he wrote two novels about Mexico, and his involvement with the labor and land movements also made questions of U.S. empire-building both relevant and pressing for him. Like Duganne, Lippard promoted the cause of land reform and even founded a secret society as a way to popularize National Reform principles. Whereas Duganne, Evans, and other land reformers opposed the war, Lippard enthusiastically supported it, despite later misgivings. In a speech before the Industrial Congress in Philadelphia in 1848, Lippard based his urbanoid, utopian hopes for the future on the existence of "free land" in the West: "I know that the day comes when the interests of the Rich and Poor will be recognized in their true light,—when there shall be left on the surface of this Union no capitalist to grind dollars from the sweat and blood of workers, no Speculator to juggle free land from the grasp of unborn generations. When every man who toils shall dwell on his own ground, and when Factories, Almshouses, Jails, and the pestilential nooks of great cities, shall be displaced by the Homesteads of a Free People."[80] In contrast to Buntline and Duganne, whose nativist beliefs made them fearful of adding large numbers of Catholics and "foreigners" to the nation, Lippard often denounced organized nativism (his work, however, is not devoid of anticlerical and anti-Catholic sentiments); as a result, Lippard was less worried about the incorporation of all or part of Catholic Mexico and more supportive of the war and annexation.[81] Lippard's views were shaped by his family's German immigrant background and his engagement with the fiercely divided artisan republican labor culture of Philadelphia.[82] Although his version of labor radicalism was a specifically Protestant one, he was less hostile to immigrants and Catholics than Buntline and Duganne were, and that paradoxically made him more approving of the project of U.S. expansion.

Denning suggests that Lippard was one of the "auteurs" in this new culture industry, "the D. W. Griffith of cheap stories: the studio system will follow."[83] That is, while in the 1840s and 1850s authors such as Lippard were able to retain some creative control of their cultural production, in the field of cheap, sensational literature there were also increasing pressures on individual authors to respond to the emerging conventions of commercial publishing: to write stories of a certain length that conformed to popular formulas that, in Christine Bold's words, left "no room for the usual authorial decisions or opportunities for original creation."[84] This does not mean that authors of sensational literature were automatons who simply followed the dictates of the "fiction factory." Especially in the decades before the Civil War, the relationships between authors and publishers were much more complex than that; authors, after all, helped to develop the very conventions and genres that eventually became dominant, and in the earlier period, writers were rarely given specific instructions about what to write.[85] But although *American Sensations* focuses on particular authors of sensational literature, such as Lippard, Buntline, Duganne, Edward Ellis, Mary Denison, Metta Victor, and John Rollin Ridge, this study is also an analysis of various forms and genres of early sensational popular and mass culture. In the chapters that follow, I examine labor and land reform newspapers; Lippard's and Buntline's politically engaged story papers; the avowedly depoliticized but nonetheless still political mass-produced story papers of the late 1840s and 1850s, such as the *Flag of Our Union;* the pamphlet novels, where story-paper literature was often reprinted; the dime novels produced after 1860; crime gazettes and outlaw stories; and the *corridos,* or ballads, produced by diasporic *mexicano* communities. In each case, I explore the relationships among the various forms of popular and mass culture, contemporaneous social movements, and the larger political culture, and I argue that although some of these forms are more explicitly pitched to a working-class audience, others strive for a mass audience that cuts across classes.

In chapter 2, "George Lippard's 1848: Empire, Amnesia, and the U.S.-Mexican War," I read several sensational novels by Lippard in relation to his journalism for the *Quaker City,* the labor story paper that he edited from late 1848 through early 1850, as well as to *The White Banner,* a collection of some of the writing and speeches he produced for the Brotherhood of the Union, a secret society that he organized to promote land reform and other working-class causes. I examine three different sensational genres of 1848: mysteries-of-the-city literature (*The Empire City* and *New York*); apocalyptic historical and religious fantasy (*The Entranced* and *Adonai*); and U.S.–Mexican War literature (*Legends of Mexico, 'Bel of Prairie Eden*). Although critics often isolate Lippard's mysteries-of-the-city literature from these other types of writing, particularly the war novels, all of these genres come together in the *Quaker*

City weekly, for Lippard serialized all three types of literature in his story paper during the late 1840s. In the 1849 issues, excerpts from *The Entranced, The Empire City,* and *Legends of Mexico* were juxtaposed, along with news of the European revolutionaries, replies to letters from readers, remarks on land reform and local politics, and columns promoting some of the many radical projects he helped to organize, including the Brotherhood of the Union and a cooperative for seamstresses. This chapter argues that despite the mass appeal of novels such as *The Quaker City; or, The Monks of Monk Hall,* much of Lippard's literature was closely tied to the working-class communities that he tried to represent, but it also insists that working-class politics and empire-building were inextricably knotted together in Lippard's vision of 1848.

Part 2 focuses on story papers such as the *Flag of Our Union,* the *Star Spangled Banner,* and the *Flag of the Free,* which were widely disseminated in the late 1840s in the wake of the print and transportation revolutions. In chapter 3, "The Story-Paper Empire," I suggest that these mass-produced story papers were very different from Lippard's labor story paper: the publishers cut back on news coverage, tried to please an audience composed of multiple classes, and sometimes claimed to exclude offensive subjects. Nonetheless, these papers still included various sorts of political commentary, and the stories that they serialized during the years of the U.S.-Mexican War were often about the war itself, as well as imperial adventure in other foreign lands. In chapter 4, "Foreign Bodies and International Race Romance," I compare these story-paper novels about the U.S.-Mexican War with congressional debates about the annexation of all or part of Mexico and the amalgamation of "foreign" peoples. I argue that boundaries of gender, sexuality, and class were crucial to reconceptualizations of the boundaries of race and nation, because the "international romance"—a subgenre of imperial adventure fiction—positioned women as symbols of the Mexican nation and tried to construct cross-class coalitions between native-born U.S. white men at the expense of immigrants and nonwhites. Chapter 5, "From Imperial Adventure to Bowery B'hoys and Buffalo Bill: Ned Buntline, Nativism, and Class," builds on this discussion by foregrounding Buntline's story-paper novelettes as well as some of his other novels of imperial adventure, particularly those that involve Cuban filibustering. I conclude that the white Protestant constructions of manhood and fraternity that Buntline champions in his imperial adventure fiction also shape the working-class nativism that he advocated in his story paper *Ned Buntline's Own.*

Part 3 addresses the labor and land reform press of the late 1840s, the dime novel of the early 1860s, and the "Western" as a subgenre of cheap sensational literature. Chapter 6, "The Contradictions of Anti-Imperialism," assesses the significance of nativism and white egalitarianism in the anti-imperialist literature produced by land reformers and others during this period. Chapter 7, "The Hacienda, the Factory, and the Plantation," examines Duganne's two dime novels about Mexico and argues that this kind of literature established many of the conventions that would later reappear in twentieth-century "Western" movies set in Mexico. Finally, chapter 8, "The Dime Novel, the Civil War, and Empire," explores the relationships between inter-American conflict and the sectional battle over slavery in several dime novels published during the Civil War years. One of the central claims of this chapter and section is that the complex, hemispheric dynamics of expansion that are represented in this fiction, which engage multiple contemporaneous internal and inter-American conflicts in the U.S. South, Minnesota, Cuba, Nicaragua, and Texas, largely disappear in discussions of the dime novel Western that place the West squarely within a national frame. This chapter looks especially closely at the substantial number of early dime novels that were written by women, and it suggests that although the "mechanic accents" that Denning has taught us to listen for are still audible in this literature, Northern white women and other dime novel authors often promoted a more "middling" version of white egalitarianism that did not entirely support the leveling of class distinctions among whites; instead, they championed an expansive "middle" position that was opposed to the perceived excesses of both the lower and upper classes.

The final chapter, "Joaquín Murrieta and Popular Culture," which comprises Part 4, "Beyond 1848," is about inter-American sensational crime literature, including outlaw novels, police gazettes, and *corridos* that focus on the California social bandit. I also draw on various discourses about racial categories and citizenship rights in order to explore the complicated relationship between popular cultural forms and the state's attempts to impose and stabilize a racial order. John Rollin Ridge's 1854 novel influenced many retellings of the Murrieta story, including the *corridos;* several dime novel versions; the 1936 movie *The Robin Hood of El Dorado;* plays in both English and Spanish; and revisions published in Mexico, Spain, France, and Chile. Paying special attention to the Murrieta *corridos* produced by diasporic working-class communities, as well as the *California Police Gazette* (1859) version, I argue that as this sensational crime story migrates across national boundary lines, it showcases the violence of U.S. nation- and empire-building, incessantly registers and sometimes crosses emerging class and racial boundaries, and thereby foregrounds the complex relationships between newly defined groups of "natives" and "aliens."

THE CULTURE OF SENSATION

As my title indicates, *sensation* is a key word in this study. When I refer to the culture of sensation, I mean to indicate two related and often overlapping spheres of popular culture. First is a specifically literary sphere: the sensational literature that began to proliferate in the 1840s and that was roughly classified as a "low" kind of literature in relation to a more middlebrow popular sentimentalism as well as to the largely nonpopular writing that would subsequently be enshrined as the classic literature of the American Renaissance. Second, the culture of sensation references a wider spectrum of popular arts and practices that includes journalism, music, blackface minstrelsy, and other forms of popular theater such as Yankee, Bowery B'hoy, and frontier humor as well as sensational melodrama and, in the broadest terms, the political cultures that were aligned with these popular forms. Although in this book I give a good deal of attention to sensational literature, one of my premises is that literary sensationalism cannot be understood in isolation from the larger culture of sensation that surrounded it. For this reason, I explore the formats (newspaper, story paper, crime gazette, dime novel series) that provided reading contexts for sensational literature as well as the connections between these publications and the wider arenas of political life and social movements, especially the labor, abolitionist, nativist, and land reform movements of the era.[86] Throughout, I investigate the diverse "body politics" of this culture of sensation, and I assume that, although sensationalism is the idiom of many mid-nineteenth-century working-class cultures, it is also a racializing, gendering, and sexualizing discourse on the body.

It is important to remember, of course, that the popular is, as Néstor García Canclini suggests, "something constructed" rather than "preexistent," and that the culture of sensation, like other forms of popular culture, offers what Canclini calls "stagings of the popular" rather than access to a fictive, unified body of the nation-people.[87] In addition, I agree with Canclini and others that popular cultures exist in tension with capitalist modernity rather than outside it, and so I would also question judgments that define "authentic" popular culture as that which escapes "industrialization, massification, and foreign influences."[88] Although some might contend that the term "mass culture" would be more appropriate for the objects of my analysis and although I do indeed use it at times in this book, I tend to reserve it for cultural forms that try to suppress class antagonisms in order to appeal to a broad, cross-class audience. The conjunction of the terms "sensation" and "mass culture" might misleadingly suggest, moreover, that I am about to make a Frankfurt School–style argument about the always mesmerizing and pernicious effects of the new mid-nineteenth-century culture industries; it should be clear by now that I am not going to do that. This does not mean, however, that I will simply celebrate sensational popular cultures as sites of resistance and discount the effects of industrialized and commodified modes of cultural production and reception, as cultural studies scholars have sometimes been accused of doing.[89] The culture of sensation does indeed bear some of the responsibility for the long U.S. history of nativism, empire-building, and white egalitarianism. Although I argue that the responses to these issues among the producers and consumers of the culture of sensation were diverse rather than routinized and utterly predictable, it nonetheless remains generally true that, as Rogin suggests, early forms of U.S. popular culture "created national identity from the subjugation of its [nonwhite] folk."[90] I would only add that this makes it even more necessary to come to terms with the culture of sensation and its effects on U.S. history and culture.

Toward that end, I need to say more about how sensational literature became widely popular in the 1840s and after, largely as a result of changes in print technology and transportation. In *Cultures of Letters,* Richard Brodhead suggests that in the mid–nineteenth century the literary field began, slowly and unevenly, to be stratified into three different modes of literary production: a nonpopular "high" culture, a domestic or middlebrow world of letters, and a "low" culture comprising story-paper fiction and dime novels.[91] In *Beneath the American Renaissance,* David Reynolds similarly distinguishes between the "classic" literature of the American Renaissance writers, a "genteel sentimental-domestic genre," and the sensational literature that proliferated in the wake of the penny press: "seamy social texts such as penny papers, trial reports, and crime pamphlets; Romantic Adventure fiction (much of it quite dark) and the more politically radical genre of Subversive fiction; and erotic and pornographic writings."[92] Reynolds claims that between 1831 and 1860, improvements in print technology spurred the publication of cheap sensational literature, so much so that the proportion of sensational novels increased to almost 60 percent of the total number of novels published, and the proportion of "genteel-sentimental" novels dropped to around 20 percent.[93]

Finally, Denning also argues for a "three-tier" public in his account of this period.[94] He emphasizes that the relatively low price of this literature—story papers usually cost five or six cents, although pamphlet novels were sold for twelve to twenty-five cents, and books in Beadle's famous series could be purchased for a dime—made it much more affordable for a wide audience, including many working-class readers, than other forms of literature.[95] According to Ronald Zboray, even paperbound books were a luxury in these years; cheap literature was much more accessible to urban dwellers than to those in rural areas, but the low price of penny papers and story papers "put reading material in reach of even poorer farmers and the working class."[96] These "three tiers" were not entirely separate worlds, for especially in the 1840s and 1850s audiences overlapped, writers might contribute to different types of publications or issue their work in different formats, and various literary modes, conventions, genres, and devices crossed over or were mixed together within the different tiers. Still, within emerging literary hierarchies these types of literature occupied different positions, even though the differences were not absolute and even though such distinctions were still in the process of being elaborated and institutionalized.

It may be helpful to compare the popularization of sensational literature in the United States during the nineteenth century with its popularization in Europe. In *Mixed Feelings*, her study of British Victorian sensationalism, Ann Cvetkovich suggests that the late-nineteenth-century middle-class sensation fiction that she analyzes was "the target of attack" by critics "because it represented the entry into middle-class publishing institutions of the sensationalism that characterized the working-class literature of the preceding decades, such as G. M. W. Reynolds's *Mysteries of London*, and the stage melodrama."[97] In the United States, cheap sensational literature, theatrical melodramas, and other low, sensationalized body genres of the 1840s and 1850s were the equivalents of this early sensational British cultural production.[98] In his work on what he calls "the cinema of attraction," which focuses especially on early silent films that seek to deliver a series of visual and sensory shocks, Tom Gunning has emphasized its roots in sensational European theatrical melodrama. Around 1860, he suggests, "the term 'sensation' migrated from its primary meaning of the evidence of the senses to describe the centre-piece of a new form of theatrical melodrama," which soon became known as the "sensation drama": "The new theatrical use

of the term targets the spectator as the key in this modernisation of melodrama, focusing on the effect of the scene, its powerful assault on the
senses of the audience." Although Gunning suggests that the term seems
to have originated in the theater, he also links it to late nineteenth-century
sensation novels and the sensation press. "One could argue," he claims,
"for the term being one of the key words of the popular culture of
modernity."[99] The history of this popular culture of modernity must be
pushed back at least to the 1840s, however, for the penny press, sensational theatrical melodrama, and cheap sensational literature were already important parts of the cultural scene in the United States during
that decade.

In his essay "An Aesthetic of Astonishment," Gunning links this sensational popular culture of modernity to "urbanisation with its kaleido-
scopic succession of city sights, the growth of consumer society with its
new emphasis on stimulating spending through visual display, and the
escalating horizons of colonial exploration with new peoples and new
territories to be categorised and exploited."[100] He suggests that as a distinct aesthetic mode it emphasized a mixture of fear and thrills; presented
a series of visual or sensory attractions, moments of revelation, and non-
narrative spectacle rather than offering a psychological narrative of development; reached "outward" to "confront" the spectator through a
"marked encounter, a direct stimulus, a series of shocks" instead of encouraging detached contemplation; and frequently showcased the un-
beautiful, the grotesque, and the freakish.[101] It is not difficult to see the
continuities between Gunning's sensational theater and cinema of attractions, on the one hand, and the sensational popular culture of the
mid–nineteenth century, on the other, which similarly combined thrills
and terror; frequently showcased visual tableaux and action scenes
rather than emphasizing domestic scenes and the interior, psychological
development of rounded characters; aimed to provoke extreme embodied responses in readers; and often lingered on the grotesque and the horrible. Gunning's observation that "city street scenes" and "foreign
views" were two of the most important genres of an early cinema of attractions should also recall the sensational literature of the previous century, which, as I have argued, focused especially on the mysteries of the
city and imperial adventure in Mexico, Cuba, and the U.S. West. That
is, city and empire have long been a double feature of sorts in the sensational popular cultures of U.S. modernity.

Although U.S. sentimental-domestic literature often includes glimpses
at least of urban scenes and foreign views and although the urban and

the foreign are frequently crucial to the plots, they are rarely the central focus in the way that they are in a good deal of sensational literature. Certainly sensational literature lingers on potentially shocking and disturbing aspects of such scenes and views more than sentimental literature does. That is part of what distinguishes sensationalism from sentimentality as a structure of feeling: sentimentalism generally emphasizes refinement and transcendence, whereas sensationalism emphasizes materiality and corporeality, even or especially to the point of thrilling and horrifying readers.[102] In his study of Edgar Allan Poe and mass culture, Jonathan Elmer has suggested that although sentimentalism tries to regulate the feelings and to disincarnate the bodies that it invokes, literary sensationalism more often works at a distance from "the openly recuperative didacticism of sentimentalism" and revises sentimentalism's "dropping out of the materiality of discourse" by insisting upon "a corporeal or material or affective leftover," the "remains" that cannot be refined or transcended.[103] This interest in the material and the corporeal makes sensationalism an aesthetic mode that supports an emphasis on laboring bodies and the embodied relationships that workers have to power; I take up this point in the next chapter, which is about George Lippard's sensational "body politics" in the American 1848.[104] Although Lippard's sensationalism contributes to an attack on class hierarchies, however, he also "sensationalizes" constructions of race and nation and thereby promotes empire as the antidote to such hierarchies despite the doubts and contradictions that haunt his war literature. This brings us back to a point that I have repeated in this introduction, that the emphasis on the body in the culture of sensation must be assessed in relation to a politics of not only class but also race and empire.

Blackface minstrelsy is probably the most widely discussed sensational body genre of the mid–nineteenth century. Recent debates among Saxton, Lott, Roediger, Rogin, and others have helped us to understand how nineteenth-century working-class men, many of whom were Irish immigrants, constructed white identities by staging blackness. As Rogin puts it, blackface "made new identities for white men by fixing the identities of women and African Americans."[105] This form of sensational popular culture was generally aligned with a post-Jacksonian Democratic coalition that incorporated many working-class European immigrants by promoting a more expansive whiteness defined in opposition to blacks and other nonwhites. But the sensational body genres of empire were also significant racializing discourses, and, as in the case of blackface, race, gender, and sexuality were often complexly entangled. In Part 2, I show

how boundaries of race and nation were drawn and redrawn in relationship to boundaries of gender and sexuality and how some authors
of sensational U.S.–Mexican War romances appealed to nativist ideologies of white Protestant manhood to construct cross-class affiliations
at the expense of Mexicans. Although despite his scorn for party politics Lippard generally promoted the more expansive whiteness that was
also championed by the Democrats, authors such as Ned Buntline articulated more fears about the incorporation of "foreign" bodies into
the republic and constructed whiteness differently. In Part 3 I examine
how sensational ideologies of race, gender, and sexuality figure in literature opposing the U.S.-Mexican War as well as in the dime novels of
the Civil War era, and in Part 4 I argue that post-1848 California crime
literature imports sensational racial stereotypes from U.S.–Mexican War
romances in order to collapse differences between "native" and "immigrant" Spanish-speakers in California and to racialize them as essentially
alien. Each part of *American Sensations* suggests that the sensational
popular cultures of the American 1848 racialized bodies in ways that are
irreducible to black/white binaries.

As my examples imply, a good deal of sensational literature was written by men, and much of it promotes competing ideologies of heroic
masculinity and mobilizes representations of women's bodies as symbols
of race and nation. That is true of both pro- and anti-imperial literature,
including the sensational *corridos* about Joaquín Murrieta that I discuss
in my conclusion. This raises the question: is sensationalism basically a
male discourse? That is, could we characterize sensationalism as a set of
genres written exclusively by, for, and about men? In Parts 2 and 3, especially, I show how publishers of sensational story-paper literature and
early dime novels appealed to a female as well as a male audience. And
throughout the book, I insist that sensationalism is not just about men,
for constructions of womanhood and sexuality are also central to this
literature. Nonetheless, tropes of masculine violence certainly recur in
many sensational texts. Part of this has to do with the ways in which
sentimentality was increasingly being identified with middle-class women
and with feminization in the mid–nineteenth century, even as sensationalism was more often associated with a masculine, working-class resistance to sentimentality. Although it is certainly true that many men deployed the discourse of sentimentality, ideologies of separate, gendered
spheres and of essential gender differences, which intensified in the
mid–nineteenth century, still exerted pressures on definitions of popular body genres in this period.[106] It is also the case that working-class

masculinity was often defined in opposition to what were constructed as "feminized" middle- and upper-class men who participated in the culture of sentiment.

This emerging opposition between a "feminized" sentimentality and a "masculinized" sensationalism can be observed as early as 1845 in George Lippard's novel *The Quaker City.* As Lippard describes a horrible pit beneath Monk Hall where his character Devil-Bug keeps the loathsome corpses of his victims, he suddenly interrupts the action to denounce male sentimentalists:

> Shallow pated critic with your smooth face whose syllabub insipidity is well-relieved by wiry curls of flaxen hair, soft maker of verses so utterly blank, that a single original idea never mars their consistent nothingness, penner of paragraphs so daintily perfumed with quaint phrases and stilted nonsense, we do not want you here; Pass on sweet maiden-man! Your perfumes agree but sorrily with the thick atmosphere of this darkening vault, your white kid-gloves would be soiled by a contact with the rough hands of Devil-Bug, your innocent and girlish soul would be shocked by the very idea of such a hideous cavern, hidden far below the red brick surface of broad-brimmed Quaker-town. Pass by delightful trifler, with your civet-bag and your curling tongs, write syllabub forever, and pen blank verse until dotage shall make you more garrulous than now, but for the sake of Heaven, do not criticise this chapter! Our taste is different from yours. We like to look at nature and at the world, not only as they appear, but as they are! To us the study of a character like Devil-Bug's is full of interest, replete with the grotesque-sublime.[107]

As David Reynolds notes, Lippard often combines sentimental and sensational modes in order to attack the former: he not only undercuts an idealizing discourse of domesticity by emphasizing "the shattering of homes as the result of obsession, betrayal, lust, and greed" but also identifies middle-class sentimental literature with "the bourgeois world of trite morality."[108] In this passage, we can see how Lippard depicts this world of sentimentality as feminized, emasculating, and bourgeois, while he describes his own sensational style, "replete with the grotesque-sublime," as a more masculine and realistic form of representation. This passage is suggestive of the ways that sensational literary modes were often identified with men and with a "masculine" resistance to feminization, middle-class pieties, and a genteel sphere of sentimental literary production.

Nonetheless, just as men participated in the culture of sentiment, so too did women contribute to the culture of sensation. During the 1850s and 1860s, in the years following the U.S.-Mexican War, female writers such as E. D. E. N. Southworth, Louisa May Alcott, Mary Denison, and

Metta Victor used the U.S. borderlands, Mexico, Cuba, and other sites of international conflict in the Americas as settings for sensational stories of passion, revenge, and adventure. As Amy Kaplan has pointed out, in *The Hidden Hand,* certainly one of the most popular novels of the nineteenth century, Southworth traces connections among the slums of New York City, a plantation in Virginia, and the battlefields of the U.S.-Mexican War.[109] And in Alcott's short story "Pauline's Passion and Punishment" (1863), which was published in *Frank Leslie's Illustrated Newspaper,* the relationship between the passions and the foreign has much to do with the place of Cuba in both imperial and anti-imperial fantasies and of the "Spanish" within U.S. racial economies. In one of Mary Denison's many dime novels, *The Prisoner of La Vintresse; or, The Fortunes of a Cuban Heiress* (1860), her characters move back and forth between Cuba, New York City, and rural New York; while in *The Two Hunters* (1865), dime novelist Metta Victor connects New Orleans to Spain, New York City to St. Louis, and St. Louis to Mexico via the Santa Fe trail. Reading these stories in their original forms, in newspapers, illustrated story papers, and dime novels, makes it especially apparent that these stories of female power and passion were also attempts to represent bodies along racial lines that were strongly shaped by the long nineteenth-century history of imperialism in the Americas.

Racial hierarchies that are inseparable from empire-building are on full display, for example, in the pages of *Frank Leslie's Illustrated Newspaper,* in which Alcott's prize-winning story "Pauline's Passion and Punishment" was first published in January of 1863. During the late 1850s and the 1860s, the paper included editorials on the Monroe Doctrine and on the U.S. rivalry with Spain and Britain over Central America and the Caribbean, as well as many articles supporting William Walker, the notorious filibuster; sketches of exotic, desirable lands in places such as Nicaragua, Guatemala, and San Antonio, Texas; and articles on Haiti and Mexico. Although the paper claimed during the Civil War years that all attempts "at aggression on Spanish rights...originated and [were] supported from the South alone" (28 September 1861), in fact throughout the 1850s the paper repeatedly advocated the takeover of various sites throughout the Americas controlled by Britain as well as Spain. For example, an editorial of 6 November 1858 suggested that but for a "foreign element in our midst, we should have had Cuba and Central America long ago." Advocating the cause of Walker in Nicaragua, one writer concluded that "the fairest portion of the world, the transit between two great oceans, the highway connecting our Atlantic and Pacific ports, must be in the hands of a vigorous race, and...American institutions, and American spirit, if not the American flag must wave over Central America" (5 January 1856). Although in the 1850s the paper's writers explicitly longed for the U.S. flag as well as U.S. influence to wave over the Americas, during the 1860s they more often cast the United States in the role of the "natural head and protector of the American republics" (1 February 1862). The many references in the paper's pages to the "mongrel republics" of the Americas (for example, 2 July 1859) should make us ask, however, just what and whom the United States was try-ing to protect: the paper's writers even suggest that "Spanish blood," whether "pure Castilian" or "mixed with other races," is a curse "wher-ever it is the predominant fluid, if, indeed, such a filthy puddle can ever rise to the dignity of a liquid" (2 July 1859). Judgments such as that are typical of the newspaper, and they suggest that an emergent Northern commercial imperialism was far from free of the white supremacist val-ues that also underpinned newly repudiated (but not for long) forms of territorial expansionism.

"Pauline's Passion and Punishment" begins on a Cuban coffee plan-tation and involves an ill-fated marriage between a Cuban man, Manuel, and Pauline, a companion to the daughter of Manuel's guardian. In many ways Alcott undermines the racial hierarchies that the story paper pro-motes, but she still identifies "southern" races with the passions. At the outset, Pauline burns with passion and plots revenge because she has been betrayed by her lover, who has married another woman for her money. Initially, she is described as a distinctively northern-European type—the "carriage of [her] head," for instance, reveals "the freedom of an intellect ripened under colder skies"—which is defined in opposition to the "southern": "[T]here was no southern languor in the figure, stately and erect; no southern swarthiness on fairest cheek and arm; no southern darkness in the shadowy gold of the neglected hair."[110] But as she indulges her passions and carries out her revenge, which involves marrying the handsome, wealthy Manuel and making her former lover mad with jealousy and ill-founded hopes, she changes dramatically. Not only do her eyes and face become dark or black when she gives way to passion, but she is also explicitly compared to an "Indian on a war trail" (6) and "an Indian on the watch" (22). What is more, Manuel himself is defined by his "southern temperament" (5), which makes him more sen-sitive, expressive, emotional, and graceful, but which is also said to in-clude a "savage element that lurks in southern blood" (6). Although she initially married Manuel because of the money and social position he could give her, at the end she realizes that she truly loves him. When her former lover pushes Manuel off a cliff just as she achieves her ultimate revenge, the story ends and Pauline's "long punishment" begins.

Alcott makes Manuel into an ideal masculine type, despite or perhaps because of his "southern blood." This ideal masculinity, however, paradoxically involves a certain feminization. In other words, Manuel is a superior man precisely because his southern "blood" brings with it many traits that were conventionally coded as womanly. In this way, Alcott reverses the judgment of the international romances of 1848, which as we shall see in Part 2, often implied that the feminization of the man of Spanish or Mexican origin made him an undesirable mate. She also complicates the racial orthodoxy of Leslie's writers that identified Spanish "blood" with degradation and pollution. But she continues to identify "southern" races with savagery and the passions, even as she at times countervalues those traits. And despite the quite idealized representation of Manuel, he remains subordinate to the imperious Pauline, obeying her every command. So although Alcott revises gender orthodoxies, that revision depends upon ideas about race and "blood" that are inseparable from imperial and inter-American rivalries.

Brodhead has shown how later Alcott repudiated her earlier sensation fiction in order to focus on producing sentimental-domestic literature because sensationalism was viewed as "the literary emanation of lower-class culture." Brodhead suggests that a woman could "cross over into this genre and social culture, but not without violating the shieldedness from indecent knowledge that establishes the proper 'women' of middle-class society."[111] Certainly there were more risks for women in writing this kind of sensational literature, since it could be viewed as both unwomanly and declassing, and so it is not surprising that there are far fewer female-authored than male-authored sensational texts in the mid–nineteenth century. As a result, when women publish sensational forms of literature, such as the many dime novels that I examine in chapter 8, they often combine sentimental *and* sensational modes to quite different ends than those of George Lippard: sensational aspects of the text, which focus on violence, shocking scenes, bodies, and the grotesque are often framed by sentimental devices that reassert genteel values and middle-class respectability. As we shall see, sensational women's writing also qualifies the white egalitarianism promoted by male sensationalists. Female authors of dime novels often refuse to dismantle class hierarchies completely, instead valorizing a middle position opposed to the perceived excesses of both the upper and lower classes.

This different take on class corresponds to women's greater vulnerability, I would suggest, to charges that a familiarity with "low" life, whether in urban or foreign spaces, was irredeemably degrading. This should not, however, blind us to the fact that many women wrote sensational literature despite the threat of stigma: almost one-third of the Beadle's dime novels published during the Civil War years were written by women.

Throughout *American Sensations,* I focus on a host of neglected and out-of-print sensational texts, such as the substantial body of early dime novels written by women, in an effort to revise both literary history and historical paradigms. Although important work on sensational popular cultures has been published in the last two decades, the relative critical neglect of sensational literature, along with the isolation of sensational urban genres from imperial genres, has contributed to an amnesia about the connections among working-class culture, popular culture, and imperialism in nineteenth-century U.S. history. As we move away from narratives that posit the working class as the privileged actor in a universal history, it is important to revise our models of class so that we can better understand the historically contingent relationships among class, gender, race, sexuality, and empire. I hope that this book as a whole will contribute to a reconsideration of the centrality of entanglements of class, race, gender, sexuality, and empire in nineteenth-century U.S. culture.

TWO

George Lippard's 1848

Empire, Amnesia, and the U.S.-Mexican War

[T]he dead men, piled in heaps, their broken limbs, and cold
faces, distinctly seen by the light of the morning sun, still
remained, amid the grass and flowers, silent memorials of
yesterday's Harvest of Death.
> —George Lippard, *Legends of Mexico*

They are strangely superstitious, these wild men of the
prairie, who, with rifle in hand, and the deep starlight of the
illimitable heavens above, wander in silence over the trackless
yet blooming wilderness. Left to their own thoughts, they
seem to see spectral forms, rising from the shadows, and hear
voices from the other world, in every unusual sound.
> —Lippard, *'Bel of Prairie Eden:*
> *A Romance of Mexico*

In one of several scenes pictured in the complicated conclusion to *New York: Its Upper Ten and Lower Million* (1853), George Lippard focuses on a band of "emigrants, mechanics, their wives and little ones, who have left the savage civilization of the Atlantic cities, for a free home beyond the Rocky Mountains." As their leader, the socialist mechanic-hero Arthur Dermoyne, gazes upon the moving caravan, he sees his followers as "three hundred serfs of the Atlantic cities, rescued from poverty, from wages-slavery, from the war of competition, from the grip of the landlord!" For just a moment, the eastern U.S. class divisions that Lippard foregrounds in his mysteries-of-the-city novels promise to recede as his sensational story moves westward. That is to say, when in the early 1850s

Lippard finally finished the novel that he had begun in 1848, the year that the U.S.-Mexican War officially ended, he tried to resolve the violent, tangled urban gothic plots of *The Empire City* and *New York* by appealing to a utopian vision of a migrant band of white colonists moving across "the boundless horizon and ocean-like expanse of the prairies" toward "a soil which they can call their own."[1] But if this vision of a boundless expanse of vacant Western land replaces the Eastern class inequalities that loom large in *New York,* Lippard's two gothic U.S.–Mexican War narratives, *Legends of Mexico* (1847) and *'Bel of Prairie Eden: A Romance of Mexico* (1848), expose the violent scenes of empire-building that supported this nationalist fantasy of white working-class freedom.

Lippard's two war novels are only part of a huge body of printed texts and visual images that circulated widely during the years of the U.S.-Mexican War, for the print revolution of the late 1830s and 1840s directly preceded the war.[2] During the war, formulations of a fictive, unifying, "Anglo-Saxon" national identity were disseminated in sensational newspapers, songbooks, novelettes, story papers, and other cheap reading material.[3] Through this popular literature, a heterogeneous assortment of people imagined themselves a nation, staging their unity against the imagined disunity of Mexico, which was repeatedly called a "false nation" in the penny press.[4] But the existence of such a unified U.S. national identity was anything but self-evident during this period, for the 1840s were also marked by increasing sectionalism, struggles over slavery, the formation of an urban industrial working class, and nativist hatred directed at the new, mostly German and Irish immigrants whose numbers increased rapidly after 1845. If the war sometimes concealed these divisions by intensifying a rhetoric of national unity, it could also make differences of class, religion, race, and national origin more strikingly apparent. For although sensational war literature such as Lippard's may have promoted a unifying nationalism as well as the paradoxical idea of a nonimperial U.S. empire, it also often unleashed uncanny, spectral forms that troubled exceptionalist fantasies of free soil, a vacant Western landscape, and a united American people.[5]

Because this fiction was produced so quickly and because it is both highly formulaic and highly dependent on newspaper accounts, it has been largely dismissed by scholars. Even Richard Slotkin, who examined some of this literature in an excellent chapter of *The Fatal Environment: The Myth of the Frontier in the Age of Industrialization, 1800–1890* (1985), calls it "The Myth That Wasn't." According to Slotkin, some "quality in the historical experience itself appears to have doomed to failure the attempts of writers to assimilate the experience to the existing language of literary mythology."[6] But I want to suggest that it is precisely this "failure" of literary mythology to "assimilate" the historical experience that makes popular sensational war literature especially revealing. In other words, this fiction's mode of production, which accounts for its relative immediacy, its closeness to the "news" functions of the penny press, and the uneasy fit between literary conventions and historical experience, often has the effect of foregrounding the gaps, contradictions, and seamy underside of the ideological projects of white settler colonialism and Manifest Destiny.

Lippard's sensational U.S.–Mexican War novels are also particularly interesting because they are a part of his body of work that is rarely emphasized, although there are many connections between this fiction and the other literature he produced. As I suggested in the introduction, critics such as Michael Denning and David Reynolds have focused on Lippard as an advocate of the working classes and as the author of sensational mysteries-of-the-city novels. But if Lippard is, as Denning suggests, "the most overtly political dime novelist of his or subsequent generations," then it is important to address the significance of empire in his politics, especially since such questions have remained largely unasked because Lippard has most often been classified as a writer of urban literature.[7] In what follows, I attend to the double significance of 1848 in Lippard's journalism and fiction: the year 1848 marks the short-lived hope for a fundamental transformation of both European and U.S. society that was inspired by the European uprisings of that year, as well as by belief in "America's" imperial mission. Those hopes were both revivified and threatened by the U.S.-Mexican War and the incorporation of northern Mexico into the United States.

During the early 1840s, Lippard was a member of what Pierre Bourdieu, following Max Weber, calls the "proletaroid intelligentsia"—those who "make a living, however precarious, from all the minor jobs tied to 'industrial literature' and journalism": he started out as a writer of news stories, political essays, literary criticism, and gothic narratives for local papers such as the Philadelphia *Spirit of the Times* and the *Citizen Soldier*.[8] In 1843 and 1844, however, Lippard's sensational novel *The Quaker City* was published as a series of pamphlets and quickly became one of the most popular and controversial novels of the age. Lippard was subsequently able to earn three thousand to four thousand dollars a year as a writer—a fantastic amount for an author in the 1840s.[9] As Denning

suggests, Lippard was one of the stars of this new culture industry, combining "the production techniques of the fiction factory with working-
class ideologies of republicanism and socialism."[10] Indeed, the success
of *The Quaker City* made it possible for him to take more control over
his various literary projects, and after 1844, Lippard's writing became
more overtly political. During the next decade, he produced two novels,
The Nazarene; or, The Last of the Washingtons (1846) and *The Killers.
A Narrative of Real Life in Philadelphia* (1850), which addressed the
sectarian and race riots that divided Philadelphia during the decade.[11]
And from 1848 to 1850 he also edited his own labor newspaper, the
Quaker City weekly, which included the serials *Memoirs of a Preacher,
The Empire City, The Entranced; or, The Wanderer of Eighteen Centuries,* and *The Killers;* selections from *Legends of Mexico* and *Legends
of the Revolution;* as well as lengthy political editorials, book reviews,
and responses to letters from readers.

The *Quaker City* weekly was a five-cent paper with oversized pages,
advertised as "A Popular Journal, devoted to such matters of Literature
and news as will interest the great mass of readers."[12] Although during
the 1840s and 1850s most story-paper publishers, such as those that I
will discuss in Part 2, tried to reach a mass audience comprised of multiple classes by focusing on stories and minimizing controversial political commentary, in Lippard's hands the story paper was a popular form
with close ties to active communities such as the antebellum labor and
land reform movements: Lippard addresses a diverse and internally divided print community as he "hails" male and female workers, promotes
new working-class institutions, and comments on local and national politics. He decided to edit his own paper because he wanted to communi-
cate more directly with his audience, to bypass "Model Editors, or Moral
Editors, or Huckstering Publishers" and "to write no more for these
mere Agents between the author and the Reader." He claimed that his
work for the *Quaker City* weekly was especially gratifying because it
was "widely circulated and eagerly read in the Homes of the Poor, not
only in New York, but in the city which is more directly the scene of our
labors" (29 January 1849). Although he printed the work of a few other
columnists and writers (especially in the 1850 issues), Lippard did almost all of the writing himself. The purpose of the paper, he said, was
to promote the "development of certain views of social reform," especially "the defence of the Laborer against the exactions of the Capitalist," through "the medium of popular literature" (30 June 1849). "What
is literature good for," he reflected in another issue, "if it is not to be

used in the cause of humanity? ... A literature which does not work practically, for the advancement of social reform, or which is too dignified or too good to picture the wrongs of the great mass of humanity, is just good for nothing at all" (10 February 1849). During the late 1840s, Lippard hoped to promote social reform through the medium of popular literature, but just before his death in the early fifties he cut back on his literary endeavors in order to put more energy into a new project, his Brotherhood of the Union. The Brotherhood was a secret society that he described as "a practical, everyday Worker—in the cause of Labor" (5 January 1850). Dedicated to the idea that "this Continent was given by God to toiling Men, as the Palestine of regenerated Labor" (10 February 1849), the Brotherhood was, according to historian Jamie Bronstein, "the premier nonpolitical land-reform organization of the 1850's."[13]

Lippard's commitment to the dissemination of land reform principles was certainly one of the factors that encouraged him to see the U.S.-Mexican War in exceptionalist terms, as an opportunity to secure more lands for the landless and to bring freedom and democracy to other parts of the New World. But Lippard's anticlericalism and fears of Catholic conspiracies, both of which were conjoined to a radical Protestant republicanism influenced by French utopian socialists and German immigrants, also reinforced his willingness to find an imperial solution to the problem of industrial capitalism in Northeastern cities. In the next section, I explore some of the ways that sensationalism, Protestantism, and republicanism are reconfigured and recombined in Lippard's writing, especially in his short novel *The Entranced; or, The Wanderer of Eighteen Centuries,* which was serialized in the *Quaker City* weekly in 1849 and then published later in a slightly revised form under the title *Adonai: The Pilgrim of Eternity* in *The White Banner,* a collection of some of his more militant pieces that he circulated among the membership of the Brotherhood. Edited and published by Lippard himself in 1851, *The White Banner* contained "Legends of Everyday Life" (brief stories about corrupt rich men, the suffering poor, the demonization of socialism in the press, and other topics); a lecture on the history of Protestantism; various materials relating to the Brotherhood; and the text of *Adonai,* a wild and bloody historical and religious fantasy that moves from the time of Nero and the Roman Empire to the nineteenth-century United States by following the intermittent "awakenings" of Lucius, or Adonai, a Christian martyr who falls into a magnetic trance that lasts for centuries. Grafting a fictionalized history of Protestantism onto a dystopian, apocalyptic narrative that surveys key New World sites such as a prison, a factory, and a slave mart in Washington, D.C., Lippard exposes the nation's corrupt republican institutions and juxtaposes abstract formulations of liberal-democratic personhood with the bodies of slaves, factory workers, prisoners, and the poor of the world.

But Lippard's "sensational" focus on embodiment also has its costs. Although his emphasis on bodies and sensations responds to contemporaneous formulations of a disembodied soul and an abstract citizen, it also risks obscuring the constructedness of bodies and reifying "differences" of race, gender, and sexuality. Dana D. Nelson has argued, for instance, that in the seduction and rape-revenge narratives that pervade his fiction, "Lippard locates questions of civic order in women's mysterious interiors" and maps male dramas "across female bodies."[14] And as we shall see, antebellum ideologies of race drawn from a variety of sources, from nineteenth-century race science to the histories of William Hickling Prescott, also shaped his representations of racialized bodies. So Lippard's "body politics" are complicated and contradictory; they make the body, in Bruce Burgett's words, "both a ground and a site of political debate."[15] Although on the one hand his emphasis on bodies may threaten to naturalize some forms of inequality insofar as he suggests that differences of gender and race are fixed and objective, his "sensational" focus on working-class and poor people's embodied relationship to power is on the other hand a meaningful response to the rise of body-transforming institutions such as the prison and the factory and disciplinary practices aimed at the body in the nineteenth century.[16] In what follows, I examine Lippard's *Entranced* and *Adonai* in relation to the emergence of such institutions and practices, as well as to the European revolutions of 1848. Then, in the concluding sections, I place Lippard's sensationalism and the events of 1848 in an inter-American frame as I focus on Lippard's two U.S.–Mexican War novels. In *Legends of Mexico*, Lippard makes manifest a sensational, racialized definition of the nation-people and labors to justify exceptionalist theories of U.S. empire as uniquely progressive and beneficent. The history of class conflict and aggressive empire-building that Lippard tries to disavow by projecting it onto Spain and Mexico erupts forcefully, however, in *'Bel of Prairie Eden,* a romance that moves from the colonization of Texas in the 1830s to the invasion of Vera Cruz during the War and then to postwar Philadelphia, which is the focus of the final section of this chapter.[17] I conclude that Lippard's war literature makes especially evident the limits of his sensationalism—particularly as it racializes and genders individual and collective bodies—even as it foregrounds a history of U.S. empire in the Americas that has been marginalized in many accounts of U.S. labor cultures.

SENSATIONAL BODIES

In an editorial in the first issue of the *Quaker City* weekly, which was published on 30 December 1848, Lippard rejoiced that Louis Philippe had been "tumbled from his Kingdom and his wealth" in France, that other nations had caught "the electric thrill of Regeneration in their dead bosoms," and that "the People of the world" were "in arms for their rights." "Will 1849 tell a more sublime story than has been told by 1848?" he wondered. "Will the Kings be able to manacle the People, and tread them into slavery once more?" Then, turning his focus from Europe to the United States, he asked his readers: "And our land—is there no cloud upon its horizon? Does not Black Slavery sit brooding in our very Capitol—are not our Great Cities thronged with Armies of white slaves? Who shall tell the deeds which are to come—who shall read the mysterious scroll of 1849?" In the same issue, he began to serialize a sensational story, *The Entranced,* that addressed those very questions. Over the course of the next few years, the sections of the narrative that he continued to publish in his paper, and especially the revised version that he reprinted in *The White Banner* under the title *Adonai,* reflected both his disappointment at the containment of the European revolutions and his sense that the United States was far from free of the forms of inequality that had provoked the uprisings in Europe.[18]

Although, as we shall see, in his U.S.–Mexican War fiction Lippard tried to justify the war by promoting an exceptionalist interpretation of "America's" mission, in *Adonai* he suggests that the U.S. "Empire" uncannily resembles the Roman Empire; the "Senate of a free people," for instance, has become "the Senate of a land of tyrants and slaves, governed by the Sceptre of some new Nero, who is counselled by Senators fond of human blood."[19] Lippard's weird bloody allegory comes to an apocalyptic close on the Day of Judgment, which takes place in the wake of the failed European revolutions of 1848, when the poor of the world rise up against the priests, kings, and rich men of all nations. Although Lippard concludes by affirming that society is capable of social reorganization, this violent climax underlines a prophecy made earlier in the novel that "[w]hen the robbers of the Poor are not moved to mercy by the Book of God, or the Declaration of our fathers, then must the Poor teach unto these Robbers the Gospel of the Rifle" (79).

In Lippard's account, the "Book of God" and the "Declaration of our fathers" fail to protect poor and laboring people because the "robbers of the Poor" exploit, crush, and cannibalize their bodies and then interpret those two documents in self-serving ways by emphasizing a disembodied soul and an abstract citizen, the rewards of the afterlife and the sanctity of "Commerce and Manufactures." Although elsewhere Lippard is more optimistic about the possibility of reinterpreting and reclaiming republicanism, in *Adonai* the disembodied abstractions of republican reformism are rejected decisively by Lippard's "Arisen People."

In this narrative, the Christian convert Adonai falls into a magnetic trance after predicting that in sixteen hundred years Christianity will have transformed all men into brothers; that there will "not be a Priest or a King or a Rich Man left upon the face of the globe"; and that land will no longer "be held by the FEW, for the MANY to make fertile with their sweat and blood" (6 January 1849). When he awakens in 1525, however, he sees a world in which "Popes, Priests, and Kings" are "elevated into a horrible Godhead, while the great mass of mankind [are] brutalized into Devils." When Adonai wanders on to Germany, he hears a crowd of people asking the reformer Martin Luther to preach "the freedom of the body" as well as "the freedom of the soul," but Luther angrily responds that the "body is born to suffer and die" (13 January 1849) and that they must place their hopes in the next world. Exasperated, Adonai calls Luther's reform a Half-Way Gospel, predicts that it will strangle Luther's Reformation, and then returns to his cell in the catacombs to sleep again.

When Adonai awakens in 1848, he is pleasantly surprised to witness the uprising of the "People" in Rome. So he dons the Tunic of Labor and wanders around Italy, Germany, and France. Eventually he arrives in Paris, where he listens to the "Prophets of the Poor"—Georges Sand, the socialist Louis Blanc, radical democrat Ledru-Rollin, and others—argue with the "Men of Money" (20 January 1849) over the new form of government. Ultimately the latter take control and try to give new life to a dead social system, represented here by a corpse that the Men of Money try to rejuvenate by applying shocks from a galvanic battery. The lesson in all of this, Lippard suggests toward the end of *The White Banner,* is that "Europe cannot pass to Liberty but through the Red Sea" of revolution. "When her people rise again they must strike and spare not," Lippard warned. "Mercy to the tyrants is death to the People. You were merciful in 1848, were you not brave People? How have you been rewarded? Europe dead in the night of despotism gives the answer" (146).[20]

In case any of his readers might imagine that the horrors he is describing are confined to Europe or that they are the relics of a superseded
past, Lippard reanimates them in mid-nineteenth-century America as
Adonai visits the New World. By comparing sites of struggle in the Europe of 1848 with similar sites in the United States, Lippard countered
theories of American exceptionalism that posited the United States as a
fluid society free of the inequalities that had plagued the Old World.
Adonai expects America to be the land of a "free people, dwelling in
Brotherhood, without a single slave to mar their peace, or call down
upon their heads the vengeance of God" (42), but the first sight he sees
in Washington, D.C., is a slave-mart run by a man who proudly claims
that his grandfather fought for liberty under Washington. Reeling from
"a horror, too deep for words" (47), Adonai goes on to visit several different body-transforming republican institutions, including a prison—
"embodiment" of "the Law of the New World" (65)—and a factory, a
temple devoted to CAPITAL, "the God of the Nineteenth Century" (59),
"whose worship is celebrated upon the very corses of murdered Labor"
(61). While visiting the factory, Adonai recognizes the Executioner, a
malign figure who has shadowed him through his various awakenings,
performing a new role as the overseer of the factory. Reversing contemporaneous narratives that represented "America" as the culmination of
a westward-moving history of perpetual progress, Lippard's strategic positioning of the Executioner within a U.S. factory suggests that the exploitation engendered by nineteenth-century U.S. liberal capitalism gives
new life to old forms of oppression. As the Executioner puts it, "I am
better off, as the Overseer of a Factory, dedicated to Capital, and kept in
motion by the murder of Labor, than I have ever been, during the course
of eighteen hundred years!" (60).

When Adonai moves on to the U.S. Senate, other republican institutions come under fire as Lippard suggests that capitalism, the state, and
the men who foster the symbiotic relationship between the two effectively control the meaning of the Declaration of Independence and the
Constitution of the United States, so that democratic-republican promises of equality and freedom become empty words masking the return of
supposedly superseded forms of inequality.[21] Again, Adonai discovers
that the old has returned in the guise of the new. If the Constitution establishes "a thousand and ten thousand petty tyrants, Lords of the Mart
and Lords of the Loom" (53) in place of the king, the president is himself a force more powerful than a king, holding "a power such as no
Monarch of the Old World ever grasped" (55). If Liberty is simply the

freedom "to obey laws which, made for Capital and through Capital, drive Labor to the jail, the gibbet or the grave" (71), then republican institutions are simply a kind of machinery that helps the powerful to govern workers by "transforming Labor into Coin and Strips of Paper" and by "drain[ing] the sap and blood from its heart" (72). In other words, capitalism drains the sap and blood from the heart of republican institutions and entitlements, transforming words such as "freedom" and "equality" into meaningless abstractions and making U.S. democracy a more murderously efficient engine for powerful exploiters of bodies rather than a vehicle for the transcendence of inequalities.

The solution as Lippard imagines it here is an apocalyptic world revolution. Near the end of the narrative, Adonai encounters "a multitude of people, gathered from all the nations and tribes of the earth" (84) on a plain in the desert. These people, "all the Poor of the world," are gathered around a sepulchre containing Christ's body that is guarded by a circle of priests, kings, and "Rich Men of all Nations" (85). While the poor crave Christ's body and the healing rays of light that emanate from it, they are told that only the rich have the right to the body of the Lord. Even as Adonai wonders why the multitude don't thrust the kings, the rich, and the priests aside, one poor man runs up and hurls his body against the wall of men. Instantly, however, a priest zaps him with a cross and kills him, and in a satanic inversion of the Last Supper, the kings and rich men divide his body among themselves and feed upon the flesh. As others try to break down the human wall, they are "rent to pieces and devoured" (87). Finally, a man "clad in rags," with limbs "distorted by labor," knotted hands, and a face "covered with scars" exhorts the poor of the world to revolt against their masters: "You have prayed to these priests—they have answered you with death. You have shed your tears at the feet of these kings—they have fed upon your flesh. You have clutched the garments of these rich men—they have quenched their thirst with your blood.... NOW THE DAY OF PRAYERS AND TEARS HAS PASSED. THE DAY OF JUDGMENT HAS COME" (86). As the chapter ends, the Arisen People, inspired by a glimpse of the blood of Holy Revolution, advance upon the trembling rich men, priests, and kings. Although elsewhere Lippard focuses more narrowly on poor and working people in Northeastern cities, here his vision of the Arisen People includes "Negroes, Caffirs, Hindoos, Indians" as well as people from China, Japan, the "islands of the sea," Europe, and the New World (84).

Although the contradictions and limits of this vision of world revolution must be emphasized, it is important to understand that the body

of Christ possessed a meaning for Lippard and for many of his readers
that could, under certain circumstances, underwrite powerful appeals
for radical social, economic, and political changes. Although Lippard
argued that most versions of Protestantism had focused on the freedom
of the soul at the expense of the freedom of the body, he read a counter-
tradition in the New Testament that he interpreted as the story of a militant mechanic Christ who fought to advance the temporal and corporeal as well as the spiritual interests of the poor. As Lippard interpreted
them, the Gospels provided a sort of textbook for revolutionary laborers. In widely disseminated stories such as "Jesus and the Poor," "The
Imprisoned Jesus," and "The Carpenter's Son," and in religious goth-
ics such as *Adonai,* Lippard focused on the material body and the
earthly suffering of an incarnated Jesus. Lippard's Jesus is "the only Redeemer of the poor," a "son of toil" clad in "the coarse garb of labor,"
who, "the other day, was toiling with his father, at the carpenter's
bench," wiping the "laborer's sweat from his brow."[22] Lippard lingers
over his representations of Christ's laboring, sweating, suffering, wounded
body because he wants to use the apocalyptic temporality of the New
Testament to interrupt what he sees as an eighteen-century-long history
of exploitation and oppression.[23] Although others had described religion
"as a matter far-off from the masses," Lippard argued, the "Carpenter's
Son" proved that "it was a part of the life of every Man and Woman...
ending in a re-created earth, a re-organized social world...[n]ot an ideal
Kingdom, but a real Kingdom, whose existence would be attested as
much in the physical comforts as in the moral improvement of the
human race."[24] Lippard imagined fundamental social change, and he
believed that this question should be settled on earth, and not deferred
to some future state: "The Kingdom of God is plainly that state of temporal affairs which, by a proper distribution of labor, enables the entire
human family to cultivate their best faculties. The Kingdom of God com-
mences in this world, will progress in the next, and in all other worlds"
(30 March 1850).

Lippard's sensational emphasis on the body and on a revolutionary
interpretation of the New Testament was in part a response to the rigidly
Calvinist doctrines of conservative, orthodox Philadelphia Presbyterians
who, according to Bruce Laurie, championed "hierarchical social
arrangements in which each man knew his place."[25] In *The White Banner,* Lippard chose "John Calvin, with his hollow eyes, his granite heart,
and hands dripping with the blood of souls" (135) as the exemplar of a
"coldly intellectual form of Protestantism" (133). "If he presented an

image of Christ at all," Lippard charged, "it was an image which wore a lurid smile in the face,—which seemed to woo the sick and suffering with its smile,—but once embraced, sharp knives started from the arms and breast of the image,—and mangled and tore the worshipper to bloody fragments" (134).[26] But if Lippard attacked Calvinist orthodoxies, neither did he simply echo contemporaneous versions of an Arminian theology that emphasized self-help and an "industrial morality" that "promised to create a sober and tractable working class."[27] Instead, the Protestant vision that informs writings such as *Adonai* authorizes collective action and social transformation, and Lippard claimed that it was influenced by immigrant German communitarians and socialists who had founded Pennsylvania religious colonies such as Ephrata as well as by Johannes Kelpius's "The Woman of the Wilderness."[28]

At the same time, however, in *Adonai* Lippard's dark allusions to the pope as well as Henry VIII and Calvin, along with his references to the Priests who keep the People from Christ's body, should make it clear that this version of radical Protestantism brings with it a complex of anti-clerical and anti-Catholic beliefs. Even though he uses the word "priest" here to refer not only to Catholics but also to other religious leaders who use "iron books" or "crosses" or "images" to separate Christ from the People, these representations still align Catholicism with religious tyranny and the oppression of the poor. In part, this was a response to the intensified post-1848 conservatism of the Catholic Church in Philadelphia. According to Laurie, the European uprisings "ripened" the "inchoate political conservatism" of U.S. prelates: "They tarred radical republicanism with the brush of 'red revolution' and extrapolated the lessons of 1848 in Europe to the politics of their adopted city. They took a dim view of any tinkering with the established order or any form of collective action in redress of social injustice. Clerics insisted that the aggrieved resolve class conflict through 'moral suasion.' "[29] Even if Lippard was trying to counter this political conservatism, however, such anticlericalism also had the power to divide working-class people, inasmuch as Philadelphia had repeatedly witnessed violent confrontations between working-class Protestants and immigrant Catholics during the 1840s.

In the *Quaker City* weekly, Lippard claimed to have "always opposed political and sectarian Nativeism" (11 August 1849). In response to a letter from a reader who sent him an article "abusing our citizens of foreign birth," he replied that the "true American (whether native or adopted,) can never build up himself, by raising a prejudice, against a particular race" (28 April 1849). *The Quaker City; or, The Monks of*

Monk Hall includes a withering satire of the hypocritical nativist Reverend F. A. T. Pyne, who preaches "a gospel of fire and brimstone and abuse o' the Pope o' Rome, mingled in equal quantities," while in *The Nazarene* Lippard blames an evil "Holy Protestant League," among others, for the bloody 1844 riots in Kensington and Southwark that claimed at least twenty lives.[30] But although Lippard refused to support restrictions on immigration and naturalization, condemned nativist violence, and insisted that "the largest portion of Catholics in this country are deeply imbued with the love of liberty," he still maintained "that a body of men exist in the [Catholic] Church, who have sworn eternal wrath against every form of human liberty and democratic truth" (12 May 1849).[31] Increasingly, Lippard distinguished Catholic laymen from rulers and claimed that although the former were most often true Christians and citizens, the latter threatened the republic.

In *New York,* the revised and expanded version of *The Empire City* that Lippard published shortly before his early death, he represents the Catholic Church as a rival empire that initially threatens to take over the Western lands that are settled by the socialist-mechanic Arthur Dermoyne and his white working-class followers at the end of the novel. One Catholic conspirator, a Prelate, argues that since the United States is certain to "finally absorb and rule over all the nations of the Continent," the policy of the Church must be to "absorb and rule over the Republic of the North" (68), for "ours is not so much a church as an EMPIRE . . . which, using all means and holding all means alike lawful, for the spread of its dominion, has chosen the American Continent as the scene of its loftiest triumph, the theater of its final and most glorious victories" (69). When it is revealed that gold has been discovered in California, the struggle for the Western lands takes on even more significance. Although the Prelate hopes that the gold will fortify the earthly power of the Catholic Church, the pope's legate—who is really one of Lippard's heroes in disguise— vows that within this corrupt church "there is another Church of Rome, composed of men, who, when the hour strikes, will sacrifice everything to the cause of humanity and God" (73). Meanwhile Dermoyne, one of several possible heirs to these Western lands, dreams of taking a party of workmen to a spot in the West "unpolluted by white or black slavery," where they can build a utopian community devoted to "the worship of that Christ who was himself a workman, even as he is now, the workman's God" (108).

All of this helps to explain how the sensational, radical Protestant vision of world revolution that Lippard offers in *Adonai* could also be used to support U.S. imperial expansion. Since Lippard imagined that the Catholic Church was at the heart of an international conspiracy to take over the Americas, he saw the conflict with Catholic Mexico as an opportunity to extend the principles of freedom and democracy rather than as a war of conquest. And despite his fears that these ideals had been debased and corrupted by capitalism, he still identified them with "America." In short, Lippard often promoted a working-class myth of America by trying to wrest "America" as a utopian symbol away from capitalism.[32] Although the collective protagonist toward the end of *Adonai* is "the Poor of all Nations," rather than U.S. workers as such, George Washington's ghost—the "Arisen Washington"—is Adonai's companion in the final chapters, and at the end he gives the sword he used at Valley Forge to "THE LABORERS OF A WHOLE WORLD" to fight their battle against their oppressors.

As I suggested above, Lippard's utopian investment in the project of land reform also predisposed him to favor the annexation of new lands as a way to provide more territory for landless workers. Although he frequently expressed his contempt for party politics, he was closer to the Democrats than the Whigs: he generally endorsed the Democratic policies of welcoming new immigrants and promoting imperial expansion as a way to reduce crowding and competition for jobs and other resources in the East. And even as he broke with Democratic orthodoxy by repeatedly denouncing chattel slavery, he also deployed the problematic metaphor of "white slavery," which, as David Roediger argues, often led to an insidious "prioritizing of struggles by whites."[33] Although both the fugitive slave Randolph Royalton and the socialist mechanic Arthur Dermoyne are portrayed sympathetically in *New York,* at the end of the novel Randolph and his sister go "abroad" (279) while the story of the white workingman moves to the foreground as Dermoyne and his followers find a "free home" in the West. In other words, Lippard concludes with a scenario (former slaves leave the country, white working families go West) that recalls the white egalitarianism of the Wilmot Proviso, the measure that would have banned slavery in newly acquired lands so as to preserve a "home" for free white laborers. Thus although in *Adonai* and in his other writings Lippard countered one version of American exceptionalism—what could be called a Hartzian theory that the United States is a fluid society free from the forms of institutionalized inequality that plagued Europe—he placed his hopes in another version of (Turnerian) exceptionalism based on the premises that "free" Western lands might serve as a safety valve for such domestic social and economic antagonisms and that U.S. expansion would mean the extension of the area of freedom rather than the violent conquest of other nations.[34] In the next section, we will see how Lippard mobilized sensational ideologies of race and nation in a desperate effort to shore up this second version of American exceptionalism.

AMERICAN SENSATIONS

In *Legends of Mexico,* Lippard celebrated the bloody events that "aroused a People into arms," "spoke to the hearts of fifteen millions people," "startled a People into action, and sent the battle-throbs palpitating through fifteen millions hearts."[35] In the first chapter, Lippard envisions the nation-people as a single human body that comes to life when it hears a "Cry, a Groan, a Rumor" "thundering" (11) from the shores of the Rio Grande. Lippard makes a sensational appeal to his readers, an appeal that records a visceral, mass response to war to which his *Legends of Mexico* also aims to contribute. This sensational appeal is meant to arouse and startle, to provoke a collective bodily response to the battles being waged over national borders. As Lippard mobilizes sensationalism in the service of U.S. empire, differences of class and status (the "hardy Mechanic" [12], the "working people" [13]) appear only to disappear within the collective body of the "free People of the American Union" (16), which is united precisely in opposition to the mixed-race peoples of Mexico. Here, Lippard's war sensationalism emphasizes intensely nationalist affects and feelings at the expense of class: he tries to subsume class within race and nation by urging his readers to identify with a fictive, white U.S. national body.

The mass response, the "wild excitement" (12) that Lippard both recorded and tried to reproduce, was a relatively novel sensation, made possible by the print revolution. As Robert Johannsen suggests, because of these changes in print culture, the U.S.-Mexican War would be "experienced more intimately, with greater immediacy and closer involvement than any major event in the nation's history. It was the first American war to rest on a truly popular base, the first that grasped the interest of the population, and the first people were exposed to on an almost daily basis. The essential link between the war and the people was provided by the nation's press, for it was through the ubiquitous American newspaper that the war achieved its vitality in the popular mind."[36] In other words, the penny press and other forms of popular culture helped to produce feelings of intimacy, immediacy, and involvement in the war as papers reported, for the first time on an almost daily basis, the details of battles in Mexico, and as songs, images, novels, and histories were widely disseminated.

The opening of Lippard's *Legends of Mexico* focuses on this very process whereby news of events in Mexico serves as the catalyst for a sensational, intensely nationalist response to the war. U.S. newspapers speculated about the possibility of war for months after Polk sent an Army of Observation in February 1846 to the Rio Grande, which the United States claimed on specious grounds as its new southern border after it annexed Texas in 1845.[37] Then in May 1846, when Polk declared war, prowar demonstrations were staged in every major U.S. city, including a rally attended by twenty thousand people in Philadelphia, Lippard's Quaker City.[38] But war supporters waited nervously for nearly two weeks for news about Zachary Taylor's forces. Lippard describes this situation in the beginning of *Legends of Mexico:* "In the spring of 1846, from the distant south, there came echoing in terrible chorus, a Cry, a Groan, a Rumor! That cry, the earnest voice of two thousand men, gathered beneath the Banner of the stars of a far land, encompassed by their foes, with nothing but a bloody vision of Massacre before their eyes" (11). Popular representations of embattled U.S. troops must have excited feelings of fear, anxiety, and identification in many readers. Thus when news of victories at Palo Alto and Resaca de la Palma finally reached the United States, nationalist celebrations erupted throughout the country. According to Lippard, as "thunder at once, convulses and purifies the air, so that Rumor [of U.S. victories in battle] did its sudden and tempestuous work, in every American heart. At once, from the People of twenty-nine states, quivered the Cry—'To Arms! Ho! for the new crusade!'" (12). As Lippard represents it, war reports convulse and purify "American" hearts, engendering a unified national body.

Benedict Anderson suggests that representations of national simultaneity indicate a radically changed form of consciousness decisively linked to the spread of print capitalism. Newspapers in particular, he argues, encouraged readers to imagine themselves part of a national community reconstituted by the "extraordinary mass ceremony" of "almost precisely simultaneous consumption."[39] During the 1840s, the invention of the telegraph facilitated the rapid transmission of news, supporting collective nationalist responses to the war on an unprecedented mass scale.[40] In *Legends of Mexico,* Lippard represents such a scene of national fantasy as he imagines the nation-people simultaneously responding, in different places, to news of battles in Mexico:

From the mountain gorges of the north, hardy birds of freemen took their
way turning their faces to the south, and shouting—Mexico! In the great
cities, immense crowds assembled, listening in stern silence, to the stories of
that far-off land, with its luxuriant fruits, its plains of flowers, its magnificent
mountains overshadowing calm lakes and golden cities, and then the cry rung
from ten thousand throats—Mexico! The farmhouses of the land, thrilled
with the word. Yes, the children of Revolutionary veterans, took the rifle of
'76 from its resting place, over the hearth, and examined its lock, by the light
of the setting sun, and ere another dawn, were on their way to the south,
shouting as they extend their hands toward the unseen land—Mexico! (12)

Here, the "word" reaches the "mountain gorges of the north," the "great
cities," the "farmhouses of the land," and "the children of Revolutionary veterans" everywhere, linking together these diverse sites on the basis
of their common response to the news of war. This vision of bodies in
different locations simultaneously turning "south" and shouting "Mexico" seeks to reconcile differences of region and occupation within a
larger national unity. Although Anderson understands this process of
imagining the nation through the medium of print in relatively abstract
terms, Lippard represents the national community as a collective body
that convulses, quivers, and thrills to the news of the U.S.-Mexican War.
That is to say, if for Anderson the nationalist "meanwhile" (25) produces a sense of "community in anonymity" (36) as it connects different
parts of the nation, Lippard's war literature shows how nationalism
works by also particularizing and foregrounding bodies rather than simply abstracting from and decorporealizing them. If the "skeleton" of national history must be clothed "with flesh and blood" (26) in order for
people to respond to it, then nationalism as mediated by print capitalism
also depends upon thrilling sensations of embodiment.

In the opening chapter of *Legends of Mexico,* these sensations of embodiment are distinctly racialized. Reginald Horsman argues that during
the U.S.-Mexican War "the Americans clearly formulated the idea of
themselves as an Anglo-Saxon race." He adds that although many U.S.
commentators thought of this "race" as primarily English and distinguished it from an inferior Celtic race, for example, others viewed the
"American" as "a unique blend of all that was best in the white European races."[41] In *Legends of Mexico,* Lippard rejects the identification
of whiteness with Englishness as he defines the American people as fundamentally Northern European: "We are no Anglo-Saxon people. No!"
Lippard asserts. "All Europe sent its exiles to our shore. From all the nations of Northern Europe, we were formed. Germany and Sweden and

Ireland and Scotland and Wales and England, aye and glorious France, all sent their oppressed to us, and we grew into a new race" (16). By extending the boundaries of this new American race beyond the Anglo-Saxon, Lippard promotes a more inclusive definition of white Americanness that also welcomes, for instance, Irish immigrants, whose numbers were increasing rapidly during the 1840s.[42] But this more expansive definition of white American unity crucially depends upon the construction of Mexicans as a "mongrel race, moulded of Indian and Spanish blood," that is destined to "melt into, and be ruled by, the Iron Race of the North" (15). The incorporation of Mexicans into the U.S. national body clearly involves the reinforcement, rather than the erasure, of racial hierarchies, for Lippard imagines a form of union in which Mexicans continue to be ruled by white Americans. So if the Irish, Germans, and other Europeans Lippard includes in this "new" American race are admitted to the union as equal partners, Mexicans remain subordinated to white America. This vision of a united, more inclusive, white American race defined through a hierarchical relationship to Mexico is entirely consonant with the politics of Manifest Destiny, as Lippard himself makes clear: "Our lineage is from that God, who bade us go forth, from the old world, and smiled us into an Empire of Men." He concludes, "Our destiny is to possess this Continent, drive from it all shreds of Monarchy, whether British or Spanish or Portuguese, and on the wrecks of shattered empires, build the Altar, second to the BROTHERHOOD OF MAN" (16).

As this passage suggests, Lippard attempts to identify "America" with a particular racially defined community in order to justify U.S. empire-building. That is to say, in *Legends of Mexico* the body of the nation-people is placed within both a sacred and a European lineage as Lippard appeals to a white democratic utopianism that he opposes to European monarchy. Unlike other past empires that have been subject to the vicissitudes of history, Lippard contends that U.S. empire will be unique, a holy, antimonarchical community dedicated to the brotherhood of man. But this conception of America as immanent utopia is fundamentally grounded on racial hierarchies and the dynamics of violent expansion: Lippard's radical Protestant millennialism sanctions U.S. imperialism as he imagines history culminating in a U.S. empire that he describes elsewhere as a Palestine for redeemed labor.[43] In this utopian fantasy, the contradictions of history, class conflict, and violent conquest are displaced by a vision of the American "race" as a chosen people and the U.S. empire as a sacred community.

Such a reading of U.S. empire as uniquely beneficent and egalitarian is foregrounded on the cover of the 1847 T. B. Peterson edition of *Legends of Mexico,* where a citation from Thomas Paine's *The Crisis* (1777) appears: "We fight not to enslave, nor for conquest; But to make room upon the earth for honest men to live in." In 1847, in the middle of the U.S.-Mexican War, this reference to Paine's Revolutionary War writings suggested multiple meanings. First, it set up the U.S.-Mexican War as a repeat performance of the Revolutionary War (recall the "children of Revolutionary veterans" picking up the "rifle of '76" and setting out for Mexico). Although many opponents of the U.S.-Mexican War argued that it invited the extension of slavery and was an unjustified war of invasion, this citation implicitly appealed to the republican ideals of freedom and independence and explained the conflict with Mexico as another battle against tyranny.[44] Second, the use of this quotation supported the exceptionalist premise that U.S. empire was fundamentally different from the "shattered" New World empires of Britain, Spain, and Portugal. More specifically, it implied that the U.S.-Mexican War was a different sort of project than the Spanish conquest of Mexico, which had enthralled U.S. readers for years, most notably in the form of William H. Prescott's massive and massively popular *History of the Conquest of Mexico* (1843). The passage from *The Crisis,* however, is actually misquoted; the original reads: "We fight not to enslave, but to set a country free, and to make room upon the earth for honest men to live in."[45] The substitution of the phrase "nor for conquest" for "to set a country free" shows how important it was to U.S. imperialists to establish distinctions between the U.S.-Mexican War and the Spanish conquest of Mexico, even as the parallels between the two remained a source of endless, if uneasy, fascination.

During the 1840s in the United States, the Spanish conquest of Mexico was generally interpreted as necessary, since it brought Christianity to the so-called New World. But it was also viewed as ultimately flawed because the Spanish were not Protestants but Catholics; because Spaniards as a people were said to be characterized by superstition, avarice, cruelty, and tyranny; because they were not considered racially pure, but rather were disposed to mix with conquered peoples; and because they were not the chosen people who, according to millennialists, were destined to lead the world to the utopia at the end of history.[46] Prescott was himself deeply ambivalent about Spain: he opposed the annexation of Texas and the U.S.-Mexican War and seems to have worried that the United States was not exempt from history, that it too might be subject to the instabilities of empire and fall.[47] Despite the complexities and paradoxes of the *History of the Conquest of Mexico*, however, readers often interpreted it as a sort of guidebook to Mexico for U.S. military forces and as an historical model for the U.S.-Mexican War, with the Spanish conquest prefiguring the victory of the United States over Mexico, though the Spanish were widely considered to have been excessively cruel and "motivated by greed and avarice."[48] According to this logic, as the misquotation of Paine's words suggests, because the United States fought "not to enslave, nor for conquest," it could escape Spain's fate and usher in utopia.

And yet, this belief in the exceptional status of U.S. empire was by no means untroubled by doubts and contradictions. The ideological legacy of eighteenth-century republicanism, for instance, continued to powerfully shape ideas about empire in the 1840s. According to republican beliefs, the pursuit of empire always threatened a republic with corruption and decline through overextension and by engendering luxury, bringing in foreign populations, and encouraging the establishment of professional armies.[49] This republican "drama of imperial decline," as Angela Miller calls it, is staged in Thomas Cole's famous series of paintings entitled *The Course of Empire* (1833–1836). Cole depicts what he and many of his contemporaries understood to be the five stages of empire: the Savage State, the Arcadian or Pastoral State, Consummation, Destruction, and finally Desolation. As one contemporary writer put it, Cole's paintings represented "the march of empire, or the rise, decadence, and final extinction of a nation, from the first state of savage rudeness through all the stages of civilization to the very summit of human polish and human greatness, to its ultimate downfall."[50] Miller suggests that many of Cole's contemporaries responded enthusiastically to the paintings, even as they struggled to deny the relevance of this narrative for U.S. empire; they maintained that the "exceptional conditions of its expansion—peaceful, nonaggressive, republican, and blessed with an inexhaustible wilderness—guaranteed that the nation would avoid the fate drawn by Cole."[51] But during the war years, the fiction of peaceful and nonaggressive U.S. expansion became much more difficult to maintain, and the rhetoric of republicanism often contributed to contemporary languages of antiimperialism.

All of this suggests that assertions of American exceptionalism cannot always be taken at face value, but rather should often be seen as nervous attempts to manage the contradictions of ideologies of U.S. empire-building, contradictions that pervade war literature such as Lippard's. In other words, efforts to forget or redescribe the project of empire-building are often attempts to ward off evidence showing that U.S. expansion is not peaceful, nonaggressive, benignly republican, or directed toward an inexhaustible wilderness. This sort of evidence proliferated in war representations, which inevitably revealed that Mexico was not a vacant wilderness, that many different peoples already lived there, and that violence would be required to displace them. This is the problem that the citation from *The Crisis* tries to solve. Moving from the double negation of slavery and conquest to a utopian vision of room upon the earth for all, the placement of Paine's words on the cover of *Legends of Mexico* urges readers to forget about those who were being displaced, as well as the bloody scenes of displacement that cleared the earth for "honest men" to live in. If we judge this book by its cover, then, Lippard's legends suggest a paradox. He wants us to forget, or at least to remember differently, the very scenes that he is committed to picturing in explicit and disturbing detail. How does he hope to convert military conquest into a benign "making room"? That is, how does he try to make the violence of empire-building disappear within a vision of white America as utopia?

First, he invokes the Black Legend. This system of beliefs was supported by anti-Catholic sentiments, accounts of the Spanish Inquisition, reports of Spanish atrocities in the New World, and ideas about the horrors of racial mixing. After the Black Legend traveled across the Atlantic with the early colonists, it was reinforced by the anti-Catholic nativism of the 1840s as well as the war with Mexico.[52] Lippard draws on the Black Legend when he identifies tyranny, luxury, and avarice with Spain, introduces rapacious Spanish villains, and contrasts an evil Spanish conquest with a liberating U.S.-American presence in Mexico. In the opening chapter, for instance, Lippard implicitly distinguishes northern European colonists of the Americas from the Spanish when he insists that the northern Europeans crossed the Atlantic "not for the lust of gold or power, but for the sake of a Religion, a Home" (15). By identifying Spanish conquerors with the lust for gold and power that he deplored in both journalism and urban gothic literature, Lippard struggles to distance himself from the very analogy between Spain and the United States that his words repeatedly suggest.[53] Even though he tries to distinguish the two, however, U.S. empire becomes, as we shall see, an uncanny double of the Spanish empire in this text. For if the United States displaces and replaces the remnants of the Spanish empire in Mexico, it also inherits the curses heaped on Spain: as the violence depicted in this novel escalates, it becomes difficult to separate Spanish tyranny from U.S.-American freedom.

Lippard's second major strategy is to unify the U.S. nation-people by repeatedly sketching pictures of endangered, mutilated, or destroyed U.S. bodies. He often uses bloody, gothic language and imagery to illustrate the horrors of war. Lippard zooms in on gory scenes in which a Mexican cannonball is unroofing the skull of a U.S. soldier (55); or in which U.S. troops advance through a battlefield strewn with their comrades "in mangled masses" (82); or in which a soldier's lower jaw is torn away "by the blow of a murderous lance" (128). Like other prowar writers, he represents evil Mexican soldiers mangling and robbing the U.S. dead and wounded as they lie helpless after the fight. By representing Mexicans as a threat to the bodies of the nation-people, Lippard urges readers to unite despite their differences.

In one especially telling instance, he focuses on an Irish immigrant, a common soldier, who came "from the desolated fields of Ireland, across the ocean, then into the army" (55). As he often does in his war fiction, Lippard lingers on the manly body of the soldier, "attired in a blue round jacket, his broad chest, laid open to the light." As he listens to the words of his commander, his "swarthy face is all attention, his honest brow, covered with sweat, assumes an appearance of thought." Then suddenly, as one example among many of "the infernal revelry of war," Lippard depicts a grotesque battle scene in which "the soldier is torn in two, by a combination of horrible missiles, which bear his mangled flesh away, whirling a bloody shower through the air. That thing beneath the horse's feet, with the head bent back, until it touches the heels, that mass of bloody flesh, in which face, feet, and brains, alone are distinguishable, was only a moment past, a living man" (54). The intentness with which Lippard focuses on the mangled body of the Irish soldier suggests a number of possible readings. The sensational excessiveness of this account may appeal, for instance, to a ghoulish voyeurism that takes pleasure in scenes of bodily destruction. Indeed, the scene might attract a reader who particularly enjoys reading about the destruction of the Irish immigrant body, a liminal figure serving as a scapegoat through which the fantasy of bodily destruction can be more easily staged.[54] But Lippard frames the incident with a sentimental narrative about the soldier's wife, who followed him with baby in arms from Ireland to the battlefield and who holds onto his festering body all night until the army gravediggers bury it. Lurid as even this detail is, the inclusion of it along with the initial description of the soldier suggests that Lippard is also trying to provoke sympathy in his readers by focusing on the bereaved family as well as the destruction of the "good" soldier's body.

Inasmuch as Lippard urges readers to feel for this Irish immigrant soldier, he implicitly responds to nativist prejudices against the Irish. That is, such a representation of the immigrant body could be said to symbolically incorporate marginal whites such as the Irish into the American "race," since Lippard makes the soldier into a martyr for the white nationalist cause. Once again, however, this incorporation of marginal whites takes place at the expense of Mexicans positioned as a threat to the white family and the bodily integrity of the Irish soldier.[55] And if Lippard's representations of bodies endangered or shattered by Mexican forces extend Americanness to the Irish immigrant, they are also meant to unite readers at home. Lippard even pictures for his audience the sensations of nationalist unanimity that he wants them to feel in response to these war scenes: "At this very hour, in the American Union at least one hundred thousand hearts, are palpitating in fearful anxiety for us, afraid that every moment may bring the news of the utter slaughter of Taylor and his men" (77).

But as Lippard seeks to mobilize gothic sensationalism in behalf of U.S. nation- and empire-building, the goriness of his battle scenes transgresses the very racial and national boundaries that he in other ways tries to establish. As the scene shifts from the first battles of the war at Palo Alto and Resaca de la Palma to the fighting in the city of Monterrey and then to the war's bloodiest battle, Buena Vista, Lippard represents more and more scenes in which Mexican homes are invaded, Mexican families are destroyed, and Mexican bodies are "splintered into fragments" (96) and mowed "into heaps of mangled flesh" (101). Instead of converting conquest into liberation, this focus on Mexican losses registers the spectacular acts of violent displacement that supported the nationalist dream of white freedom.

As Lippard labors to distinguish U.S. empire from Spanish empire, he often adapts rhetorical strategies from mysteries-of-the-city novels. In novels such as *New York* and *The Quaker City,* Lippard frequently contrasts the high life of the rich and powerful with the lowly life of the poor and oppressed. This strategy is so common in mysteries-of-the-city literature that it is one of its defining features. Mysteries-of-the-city novels also often attack wealthy nonproducers by misrecognizing capitalism as the intrusion of a feudal/aristocratic mode of production into liberal democratic America. Here, however, Lippard uses contrasts and the language of feudalism to cast Mexicans in the role of wealthy oppressor. When Lippard first introduces General Arista before the battle of Palo Alto, for instance, he uses the same kind of language, along with the supplement of a racialist orientalism, that he deploys to characterize evil rich seducers

THE DEATH OF RINGGOLD:
A LEGEND OF MEXICO.
BY GEORGE LIPPARD.

Figure 1.   Detail, "The Death of Ringgold," from the *Quaker City*, 13 January 1849. (Courtesy American Antiquarian Society)

such as Gus Lorrimer in *The Quaker City*.[56] The description of the interior of Arista's tent is the key to his character, as Lippard defines it: "Within the tent, seated on a luxuriously cushioned chair, near a voluptuous bed, glistening with the trappings of oriental taste, you behold a man of warrior presence, his gay uniform thrown open across the breast, while he holds the goblet of iced champagne to his lips" (22). The "gaudy uniforms" (23) of the Mexicans are akin to the expensive, fashionable outfits worn by the East Coast libertines that Lippard lampoons elsewhere. By identifying the Mexican general with luxury, voluptuousness, exotic tastes, and excessive pleasures, Lippard aims to arouse the class-based sensations that he stimulates in his urban gothic fiction. In other words, rhetorical strategies used in mysteries-of-the-city novels to explain class relationships are translated into the context of relationships between nations. For if Arista and his men are reconstructed as wealthy oppressors, U.S. officers are cast as lowly but heroic class Others, as Lippard contrasts the sumptuous scenes in the Mexican camp to the U.S. quarters in which leaders, sleeping on "rude" camp beds and attired in "plain apparel" (23), rest in preparation for the next day's march.

Lippard also maps a language of class onto nation when he moves from descriptions of battle scenes to the legends of "passion, of poetry, of home" (27) that "clothe the skeleton" of history "with flesh and blood" (26). In one of these legends, Lippard tells the story of a beautiful mestiza named Inez who has secretly married a U.S. soldier only to be separated from him by her tyrannical Castilian father. The extravagant luxury of the settings that Inez inhabits suggests parallels between the elite Mexicans and the mansion-dwelling capitalist aristocracy of Lippard's mysteries-of-the-city fiction. Inez's bedroom is paved with mosaic slabs of marble and includes a "fountain, bubbling from a bath, sunken in the centre of the place, while four slender pillars supported the ceiling" (28). And when she dreams of her marriage to the U.S. soldier in the Cathedral of Matamoras, we learn that the altar is made of solid silver, with a candelabra of gold above it and a balustrade of precious metals extending on either side. "Count the wealth of a fairy legend; and you have it here, in this solemn cathedral," Lippard advises us. "And yonder—smiling sadly over all the display of wealth—stands the Golden Image of the Carpenter's Son of Nazareth, and by his side, beams the silver face of his Divine Mother" (29). Here Lippard's Protestant iconoclasm combines with a radical republican fear of luxury to position these Mexican Catholics, with their fashionable churches and excessive displays of wealth, as the counterparts of the "upper ten" that he attacks in his mysteries-of-the-city novels.

Despite the many parallels between the Mexican ruling class and the "upper ten" that Lippard demonizes in his mysteries-of-the-city fiction, his desire to unite the U.S. nation-people along racial lines prevents him from explicitly comparing the privileged classes of Mexico and the United States in *Legends of Mexico*. Instead, elite Mexicans take on the role almost exclusively of the evil rich, while elite U.S. officers, many of whom are the sons of wealthy and influential men such as Henry Clay, become heroes.[57] For the most part, then, Lippard's critique of U.S. class relations is rerouted as he foregrounds heroic regional, national, and racial types. For instance, the U.S. soldier that Lippard calls the Virginian, who is presented as a point of readerly identification and as the appropriate partner for Inez, is characterized only by his region, his race, and his beguiling masculinity, which is showcased by his attire, "the plain blue undress of an American officer, which revealed every outline of his slight, yet sinewy frame" (31). Class almost disappears as a marker of moral value in Lippard's descriptions of U.S. characters; introducing it would fragment the very national community that he is trying to consolidate.[58] On the other hand, class is mapped onto nation and used to demonize Inez's father, who plots to wed his mestiza daughter, a symbol of the Mexican nation-people, to another Spaniard. By constructing a romance that brings together Inez and the Virginian despite the opposition of her wealthy father, Lippard suggests that the United States, rather than Spain, is the appropriate partner for Mexico and that U.S. empire must and should replace Spanish empire there.

Although Lippard avoids making explicit comparisons between wealthy U.S. and Spanish oppressors in *Legends of Mexico,* his animus against the Spanish and his use of the mestiza Inez as a symbol of the Mexican nation might suggest parallels between the oppressed Indians, who are victimized by the Spanish dream of gold, and the exploited lower million in the United States. That is, even though Lippard struggles to redirect class identifications in *Legends of Mexico,* he evokes a certain amount of sympathy for Mexican Indians by placing them in a position that is symbolically similar to that of aggrieved groups within the U.S. These kinds of parallels are frequently explored, however tentatively, in the popular literature of the period. In many of the accounts of the conquest that circulated during these years, Mexican Indians were represented much more sympathetically than were the Spanish conquerors, even though many of these representations also included racist allusions to human sacrifice and other exotic rituals. These more sympathetic representations of Mexican Indians often, however, supported hispanophobic responses that justified U.S. intervention in Mexico. In *Legends of Mexico,* for instance, Lippard includes a romanticized representation of an Indian tribe that has fled to the mountains bearing torches that were lighted at the eternal flame of Montezuma: "When the Hero-Priest Hidalgo,—descended from the Aztec race—raised the standard of revolt, and declared the soil of Anahuac, free from European despotism," Lippard writes, "that torch blazed in the faces of the Spaniards and lit them to their bloody graves" (34). In this passage, Lippard identifies the Mexican War of Independence with Indian struggles against Spanish despotism and thereby seems to endorse Indian resistance, though he quickly moves on and focuses once again on white North Americans as the agents of change in Mexico.

Even though Lippard extends some sympathy to Mexican Indians, he never represents them as equals. Instead, he tends to identify them with the dead past, so that his largely Prescott-derived pictures of Indian enclaves have a "land-that-time-forgot" feel to them; they also recall James Fenimore Cooper's "vanishing Americans" in novels such as *The Last of the Mohicans*.[59] The Indian tribe that he focuses on in *Legends of Mexico* is completely cut off from modern Mexico, "fenced in from civilization by impenetrable thickets swarming with wild beasts" (34); he describes them as "one of those remnants of the Aztec people, which have been hidden in the desert, from the eye of the white man, for three hundred years" (35). Even though Lippard is implicitly critical of "civilized" values here, his representation of Indians as relics of the past suggests that they will not play a significant role in Mexico's future. What is more, with the exception of Inez, Lippard usually represents the racial heterogeneity of Mexico negatively. For example, like most other writers for the penny press, Lippard describes "the Ranchero" as "that combination of the worst vices of civilization and barbarism" (25). Drawing on the dominant strain of the race science of the time, Lippard suggests in this passage that racial mixtures, particularly the mixture of Spanish and Indian blood, result in offspring combining the worst of both races.[60] Once again, Lippard appeals to racial distinctions to override the parallels between internal hierarchies in the United States and Mexico that his words might otherwise suggest.

Although Lippard generally condemns racial mixtures and tries to distinguish between the United States and Mexico on grounds of racial purity, however, his fantasy solution to the conflict between the two nations is a marriage between a U.S. soldier and the mestiza Inez. This plot device recurs in much of the war literature, although most of the heroines are creoles. International romances between U.S. soldiers and elite Mexican women were often represented in the popular literature as a benign form of imperial conquest or as an alternative to it: the romance plots of a good deal of cheap war fiction were echoed by contemporary calls to conquer Mexico by "whitening" it through transnational heterosexual unions. In November of 1847, a writer for the *Democratic Review* even suggested that a postwar U.S. army of occupation in Mexico could result in the "strong infusion of the American race," which "would impart energy and industry gradually to the indolent Mexicans, and give them such a consistency as a people, as would enable them to hold and occupy their territories in perfect independence.... The soldiers succeeding each other for short terms would most of them, as they were discharged, remain in the country, and, gradually infusing vigor into the race, regenerate the whole nation."[61] Although this writer ostensibly hopes to see an independent Mexico, he reinforces stereotypes of Mexican men as indolent and Mexican women as both sexually available and naturally attracted to U.S. men.[62]

As popular writers fantasized about heterosexual union between a feminized Mexico and a masculinized United States, they appealed to narratives of gender and sexuality to turn force into consent and conquest into international romance.[63] In this way, they tried to establish distinctions between a rapacious Spanish conquest and an idealized, peaceful, and nonaggressive U.S. relationship to Mexico. But as we shall see in Part 2, these romances rarely conceal the coercive power relations that lie at their heart, and they also raise issues about racial mixture that undermine the precarious distinction between a united white American race and a racially heterogeneous Mexico. For if the mixture of Spanish and Indian blood is said to result in offspring that combine the worst of both races in the case of the demonized *ranchero,* then the marriage between the mestiza Inez and the Virginian, for instance, might well threaten to corrupt the fictive purity of white America, despite the optimism in some of the literature about the possibility of "improving" the Mexican "race" through pairings between U.S. men and Mexican women. Although Lippard never addresses this inconsistency, these kinds of contradictions plague his efforts to distinguish clearly the U.S. and the Spanish empires and therefore threaten to undermine his exceptionalist vision of "America."

One of the most complicated convolutions of this distinction-forging logic occurs when Lippard tries to represent the U.S.-Mexican War as a just retribution for the atrocities committed during the Spanish conquest of Mexico. On the eve of the battle of Palo Alto, for example, an old Aztec priest in a remote Indian community lights a torch at the flame of Montezuma and proclaims the doom of the Spaniards. Just as the Spaniards conquered the Aztecs, the priest declares, so will "a new race from the north" defeat the Spaniards in battle. "That Murder done by the Spaniard, returns to him again; and the blood that he once shed, rises from the ground, which will not hide it, and becomes a torrent to overflow his rule, his people, and his altars!" (47). The gothic language of uncanny, bloody revenge heightens as the chant continues:

> Montezuma, from the shadows of ages, hear the cry of thy children! Arise! Gaze from the unclosed Halls of Death, upon the Spaniard's ruin, and tell the ghosts to shout, as he dashes to darkness in a whirlpool of blood:

Montezuma, and all ye ghosts, sing your song of gladness now, and let the
days of your sorrow be past! Even, above the ocean of blood, which flows
from thy mouth, over the land of Anahuac, behold the Dove of Peace, bearing her green leaves and white blossoms to the children of the soil! (47)

In this passage, the ghosts of Indians who died during the Spanish conquest lurk in the shadows of the unclosed Halls of Death, mutely wit-
nessing the preparations for the battle between Mexico and the United
States. Lippard suggests that the victory of the U.S. forces will exorcise
these ghosts by bringing about the Spaniard's ruin. He figures the United
States as the savior of Montezuma's children; paradoxically, the ocean of
blood that is spilled as the United States fights Mexico impels the Dove
of Peace to greet the long-oppressed "children of the soil" with green
leaves and white blossoms.

The irony of this passage is that the United States must imitate the
Spanish conquerors in order to replace them and put the ghosts of the
earlier conquest to rest. For if U.S. forces dash the Mexicans to darkness
in a whirlpool of blood, what ghosts will this second bloody conquest
engender? By raising the ghosts of conquests past, Lippard invokes
specters that trouble the exceptionalist premise that the U.S.-initiated
war was not an act of aggressive expansionism but rather the extension
of freedom to oppressed peoples. For even as he tries to represent the
United States as the redeemer of Mexico, bringing peace to the indigenous "children of the soil," the paradoxes that he encounters and the
bloody battle scenes that directly follow threaten the distinction he is
trying to make between the Spanish and U.S. empires: Lippard's war
pictures foreground the instability of empire, the contradictions of history, and the violence of U.S. conquest despite his desire for us to remember things differently.

WAR PICTURES

The going forth is beautiful. To see those flags flutter
so bravely from the lances, like the foliage of those
trees of death, to hear the bugles speak out,—but the
morrow? The coming back? Hark! through the
darkened air, did you not hear a sound, like the closing
of a thousand coffin lids?
                    —George Lippard, *Legends of Mexico*

Most of *Legends of Mexico* is devoted to the display of sensational pictures of battle scenes—it was even advertised in the pages of the *Quaker City* as "the most graphic and readable book ever written on the war with Mexico" (30 December 1848). The narrative moves from the opening border skirmishes in May 1846 to the first battles at Palo Alto and Resaca de la Palma and the attack on Monterrey in September 1846, before concluding at Buena Vista on 22 and 23 February 1847. Notably, Lippard leaves out other battles fought during this period, battles that were more difficult to glorify, including the "confused and costly" encounters at Contreras and Churubusco and the "ill-advised" battle of Molino del Rey.[64] Despite such telling omissions, however, his *Legends of Mexico* reveals much about popular responses to the war as it took place, for Lippard incorporates the language of contemporaneous newspaper accounts and frequently references war pictures that were staged as panoramas in theaters, reprinted as illustrations in papers, and sold on the street as popular prints.

Bill Brown proposes that Stephen Crane's *The Red Badge of Courage* (1895) "registers a shift in the mass mediation of war," reinterprets the Civil War "through the cultural lens of the [camera] lens itself," and thereby illuminates "a particular history of American seeing."[65] It could be argued that Lippard's war literature also registers such a shift but at an earlier moment, a moment when improvements in communications and print technology made it possible for pictures, news, books, and other printed, war-related material to circulate throughout the nation shortly after the important battles of the U.S.-Mexican War took place. We can glimpse the effects of these new technologies in Lippard's writing as they structure the framing of the visible in *Legends of Mexico*. He begins his long account of the battle of Palo Alto by painting a panoramic picture that resembles, in its representational strategies, the bird's-eye views of battlefields and military lines that were also on display in popular lithographs and in moving panoramas, a new form of popular theatrical entertainment that featured scenes painted on giant canvases that were unwound on rollers.[66] As he leads the gaze of the reader from point to point through interjected instructions—"look yonder," here "you see," "there, you behold"—he describes the battlefield in terms of its vision-accommodating possibilities: "No hillocks to obstruct the view, no ravines for ambuscade, no massive trees, to conceal the tube of the deadly rifles...it seemed the very place for a battle, the convenient and appropriate theatre for a scene of wholesale murder" (49). And viewed from a distance, before the action has begun, he sees the "imposing array" of the armies as "very beautiful" (50).

This panorama of war clearly depends upon a proprietary aesthetic—
a vision of the Mexican landscape as open and available to the reader's
controlling, colonizing gaze. But *Legends of Mexico* also contains many
scenes that focus on Mexican injuries and war losses, and often those
passages lead in unexpected directions. For instance, as the battle of Resaca de la Palma nears its close, Lippard focuses on the road to Fort
Brown, "paved with corses, roaring with thunder, blazing with the lightning of cannon." Although earlier he invited the reader to gaze at the
"beautiful" array of troops preparing for battle, here he directs us to
"[g]aze there, and see the Mexicans go down at every shot, by ranks, by
platoons, by columns. It is no battle, but a hunt, a Massacre!" As the
U.S. troops set fire to the prairie, the movement of the flames "crushes
and hurls and burns the Mexicans toward the center of death, the Rio
Grande." And yet, instead of describing this as a glorious sight, the narrator seems to shrink from it: "The heart grows sick of the blood. The
chaparral seems a great heart of carnage, palpitating a death at every
throb. Volumes would not tell the horrors of that flight!" (99). And then,
when Mexican soldiers try to crowd onto a raft and escape down the
river, the boat capsizes, "and where a moment ago was a mass of human
faces, lancers' flags and war-horse forms, now is only the boiling river,
heaving with the dying and the dead" (100). For days afterward, "those
bodies, festering in corruption, floated blackened and hideous, upon the
waters of the Rio Grande" (100). At this point, as the battle turns into
a massacre, it becomes difficult to distinguish scenes of U.S. empire-
building from the "blackest" legends of the Spanish conquest.

Although Lippard quickly moves to place this battle scene within the
context of Zachary Taylor's march to "redeem" the continent, his
panoramas of death undermine the already difficult to sustain distinction between an evil Spanish and a benign U.S. conquest. Indeed, the carnage suggests parallels between U.S.–Mexican War battles and infamous
episodes of the Spanish Conquest such as the massacre at Cholula, where
more than three thousand Indians were slaughtered. This is especially
true when battles are fought in densely populated areas, such as the city
of Monterrey, where almost ten thousand people lived. According to
Prescott and other historians, the massacre at Cholula had been particularly horrible—an encounter that "left a dark stain on the memory of
the Conquerors"—because it involved noncombatants, "townsmen"
who "made scarcely any resistance" to the Spaniards who sacked and
burned the city, leaving corpses "festering in heaps in the streets and
the great square."[67] During the four-day battle at Monterrey in late

September 1846, U.S. soldiers advanced through the city by invading the homes of townspeople, knocking down walls between connected dwellings, and then moving on through to the next house. This battle plan inevitably involved noncombatants and caused massive destruction. According to the fifteen Mexican writers of the war history that was translated into English in 1850 as *The Other Side; or, Notes for the History of the War Between Mexico and the United States,* after the battle "Monterey was converted into a vast cemetery. The unburied bodies, the dead and putrid mules, the silence of the streets, all gave a fearful aspect to this city."[68]

Although most of the visual artists chose to ignore this aspect of the battle and to focus instead on remote views of the city or panoramas featuring the dramatic landscape, a few did try to picture the devastation that took place. In a lithograph entitled "Third Day of the Siege of Monterey" (1846) and in Nathaniel Currier's "Battle of Monterey" (1846), U.S. soldiers are depicted fighting in the streets and breaking through stone fortifications, with homes and the cathedral in the background.[69] But in *Legends of Mexico,* U.S. soldiers invade Mexican homes, and as Lippard pictures the fighting, images of rape, death, and violence directed at noncombatants dominate the narrative. For from his perspective, war on the battlefield "where the yell of the dying, rings its defiance to the charging legions, wears on its bloodiest plume, some gleam of chivalry, but War in the Home, scattering its corses, besides the holiest altars of life, and mingling the household gods, with bleeding hearts and shattered skulls—this, indeed, is a fearful thing" (116).

In the beginning of this chapter, as Lippard describes Monterrey and its environs, he adopts the representational strategies of the popular prints that offered panoramic views of the city's spectacular setting: "They tell me that Monterey is beautiful; that it lies among the snow-white mountains, whose summits reach the clouds."[70] As he focuses on the lands surrounding the city, he emphasizes images of material abundance—tropical fruit and foliage, the green cornfields, and "the rich garniture of the soil"—that would appeal to prospective U.S. colonists. Lippard imagines the city as a woman, an "Amazon Queen," with orange groves that "girdle her dark stone walls, with their white blossoms, and hang their golden fruit above her battlemented roofs." "From this elevated grove, towards the south, around the sleeping city," he writes, "winds the beautiful river of San Juan, now hidden among the pomegranate trees, now sending a silvery branch into the town, again flashing on, besides its castled walls" (107). As he speculates on the difficulties of conquering the city (it seems "impregnable," "No arms can take it; no cannon blast its impenetrable

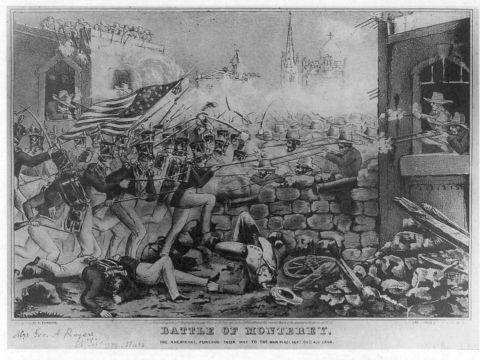

Figure 2.   "Battle of Monterey" lithograph by Nathaniel Currier. (Courtesy American Antiquarian Society)

walls" [108]), the gendered rhetoric of war and conquest that he deploys suggests the invasion of the city would be a metaphorical rape of Monterrey, the Amazon Queen. And when he finally zooms in on the besieged city, a bloody vision of war transforms the pastoral landscape into a gothic nightmare: the reader is drawn into a scene that is marked by violent struggle and the suffering of the city's inhabitants. As the orange groves that girdle the city are mowed down, the romantic picture of the city as a virgin Amazon Queen is displaced by images of violation and rape. As the beautiful San Juan becomes a river of blood, the shame registered by its "crimson blush" (109) betrays the violence of U.S. empire-building. And as a woman in her home is crushed and splintered by the weapons of war, Lippard revises popular representations of the battle of Monterrey that cut the besieged city-dwellers out of the picture. As clouds of battle smoke stretch "like an immense shroud along the western sky" (109), such gothic transformations unsettle exceptionalist formulations of U.S. conquest as uniquely good or benign.

Lippard further emphasizes a gendered reading of conquest by pairing this picture of the transformation of the landscape with a story that takes the reader into a Mexican home where two young women, virgins of course, wait for their father and brother to return from the fighting. Lippard places the reader inside the house with the women, instead of with the U.S. soldiers, as the battle intensifies: "And the storm grew nearer their house; it seemed to rage all around them, for those terrible sounds never for one moment ceased, and the red flash poured through the narrow window, in one incessant sheet of battle lightning" (111). Finally, the door to their chamber gives way, "the red battle light rush[es] into the place" (113), and their dying father falls backward into their home, with blood pouring from a wound in his chest. Once again, Lippard figures the invasion of the homes of Monterrey as a symbolic rape. The U.S. volunteer who "fired for the first time, with the lust of carnage" (113), and who killed the father and receives the latter's dying curse, is thus figured as invader, rapist, and murderer all at once. For as the soldier "saw the unspeakable agony, written on each face," he "knew himself, a guilty and blood-stained man" (113).

While it might be possible for the U.S. reader to distance himself/herself from the scene by reflecting that these horrors are happening to Mexicans, the volunteer does not make such a distinction. In fact, he compares this Mexican home to the home he left behind in Pennsylvania: "I have a father, too, away in Pennsylvania, and sisters, too, that resemble these girls" (114). As the Mexican home that he has invaded becomes an uncanny double of his home in Pennsylvania, the entire battle scene takes on a ghastly hue. Unable to bear the horror of the murder scene, "only wishing to turn his eyes away from that sight," he escapes to the roof and witnesses the end of the battle of Monterrey. But even the panoramic view of the city that meets his gaze provides no real distance from the scene he has left, for, "sick of the battle," he sees only "one great lake of carnage" as "three days battle rolls by every street and avenue, along these roofs, and through yonder smoking ruin" (114). Everywhere he looks, "the dead looked so ghastly up in his face!" (115). The violence extends to noncombatants, too, for the soldier also sees a dead woman, "clotted with blood, while her frozen features, knit so darkly in the brow, and distorted along the lips, told how fierce the struggle in which she died" (115). And when he returns to the room where he left the sisters and their dying father, it seems "like a death vault." As he feels his way through the pitch-black chamber, his hands touch the cold faces of the dead, which leave his fingers wet with clotted blood. When finally the glare

THE SISTERS OF MONTEREY:
A LEGEND OF MEXICO.
BY GEORGE LIPPARD.

Figure 3. "The Sisters of Monterey" detail in the *Quaker City,* 27 January 1849. (Courtesy American Antiquarian Society)

of battle momentarily lights up the room, he sees three corpses instead of one, for a single bullet has pierced the skulls of one sister and the brother who had returned from battle and, with his head close to hers, had tried to console her. And this "picture" was only "one of the thousand horrible sights which the light of battle, revealed in the Homes of Monterey" (117).

Lippard ends by trying to give the chapter a redemptive conclusion, one that rings resoundingly hollow after the pages of horror that preceded it. First, he pulls back from the battle scene, takes a remote perspective, and pictures the landscape restored and transfigured, the river no longer blushing with blood, the homes of the town framed in gardens of flowers. "Over the Bishop's palace waves the Banner of the Stars," Lippard writes, "symbol of that Democratic truth, which never for a moment ceases to speak, 'This continent is the Homestead of free and honest men. Kings have no business here. Hasten to possess it, Children of Washington!'" (119). Second, he marries the bereaved Mexican woman to the murderer of her father, and describes her as both "a true woman" and a trophy of war, a "gift" sent "from Paradise," which the soldier's father and sisters take "to their hearts" (121). In both of these ways, Lippard tries to banish scenes of invasion by promoting a vision of consensual relations between the United States and Mexico. In the first instance, he invokes the ideals of democracy to rewrite the story of violent conquest as a narrative about the extension of freedom. In the second, he attempts to turn force into consent and symbolic rape into marriage, making his readers feel at home in Mexico by replacing disturbing images of the invasion of Mexican homes with a romantic wedding picture.

But if Lippard repeatedly tries to turn force into consent, most of *Legends of Mexico* reveals that, as the Mexican writers of *The Other Side* argued, the age of U.S. empire-building, which was called "one of light," was "notwithstanding, the same as the former—one of *force and violence.*"[71] And in Lippard's second novel set in Mexico, *'Bel of Prairie Eden,* which was published the next year, representations of international romance are displaced by dramas of seduction, rape, and revenge as his utopia for redeemed labor becomes a haunted homestead in the Texas borderlands.

WHITE UTOPIA IS A HAUNTED HOMESTEAD

In the first chapter of *'Bel of Prairie Eden,* Lippard initially represents the Texas prairies in idealized terms, as a boundless, utopian space where emigrants can escape the past and realize their dreams of freedom by settling on virgin, vacant land. In the opening chapter, two brothers, the sons of wealthy Texas colonist Jacob Grywin, gaze at a beautiful view: "the prairie, bathed in the light of the setting sun" (7). By calling their home Prairie Eden and by describing the Texas landscape in literally glowing terms, Lippard echoes the extensive literature written during the 1830s and 1840s to encourage prospective settlers from Europe and the United States to relocate in Texas.[72] During the 1820s, Mexico passed colonization laws allowing foreigners to buy land in Texas more cheaply than it could be purchased in the United States. For the next two decades, beginning in the Mexican period and continuing after the United States annexed Texas in 1845, emigrants from the southern United States, especially, but also from eastern U.S. cities, Ireland, Germany, and other parts of Europe flocked to the area, often settling in small colonies founded by land agents called *empresarios.*[73] In order to sell their vision of a colonized Texas to emigrants, land companies and speculators represented the region as a utopia for the landless, an Edenic place where settlers could escape the class constraints of Europe and the United States and establish equality and independence through land ownership.[74] But Lippard's Texas is haunted by the race wars that mark its foundation as well as by volatile, shifting national sentiments and the very forces of the capitalist city that some emigrants sought to escape.

From the beginning, many ominous signs indicate that all is not well in Prairie Eden. Grywin, the founder of the colony, is a "broken bank director of Philadelphia, who turned traitor to the trust of some thousand widows, and then fled the city, seeking refuge for his guilty wealth in the prairie of Texas."[75] Instead of providing utopian spaces that allow immigrants to escape the capitalist relations of the city, Texas here serves as a refuge for the corrupt capitalist who wants to leave his crimes, but not the profits they yielded, behind him in the East. Although he is a Northerner, Grywin also brings slaves with him to Texas, and Lippard thereby references widespread fears that the incorporation of new territory into the Union would mean the extension of slavery. An *empresario*-like figure, Grywin arrives in Texas in 1840, accompanied by fifty "retainers," including "forty white laborers—some civilized people from the States, others German emigrants—and ten black slaves" (8) who build a mansion for him on the prairie and surround it with their own "small huts" (16). The luxurious mansion resembles those described in urban gothic literature, especially when it is contrasted with the lowly huts on its borders; it could have been lifted from *New York* or *The Quaker City* and dropped on the Texas prairie. Lippard repeatedly uncovers uncanny resemblances and traces connections between the capitalist U.S. city and scenes of empire-building in Texas and Mexico in a novel which, as the book's cover tells us, "begins on the wild prairie—goes on in the city of Vera Cruz—winds up in Philadelphia." But moss hangs like a silvery shroud around Grywin's mansion; the prairie is inhabited by spectral forms that prophesy "evil, nothing but evil" (13); eerie buzzards silently circle over the rooftops of Vera Cruz on the night that U.S. troops land in the city; and remorse for acts of seduction and revenge committed in Mexico pervades the gloomy conclusion that takes place in Philadelphia.

Even at the outset, this novel implies that this colony, and also perhaps the colonization of Texas, are based on shaky foundations. This premise haunts the narrative, suggesting that everything that subsequently happens to Grywin's house might result from his original guilty acts as well as from his attempts to escape their consequences. For Grywin's house is soon in danger—literally, when it is invaded by his overseer and former clerk, Red Ewen, in league with troops from the Mexican army, which he has joined—and symbolically, when the Mexican officer Don Antonio Marin offers Grywin's daughter, 'Bel, a choice between her honor and her father's life. Although in *Legends of Mexico* Lippard juxtaposes battle scenes and romance plots, in *'Bel of Prairie Eden* the conflict between the United States and Mexico is translated into dueling narratives of seduction, rape, and revenge, in which women's bodies condense tangled webs of complex issues that are never resolved.

Even though Lippard initially stigmatizes the Texas colonizer, he soon turns the tables by demonizing the Mexican Marin. We discover that Marin knew 'Bel and her family before, in Philadelphia, when he was the attaché of the Mexican legation. At that time, he had asked to marry 'Bel and was refused; to that refusal her father "added some words, at once needless and bitter" (22). But if this contemptuous refusal seems at first to partially justify Marin's vengeful feelings, attempts to represent him as anything other than monstrous disappear after he threatens 'Bel's virginity. Soon thereafter, he drugs her with opium, gets her to consent to have sex with him in order to save her father's life, and then hangs Grywin anyway. Later, Marin also orders his soldiers to murder Grywin's younger son, Harry. At these moments, Lippard blames Mexico for the war and encourages readers to feel for white settlers on the Texas borderlands. By making Ewen and the Mexican soldiers a threat to the white family and the homestead in Texas, Lippard mobilizes sensations of fear and horror in behalf of the Texas colonizers that may override his representation of the colonization of Texas as a morally tainted enterprise.

But the vengefulness of Grywin's remaining son, John, is just as monstrous, and it leads to an ending that is anything but happy. After John learns what has happened to his family, he begins to plot his sadistic revenge. First, as Marin and his father walk together one evening, a bullet from an unknown source pierces his father's brain. John, of course, is responsible. Second, John seduces Marin's sister, Isora, and then arranges it so that Marin is forced to watch from a hidden aperture while John has sex with her. Finally, John tricks Ewen into murdering Marin by plunging a knife into his heart as part of an initiation rite. But this "Satanic revenge" (70) returns to haunt John after he falls in love with Isora, even though she never learns that John's enemy was her brother or that her brother is dead. John marries Isora and takes her back to Philadelphia, but she soon becomes unhappy and thinks only about seeing Marin again; meanwhile, John is tortured by the thought that she is pining away because of his excessive revenge. At the novel's end, Isora dies of grief and John is left alone with his remorse.

As I have suggested throughout Part 1, Lippard's invocation of a panoply of gothic effects—"haunted houses, evil villains, ghosts, gloomy landscapes, madness, terror, suspense, horror"—to narrate the U.S. presence in Texas and Mexico has contradictory effects.[76] On the one hand, it contributes to the demonization of Mexicans and may thereby feed the war frenzy of readers. There is also plenty of lurid material here to stimulate a voyeuristic response at some distance from a well-defined, coherent position on the war. But the novel also suggests that romance cannot heal the wounds of war: the marriage plot that Lippard uses at the end of *Legends of Mexico,* and that so many writers employed to make the conquest of northern Mexico appear to be consensual, fails as a way of resolving international conflict. Force is never plausibly transformed into consent; the violence that structures most of the narrative does not disappear but instead fully implicates the Texas colonizer in the bleak conclusion. It is even possible to read this as an antiwar novel if one emphasizes the ending and interprets the escalating revenge plots as an allegory about the futility of the violence between the United States and Mexico.

Lippard apparently began to have second thoughts about his war fiction soon after the conflict ended. In the brief sketch "A Sequel to the Legends of Mexico" that appeared in *The White Banner* in 1851, Lippard worried about whether the "very pictures of war and its chivalry" that he had drawn a few years earlier "might not be misconceived and lead young hearts into an appetite for blood-shedding" (108). So a few years after the signing of the Treaty of Guadalupe Hidalgo, he imagined Taylor and his army of conquest transformed into an "Industrial Army," with spades instead of muskets, and plows instead of cannons, transforming the Pennsylvania desert "into a very garden, adorned with the homes of one hundred thousand poor men, who before the campaign began, had been starving in the suburbs of the Great Cities" (109). In this sketch, Lippard tries to make two haunting visions of war disappear: the class warfare threatened by poor men accumulating in Northeastern cities, and the violent, bloody scenes of the U.S.-Mexican War that he and other writers had drawn for the sensational press during the 1840s. Although he hoped to banish these disturbing images of U.S. expansion and domestic unrest by sketching a Jeffersonian picture of an agrarian republic transforming poor men and artisan radicals into virtuous and useful U.S. settlers, most of his writing betrays the impossibility of escaping the nightmare of capitalist industrialization and violent empire-building into a free space of egalitarian possibility. Although, with the important exception of Slotkin, critics who have begun to recover Lippard's work and to discuss his class politics have had little to say about his U.S.–Mexican War novels, it is impossible to understand the connections between class formation and empire-building without reading this literature.

For if, as Amy Kaplan argues, the role of empire has been largely ignored in the study of U.S. culture, then efforts to foreground the construction of "American nationality" through "political struggles for power with other cultures and nations" must also focus on the war with Mexico.[77] Although scholars often locate the origins of U.S. imperialism at the end of the nineteenth century, the past that is reanimated in sensational war literature should provoke the re-examination of a longer history of empire in the Americas, because the events of 1848 make it clear that U.S. class and racial formations throughout the nineteenth century were decisively shaped by international conflict and both the internal and the global dynamics of empire-building.

PART 2

Foreign Bodies and International Race Romance in the Story Papers

THREE

The Story-Paper Empire

The subject of war, diplomacy, and high politics frequently comes up when traditional political historians question the utility of gender in their work. But here, too, we need to look beyond the actors and the literal import of their words. Power relations among nations and the status of colonial subjects have been made comprehensible (and thus legitimate) in terms of relations between male and female. The legitimizing of war—of expending young lives to protect the state—has variously taken the forms of explicit appeals to manhood (to the need to defend otherwise vulnerable women and children), of implicit reliance on belief in the duty of sons to serve their leaders or their (father the) king, and of associations between masculinity and national strength. High politics itself is a gendered concept, for it establishes its crucial importance and public power, the reasons for and the fact of its highest authority, precisely in its exclusion of women from its work. Gender is one of the recurrent references by which political power has been conceived, legitimated, and criticized. It refers to but also establishes the meaning of the male/female opposition.

> —Joan Scott, "Gender: A Useful Category
> of Historical Analysis"

[My concern here is to] locate an erotics of politics, to show how a variety of novel national ideas are all ostensibly grounded in "natural" heterosexual love and in the marriages that provided a figure for apparently nonviolent consolidation during internecine conflicts at midcentury. Romantic passion, on my reading, gave a rhetoric for the hegemonic projects in Gramsci's sense of conquering the antagonist through mutual interest, or 'love,' rather than through coercion....It will be evident that many romances strive toward socially convenient marriages and that, despite their variety, the ideal states they project are rather hierarchical.

> —Doris Sommer, *Foundational Fictions*

One of the major contradictions of imperialist expansion was
that while it strove to nationalize and domesticate foreign
territories and peoples, annexation incorporated nonwhite
foreign subjects in a way perceived to undermine the nation
as a domestic space.

—Amy Kaplan, "Manifest Domesticity"

Issues of gender, sexuality, and race were clearly at stake in political debates about imperial expansion and in popular sensational adventure literature published during the 1840s and 1850s. This was so, first of all,
because both champions and critics of imperial expansion appealed to ideologies of manhood. In the 1840s, the "volunteer"—the virtuous citizen-
soldier who defended the nation out of a love for his native land—was
often championed as a manly ideal and as a symbol of the United States
in the popular press. But other men, including the large numbers of immigrants and propertyless men in the U.S. military forces and in the nation, as well as Mexican men of all types, were frequently viewed as
threats to such conceptions of manhood and national identity. The war
literature displays intense anxieties, moreover, about whether Irish and
other immigrant men can be subordinated within U.S. military hierarchies or whether they will instead turn out to be weak links in the chain
of imperial manhood.[1] On the other hand, although a few U.S. writers
idealized international bonds between elite U.S. and Mexican men, Mexico was generally subordinated to the United States within such visions
of inter-American reconciliation.

Eligibility for such subordination crucially depended on how the
boundaries of whiteness were constructed; in other words, on whether
various types of working-class, immigrant, and Mexican men were
thought to be white. These were often real questions during the 1840s,
for during those years the place of the Irish and especially of Mexicans
within emerging racial (re)classifications was by no means clear. Although writers of popular adventure fiction occasionally imagined elite
Mexican men who might enter into political or business relationships
with U.S. men or, more rarely, who might marry white U.S. women,
Mexican men were more often viewed as racially other and as either ex-

cessively or inadequately manly. Immigrant Irishmen were represented in similar ways, but some of the war literature, as we shall see, emphasized the assimilation of the Irish into white America through military service. Finally, native-born, working-class men were sometimes idealized in popular novels, but they were more usually subordinated to the merchants' sons and other elites who were often the heroes of imperial adventure fiction. Although the most influential accounts of entanglements of ideologies of U.S. manhood and empire focus on the late nineteenth century, all of these examples suggest that mid-nineteenth-century U.S. conceptions of manhood were tried and recast in the crucible of empire.[2]

Mid-nineteenth-century imperialism also crucially affected women and engaged ideologies of womanhood. The U.S.-Mexican War dramatically and violently transformed the lives of the women who lived where battles were fought and where military forces were present. Many women followed men to the battlefields, and some, according to popular legend, even fought in the war. Women also labored in the camps, foraging, cooking, doing laundry, and nursing the wounded. Although some U.S. women, notably Irish immigrant women, followed the army to Mexico, for many U.S. observers the visible presence of women in Mexican military camps was apparently a remarkable sight.[3] When in the early 1840s the relatively privileged and comfortable Frances Calderón de la Barca, a Scottish-born Chilean diplomat's wife who migrated to the United States in the 1830s, encountered women in a Mexican army unit during the early 1840s, she scathingly described them as "masculine women" and as "mounted Amazons, who looked like very ugly men in a semi-female disguise."[4] From Calderón de la Barca's elite perspective, these *soldaderas* unsettled the boundaries of gender, so much so that they "looked like" men.

On the other hand, during the war some U.S. writers depicted Mexican women as models of womanhood who selflessly nurtured men on both the U.S. and Mexican sides. In John Greenleaf Whittier's popular poem "The Angels of Buena Vista," for instance, "holy" Mexican women minister with "tender care" to wounded soldiers left on the battlefield after the fight has ended.[5] But if this image of Mexican women as ministering angels mirrored influential U.S. domestic ideals of womanhood, many popular authors of story-paper literature depicted Mexican women, as Calderón de la Barca did, as blurring the boundaries of gender. Indeed, many of their novels feature Mexican women who disguise themselves as men in order to participate in the war. And yet, although Calderón de la Barca viewed the crossing of gender boundaries as threatening and disgusting, sensational story-paper novelists, as we shall see, more often suggested that the exploits of boundary-crossing heroines were thrilling and heroic, even though the endings usually emphasized the heroine's return to a more stereotypically feminine role.

As these examples suggest, besides directly involving women, the war also significantly involved ideas about women. Indeed, relations between the United States and Mexico were often imagined as relations between male and female. In a wide range of discourses, U.S. national strength was metaphorically aligned with manhood, and Mexico was figured as a woman.[6] In this case, too, ideologies of womanhood were inseparable from those of race and empire. That is, questions about the boundaries of gender, about what type of "woman" Mexico was, and about whether "she" was an appropriate romantic partner for the United States were inseparable from debates about the boundaries of race and the significance of empire for the white republic.

These debates focused on sexuality as well as gender. When relations between the United States and Mexico were recast as erotic relations, narratives of sexuality were also involved, for the key question in many wartime discourses was whether a "feminine" Mexico could be "married" to the implicitly male United States.[7] Although advocates of empire struggled to ground imperial relations in male/female desire, anti-imperialists were more interested in showing why a marriage between nations was impossible, ill advised, or unnatural. Both sides, however, appealed to a complex of ideas that we might associate with emergent conceptions of heterosexuality in order to legitimate their positions on international relations.[8] But in this period, which directly preceded the late-nineteenth-century codification of a "homosexual" identity in medical and legal discourses, ideas about the boundaries of sexuality were in flux. And yet, even though what Eve Kosofsky Sedgwick has called "the crisis of homo/heterosexual definition" did not at this moment, as it would soon, structure "the major nodes of thought and knowledge" of Western culture, U.S.–Mexican War literature certainly marked an "impending crisis" in discourses of sexuality as well as in sectional relations between North and South.[9]

Although war literature often reasserted the legitimacy and naturalness of male/female desire, however, it also registered nonnormative forms of desire and intense affective bonds between men. In a similar context, Ann Laura Stoler has argued that if "the colonies were construed as sites where European virility could be boldly demonstrated it

was because they were also thought to crystallize those conditions of isolation, inactivity, decadence, and intense male camaraderie where heterosexual definitions of manliness could as easily be unmade."[10] During
the U.S.-Mexican War, relationships between men, as well as the pull of
the military hierarchies that structured many of these relationships, were
dramatically intensified. Moreover, though Mexico was not a colony, it
was often imagined as an exotic space teeming with alternatives to middle-
class U.S. ideals of gender and sexuality.[11] So as Stoler suggests, it would
be a mistake to assume that dominant ideals of gender and sexuality
were "merely confirmed" by imperial projects, not only because imperial activity was sometimes thought to threaten these ideals but also because imperial "discourses of sexuality were productive of class and
racial power, not mere reflections of them."[12] These sexual dynamics
were of course overdetermined by imperial hierarchies: U.S. empire-
building in Mexico was one of the fields within which the boundaries of
an emergent heterosexuality as well as its excluded alternatives were
elaborated. In what follows, I examine how authors of sensational story-
paper fiction reconstructed the boundaries of race, gender, and sexuality that the U.S.-Mexican War both unsettled and reinforced.

During the late 1840s and 1850s, producers of story papers and cheap
pamphlet literature helped to organize a new sphere of sensational mass
culture by publishing adventure fiction written mostly by "native" authors. Even as literary entrepreneurs and Young Americans such as John
O'Sullivan promoted a cultural nationalism that was conjoined to ideologies of Manifest Destiny, so too did these early purveyors of popular
literature.[13] In the second half of the 1840s, the Boston-based weekly
story paper the *Flag of Our Union* dominated the field of cheap literature; the publishers, Frederick Gleason and Maturin Murray Ballou, offered prizes to prospective authors, and, according to Henry Nash Smith,
"pioneered the development of a national system of distribution" and
"developed the standard procedures of the popular adventure story."[14]
As one of the most important early forms of mass culture, these story-
paper adventure novels reveal the intimate relationships between U.S.
empire-building in the American 1848 and (re)constructions of class,
race, gender, and sexuality in the mid–nineteenth century and beyond.

Alexander Saxton has suggested that the extension of white male suffrage in the early part of the century, along with improvements in print
technology and literacy rates, inaugurated a new era of mass political
culture in which the Democrats and the Whigs competed for the allegiance of potential voters with smaller parties such as the many nativist

organizations that intermittently flourished during the late 1840s.[15] In other words, the new mass culture of which the story paper was an important part helped to mobilize the changing coalitions that congealed tenuously at election time. Although the story papers claimed to be politically independent or neutral and tried to appeal to a diverse audience, during the late 1840s they included many stories, editorials, and reports about the war and engaged questions about the extension of slavery, the annexation of all or part of Mexico, and the incorporation of foreigners and nonwhite people into the nation. The story papers also presented models for relationships among different types of U.S. men, and developed the conventions of what I am calling international race romance—stories that try to "reconcile the irreconcilable" and transform U.S. force into Mexican "consent" by recasting violent inter-American conflicts as romantic melodramas.[16]

Story papers such as Gleason's and Ballou's *Flag,* Justin Jones's *Star Spangled Banner,* and the Williams Brothers' *Uncle Sam* and the *Flag of the Free,* which claimed circulations of up to forty thousand during the years of the U.S.-Mexican War, carried fewer news items than did the labor newspapers or the mass dailies, devoting most of their space instead to serialized sensational stories such as *The Secret Service Ship, The Volunteer: or, The Maid of Monterey,* and *The Black Avenger of the Spanish Main.*[17] These papers were very different from Lippard's *Quaker City* weekly, which I discussed in the previous chapter, or *Ned Buntline's Own,* another story paper that, as we shall see, juxtaposed serialized novels with articles and editorials that articulated working-class struggles to the nativist cause. Although the *Flag of Our Union,* for instance, declared itself the friend of the laboring classes, it rarely reported specifically on workers' issues, organizations, and conflicts.[18] Instead, it praised the dignity of labor as well as the importance of Yankee trade and manufactures, and generally aimed to accommodate a mass audience composed of multiple classes. It was advertised, after all, as a paper "published for the million, and at a cost, and in a shape that places them within the reach of all" (7 October 1847). The Williams Brothers' *Flag of the Free,* which was more Whiggish in tone than Gleason's and Ballou's *Flag* and even ran ads for a Whig paper in its columns, also claimed to be "Uncontaminated by party politics" and to exclude "all offensive subjects."[19] Although the set of beliefs circulating in story-paper literature cannot be reduced to the platform of one or the other of the political parties, the papers discuss many of the important political issues of the day even as they strive to convert the latter into the terms of romantic melodrama. These papers were irresistibly drawn to scenes of empire-building in the U.S. West and Mexico, and their efforts to attract the "million"—a mass audience made up of diverse constituencies—resembled and overlapped with the attempts of the political parties to assemble cross-class and translocal coalitions of white male voters.

But if a new mass political culture sought to win the allegiance of a heterogeneous group of white men, the audience for story-paper literature extended beyond the boundaries of that internally divided group, for the "million" clearly included women as well as men. The *Flag of Our Union* assured its female readers that it had "too many friends among the fair sex, not to heed well their interest, and to chronicle all valuable matters for their notice" (2 October 1847). "Unless we please the ladies," another editorial reported, "we shall feel that we are working in vain" (23 October 1847). The papers were widely distributed in Northeastern cities, where they were often issued under the imprint of local news agents, as well as in New Orleans, St. Louis, Cincinnati, and Detroit.[20] Apparently they followed in the tracks of empire: a soldier who corresponded with the *Flag* during the war assured the editors that "even into the heathen darkness of Mexico does the 'Flag of Our Union,' both literal and typical, penetrate" (18 September 1847). At a price of three or four cents an issue, the relative affordability of these papers would have made them accessible to many working-class readers.[21]

Many patriotic serialized thrillers (along with other similarly sensational stories that did not first appear in the story papers) were also published by these firms as pamphlet novelettes selling for twelve and a half or twenty-five cents. The novelettes circulated in even greater numbers than did the story papers. In October of 1847, Gleason claimed to have supplied "enormous editions" of up to fifty thousand for the public, and he also noted that the stories were being republished in England "by responsible houses and in large editions" (2 October 1847). For Gleason, one of the selling points of this literature was its cheapness and disposability: "Especially to those travelling on railroads or in steamboats they are capitally adapted, being so cheap that one can afford to leave them by the way after reading," read an advertisement featured in an 1847 issue of the *Flag* (27 November 1847). But according to one literary historian, "Gleason's most important boast about the *Flag* was its Red-Blooded Americanism." He claimed to print only the work of "American" authors rather than reprinting contributions to British publications, and he preferred "American heroes and heroines or, failing that, working-class protagonists in foreign countries who overcame aristocratic villains."[22] Although the story papers included an occasional selection from writers such as Eugene Sue and Alexander Dumas and although the Williams Brothers in particular reprinted many French and English favorites, the story papers overwhelmingly featured the work of U.S. writers, especially after 1845. These story-paper entrepreneurs thereby promoted a popular version of cultural nationalism as they supported a mass sensational literary culture that had as its focus the romantic adventure story, and during the next ten years or so, they developed its basic genres, conventions, and settings.[23] While John O'Sullivan coined the term "Manifest Destiny" and, as Priscilla Wald argues, "fashioned" an influential "narrative of literary nationalism" in the *Democratic Review,* the imperial fantasies distributed by cultural nationalists such as Gleason in the *Flag of Our Union* were aimed at a mass audience that was also interested in reading national literature devoted to resolving and obscuring "the contradictions and representational and political difficulties of an imperial nation."[24]

After he joined forces with Gleason in 1845, Maturin Murray Ballou, a Harvard dropout and the son of the famous New England minister Hosea Ballou, became one of the most important innovators in the field of mass-produced adventure literature. Ballou, who with Frank Leslie would go on to produce the first illustrated weekly *(Gleason's Pictorial Drawing Room Companion)* as well as several other cheap magazines, became the "guiding hand" at the *Flag* and eventually took over from Gleason in 1854.[25] He was also one of the firm's most popular authors. His *Fanny Campbell, the Female Pirate Captain* (1845) sold eighty thousand copies in a few weeks, and he wrote many other adventure stories for the paper, including *The Adventurer, or, The Wreck on the Indian Ocean* (1848); *Red Rupert, The American Bucanier* (1845); and *The Spanish Musketeer* (1847).[26] During the late 1840s, Gleason's Publishing Hall issued the work of more established authors, such as Ann Stephens, whose *Malaeska* would be revised and reprinted as the first dime novel in 1860; it also promoted new writers who soon became famous, such as Ned Buntline and Charles Averill, author of *Kit Carson, the Prince of the Gold Hunters* (1849) and many other hugely successful novels.[27] The novels promoted by the *Flag* often focused on foreign spaces, sometimes in Europe but more often in the Americas, and frequently with an emphasis on "Spanish fantasy": there were stories about the Spanish Inquisition; the era of Ferdinand and Isabella; Caribbean pirates; Cuba; Panama; and many, as we shall see, about Mexico. The *Flag* also exploited what we might call the foreign-within-the-domestic, which encompassed the mysterious city (Boston, New York); as well as Indian territory, which was claimed as part of "native" America yet represented as exotically other; and the liminal spaces of the U.S. borderlands, such as Texas, which were only insecurely or recently annexed to the nation. In all of these cases, the geopolitical relations of the period—notably including urbanization, increased immigration to the United States, the violent displacement of Indians by U.S. settlers and soldiers, rivalries with Spain and England in the Caribbean, and the war between the United States and Mexico—shaped the ideas about the foreign and the domestic that appeared in the pages of story papers such as the *Flag*.

In October of 1848, when Gleason announced a new prize competition, he elaborated on his criteria for judging these stories: "We wish for such contributions as shall be strictly moral in their tone, highly interesting in their plot, replete throughout with incident, well filled with exciting yet truthful description, and, in short, highly readable and entertaining. Domestic stories, so-called, are not exactly of the class that we desire; but tales—of the sea and land—of the stirring times of the revolution—or of dates still farther back, are more in accordance with our wishes."[28] Although Gleason specifically requested stories set in the past, however, during the late 1840s story-paper heroes were often sent off to Texas and Mexico in popular romances featuring side-switching soldiers, aristocratic Mexican creole or Spanish villains, and cross-dressed Mexican fighting women. Along with their competitors, the Williams Brothers in New York City and Justin Jones in Boston, Gleason produced the bulk of the war novels in this emerging field of mass culture.[29]

Why does Gleason distinguish this "exciting" literature from a "class" of "domestic stories"? Does he mean to suggest a certain distance from the mass-produced sentimental fiction, a good deal of which was written by women, which was also popular during this period? Not entirely, for sentimental literature and sensational fiction are not completely separate spheres during this period, though as Richard Brodhead observes, "domestic fiction had its audience centered among people (often women) already possessing, or newly aspiring to, or at least mentally identifying with, the leisured, child-centered home of middle-class life," while story-paper literature also incorporated other groups such as "farmboys, soldiers, German and Irish immigrants, and men and women of a newly solidifying working class."[30] But the *Flag*, which called itself a family paper, often endorsed middle-class ("strictly moral") values, sometimes featured female writers, and appealed to female as well as male readers. This does not mean that the audience for story-paper literature must be assimilated to that often nebulous catchall category, middle-class culture; Michael Denning's sense that this fiction also registers the "mechanic accents" of working-class audiences is more responsible to the complexities of the material.[31] And as Brodhead argues, very soon within emerging literary hierarchies domestic fiction would come to be identified with a female "middlebrow world of letters," while story papers would usually be assigned to "the 'low' one that came to exist 'below' it," a sphere which, particularly with the proliferation of male-authored dime novels after the Civil War, would increasingly, though often wrongly, be viewed as monolithically male.[32] This somewhat anachronistic hierarchy, however, which was promoted by many twentieth-century literary critics, conceals the considerable overlap between the two worlds in the 1840s, including not only the partial convergence between audiences but also the interdependent relationship between notions of the domestic and the foreign in the sensational story-paper literature of the period.

In an article entitled "Manifest Domesticity," Amy Kaplan has argued that in the 1850s, "narratives of domesticity and female subjectivity" were "inseparable from narratives of empire and nation-building." We should understand the domestic, she suggests, not as "an anchor, a feminine counterforce to the male activity of territorial conquest," but rather as "more mobile and less stabilizing...expand[ing] and contract[ing] the boundaries of home and nation...to produce shifting conceptions of the foreign."[33] While the sensational story-paper literature that I consider in Part 2 moves outside the boundaries of the domestic sphere, it also foregrounds the entanglement of the foreign and the domestic and produces racialized and gendered conceptions of the foreign in response to the events of 1848 and after.

Even when they are set in traditionally male-dominated spaces, such as the ship and the battlefield, issues of gender and sexuality are central to the plots and the imaginative work of these novels. Most feature female characters, frequently cross-dressed pirates or soldiers, such as Ned Buntline's Edwina Canales in *The Volunteer: or, The Maid of Monterey*, who dresses as a man and fights for Mexico. When the story was reprinted as a cheap novelette, the publishers singled out as a special selling point the illustrated cover, which featured a "spirited engraving of the heroine of the tale, Edwina Canales, gallantly encouraging her men to the charge" (2 October 1847). The pervasiveness of cross-dressed heroines in these novels suggests that sensational adventure literature was an important site for elaborations of the female picaresque; that is, the episodic

stories about the travels and adventures of "female criminals, adven-
turesses, soldiers, and spies" that were popular throughout the nineteenth century.[34] Although Cathy Davidson is right to point to the "con-
ditional and temporary" nature of the freedoms allowed to the picara in
the early U.S. novel, it is also the case that, as Elizabeth Young has argued, stories of military masquerade in particular could function "as a
metaphorical point of exchange for intersections between individual
bodies and the national body politic," thereby opening up questions of
gender, sexuality, race, region, and nation.[35]

Particularly during the years of the war with Mexico, as debates about
the annexation of all or part of Mexico intensified, and then after 1848,
when the national "home" was remodeled to accommodate vast new
territories, definitions of the foreign and the domestic, as well as ideologies of gender, sexuality, race, region, and class, were pressured and
reconstructed. For the dispute over the boundary between foreign and
domestic space, as well as the ensuing discussions about how much, if
any, of Mexico's territory should be incorporated into the United States,
engendered intense anxieties about internal political divisions, anxieties
that sensational story-paper literature attempted to manage. And although in almost every case it would be difficult to argue that the story-
paper novels wholeheartedly endorse the war and the annexation of
Mexico, in the international race romances of 1848 the boundaries of
gender and sexuality are central to debates over the politics of empire-
building and the incorporation of "foreign" territories and peoples.

One of the ways that international race romances tried to manage
these anxieties was by appealing to and popularizing an ideology of imperial U.S. American manhood that promised to transcend internal divisions such as class and region. This story-paper fiction that circulated
so widely among emergent middle-class and working-class audiences frequently appealed to an ideal of manhood embodied by a white U.S.-
American soldier-hero whose manliness is defined in contrast to various
"unmanly" villains, usually rapacious Mexican officers who try to force
unwilling heroines into marriage. But story-paper fiction exposed U.S.
domestic divisions even as it tried to bridge them, and it thereby registered, as we shall see, not only antagonisms of class, gender, and sexuality but also conflicts between so-called natives and immigrants, the
shifting place of the Irish within white America, and the looming battle
over slavery that would culminate in the Civil War.

Although these divisions also surfaced in other columns of the story
papers, the papers generally rallied around a white egalitarian patriotism

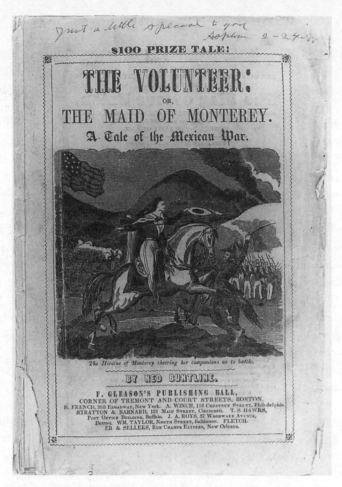

Figure 4.   Cover of Ned Buntline's novelette *The Volunteer: or, The Maid of Monterey* (1847). (Courtesy of the Bancroft Library, University of California)

fortified by the emotional intensities generated by the dynamics of empire-building. In addition to publishing patriotic war stories, for instance, story-paper entrepreneurs almost immediately integrated events and heroes from the Mexican War into their elaborate illustrated mastheads. In 1848, the *Flag of the Free* carried three illustrations under the title: the central engraving depicted a battle scene and the words "Buena Vista" (one of the most famous battles of the war), and on each side of this illustration pictures of Indians were paired with the words "Rio Grande" and "Aroostook," two places where boundary disputes had taken place.[36]

The representations of Indians could reference the many armed disputes over land that had taken place between whites and Indians, or they might simply indicate an appropriation of Indian-ness in the service of white nationalism, with the pictures of Indians confirming the "natural" boundaries of "native" America and serving as an emblem of the cultural nationalism that the paper promoted. An Indian also appears prominently on the *Star Spangled Banner*'s masthead in 1848, along with two illustrations of U.S. soldiers and a series of small drawings of U.S.-Mexican War heroes Zachary Taylor and Winfield Scott, as well as Washington, Hancock, Franklin, Lafayette, and Jackson. In the *Banner*'s title, each letter also contains the name of a famous battle, from Lexington and Concord to U.S.–Mexican War battles such as Buena Vista and Vera Cruz, ending with the word "Mexico" inside an exclamation mark. Not to be outdone, in addition to its illustrations of George Washington and two U.S. soldiers, the *Flag of Our Union* positioned each letter of the paper's title on a small sign that also included the names of all of the U.S. states, notably Texas. All of these mastheads represent the story-paper title as itself a flag, and the references to the Revolutionary War, the U.S.-Mexican War, Indians, and the names of all of the states wed U.S. nationalism to empire-building and military models of manhood.

Although the papers declared themselves neutral or independent and tried to please a mass audience, they all ultimately supported the war effort. Their positions on expansionism, however, were somewhat different. The *Flag of Our Union* was probably the most unequivocally and enthusiastically imperialist of the group. During 1846 and 1847, it included several articles in support of the war, including one that celebrated the new territory "acquired by Anglo-Saxon valor" (11 July 1846), a laudatory biographical sketch of Zachary Taylor (10 July 1847), a short piece applauding the military performance of republican citizen-soldiers (24 July 1847), and an article praising the capture of Mexico City as "an event, that in the days of Roman greatness would have indeed put the capstone to a pyramid of glorious conquests" (23 October 1847). The paper generally seemed to favor the addition of new Mexican territories to the nation, perhaps because of its "firm belief that five years from this time, Mexico will be settled largely by Yankees, and trade, and manufacture will prosper there" (15 May 1847). When the war ended, the *Flag* declared that the "United States, by virtue of its power and position, is the natural umpire of the North American continent" (13 May 1848). And just two years later, the editor advocated the annexation of Cuba, claiming that the " 'gem of the American archipelago' will be a

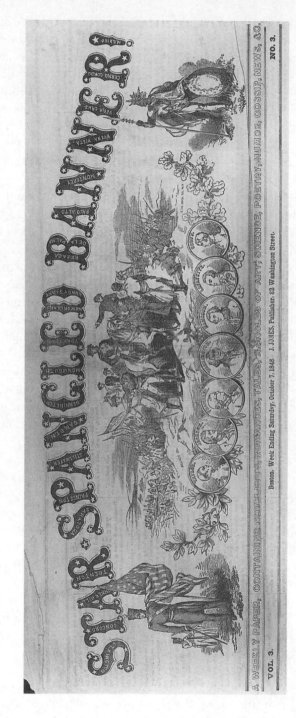

Figure 5. Masthead of the 7 October 1848 issue of the *Star Spangled Banner*. (Courtesy American Antiquarian Society)

Figure 6. Masthead of the 20 May 1848 issue of the *Flag of the Free*. (Courtesy American Antiquarian Society)

bone of contention until it is joined to this country, and probably pow-
der will be burnt before this is done" (20 July 1850).

Other papers, such as the Williams Brothers' *Flag of the Free,* however,
expressed more reservations about the annexation of new territories. Although in 1847 the paper urged the energetic prosecution of the Mexican
War (2 January 1847) and crowed that the "immense region of California
will fall into our hands like a ripe peach" (13 February 1847), after the
signing of the Treaty of Guadalupe Hidalgo in 1848 the editors rejoiced
that more of Mexico had not been taken, claiming that this "moderation"
showed that Americans were not as "tyrannical and unprincipled" as Europeans. Deeming the war "a glorious conquest," the paper claimed that
the treaty also represented "a conquest over those dangerous passions
which the intoxication of successful war has aroused in all nations, republics as well as monarchies. It saves us from the horrors incident to a
standing army of sixty thousand men in the heart of a sister republic" (17
June 1848). When a war between Indians and creoles in Yucatán led some
to advocate the U.S. occupation of the area, the writer of an editorial for
the paper objected: "Permanent occupation implies colonial government
and interminable expenses. England's colonies have been a constant drain
upon her treasury, and the source of great abuses" (20 May 1848). Some
of the same concerns no doubt caused the paper to denounce "the absurd
project" of annexing Cuba to the United States" (10 June 1848).

If the views about race expressed in another Williams Brothers publication, the *Uncle Sam,* are any indication, however, other worries about
the annexation of new territories also probably motivated this writer for
the *Flag of the Free.* At the outset of the war with Mexico, the *Uncle
Sam* expressed fears of the "mixed breed" troops of Mexico invading
the U.S. South, freeing all of the slaves, and enlisting the support of "people of color" to fight the United States:

> When we consider the peculiar population of the South, we confess we are
> not without our fears of impending evil. The troops of Mexico are of a mixed
> breed; they are mulattos, and so declining into the African. But little if any
> Spanish blood is to be found among them. Mexico is an "Anti-Slavery
> State"—she wars with all who hold the black race in subjection. There are
> three millions of slaves in our Southern country;—and the approach of a nu-
> merous body of foreigners proclaiming liberty to the people of color, and
> promising plunder and rapine as inducements to favor the advancing armies,
> is not a matter to be considered lightly. (23 May 1846)

Although story-paper editors sometimes expressed the hope that slavery
would gradually end, they certainly did not advocate abolitionism (the

Flag of Our Union even called Frederick Douglass a "black-guard" and "pet of the ultra abolitionists" [2 June 1849] for denouncing the war), and statements such as this one suggest that both antislavery and anti-annexationist sentiments were often motivated more by fears of racial contagion than idealistic concerns about republicanism.[37] "One reason why we deprecate a Mexican invasion is this," the *Uncle Sam* concluded. "The Mexicans are the nastiest race of modern times" (23 May 1846). The explicitness of the racial invective is unusual for editorials in the story papers of the time, but many similarly negative representations appear in story-paper novelettes.

The story-paper empire was more ambivalent, however, about the place of Irish immigrants within white America. Although Gleason and Ballou published two novelettes, Harry Halyard's *The Chieftain of Churubusco* and Charles Averill's *The Mexican Ranchero,* in which Irish deserters from the U.S. army join forces with the Mexicans, editorials and articles in the paper were generally fairly sympathetic toward the Irish. In part, that was because the *Flag* was virulently anti-British. The paper repeatedly attacked England for its imperialist policies in different parts of the world while denying that the United States was involved in a similar venture in Mexico. "[We] fight for right, not for conquest," one editorial announced, "therefore we have an actuating motive that never influences the British soldier" (31 October 1846). When the English criticized the United States for bombing Vera Cruz and injuring large numbers of noncombatants, the *Flag* replied that British conduct in China was much worse and that if the city been taken by the British they would have utterly destroyed it, just as they had burned and razed Washington during the War of 1812 (4 December 1847). And in response to news of military encounters between British and Indian troops, the *Flag* asked, "Who, in all Christendom, sympathizes with the British in this unexampled war of incursion and conquest, upon a foreign soil, separated from them by thousands of miles of ocean?" (7 April 1849). While the United States was involved in its own war of incursion and conquest in Mexico, the *Flag* repeatedly searched for ways to pin the charge of imperialism on Britain and thereby to make U.S. empire-building seem different—in this case on the implicit grounds that Britain sought overseas empire, "separated from them by thousands of miles of ocean." Noting that Irish emigrants fiercely hated Britain, one writer concluded, "[S]uch is British colonization" (25 December 1847). On the other hand, the paper guardedly welcomed the immigrants and implied that the United States would do a better job of ruling them than England had: "Give us good, stringent laws to govern these people, and we care not how many come" (7 July 1849).

But this equivocal editorial position on immigration was not always endorsed in the stories the *Flag* ran, which sometimes presented much less sympathetic views of the immigrant Irish who were coming to the United States in increasingly large numbers during the famine years. From the summer of 1845 through the early 1850s, the massive and repeated potato crop failures in Ireland forced the immigration of more than a million Irish to North America. These new immigrants were decidedly unwelcome to the nativists who organized political parties and participated in destructive riots during the 1840s and 1850s in Boston, New York, and Philadelphia. Irish laborers in Eastern U.S. cities generally received low wages, lived in substandard housing, worked at unskilled jobs, and tended to be concentrated in trades such as weaving that were being transformed by industrialization.[38] It is not surprising that many joined the U.S. Army and went to Mexico, where some watched Protestant soldiers destroy Catholic churches, others switched sides and fought with the Mexicans, and most completed their terms of service and returned to the United States. Although U.S. victories in battle were used to argue for the superiority of republican Anglo-Saxon America, immigrant soldiers constituted about half of the recruits in the regular army.[39] War service would in many ways help to facilitate the incorporation of the Irish into white America, but in sensational story-paper literature the Irish soldier condenses an array of anxieties about the boundaries of whiteness, about the distinction between the foreign and the domestic, and about empire and American exceptionalism.

All of this suggests that the battlefields of the U.S.-Mexican War, as represented in sensational story-paper fiction, were important theaters for stagings of a white "native" American identity. But these mass-produced imperial race fantasies have rarely been factored into accounts of mid-nineteenth-century popular culture. Michael Denning's influential study of popular literature during this period, for instance, moves from the late 1830s and early 1840s (the birth of the story paper, most notably with Park Griswold's and Park Benjamin's *Brother Jonathan*) to the mid-1850s (Bonner's *New York Ledger* and Street and Smith's *New York Weekly*), thereby skipping over the story papers and pamphlet novels of the late 1840s, the years of the U.S.-Mexican War.[40] As I suggested in the introduction, Denning rightly contends that an overemphasis on Westerns and tales of Indian fighting and the frontier within studies of popular fiction has made it difficult to appreciate how significant urban themes were in the literature of the 1840s.[41] But the omission of the story-paper literature of the late 1840s from this account makes it hard to comprehend the many connections between city and empire in this period, or to understand how inter-American conflict and U.S. imperial policies also shaped the early forms and genres of mass culture.

In the rest of Part 2, I argue that the story-paper literature of this period engendered racialized constructions of the foreign that are an important part of the story of nineteenth-century popular culture and that were subsequently recycled and transformed in dime novels and Western pulp fiction and films. In chapter 5, I consider the connections between city and empire, as well as between mass culture and working-class culture, by exploring intersections of nativism and imperialism in the work of Ned Buntline. Buntline wrote adventure fiction for the story papers during the U.S.–Mexican War years, just before he moved to New York and refashioned himself as the author of mysteries-of-the-city novels, the cultural representative of the white working-class B'hoys and G'hals of New York, and a proselytizer for nativist organizations such as the Order of United American Mechanics. Although critics tend to focus either on Buntline's literary adventures in New York or on his later role in developing the legend of Buffalo Bill, the imperial race fantasies that he elaborated in the story papers significantly shape the popular forms of nativist working-class protest that he produced in his urban reform literature, and these imperial romances both express and displace class antagonisms by recasting them in national, racial, and gendered terms.

I have suggested that Buntline's *The Volunteer* was one of many sensational Mexican War stories featuring cross-dressed female soldiers that were published as story-paper novels. In many of these romances, cross-dressed Mexican heroines lead troops heroically into battle and fight effectively, but ultimately fall in love with U.S. soldiers. As in the Latin American foundational fictions described by Doris Sommer, in U.S.–Mexican War stories the language of romantic passion provides a "rhetoric for the hegemonic projects in Gramsci's sense of conquering the antagonist through mutual interest, or 'love,' rather than through coercion." These popular U.S.–Mexican War romances try, in other words, to turn force into consent by reimagining the U.S. invasion as an international romance in which the force of erotic passion could, as Sommer puts it, "bind together heterodox constituencies."[42] These representations often imply that the crossing of gender boundaries is symptomatic of a larger crisis in Mexican national identity, a crisis that is sometimes said to justify U.S. intervention. But because these romances focus on

empire-building and international warfare rather than intranational consolidation, and because the possibility of incorporating Mexico through
annexation raises fears of race mixing, the conclusions to these novels
project a variety of possible outcomes rather than simply endorsing political union. In some, a marriage between a Mexican woman and a U.S.
soldier anticipates a more intimate postwar relationship between nations;
in others, heterosexual union must be deferred until the war ends; while
in still other cases, marriage is prevented by the violence of the war or
by other factors. But in each instance, plots that foreground the crossing
of gender boundaries and frustrated or successful international romances
manifestly display fears about the boundaries of the white republic and
U.S. expansion into Mexico.

Insofar as they both foreground tensions within ideologies of whiteness and expansionism, sensational representations of cross-dressed
Mexican women and side-switching Irish soldiers oddly mirror each
other. Although the cross-dressed Mexican female fighter is often an idealized, albeit exceptional, figure who is deemed assimilable into white
America, representations of Irish soldiers who switch sides and fight for
the Mexicans raise doubts about whether the Irish can truly be incorporated into the white nation. These negative representations of Irish soldiers in stories that also frequently feature heroic Yankee yeomen and
merchants' sons suggest how stepped-up immigration rates, the market
revolution, and early industrialization were transforming Northeastern
cities, political life, and alliances between classes during this period.[43]

Saxton argues that although "American workingmen during the Jacksonian era, skilled and unskilled, East and West, were more likely to be
Democrats than Whigs," there were notable exceptions: the Whigs gained
significant support from "native-born Protestant workers in cities where
recent immigrants, especially if they were Irish or German Catholics, became prominent in Democratic politics."[44] Even though the Whigs were
traditionally considered the party of the merchant classes, in this new
age of mass culture they tried to appeal to nonelite voters by arguing
that the tariff they championed would protect workers from foreign
competition and by sometimes joining forces with the nativists to support restrictions on immigration and naturalization. The divisions between Irish and Yankee soldiers in the story papers correspond in part,
then, to divisions between "the new and old working classes," as Amy
Bridges puts it. In New York City, support for nativism and the Whigs
came, she argues, from "the least proletarianized workers," especially
artisans in trades that had not yet been transformed by industrialization.

Focusing on the immigrant Irish as scapegoats, many native-born Protestant workers hoped to keep the transformation of work at bay by keeping immigrants out of the republic. But while nativism could, as Bridges suggests, convey a sense of class identity, it was also often the case that "Whiggish, republican, and nativist mutualist politics insisted on the primacy of American interests and the subordination of class divisions." Although working-class nativism responded to the peculiar pressures of industrialization and market revolution, the mutualist politics embraced by many nativists sought to efface class antagonisms by emphasizing ethnic solidarities, the common bonds of Protestant nationalism, equal opportunity, and "master-journeyman cohesion."[45] In chapter 5, we will see how nativism limited the version of working-class protest promoted by Ned Buntline. In the next chapter, however, I will consider how the combination of nativism in Northeastern cities and U.S. imperialism encouraged some members of the new working-classes—that is, immigrant soldiers—to construct solidarities with Mexicans rather than the Whigs or the Democrats.

FOUR

Foreign Bodies and International Race Romance

History, not biology, distinguishes ethnicity from race,
making the former groups (in the American usage) distinctive
but assimilable, walling off the latter, legally, socially, and
ideologically, to benefit those within the magic circle and
protect the national body from contamination.
> —Michael Rogin, *Blackface, White Noise*

[T]he scourge of the South and the nation was not cotton or
poor whites but whiteness itself—whiteness not simply as the
pinnacle of ethnoracial status but as the complex social and
economic matrix wherein racial power and privilege were
shared, not always equally, by those who were able to
construct identities as Anglo-Saxons, Nordics, Caucasians, or
simply whites.
> —Neil Foley, *The White Scourge*

This chapter focuses on two boundary-crossing figures in sensational literature: the immigrant soldier and the cross-dressed Mexican female fighter. The immigrant soldier who joined the U.S. military forces had already crossed at least one important boundary by migrating from Europe (usually from Ireland or Germany) to the United States; crossing over into Mexican territory posed special perils, it was feared, for immigrant men, especially the Irish, who might be seduced into switching allegiances for a variety of reasons, but particularly because most were Catholic. At the same time, however, the treacherous immigrant soldier was often represented as an exception, for much of the war literature made a point of reaffirming immigrant men's loyalty to the U.S. cause.

Indeed, the war in some ways enabled immigrants such as the Irish to move more surely into the "magic circle" of whiteness despite ongoing nativist agitation. And it might seem that sensational representations of cross-dressed Mexican female soldiers similarly helped to move Mexicans as a group into that magic circle, for the cross-dresser usually crossed back to her feminine role and sometimes even married a U.S. soldier. This may suggest that Mexicans as a group were considered "distinctive but assimilable" white ethnics rather than racialized nonwhites, an idea that is supported by the terms of the Treaty of Guadalupe Hidalgo, which offered citizenship to former Mexican nationals who remained in lands claimed by the United States after the war.[1] But the reformed cross-dresser was also an exceptional figure in the war literature. As a potentially assimilable foreign body, she was frequently contrasted with other types of Mexicans who were viewed as decidedly nonwhite and inassimilable. This helps to explain why the racialization of people of Mexican origin in the United States after the war was uneven and internally bifurcated. Although, as Neil Foley argues, "the Texas Revolution and the War with Mexico laid the foundation for racializing Mexicans as non-whites," it is also the case, as he suggests, that "whiteness fractured along class lines and Mexicans moved in to fill the racial space between whiteness and blackness."[2] Although some elite or light-skinned people of Mexican origin were (sometimes) able to construct white identities, others, such as recent immigrants and many poor and working-class people, would find themselves walled off from the magic circle of whiteness.

As I suggested in the previous chapter, narratives of gender and sexuality were crucial vehicles for the reconstruction of racial boundaries in war-era story-paper literature. In U.S.–Mexican War fiction, questions about the national and racial status of the immigrant Irish were also questions about manhood. Could the Irish be faithful "sons" to their adopted nation? Were they "manly" enough to be incorporated into a band of white U.S. brothers? Could they be subordinated within male military hierarchies, or were they too undisciplined to submit to such structures? Could Catholic men internalize models of imperial white manhood that were substantially based on anti-Catholic sentiments? On the other hand, questions about the status of Mexicans similarly engaged issues of manhood but also involved ideas about womanhood and more explicitly took up issues of sexuality. In story-paper literature, Mexican men were figured as an array of "unmanly" types: as tyrants, seducers, and libertines, as cowardly and bloodthirsty soldiers, and as evil and li-

centious priests. More rarely, Mexicans were represented as heroic and
even as possible members of a transnational inter-American family, but
that possibility usually depended upon plot twists that revealed a white,
U.S.-American parent. Representations of Mexican women were similarly split along racial lines, but U.S. writers more often used the trope
of the Mexican-nation-as-woman to define the boundaries of community and empire. Although narratives of "irresistible romance" between
U.S. soldiers and (white) Mexican women were used to legitimate empire, fears about the contamination of the white U.S. national body also
engendered narratives of blocked desire and illicit sexuality.[3] All of these
examples reveal how the U.S.-Mexican War affected the unsettling and
the reconstruction of boundaries of race, gender, and sexuality after
1848.

FOREIGN BODIES: IMMIGRANT SOLDIERS

In chapter 2, I argued that George Lippard foregrounded the mangled
body of an Irish immigrant soldier in *Legends of Mexico* as a way of
symbolically incorporating marginal whites into an American "race." In
singling out an Irish soldier for representation, Lippard was certainly not
alone, for a good deal of war literature foregrounded the participation
of the Irish. Like Lippard's *Legends,* much of the literature loudly insists
upon the exemplary patriotism of the Irish soldier, as if to drown out
nativist claims that recent immigrants were incapable of feeling binding,
intense nationalist loyalties to the United States. For instance, a sketch in
The Taylor Anecdote Book, a collection of pieces largely culled from
newspaper accounts, features a wounded Irish soldier who saves the U.S.
flag after the standard-bearer is killed in battle: "The Irishman, stunned
for a moment, raised himself, and wiping the blood which blinded him
from his eyes, saw the flag placed in his charge some rods in advance; he
rushed forward, bloody and ghastly with his wounds, and seized the
loved banner, and in his peculiar language exclaimed—'Holy Jasus! I am
worth a dozen deadmen yet!' and wounded as he was, he carried that
flag through the remainder of the fight, until it waved in victory."[4] This
representation of an Irishman's devotion to the "loved banner," intensified by the sensational focus on the soldier's mutilated body, implicitly
counters the nativists who argued that the allegiances of the Irish were
suspect; the use of dialect recalls the ubiquitous stage Irishmen of popular theater.[5] The message of this sketch was repeated in a different register by General Winfield Scott, who had previously favored immigra-

tion restrictions, when in an 1852 Whig campaign paper he praised the immigrant soldiers who through war service "proved themselves the faithful sons of our beloved country," thereby dispelling "any lingering prejudice" about "the comparative merits of Americans by birth and Americans by adoption."[6] Similar statements can be found in soldiers' personal narratives, such as the 1853 campaign sketches of Ohio officer Luther Giddings, who commended the Irish for their constancy and courage. For Giddings, "the splendid results of the Mexican War" were "admirably" expressed in a quotation from Secretary of State Everett taken from a dispatch to Britain and France on "the proposed tripartite treaty for the protection of Cuba." Everett states: "Every addition to the territory of the American Union has given homes to European destitution and gardens to European want." He continues: "Into the United States, grown to their present extent in the manner described, but little less than a half a million of the population of the Old World is annually pouring; to be immediately incorporated into an industrious and prosperous community, in the bosom of which they find political and religious liberty, social position, employment, and bread."[7] These representations suggest that European immigrants, specifically the Irish, were being admitted into the national and racial "community" at the expense of those, such as Indians and Mexicans, from whom territory was being taken away. And yet, the nervous insistence on Irish American patriotism and the incorporation of immigrants also responds to the abiding xenophobia that supported a resurgent nativist movement in the postwar period.[8]

Indeed, the figure of the Irish soldier was Janus-faced in mid-nineteenth-century war literature, for representations of the Irishman as faithful martyr to the U.S. cause were countered by images of the Irish as traitors to the white republic. Harry Halyard's novelette *The Chieftain of Churubusco, or, The Spectre of the Cathedral* (1848), for instance, features a stage Irishman, Teague O'Donahue, who is enticed to desert by a Mexican priest, as well as an entire band of Irish deserters, led by one Sergeant Riley, who unsuccessfully try to persuade a Yankee, Solomon Snubbins, to switch sides and join them. And in Charles Averill's *The Mexican Ranchero: or, The Maid of the Chapparal* (1847), a cross-dressing female guerrilla fighter for Mexico, who turns out to be the daughter of the niece of the deposed Mexican president Herrera and a U.S.-American father, joins forces with a U.S. officer to defeat the novel's two villains: the Irish deserter-chief Raleigh, who killed the maid's parents, and his henchman, a monstrous Mexican "half breed" with superhuman strength. In the novel's grand finale, the maid, dressed as a man, manages to kill both villains before agreeing to a marriage with the U.S. officer. It is also revealed that Raleigh is the "unnatural relative"—an uncle, in fact—of both the maid and the U.S. soldier; as he dies, he rejoices that "the blood of all of ye will bear the taint, for foreigner and Irishman though I am, I was yet the relative of your father's race, which originally was of European stock; so I triumph at the last."[9] The fact that Raleigh is of the same "race" as the maid and the U.S. officer implies that the Irish could be counted as part of the white U.S. family, but the emphasis on Irish blood as "tainted" and the pairing of the Irish deserter with the mixed-race Mexican monster suggests a more ambiguous status for the Irish soldier.

According to David Roediger, the 1840s and 1850s were crucial years in the making of the Irish worker into a white worker, for during those years whiteness was increasingly redefined to include the Irish.[10] It is by now well known that early race scientists often posited enduring differences between a degraded Celtic and a superior Anglo-Saxon "race" and that they frequently compared the Irish to blacks. Noel Ignatiev, Roediger, and others have documented how around the middle of the nineteenth century the Irish, largely because they could vote and were increasingly incorporated into the Democratic Party, were often able to claim the privileges of whiteness and distance themselves from black people. "Instead of seeing their struggles as bound up with those of colonized and colored people around the world," Roediger suggests, "they came to see their struggles as against such people."[11] The U.S.-Mexican War no doubt also played an important role in this process, for the many Irish who fought on the U.S. side joined forces with large numbers of Protestant, native-born, U.S. whites to fight against Mexicans who were widely perceived to be "vari-colored people...composed of all the variety of blood in the world, with specimens of all possible variety of mixtures."[12] Despite the renewed intensity of nativist agitation after the war, Irish military service probably also contributed to the increasingly common, if by no means universal, belief that the Irish were a part of a white "race" defined in opposition to people of color. But during the late 1840s, the place of the Irish within U.S. racial economies was unclear, and the fact that some Irish did, as we shall see, fight with rather than against the Mexicans no doubt heightened fears about the incorporation of the Irish into the white republic.[13]

The boundary between the foreign and domestic is also at stake in these representations. Although U.S. war supporters trumpeted the supposed virtues of the citizen-soldier, the large numbers of immigrant soldiers in the ranks of the regulars contradicted the myth that the U.S. Army was made up of patriotic, native-born volunteers who fought in defense of "home."[14] Were immigrant soldiers foreign threats to national unity, or potentially loyal U.S. citizens? In a nation in which nativist organizations flourished both before and after the war, and at a time when national boundaries were being extensively redrawn to include vast new territories, it is not surprising that the Irish soldier became a magnet for a range of fears clustered around the distinction between citizen and alien, native and foreigner.

Finally, sensational story-paper fiction displays anxieties about empire and American exceptionalism. While war supporters developed the rhetoric of Manifest Destiny to argue for the uniqueness and beneficence of U.S. empire-building, visions of rival empires—including the Spanish, the British, and an imagined Catholic empire—loom large in much of this literature. Although the Spanish empire was widely perceived to be in irreversible decline, it continued to support mass-produced fantasies about imperial adventure and conquest in which the British, a more powerful rival for whom Anglo-Americans felt a complex blend of racial loyalty, envy, and rivalry, also played significant roles. At the same time, the vision of a Catholic empire that shadowed the United States in the New World was often a component of nativist conspiracy theories.[15] For nativists, the figure of the Irish soldier reinforced fears that religious loyalties among Catholics—the bedrock of an imagined Catholic empire—might supersede allegiance to the United States or to whiteness. On the other hand, story-paper entrepreneurs such as Gleason and Ballou who attacked Britain for its imperialist policies and its treatment of Ireland risked exposing the resemblances between the United States and Britain as imperial Protestant powers invading Catholic countries. Senator John Pearce alluded to this problem in Congress when he worried that "if we should annex Mexico, she should be to us what Ireland is to Great Britain, a perpetual source of bloodshed, embarrassments, annoyance, endless disquietude."[16] Pearce's suggestion that the relationship between an annexed Mexico and the United States would be a colonial one countered and contradicted efforts by other senators, as we shall see, to describe annexation as the benevolent extension of freedom to an oppressed and welcoming people. Such contradictions undermined the exceptionalist premise that U.S. expansion was uniquely good or benign, an empire that was not one, even as they revealed connections between anti-Catholic nativism in Northeastern cities and empire-building in Mexico.

The memoirs of the German immigrant soldier Frederick Zeh suggest how nativism in U.S. cities shaped the experiences of the working-class immigrants who composed an important part of the U.S. Army. "Love of my new homeland was definitely not the reason I became a soldier," Zeh declares in the opening sentence, "because the bitter experiences of my six- to seven-month stay in the United States certainly instilled no patriotism in me."[17] After working as a day laborer near Philadelphia, almost dying from malaria, and frequently passing out from hunger, he decided to join the U.S. Army. At first he tried to enlist in an infantry regiment, but he was rejected because of his foreign birth. Although that experience "considerably dampened" his "ardor for becoming a soldier," he joined the regulars after reading a recruiting poster that promised "the best pay, provisions, and equipment." Before Zeh's war story begins, however, he interjects yet another anecdote to illustrate "the immigrants' bitter frame of mind toward the natives." Zeh writes: "Shortly after my induction, a countryman, completely unknown to me, stopped me and said: 'Aren't you ashamed to fight for these natives, who treat us worse than the blacks?! Let these fellows be the first to fight and when they're all shot to hell and need men, then we can step in.' The good man really did not understand what made me go to war."[18]

The war experiences of immigrants led, of course, to a variety of outcomes. Although Zeh never forgot his harsh experiences with the "natives," he also quickly learned to look down on his Mexican foes. Ironically, this Protestant immigrant soldier shared many of the anti-Catholic prejudices of the nativists that he so detested.[19] What is more, the remark of Zeh's countrymen that the natives treated Germans "worse than the blacks" suggests how inevitable that comparison would be for most European immigrants, as well as how many would respond by trying to distance themselves, as Roediger suggests, from people of color. Although Zeh's narrative is framed by bitter memories of U.S. nativism, war service probably encouraged many immigrant soldiers to try to "forget" the nativist prejudice they encountered in Northeastern cities and to claim a white American identity defined in opposition to Mexicans and people of color at home. Toward the end of his narrative, Zeh even exclaims, "How many Germans sealed their patriotic devotion to their adopted homeland by sacrificing their lives on the battlefields of Mexico!"[20] As usual Zeh's tone is cynical and ironic, but his emphasis on immigrants who sacrifice their lives for the nation is uncritically echoed in many of the popular texts of the period.

The other side of such a representation of immigrant self-sacrifice, however, is the image of the immigrant soldier as traitor to nation and race.
Zeh briefly alludes to this second image when he mentions, in passing, a
proclamation issued by the Mexican government in English, German, and
French and directed "to the foreign soldiers," urging them: "Join us and
fight with us for our rights and for our sacred imperiled religion, against
this infidel enemy." According to Zeh, "Several hundred Irishmen, stirred
up by religious fanaticism, went over to the enemy, thanks to this piece of
paper. They formed a battalion named 'San Patricio.'"[21]

The San Patricio regiment—a group of foreign soldiers, including
many deserters from the U.S. ranks, who fought for Mexico—especially
disturbed the fantasy of a united front of white native Americans. This
regiment, which included two hundred soldiers in August of 1846, was
led by John Riley, a native of County Galway, Ireland, who had deserted
from the U.S. Army before the war officially began. Michael Hogan suggests that some of the San Patricios were "Mexican citizens of European
birth, others were resident foreigners, some were deserters like Riley, and
most were Irish." Although historians have argued that the deserters left
the U.S. Army because of drunkenness or boredom, many of the San
Patricios, as Hogan observes, must have been struck by the irony of
"forming part of an army invading a Catholic country while their own
Catholic relatives were being beaten in the streets of Chicago, Boston,
and Philadelphia."[22] The anti-Catholic prejudices of many of their native-
born fellow soldiers, the harsh discipline enforced by officers, and the
bombing and sacking of Mexican Catholic churches might well have contributed to decisions to desert.[23] The desertion rate was higher, after all,
during this war than any other. By March of 1847, more than nine thousand U.S. soldiers had deserted, more than five times the number that
were killed in action.[24] Whatever their reasons for fighting on the Mexican side may have been, the deserters and other foreign nationals who
made up the San Patricios played important roles in the battles of Monterrey, Buena Vista, and Churubusco.

After the battle of Churubusco, eighty-five of the San Patricios were
taken prisoner by U.S. forces.[25] Later the majority were hanged, and
most of those who escaped hanging were given fifty lashes, branded on
the cheek with a "D" for deserter, and sentenced to hard labor for the
duration of the war. "Why those thus punished did not die under such
punishment was a marvel to me," reported a soldier who witnessed the
punishment of one contingent of these deserters. "Their backs had the

appearance of a pounded piece of raw beef, the blood oozing from every stripe as given."[26] In his personal memoir, U.S. officer Raphael Semmes suggested that these spectacular punishments were designed as a form of nationalist pedagogy for foreign soldiers:

> These executions, which would have been proper at any time, were peculiarly so now.... [T]here were many foreigners in our ranks; some of them not even naturalized citizens, and the enemy was making every effort still, to entice them away. The salvation of the army might depend upon an example being made of these dishonored and dishonorable men, and General Scott had the firmness to make it. The brave Irish, who remained faithful to us, and who were always among the foremost, and most devoted of our troops, were more rejoiced at this event than the native-born Americans even, as they had felt keenly the stigma which this conduct of their countrymen had cast upon them.[27]

Semmes's words betray the dependence of the U.S. forces on so-called foreigners, despite the widespread celebration of the native-born volunteer, even as they suggest how representations of the San Patricios might have been mobilized as a device to teach immigrants to imitate the "faithful" Irish and to abjure alliances with other nations or people of color.

In *The Mexican Ranchero*, Charles Averill's villainous Irish deserter-chief Raleigh is clearly modeled on the San Patricios' leader, John Riley, and much of the conclusion of the novel is devoted to a spectacular staging of the trial and punishment of "the foreign legion of deserters so famous throughout our country" (85).[28] The execution took place in the center of the city, according to Averill, so "the terrible scene of wholesale death could be visible to both armies encamped without the walls of the capital" (89). Averill paints the sensational scene in lurid shades of red, presenting the space of the execution as a kind of theater: "In a blaze of blood-red glare up rose the sun, as if dressed out in mimic mockery of the ensanguined scene it was soon to witness; and its crimsoned beams shone in fearful imagery upon the seventy and one gibbets erected upon the field of death" (89). Although the actual Riley was branded (twice) and sentenced to hard labor rather than death, Averill's Raleigh is hanged from a gibbet "more conspicuous and elevated than any of the others" (90). After the cross-dressed Buena Rejon kills Montano, the mixed-race monster, she leaps up to Raleigh's scaffold, waving the head "with its hideous blood-besmeared features awful in death," and demands the privilege of acting as the deserter-chief's executioner. Averill ends the chapter with an image of "the gibbetted corpses of the deserters [which] hung in their chains, [and] rattled horribly in the furious wrath of the gale, seeming like the dirge for the accursed dead" (92). But as if he suspects that some of his readers might find this spectacular punishment excessive and perhaps divisive, he concludes that "our country required the fearful and but too just sacrifice" (92).

Raleigh has to be "sacrificed" and spectacularly punished because he threatens the boundaries of nation and race that Averill's novel tries to stabilize. On the one hand, Raleigh has betrayed the national-imperial cause of the United States by fighting for the Mexicans. As an Irish immigrant and army deserter, Raleigh is a boundary-crossing figure who threatens the self-evidence and coherence of the principle of loyalty to the U.S. nation. Earlier, Raleigh had robbed the U.S. hero's family of their "rightful estates" and had repeatedly tried to kill the children; it is not difficult to read in this detail anxiety about the immigrant Irish stealing the national legacy of its "true heirs" (59), the natives. On the other hand, Raleigh's "taint" corrupts the "blood" of the U.S. hero and the Mexican heroine. He is paired with the "Mexican half-breed" Montano, who has black skin and a "shapeless form...all one confused jumble, thrown together in a hurry by nature, into a sort of human hash" (22). Montano and his sister Juana seem to stand in for the mixed-race people of Mexico, and so Raleigh's close relationship to them—they work together, and the hero suggests that Montano is "as much a monster in form" as Raleigh is "in soul" (86)—racially darkens him. This representation suggests that the Irish are weak links in the chain of whiteness, who may have greater affinities for the mixed-race Mexican masses than the white inter-American family that Averill tries to construct.

Like most sensational war novels, this one goes to great lengths to distinguish a white Mexican elite from the nation as a whole, which was often represented as disturbingly nonwhite. In *The Mexican Ranchero,* the cross-dressed Mexican maid is most obviously the white face of Mexico, while the "monstrous" Montano and Juana represent its dark face. Although the anticipated marriage between Buena Rejon and the U.S. hero in the conclusion of the novel seems to figure a close relationship, perhaps even a union of sorts, between Mexico and the United States after the end of the war, the demonization of Montano and Juana suggests the limits of such a relationship: most white U.S. Americans could happily fantasize about the incorporation of the foreign only as long as they imagined Mexico as white. Insofar as foreign bodies such as the nonwhite Mexican or the side-switching Irish soldier were perceived to threaten the presumed coherence of a white, native U.S. identity, they had to be spectacularly policed and punished.

During the war and in the decades that followed, however, the "foreign bodies" of the Irish would be slowly and unevenly incorporated into the white republic, while many people of Mexican origin would increasingly be racialized as nonwhite. Although some would be able to construct white identities, and although the Treaty of Guadalupe Hidalgo promised citizenship to former Mexican citizens in the new U.S. territories, many would be legally, socially, and economically marginalized within or excluded from the white national body. As I have been arguing, war literature significantly affected this reconstruction of postwar racial boundaries. Since political debates, travel narratives, and newspaper reports repeatedly characterized Mexico as a nation in which almost everyone was part Indian or black, it should not come as a surprise that fears of Mexico's racial heterogeneity haunt the international race romances of 1848 that figure the relationship between Mexico and the United States on the model of a marriage contract. Although these novelettes stake out different positions on the war and annexation, they all register questions that were also being raised in Congress, in the newspapers, and in popular culture more generally, about the boundaries of whiteness and about the incorporation of nonwhites and Catholics into the republic. To these debates and to the international race romances I now turn.

FOREIGN BODIES: "MOTLEY AND MERCILESS" MEXICAN MEN AND CROSS-DRESSED FEMALE AVENGERS

History teaches no truth more emphatically, than that
those empires, which have become powerful, have
drawn their energy from the life-vigor imparted by one
single dominant race. A State composed of a heterogeneous mixture of discordant races, held together by no
ties of a common origin, no common faith, no common
language, no common customs and habits, necessarily
contains within itself the elements of weakness and
final ruin.

—Daniel Ullmann,
"The Course of Empire"

In an 1856 speech called "The Course of Empire," delivered before the Order of United Americans on the anniversary of Washington's birthday, the New York nativist Daniel Ullmann tried to reconcile the project of

U.S. empire-building with Washington's emphasis in his Farewell Address on the importance of a "unity of government which constitutes" U.S. Americans as "one people."[29] After a few introductory remarks, Ullmann began with these words: "To form a great people in the present state of civilization requires a more comprehensive combination of elements than at any previous age of the world." Although he emphasized a variety of key elements in that combination, including geographical position, extent of territory, climate, and resources, he concluded that "pre-eminent among the elements of strength, are the characteristics of the race or races composing the people" (6–7). In order to build a great empire, he argued, there must be "a great central dominant race, with sufficient vital power to mold and absorb all the rest into one homogeneous national body" (8). In the United States, according to Ullmann, that dominant race was "unquestionably" the "Anglo-Saxon branch of the Teutonic race." He mused: "How far the mixture of foreign and discordant elements of castes and nationalities should be permitted is a question requiring the closest scrutiny of the philosopher and statesman to determine. In some nations the foreign mixture has been so great as to modify all the modes of thought, habits, and customs, to such a degree, that the original nation no longer existed" (20). Although Ullmann argued that the Spanish empire had fallen apart because it had "no real unity of race, language and territory" (12), he had high hopes for the U.S.-American empire. "It is certain that the American people must mold and absorb all other castes, races, and nationalities into one great homogeneous American race" (20), he concluded. "We seek not the empire of the sword—not the empire of the Inquisition—not the empire of despotism; but the empire of the people—the empire of the rights of man—the empire of science, art, and literature—the empire of morals and religion—the empire of obedience to God, his precepts and commands. Let then the Union of these States stand firm and solid as the everlasting hills" (21).

Despite Ullmann's guarded optimism about the ability of Anglo-Saxon Americans to "absorb all other castes, races, and nationalities," during the war with Mexico questions about how far "the mixture of foreign and discordant elements...should be permitted" were among the main sticking points for those who debated the question of annexation.[30] Which foreign elements might safely be absorbed by Anglo-Saxon America and which would fatally modify it? Ullmann's assertion that the Spanish empire's fatal flaw was that it had "no real unity of race, language and territory" tells us something about what many politicians and popular novelists of the late 1840s thought about Mexico. Even though some were powerfully attracted by the idea that contiguous Mexican territory might be absorbed into the United States, most conceived of Mexico as a "State composed of a heterogeneous mixture of discordant races" that threatened to corrupt a fictive U.S.-American unity.

Those on all political sides of the annexation issue, moreover, pondered these questions by translating them into the register of erotic and sexual relations between Mexicans and U.S. Americans. For instance, when in January of 1847 Representative Owen of Indiana argued that the inhabitants of northern Mexico were at present "unprepared" for annexation, he added that "when, it may be, the sons of our republic, attracted by the black eyes of Mexican beauty, shall have found homes and wives in those far regions of the south...then may come annexation; come, when mutually desired."[31] Here, Owen imagined the Mexico of the future as a feminized extension of the U.S. domestic sphere that might offer "homes" and "wives" for U.S. sons; in this way, he tried to ground annexation in mutual heterosexual desire. Although Owen suggested that at some point in the future Mexico might be safely absorbed into the United States, however, many other U.S. Americans adamantly opposed the annexation of Mexico, especially the densely populated sections, at any time and on any terms. Opponents of annexation, too, frequently used a sexually charged language to denounce the expansionists as rapacious conquerors who wanted to force Mexico into an unwanted union with the United States. Senator Berrien, for instance, condemned the expansionists' "sordid lust for the acquisition of territory" in Mexico, while George Badger objected to "wresting from her one inch of her domain by the exertion of any force which shall control her will."[32]

Although reasons for opposing the annexation of new lands were various, fears of the so-called amalgamation that would result from a union with Mexico figured prominently in antiannexationist arguments. And arguments that hinged on this word also had pronounced sexual and racial connotations, for as Robert Young suggests, until "the word 'miscegenation' was invented in 1864, the word that was conventionally used for the fertile fusion and merging of races was 'amalgamation.'"[33] Thus Senator Berrien tried to mobilize fears of sexual and racial mixing when he asked his colleagues: "Are you willing to put your birthright into the keeping of these mongrel races who inhabit these territories, by incorporating them into this Union? For myself, I am not. I protest against this amalgamation."[34] These kinds of ideas, moreover, were not limited to the Whig opposition. Although Indiana senator Hannegan supported the war and expansion, he shared some of his Whig opponents' views of annexation as racial amalgamation. As a result, he argued in early 1847 that the United States should seek to annex only relatively uninhabited areas, for he feared that "Mexico and the United States are peopled by two distinct and utterly unhomogeneous races. In no reasonable period could we amalgamate."[35] And in language that anticipated the nativist Ullmann's argument almost ten years later, Democrat Hunter argued that to have an extensive empire the United States needed "a homogeneous" people: "This cannot be expected if alien and hostile races are to be suddenly incorporated in our body politic."[36] All of these politicians posed the question of annexation in sexual and racial terms, and all of them viewed other "races" as threats to a fictive U.S. national body.

Other fears about annexation included worries that the acquisition of foreign lands would cause domestic dissension, specifically over the issue of slavery. During the debates over the Wilmot Proviso, politicians on both sides of the issue frequently expressed concern that foreign policy might fatally disrupt domestic peace by pushing the slavery question to the point of crisis. Pennsylvania Whig James Pollock warned that "the acquisition of territory will awaken a question, the agitation of which will shake the very foundations of the Union." "Is there no common ground to be found upon which the North and South may meet in peace and embrace each other in the bonds of common brotherhood?" he asked. "There is; and it can only be found in a firm determination on the part of Congress and the people, never to add another foot of foreign territory to that we now possess."[37] Southern Whig Thomas Corwin agreed: "Should we prosecute this war another moment, or expend one dollar in the purchase or conquest of a single acre of Mexican land, the North and South are brought into collision on a point where neither will yield."[38] And New Jersey's Senator Miller also foresaw that "your conquered peace in Mexico will become the fierce spirit of discord at home."[39] All of these politicians accurately predicted that the bonds of common (white) brotherhood would ultimately be torn apart by the struggle over slavery, which was intensified by the heated disagreements about whether lands taken through foreign conquest would be slave or free.

The international race romances of 1846–1848 both register and attempt to manage such concerns about racial amalgamation, the bonds of white brotherhood, slavery, and entanglements of the foreign and the domestic.[40] They do so, however, by seeking to anchor questions about national expansion in the bodies of men and women drawn irresistibly

together across national boundary lines. This does not mean that all of
the international romances of this period advocate annexation: like the
congressional debates over expansion, most of these story-paper novels
suggest various fears about the incorporation of Mexico and especially
Mexicans into the United States. But as they struggle to imagine a future relationship between the United States and Mexico, these novels
both appeal to and reconstruct hierarchies of gender, race, and sexuality to legitimate their respective visions of postwar inter-American power
relations.

These wartime narratives were based in part upon models developed
a little earlier to legitimate the efforts of U.S.-American men to gain land
and power in Texas and California. Antonia Castañeda has suggested
that in Anglo representations of Mexican California in the 1840s, "elite
Californianas were deemed European and superior while the mass of
Mexican women were viewed as Indian and inferior." Both images, she
argues, "formed part of the belief and idea system that rationalized the
war and dispossession of the land base," for the positive images facilitated marriages that allowed Anglo men to acquire land, while the negative ones "served to devalue the people occupying a land base the
United States wanted to acquire—through purchase if possible, by war
if necessary."[41] Similarly, many of the bifurcated representations of Mexican women in the international race romances of 1848 seek to justify the
appropriation of Mexican lands and other assets by, on the one hand,
portraying elites as, in Castañeda's words, "aristocratic, virtuous Spanish ladies" who may be appropriate marriage partners for white U.S.
men, and, on the other hand, constructing pejorative images of nonelite
Mexicanas in order to champion "Anglo America's racial, moral, economic, and political superiority."[42] But the proliferation of nonwhite or
ambiguously white characters shadows the whiteness of the elite Mexican heroines, and it often undermines or blocks, as we shall see, international romances between such heroines and U.S. heroes.

The heroine of story-paper international romances is almost always a
Mexican woman, although sometimes one parent is a U.S. citizen. In
Buntline's *The Volunteer,* the heroine Edwina Canales/Helen Vicars was
born in Mexican Texas, the child of a U.S.-American father and a Mexican mother, while in *The Mexican Spy: or, The Bride of Buena Vista,*
Annabel Blackler, the main female character, is the daughter of a
Philadelphia merchant and a Mexican woman "of Castilian extraction"
(7). In almost every case, the heroine is repeatedly, if rather anxiously, described as white. The titular character in *Inez, the Beautiful,* for exam-

ple, is "not of the blood of the Anglo-Saxons," but "the graceful deli-
cacy of her limbs strongly denoted" that "she was not a descendant of
the Aztecs"; in fact, "there was something in her every feature, and in her
finely developed figure" that told "that nought but pure Castilian blood
flowed in her veins" (16). On the other hand, *The Prisoner of Perote*'s
"beautiful, dark-haired, dark-eyed Josefa" (8), who has "warm blood,
which traced its source to the old Castilian fount" (22), is one of the rare
heroines whose desire for the hero is unreturned. Even though in most
novels "Castilian blood" would place Josefa within the magic circle of
whiteness, in this one her "southern nature" is repeatedly underlined in
ways that suggest her racial liminality. But Josefa is an exception that
proves the rule: the whiteness of Mexican women was often question-
able to U.S. observers, so much so that it had to be nervously reasserted
by authors who promoted some version of international romance. Whiteness is also inseparable from class and status, for all of these heroines are
elite, often the daughters of Spanish dons on haciendas, Mexican generals, or other rich and influential Mexicans. In *The Prairie Guide,* for instance, Isabella has inherited an "immense estate" from her father, and
it seems likely that "the fertile lands" (7) of her uncle's rancho will also
be passed on to her, while Isora La Vega, the heroine of *The Secret Service Ship,* is also poised to inherit a "princely estate" (26) from her father. Representations such as these establish the elite, white Mexican
heroine as a symbol of the material advantages—especially land—that
many U.S. men found so desirable.

But these elite white heroines are not the only female characters in
the story-paper novelettes, for they are often contrasted with nonwhite
Mexican women who do not play leading roles in the international romance. In *The Volunteer,* Edwina Canales is paired with her friend, the
half-Castilian, half-Aztec Anita Urrea, the daughter of the famous Mexican general. It is noteworthy that Anita is described as "all woman—all
tenderness" (18), while Edwina is said to be "of a sterner and more
queenly cast" (19). Although it might be expected that the former description would be reserved for the heroine, and that the second would
not be a compliment in the mid-nineteenth-century United States, Buntline clearly prefers Edwina to Anita, for Edwina's martial womanhood
wins the love of the U.S. hero, while Anita remains in Mexico and is married to Edwina's brother, a guerrilla fighter. And in *The Secret Service
Ship,* Isora La Vega is contrasted to Juana the evil giantess, whose "in-
human nature" is attributed to the fact that the "cannibal blood of
Patagonia" (90) flows in her veins. As a result, Juana strangles infants,

tries to kill the heroine, and generally preys "upon the human species" (28). Finally, in *The Mexican Spy,* the half U.S.-American heroine Annabel is compared with Marguerita, the "ill-formed, though handsome-featured" (34) daughter of a Mexican ranchero, as well as with Corita, the Mexican daughter of Annabel's uncle Jose de Villa Rica. Although as I have suggested, elite Mexican women are often figured as white and as eligible for a role in international romance, in this case even the wealthy Corita's love is slighted by the U.S. officer Henry Rowland, who prefers her "whiter" cousin Annabel.

Besides their whiteness, another characteristic that distinguishes many of the heroines of international romance is a talent for cross-dressing. Edwina Canales fiercely leads Mexican troops into battle, fights bravely and effectively, and generally relishes the "perils" and "excitements of active service" (57) until she receives a shoulder wound while fighting in the war's bloodiest battle, Buena Vista. Because she has already fallen in love with Captain George Blakey, the U.S. volunteer who lifts her from the bloody heap of bodies in which she is half-buried, she ends her military career, marries Blakey soon after, and returns with him to the backwoods settlement of Rural Choice, Kentucky. And yet for much of the narrative, she is dead set on avenging the murders of her parents at the hands of Texas bandits who coveted their land and her body, and she is represented as a "noble" and "exalted" example of female patriotism, even though she fights on the Mexican side. "This may appear singular to many of our readers," Buntline advises his audience, "but there have been many instances of the kind" (40).

Indeed, there were "many instances of this kind" in the story-paper literature of the period, for the figure of the cross-dressed Mexican maid was a nearly standard plot device in the international race romances of 1846–1848. In *The Mexican Ranchero,* for instance, Buena Rejon is "the far-famed, wide known, deep dreaded maid of the chapparal, the female avenger of Mexico" (17). Although she often fights in female dress against U.S. forces, she masquerades as a man, fools her brother, and becomes the lieutenant of his ranchero band in order to act as "fearlessly and perilously" (95) as she wishes. The heroine of *The Hunted Chief* also crossdresses in order to lead a guerrilla band with such daring skill that the U.S.-American hero longs "to measure swords with them, man for man" (4). On the other hand, the war causes *Inez, the Beautiful,* "a Mexican military prodigy," to impersonate a man in order to fight side by side with her father, a general, at the battle of Resaca de la Palma, where she wields her sword "with a consummate precision defying the most skilled swordsmen" (46). And Isora La Vega, the heroine of *The Secret Service Ship,* masquerades as a robber chief, manages to capture the U.S.-American hero with her "fatal lasso," exhibits "more than masculine prowess and heroism" (36), fights quite effectively for the Mexicans at the battle of Cerro Gordo, and even ultimately frees the U.S. hero from his captivity. Although this sort of behavior is sometimes deemed "strange," it is more usually described as "heroic" or "noble," probably because it is justified by patriotism, defense of the family, or heterosexual love.

Some of the models of womanhood in these story-paper novels complicate the idea that there are natural, fixed oppositions between male and female behavior.[43] For instance, when in *The Hunted Chief* the U.S.-American hero and the Mexican heroine are attacked by a band of robbers, Rainford notes that "he could discover nothing of the fear so natural to women, but her manner was resolute and collected, while from her eyes there gleamed the light of genuine courage. She sat as firm and erect in her saddle as a veteran warrior upon parade" (39). Here, Rainford's attribution of a "natural" fear to women is countered by the heroine's courage and firmness, although she is also represented as an exception to the norm, a kind of "wonder." Similarly, when in *The Secret Service Ship,* Isora and Rogers are attacked by bandits, Isora "wildly wielding her weapon, sprang into the thickest of the fight! . . . Rogers would have encircled her waist with his arm, the better to protect her person, but proudly she waved him off and fearlessly fought on" (32). Later, Rogers is captured by Mexicans, and Isora dons her male apparel once more to effect his rescue, explaining that "it is a duty the true woman owes to him she loves" (85). Even though Isora's crossing of gender boundaries is justified by the exigencies of warfare, her exceptional status, heterosexual love, and the ideal of true womanhood, this ideal has in this case apparently been revised to include adopting male dress, engaging in bloody physical fights, and rescuing helpless men.

Although U.S. readers in the 1840s enjoyed many stories about domestic heroines who impersonated men, these international race romances must be interpreted in light of the strong probability that the gender-bending behavior of these heroines would be attributed to their exotic, foreign status as well as to a perceived crisis in Mexican nationality. In Buntline's *The Volunteer,* Edwina Canales's inversion of gender roles is symptomatic of a larger crisis, one that sometimes is tenuously linked to the violence of U.S. empire-building but is more often attributed to the weakness of Mexican men and Mexican national sentiment. When Blakey first meets the cross-dressed Edwina in battle, he asks, "Has it come to this, that even the women of Mexico arm to repel their invaders?" and speculates that "deep must have been wrongs which could induce you thus to unsex yourself and face the fearful perils of war" (12). Although Blakey's question suggests that Edwina's gender performance is extreme and unnatural, it also implies that the invading U.S. forces have provoked such a radical response; it implicitly casts the United States in the role of the rapacious intruder who is repelled by the righteous maiden, a rape-revenge fantasy that partially derives from the popular urban gothic novels that many of these writers of U.S.-Mexican War romances also produced. But this explanation is replaced by another answer when Edwina replies, "It is time that they did so, Senor, when the *men* prove so cowardly as those who have fled and left me to your mercy" (12). The representation of the woman as unnaturally if admirably masculine, in other words, is accompanied by many descriptions of Mexican men as cowardly, weak, and unmanly. This dichotomy structures most of the international romances of 1846–1848.

Even though the reader is often quickly let in on the secret of the cross-dresser's "true" gender, sometimes the novels play with the possibility of male-male desire. Captain Bill Bruxton's claim that the cross-dresser in *The Hunted Chief,* for example, is "a perfect beauty" seemingly depends upon the chief's presumed maleness; "he" is, according to Bruxton, "the most beautiful boy you ever saw" (7). And when Josefa masquerades as a Mexican cavalry officer in *The Prisoner of Perote,* "he" quickly manages to "prepossess, if not infatuate" (27) the other soldiers. It could be argued, of course, that men are "naturally" drawn to the cross-dresser because they intuit that she is a woman; this may suggest that despite the cross-dresser's almost flawless performance of masculinity, "natural" gender differences cannot entirely be hidden. Indeed, the fact that all of these soldiers are erotically compelled by the cross-dresser may fortify the belief that men are inevitably attracted to women, so that their impulses register the female gender of the cross-dresser even though she appears to be a man. But the repetition of the fantasy in so many stories suggests that some kind of pleasure was taken in the gender confusion, and this almost all-male world in which officers are drawn to beautiful soldiers and enlisted men are infatuated with their leaders is not so different from the world depicted in soldiers' personal narratives about the war; the war theater intensified all kinds of hierarchical male-male relationships, and there is perhaps some trace of this as well in the trope of the soldier who is drawn to a man who turns out to be a woman.[44]

Many of these heroines are said to be near twins of their brothers, who are curiously feminized and whose bodies are described in ways that are often reserved for women. These descriptions also resemble those of the cross-dressers in scenes in which the latter masquerade as men.[45] In *The Volunteer,* the guerrilla chief Canales, who is the heroine's brother, is "small, but compactly, nay, elegantly formed; his features are regular and delicate as a woman's" and are "particularly expressive of a kind and womanlike disposition.... One would scarcely believe that his slight and delicate person could undergo more fatigue, exposure, and actual hardship than could any man of his company, yet so it was" (27). And although Rafael Rejon the Ranchero, the Maid of the Chaparral's brother, is a valiant "Mexican hero" (14), he is also described as small and womanlike: "Small and slender as a lady's were his graceful feet, which were encased in beautifully wrought moccasins; and a wildly picturesque appearance was given to his lower limbs by the tight-fitting buskins of the buffalo's hairy hide, which so plainly revealed their symmetrical shape and proportions" (13). These representations may be explained by theories, such as Gobineau's, which held that "lower" races were female or feminized, and that race-mixing could therefore cause a racial degeneration that made men more feminine.[46] This idea is supported by Rejon's statement that the "daughters of this benighted land of Mexico are ever more noble and brave spirited than her degenerate sons, who seem to have a blood less pure and lofty in their mongrel veins" (82). These gendered representations could be used to justify conquest, inasmuch as according to this schema Mexican men were too unmanly to defend or govern "their" women, themselves, and their nation. Descriptions of Mexican men as appealingly womanlike in novels that trumpeted the idealized manhood of U.S. men also suggested hierarchies between nations and between men that were implicitly grounded in the inequalities that were assumed and defended in dominant models of male-female relations.

Interestingly, these two feminized guerrilla chiefs are two of the rare cases where Mexican men seem to be welcomed into the U.S.-American family circle. Both Rejon and Canales turn out to have one U.S.-American parent, and that is certainly significant in the hero's decision, in both novels, to join the family by marrying the twinlike sister at the end. It also helps to explain why Rejon, for one, is not only described as ladylike but also as "noble and manly" (13). As he explains, it is only because of "this mingling of American with the Mexican blood" in his "nature" that he has perhaps "escaped the taint" of racial degradation that afflicts Mexico's "degenerate sons" (82). In other words, if he is both lady-

Rejon the Ranchero, Leaping from the Walls of Mexico.—See p. 13.

Figure 7.   "Rejon the Ranchero" illustration from Charles Averill's *The Mexican Ranchero* (1847). (Yale Collection of American Literature, Beinecke Rare Book and Manuscript Library)

like and manly it is only because he is both Mexican and "American." The novel nonetheless overrides some of the fears of racial mixture that it raises when Rejon is allowed to marry the white Southern U.S.-American hero's sister. At the end Harold's sister Alfredine, on the other hand, stays in Mexico and marries the guerrilla leader, who renounces his vow of eternal vengeance to the invader since he has "learned to LOVE our race, instead of hate" (100). If this representation seems to suggest that U.S. Americans in general viewed Mexican men as white and assimilable, however, it should be recalled that in *The Mexican Ranchero* heroic white men such as Rejon and Harold are contrasted with the villainous Irish immigrant Raleigh and the mixed-race monster Montano. This novel, moreover, is the only war-era story-paper romance I have found in which a Mexican man is allowed to marry a U.S. white woman; these novels as a whole are not interested in welcoming Mexican men into the white inter-American family. And as "noble and manly" as Rejon is, his feminization symbolically subordinates him to white U.S.-American men like Harold.

More usually, though, Mexican men were represented as unmanly because they were savage, as Indians and blacks were thought to be, or because they were decadent, as Spaniards and creoles appeared when viewed through the lens of the Black Legend. In both cases Mexican men were outside the pale of white male civility as it was defined in the mid-nineteenth-century United States.[47] Indeed, in this literature the civility and manliness of white U.S.-American men is defined in opposition to the incivility and unmanliness of Mexican men. In *Inez, the Beautiful*, for instance, Charles Devereux, an American lieutenant "just verging towards manhood" (10) exhibits his manliness by foiling the efforts of Don Jose Terceiro—a "monster bearing but the semblance of a man" (18)—to rape the heroine and to force her to marry him. Terceiro is an unmanly monster in a man's guise because his passions, which are deemed Castilian, are so easily inflamed, and so he tries to make Inez the "victim to his hellish lust" (14). But she escapes by jumping into a river, whereupon Devereux promptly rescues her. Although he, too, is sexually aroused by her, he prays to heaven for "courage to banish the polluting desire that for a moment possessed" him (20), and in the end he becomes engaged to marry her. In *The Secret Service Ship* General Ampudia is similarly represented as an unmanly "avenging fiend of hell" (12) because he is unable to control his passions; the chivalrous Midshipman Rogers, however, displays his manliness by rescuing a woman Ampudia is trying to rape and by hurling the general into a sepulchral pit. Finally, in *The Prisoner of Perote*, it is because of his timidity rather than his rapacity that the Mexican cavalry officer Don Fernando is the defining foil for the U.S. hero. Fernando fails to rescue his betrothed from a fire because he is wounded and timid, but his failure makes it possible for the U.S.-American Julius Marion to step in and display his manly courage and coolness as he rescues the beautiful Josefa, who promptly falls in love with him. In addition to this panoply of passionate, unmanly Spaniards and creoles, the novels also include many representations of lawless, savage mestizo rancheros and villainous, licentious priests.

In almost every case, the representations of unnatural genders and perverse sexualities are used to legitimate some form of U.S. involvement in Mexico. For not only are manly U.S. men often characterized through contrasts with unmanly Mexican men, but in many narratives U.S. soldiers must turn the cross-dressed heroines into women again by inspiring their love. Despite Inez's prodigious military skills, when, dressed in her male disguise, she meets the U.S. officer Devereux, with whom she has fallen in love, on the battlefield at Resaca de la Palma she immediately drops her sword and surrenders: "[T]he sword which before had been held with such a firm grasp and which had been wielded with such a consummate precision defying the most skilled swordsmen, loosened in his hand and fell to the earth, and he now stood before our gallant and invincible hero, trembling" (46). A few minutes later "he" is revealed to be a "she," the "gallant warrior" is transformed into an "Amazonian beauty" (49), her "male apparel" is replaced by "her own proper dress," and Inez hopes never to have cause to wear such "uncomfortable garments" again (49). Similarly, in *The Hunted Chief,* after the cross-dressed female ranchero meets the young American, Rainford, she repudiates her performance of masculinity as a "hollow masquerade" that "has become odious to me" (48). At the end of the novel, when she comes out as a woman to Rainford and confesses her love, she vows to "never more appear in man's apparel, or as the leader of these troops" (86). Even though Isora La Vega retains some of her manly skills and cross-dresses even after she has declared her identity and her love to Midshipman Rogers in *The Secret Service Ship,* she also exhibits new "womanlike" qualities: she becomes "as soft and yielding and womanlike in love, as she was brave and wild and fearless in her periods of passion; such is the mingled nature of the pure maiden of Mexico" (88). In each of these cases, desire for imperial U.S.-American manhood transforms masculine Mexican women into more properly "yielding and womanlike" subjects, even if they still retain an exotic, foreign "mingled nature."

The heroine's love object is almost always a U.S. officer whose manly body and status as a representative of the nation are the most important things about him. Midshipman Rogers, for instance, is initially described as a kind of walking, talking U.S. flag. In the first scene, while he is on a spy mission dressed as a Mexican, he saves the heroine from assault and then exposes his true identity:

> The cloak fell instantly from the disguised form of the unknown, revealing the graceful figure, and lordly proportions of a strikingly handsome young man arrayed in the brilliant uniform of an American Naval Officer, in a proud attitude of command, as he stood thus majestically upon the castle ramparts of San Juan d'Ulloa, his right arm rearing proudly aloft to the breezes of the

Gulf, a superb dark blue banner, on which was embroidered in bright golden
characters, the inscription "UNITED STATES SECRET SERVICE," surrounded by
a circle of thirty glittering stars, such as ever gem the Flag of Our Union; while
the azure sash which encircled his manly waist, so well stocked with a mimic
armory of poniard, pistol, and dagger, was itself a star-spangled standard,
folded into a semblance of a scarf, the extremity of which also formed the
sword-knot of the splendid Italian rapier, upon whose diamond-hilt his left
hand rested, ready at a moment's warning, to make the brave man's use of
the true friend in need. (15)

All tricked out in stars and stripes, the naval officer's body—his
"graceful figure" and "lordly proportions"—presents a spectacle at
which the heroine gazes "in involuntary admiration" (15). Generally, the
hero's role as a U.S. soldier is the key to his character. In *The Hunted
Chief,* we never learn what part of the United States Lieutenant Rainford is from, nor does the narrative reveal anything about his class of
origin; what is more important is that he possesses "an extraordinary
share of manly beauty" and that there was "a fire in his hazel eye that
could stimulate a soldier to deeds of daring, or could kindle a flame in
the heart of a susceptible maiden" (4).

Despite the emphasis on an overarching model of military manhood
that could serve as a point of identification for U.S.-American men of
different classes and as an object of desire for readers, however, domestic class hierarchies continue to be registered in much of this fiction.
Alexander Saxton has argued that the story-paper fiction of the 1840s
features "Free Soil" heroes who adumbrate "the Free Soil alliance of
yeomen, artisans, and established capital out of which sprang the Republican party" in the 1850s.[48] But during the 1840s, this coalition was
still inchoate, and story-paper literature reflects different positions on
the question of class hierarchy, from Whiggish efforts to adapt it to the
changing conditions of Jacksonian U.S.-America, with its increasing intolerance for a "politics of deference," to other efforts to liberate middle-
and lower-class male characters "from the disabilities attached to class."
And yet, despite their differences, both strategies crucially depended
upon what Saxton calls the ascendancy of a "scenario of white brotherhood purified and consolidated through the destruction of nonwhites."[49]

Examples of the first position—that is, efforts to preserve class hierarchies while acknowledging changing conditions—can be found in
those novels in which an elite U.S. officer, often a merchant's son, is
paired with a lower-class Yankee character who speaks in a dialect and

helps the hero foil the villains. In *The Chieftain of Churubusco,* Charles
Warren, the romantic hero, who is a West Point graduate and a "young
gentleman of good family" (11) from New York, is paired with Solomon
Snubbins, an "honest Yankee" (53) from Maine who plays an even big-
ger part in defeating the English and Mexican villains than Warren does.
And in *The Mexican Spy,* Major Henry Rowland, the son of a coal merchant in Philadelphia, teams up with a Connecticut Yankee, Pelatiah P.
Shattuck. But perhaps the most explicit attempt to construct a scenario
of white brotherhood that preserves and adapts class hierarchies in
changing conditions can be found in Arthur Armstrong's *The Mariner of
the Mines.* This novel features two U.S. captains who serve as the romantic heroes: Harold Redwood, a New Hampshire volunteer, and
Campbell, who is from New York. Redwood's father is a retired merchant who "possessed many strong and aristocratic prejudices against
those whom he termed common people" (12), prejudices that are shared
by his wife. Although it might be expected that Harold would inherit
these prejudices, he prefers the society of the common people to "that
of the exclusive aristocrats who generally visited his father's house"
(12–13). Campbell, on the other hand, is a foundling who was adopted
by a wealthy benevolent gentleman. Although he wins the love of Adelia
Sherwood, "the daughter of a rich and very aristocratic merchant" (51)
in New Orleans, her father initially objects to their courtship because
his "prejudices in favor of a pure and unspotted lineage were great and
insurmountable" (52). Later, he changes his mind when he receives news
of Campbell's heroism on the battlefield, but in the end Campbell turns
out to be the son of wealthy, distinguished parents anyway. These two
heroes are paired with two vernacular types, a New Hampshire Yankee
named Zephaniah Sniggins, and Caesar Burney, Campbell's black servant. Even though the servant and the Yankee both speak in dialect, fight
together, and are referred to by the Mexicans as "two common soldiers"
(70), the Yankee is extremely condescending to Burney, repeatedly re-
ferring to him as "blackee"; at the end the Yankee returns to New
Hampshire to marry his sweetheart, while Caesar "remains with his master, Captain Campbell" (84), who marries Adelia Sherwood in New Orleans.

These pairings of elite and nonelite men have a long history that goes
back at least as far as Royall Tyler's 1790 play *The Contrast,* in which
Colonel Manly, the romantic hero, was paired with his servant, the yeoman Yankee Jonathan. Saxton explains that the premise was that Manly,
who "spoke for the landlord-merchant oligarchy that had led the Revo-

lution and dominated the economic, political and social life of the new nation," would serve as a point of identification for elites as well as for members of the lower class, who were expected to look "habitually to their betters for moral and intellectual tutelage."[50] Jonathan's servile relationship to Manly reflects this expectation, despite his attempts to "discount the class distance between himself and Colonel Manly" by focusing on racial disparities between himself and blacks.[51] But by the 1830s, as Yankee characters proliferated in the theater and in popular fiction, Saxton argues, the elite class status of the romantic heroes "took on negative reference as the Jacksonian upsurge restructured American culture and politics" and the Yankee "left his original politics of deference behind him."[52]

The pairings of romantic heroes and Yankee vernaculars in U.S.–Mexican War novels reflect efforts to construct cross-class alliances between a merchant elite and a lower class of yeomen and artisans in the wake of the Jacksonian upsurge. In *The Mariner of the Mines* the merchant's son Redwood even explicitly repudiates the aristocratic prejudices of his father and opts for the society of the "common man." Although Campbell also turns out to be a merchant's son, his status as a foundling of unknown origin for much of the novel provides opportunities for an assault on the merchant Sherwood's similarly aristocratic prejudices; and Sherwood's change of tune after reading of Campbell's valor on the battlefield suggests that manly military merit, as demonstrated by participation in U.S. empire-building abroad, can compensate for an obscure or lowly class origin. On the other hand, the Yankee Zephaniah Sniggins exhibits none of the deference that marked the behavior of earlier Yankees such as Tyler's Jonathan. He still, however, tries to negate differences of class and status by making fun of blacks; even though he is paired with Caesar, he reasserts a hierarchy between himself and the servant that replicates and displaces the earlier hierarchy between white master and white servant in plays such as *The Contrast*. Indeed, the bonds of white brotherhood between the yeoman Yankee and the merchants' sons are forged at the expense of Caesar, who remains literally bound in a servile relationship to Campbell at the end of the novel, as well as the "motley and merciless" (11) Mexicans against whom the white brothers battle.

Significantly, the bonds of white brotherhood are also forged in opposition to the immigrant Irish. In *The Mariner of the Mines,* the patriotic Yankee is contrasted with Dennis O'Finnegan, a side-switching sergeant in the Mexican infantry who, when asked if he is a Mexican, replies that "I'm jist anything I can git the best pay for" and is denounced as a "darn traitor" (39) by the Yankee. And in *The Chieftain of Churubusco,* when Riley and his band of Irish deserters try to talk the Yankee into deserting, he replies that he would rather be "torn chock into ribbins by wild horses, have my tongue cut smack smooth out of my head, and be ground all up intew etarnal smash" (47). These representations suggest that in the 1840s an emerging cross-class coalition among artisans, yeomanry, and an important sector of the merchant elite was built on the foundation of nativism as well as the subordination of nonwhites. That was in fact often the case: during the 1840s and early 1850s, nativist small producers and a minority of nativist workingmen sometimes threw their support to the Whigs against the Democrats, the party of the immigrants. The success of such a coalition depended on a politics that, in Amy Bridges's words, "insisted on the primacy of American interests and the subordination of class divisions."[53] One of the ways that class divisions were subordinated and "American" interests promoted was precisely through the construction of mass cultural representations of white Protestant imperial manhood and fraternity such as these.

And yet, these strategies for turning representatives of different classes into a band of white brothers do not completely succeed in obscuring class differences. They continue to be strongly marked, especially in the contrast between the Yankee's peculiar dialect and the refined, proper speech of the romantic heroes. It is also noteworthy that the Yankee in *The Mariner of the Mines* is paired with Caesar Burney instead of simply being assimilated to a trio that includes Redwood and Campbell; despite the hierarchy that structures the relationship between Caesar and the Yankee, as "common soldiers" they are distinguished from the officers, and the text establishes a mirroring relationship between them through the use of dialect and by making them the sources of comic relief. Finally, what Saxton calls "the problem of marriageability" continues to haunt these novels, underlining the class differences that the authors in other ways try to obscure and soften. In *The Mexican Spy* the Yankee is entirely ineligible for romance; he returns home to Vermont while the elite romantic hero, Major Rowland, is married to the merchant's daughter, Annabel Blackler. And in *The Chieftain of Churubusco,* the Yankee weds Vanilla Hartville, a blind girl who in the beginning is the heroine's servant and is said to be the daughter of a Mexican "lepero," although she turns out to be the daughter of a poor Texas settler. The elite hero Charles Warren, however, marries the wealthy and aristocratic Lauretta Varere. Similarly, in

The Mariner of the Mines, the Yankee returns home to marry his lowly Yankee sweetheart while the two officers and merchants' sons marry rich women. These representations to some degree qualify Saxton's claim that before the Civil War, "[r]omantic love was not for vernaculars" even as they establish boundaries between the classes that cannot be bridged by marriage.[54]

Saxton argues that only later, after the U.S.-Mexican War period, is "equal access to privileges of the upper class, including acquisition of wealth and marriageability," extended to characters of lower-class origin.[55] Significantly, the example he cites is Ned Buntline's Buffalo Bill, who, despite his relatively humble origins, gets to marry a banker's daughter. But Buntline was already working toward such a solution to the problem of marriageability in *The Volunteer,* in which he makes the hero, George Blakey, a backwoodsman from Kentucky. George's father, a self-made man, had come to Kentucky "with no property save his axe, rifle, and a healthy young wife [!]" (8) but soon became a successful shopkeeper. As a Westerner and a shopkeeper's son, George is considerably removed from the merchant elite of New York and Philadelphia, but he is the hero of international romance nonetheless, for he wins the heroine's love despite the fact that "his line of descent" is not "so haughty as her own" (70). In Newton Curtis's *The Prairie Guide,* also, the "handsome and noble-looking" Charles Fanchette impresses the rich Mexican heroine "despite the rough teachings of his early education" (24), and a U.S. officer notes, "[If] he does not make a noise in the world yet, then I am no prophet. One may look a long time for his equal" (7). But such a white egalitarian position, which emphasizes equal opportunity and class mobility for nonelite men, is grounded in the ideal of white "native" military manliness tested and displayed through violent encounters with foreigners and nonwhites. This is true of all of the story-paper novels that obscure or negate the hero's class origins in favor of an overarching model of imperial manhood and international romance.

Another way that these novels try to mitigate class differences among U.S.-American men is by contrasting them with foreign villains who are also wealthy aristocrats. In *The Hunted Chief,* the Chevalier Rijon, who wants to force a marriage with the heroine, is a sensual, rich, Spanish native, the descendant of a noble family who nonetheless exhibits "no true nobility" but is rather "an unprincipled villain" (16). In Buntline's *Magdalena,* the villain is Colonel Gustave Alfrede, a rich Mexican officer who rapes and kills the U.S. hero's mother and sister and then tries to use the leverage of debt to force Magdalena's father to pressure her to marry him. And *The Prairie Guide* features yet another villainous Mexican officer, Captain Minon, who is "a Captain of lancers, a rich man, and a descendant of the aristocracy of Iturbide's days" (10). This emphasis on aristocratic foreigners as the antagonists makes the class distinctions between merchants' sons, Yankee yeomanry, and Western settlers seem less significant; the villainous foreign aristocrat serves as a scapegoat for class resentments that might otherwise be directed at the sons of U.S. elites. Instead, class rivalries are to some extent displaced by imperial rivalries between men over access to the women.

Force and consent are key words in these international romances. Although Donna Isabella Xera, the heroine of *The Prairie Guide,* despises him, Captain Minon pressures her guardian and even kidnaps and imprisons her in an effort to force a union. Even though her uncle initially consents to the marriage, however, Isabella insists that "I ought to be permitted to make my own choice" (17). When in *The Chieftain of Churubusco,* Don Jose de Varere—"a rich and influential citizen of Puebla"—says that his will is his daughter's law and that he can determine whom she will marry, her servant girl replies that it "may be so in everything else but love" (11); the heroine, Lauretta Varere, indeed refuses to consent to the unwanted marriage in spite of her antagonists' efforts to force her to do so. And in *The Texan Ranger,* Adela refuses to agree to marry Don Eugenio, "a lover chosen for her by her father, rather than by her own will" (92). By identifying Mexico and Spain with patriarchy and coercive force, these narratives represent the United States, by contrast, as the land of modernity and relative freedom for women. Since in these novels romantic and political discourses are mapped onto each other, these scenarios also construct the Mexican government as despotic and U.S. government as consensual, democratic, and "free."

Scenes in which Mexican heroines and U.S. heroes are magnetically attracted to each other and almost instantly fall in love reinforce this dichotomy between force and consent, imagined as a contrast between Mexico and the United States. When Xelima and St. James quickly fall for each other in *The Vidette,* the narrator defends love at first sight: "True love is to the human soul, what the spark of fire is to the magazine, and equally as instantaneous in its effects" (79). And when Fanchette, the prairie guide, first sees Isabella, he "started, as if he had received an electric shock" (24) and soon harbors a "deep and fervent attachment" to her, while after only a few hours, "with all the ardor of a soul capable of the greatest extremes of passion—she loved him!" (25). By making the U.S. hero the Mexican heroine's romantic choice, and by dramatizing heterosexual love as intense, almost instantaneous, and natural, these narratives try to justify, present an alternative to, or compensate for the military invasion of Mexico by displacing scenes of force and coercion with a vision of loving, consensual relations between the two nations, albeit one that still depends upon the gendered hierarchies and inequalities that structured the marriage contract in the United States.[56]

This ideological work was especially urgent because U.S. opponents of the war were increasingly arguing that the invasion of Mexico violated the liberal democratic ideal of consent, although occasionally the principle of consent would be invoked to explain why the United States could in good conscience annex all or part of Mexico. The expansionist Democrat senator Dickinson, for one, argued that as a republic, "deriving its just powers from the consent of the governed," the U.S. form of government was "admirably adapted to extended empire," inasmuch as "its influences" were "as powerful for good at the remotest limits as at the political centre."[57] More often, though, when the question of annexation came up, the ideal of consent was cited as a reason why the incorporation of Mexico would be hypocritical and wrong. The Whig C.B. Smith, for instance, argued in the House of Representatives that the U.S. government was based on the principle of "consent of the governed" and that imperialists sought "in violation of this principle, to extend our government, by force, over a reluctant and unwilling people."[58]

In practice, of course, liberal democratic theory often conflates consent and submission, and it thereby fails, as Carole Pateman argues, "to distinguish free commitment and agreement by equals from domination, subordination, and inequality."[59] In a critique of consensual paradigms as they have been applied to Chicanas/os, Carl Gutiérrez-Jones has persuasively argued that since "the history of Anglo and Mexicano/Chicano interaction is one of territorial occupation through legal manipulation working in concert with violence, it comes as little surprise that consent, as framed in the mainstream manner, is significantly challenged by Chicano texts: consent cannot be the cornerstone of justice where choice has not played a significant role."[60] In the mid–nineteenth century, the question of empire forced some of these contradictions to resurface in the sphere of politics as well as in mass literary culture. In response to the war, in other words, congressmen found it necessary to return to questions of consent and to debate the meaning of a principle that was more often left unexamined. And although advocates of expansion would of course want to represent the U.S. annexation of all or part of Mexico as consensual, opponents tried to present alternative models for postwar relations—more intimate commercial relations without political union, for example—by representing other sorts of arrangements as both consensual and superior to the use of military coercion in support of a project of territorial expansion.

Many of these novels symbolically attempt to reverse the U.S. invasion of Mexico by representing international romance as the Mexican heroine's conquest of the U.S. hero. After Charles Devereux falls in love with Inez, he thinks of her as "the being who had taken captive his heart" (22). And in *The Secret Service Ship,* Midshipman Rogers not only tells Isora that she has made "a full conquest" of his heart but also adds, "You had made a breach in the walls, the first glance I received from your dark eyes on the ramparts of San Juan d'Ulloa!" (63). Although U.S. soldiers were invading the homes of Monterrey and bombing the city of Vera Cruz, narratives such as this one try to invert the terms of military conquest and occupation by making the Mexican woman the conqueror. Midshipman Rogers also tries to heal the wounds of war and turn force into consent by suggesting that love transcends national enmities: "By *nationality* we are enemies, 'tis true, dear lady, but O! say not that in *feeling* and in LOVE we are foes!" (63). Other strategies that are deployed to justify a U.S. presence in Mexico include the emplotment of a pre-existing relationship between the romantic hero and heroine. In *The Mexican Spy,* the half-Mexican Annabel Blackler observes that "the affections of my heart were pre-engaged long before I first came to this unhappy country" (62); and in *The Texan Ranger,* Marguerita fell in love with a U.S. officer at a military ball while her father was exiled in New Orleans: "[F]or his sake," she "loved the whole nation" (102). These representations try to override the military hostilities between nations by resolving them into loving bonds that derive from pre-existing transnational connections between elites in Mexico and the United States.

Although many of these novels promote international romance as the symbolic resolution to the war, the conclusions present a number of different outcomes. In *The Prairie Guide,* the Mexican heroine Isabella dresses as a man and follows her lover to Matamoras, where he has rejoined the U.S. forces. Once it is revealed that she is a female in disguise, the two are married at once, making it possible for the humble guide to share her "immense estate" (8) and incredible wealth. This ending is obviously suggestive of the land-grab that accompanied the ending of the war, when the United States increased its size by more than one-fifth at the expense of Mexico. And in *The Mexican Ranchero,* the half-Mexican Buena Rejon's desire for and marriage to the U.S. soldier seems to figure Mexico's "consent" to an intensified relationship with the United States, once the mixed-race monster and the Irish Catholic renegade have been dispatched. At the end of the novel, she marries Herbert Harold and moves to a plantation in Virginia. As we have seen, Harold's sister Alfredine stays in Mexico and marries Buena's brother Rafael, who renounces his vow of eternal vengeance to the invader and seeks "the national reconciliation of the hostile lands" (100). Similarly, when the wealthy St. James marries the Mexican Xelima at the end of *The Vidette,* their romance makes him renounce "ambition, a desire for military distinction, a niche in the temple of his country's fame" (96). Because now "the very mention of war sickened him" (96), he resigned his commission and left his Yankee second-in-command in charge of his troops. In this case, international romance is used to criticize the war rather than to justify it. Or at least it suggests that wars should be fought by lower-class types such as the Yankee rather than the refined St. James.

Although a significant number of these novels end in marriage, in others marriage must be deferred until the war ends. *Inez, the Beautiful,* for instance, ends with a "contract of marriage" between hero and heroine that is "not to be consummated until peace is concluded between the United States and Mexico" (50–51). The narrator concludes that this is "a consummation devoutly to be wished" by "that respectable class of citizens who embrace the strongest PEACE views" (51). And at the end of *The Secret Service Ship,* Midshipman Rogers and Isora La Vega are engaged and plan to marry at the end of the war, when "there will be no bar of nationality" between the "union" (100). At the conclusion of *The Light Dragoon,* too, the U.S. officer Allston and the heiress Elvira are engaged but not yet married, and Elvira is revealed to be the lost child of a U.S. officer in the Seminole War and his Spanish wife, who was murdered by Indians (rather than the daughter of the rich Mexican Espindola, who adopted her). After they marry, Allston plans to return to Mexico as soon as that country is "conquered" in order to claim the deceased Espindola's estates "in the name of the heiress, Elvira" (100). This conclusion seems to indicate a desire for Mexican lands without the Mexicans, since Elvira turns out to have only a legal relationship to her "adopted" nation.

In still other novels, however, the consummation of international romance is prevented by the violence of war or by other obstacles, such as the previous engagement to a U.S. woman that makes it impossible for

Julius, in *The Prisoner of Perote,* to return Josefa's love. At the end of the novel, during the siege of Vera Cruz, Josefa is killed by a bomb, and as she dies she bequeaths a ring to her friend, Julius's fiancée, which becomes "the sacred bond of their marriage" (40). And *The Mariner of the Mines* completely rejects the possibility of international romance by wedding Campbell to the daughter of a New Orleans merchant and pairing the wealthy Redwood with the foundling Charlotte Archington, who turns out to be the daughter of a rich U.S. merchant and an Englishwoman whose father traded in Mexico and later became a Mexican citizen. Moreena, a "native Mexican girl," falls in love with Redwood, and when she is rejected by him her love turns to hatred and she tries to kill both him and Charlotte, although she is ultimately foiled. Her brother Francisco, who tries to force Charlotte to marry him, fares no better. This novel apparently refuses any form of amalgamation between the United States and Mexico, although it does underline the advantageous trading relationships that might be established in Mexico by foreign merchants.

Some of these novels end by trying to harmonize relations between North and South. At the conclusion of *The Mariner of the Mines,* when Caesar Burney remains with "his master" Campbell in New Orleans, Campbell's marriage to the Southern merchant's daughter in that city anticipates the reunion of Northern and Southern interests—at the expense of Burney, of course, as well as the Mexicans who are vilified in this novel. And when the death of the evil Irishman Raleigh allows the dispossessed Captain Harold in *The Mexican Ranchero* to recover "the old family plantation" in Virginia and to move there with his Mexican bride, the narrative seems to be responding to Southern objections to the war by incorporating the South into its vision of postwar reconciliation, although the question of slavery is repressed. When the issue is explicitly raised in *The Mexican Spy,* the conclusion seems forced and hollow. That novel features a black character, Brutus, a former slave in Alabama. Brutus, who was freed by his master, is a servant to a rich Mexican don, but at the end he returns to Alabama and becomes the "overseer on a plantation there" (100). In the novel, Brutus, who is paired with the Yankee vernacular character Pelatiah Shattuck, is used as comic relief (as part of a spy mission, he cross-dresses as a nun, for example) in ways that are reminiscent of blackface minstrelsy.[61] The fact that he returns to Alabama and becomes an overseer on a plantation, along with his view of his former master as a benign, fatherly presence, suggests that the novel is struggling to put to rest fears raised by debates over slavery through the promotion of what Eric Lott calls "the mythology of plantation paternalism."[62] This strategy reflects a general desire among most Democrats and many Whigs to bury the subject of slavery, especially as election time neared, in order to maintain a tenuous hold on white national unity.

If these novels strain to manage the incipient crisis, in other narratives the question of slavery erupts from within plots that otherwise try to marginalize the issue. In *The Texan Ranger,* for example, Marguerita helps two U.S. officers escape from the Mexicans, but she is betrayed by "a Texan slave whom she had trusted, for he had been a servant of her uncle's ever since his flight from Texas, and she believed that he was faithful" (101). But he asked her for more money to keep her secret because he wanted to buy his wife and two boys in Bexar, and when she refused he turned her in to the Mexican authorities. This vignette is particularly interesting because some proannexationists, according to Michael Holt, tried to convince "reluctant Northern Democrats opposed to slavery extension and a growing black population" that adding new territory to the Union would "benefit the anti-slavery cause" by drawing slaves to Texas and eventually to Mexico, thus eliminating "the twin problems of slavery and race adjustment" in the older states.[63] In other words, these Northern Democrats argued that U.S. expansion would mean that slavery would move even farther south and therefore farther away, and that slaves would gravitate across the border to whatever was left of Mexico, where slavery had been abolished. Although such a representation of runaway slaves in Mexico might have comforted the many Northern Democrats who wanted black people removed as far away as possible, it could hardly, however, have been reassuring to Southerners who worried, during the debates over the Wilmot Proviso, about the protection of the peculiar institution.

In *The Volunteer,* on the other hand, the Mexican heroine's brother, the guerrilla Canales, also employs a black "body servant," Matteo, who accompanied him from Texas to Mexico and whose son, Roberto, joins Canales's band. Even though Matteo's continued service to Canales might suggest to supporters of slavery that racialized labor relations akin to slavery could be maintained in Mexico, Roberto's assimilation into Canales's guerrilla band is treated more ambiguously. In fact, this portrayal of the black son of a slave allied with Mexican guerrillas recalls the fears raised in the Williams Brothers' story paper the *Uncle Sam,* quoted in the previous chapter, to the effect that mixed-blood Mexican soldiers "proclaiming liberty to the people of color" might enlist Southern slaves to fight against U.S. whites. At the very

least, these representations support Michael Rogin's argument that the
internal stresses that the ideology of Manifest Destiny was meant to al-
leviate reappeared with even greater fractiousness in the American
1848: "Escaping from the past into the West, from social crowds into
nature, from class conflict into racial domination, America escaped
into a bloody Civil War."[64]

And what of the "internal stresses" of Indian/white relations? Despite the recent history of Indian Removal, the Seminole Wars, and the
Black Hawk War, those who supported annexation in Congress sometimes optimistically suggested, as did Senator Sevier, that "[we] can get
along with those Indians with as little trouble as we do with our own"[65]
Some of these, like Senator Breese, thought that Mexican Indians were
"apt to learn, and willing to improve, and, if not possessed of all the
manlier virtues, have at least those which fully ensure their cheerful ac-
quiescence to our control and rapid advancement under it."[66] Others,
such as Senator Dickinson, took the harsher view that like "their
doomed brethren, who were once spread over the several States of the
Union, they are destined, by laws above human agency, to give way to a
stronger race from this continent or another."[67] Although Democrats
generally endorsed one of the poles of the "civilization or extinction"
dyad, Whigs who opposed annexation tended to argue that Mexican Indians were not likely to disappear anytime soon, and almost all of them
worried about the incorporation of Indians into the white nation.[68] Senator Bell, for instance, warned that even if U.S. whites immigrated to
Mexico, "[Y]ou will still have five millions of Indians on hand, to be an
ever-eating canker on your system."[69]

The international romances of 1846–1848 usually focus most centrally
on Mexican creoles, but some Indian characters do appear in these texts
in subordinate roles. In Buntline's *Magdalena,* the Indian boy Zalupah,
who is Magdalena's servant, is so intensely loyal to her that he sacrifices
his life to save the U.S. officer that she loves. Although his behavior is
described as "brave" and "noble" (63), this representation naturalizes
hierarchical master/servant relations and constructs what we might call
a mythology of hacienda paternalism that implies that creole/Indian relations in Mexico resemble (white fantasies of) white/black relations in
the South. Zalupah is also used to define Magdalena's whiteness
through contrast. When she decides to disguise herself and to team up
with Zalupah in order to save her beloved, she must stain her face and
hands "as dark as a New Orleans quadroon, or a Seminole Indian"
(59) in order to be of "the same hue" (59) and to pass as an Indian

peon. But if this representation suggests that Indians are easily con-
trollable, cheerfully subordinate to whites, and perhaps destined to fade
away, in other narratives they are more autonomous and potentially
threatening. In *The Texan Ranger,* the Comanche Prince Cima offers to
bring his three thousand warriors to the aid of the Mexicans against the
"American invader" (68) if the beautiful Adela, the Rose of the Rio
Grande, will marry him, while in *The Chieftain of Churubusco,* Comanches capture a U.S. American who is on his way to Mexico and initiate him "into their wild and warlike tribe" (39). In still other narratives, as we have seen, when heroines are of Indian descent, international
romance is usually repudiated as a way of figuring postwar relations between nations. Although *The Heroine of Tampico* is in some ways an
exception, since in it the daughter of Seminole Indians marries a U.S. officer, in this case the fact that she is not a Mexican Indian is significant.
Since the novel features no international pairings, and on the contrary
doubles the Seminole Indian/U.S. officer romance with a marriage between the officer's brother and an Anglo-American heroine, the novel
apparently prefers an interracial, intranational romance to one between
U.S. Americans and Mexicans.

Although it might be expected, then, that story-paper romances
would promote annexation, many of them support the U.S. military presence there but express reservations about the incorporation of all of
Mexico, and especially of Mexicans, into the white U.S. republic. Of
course, some of these novels, such as *The Vidette,* end by criticizing the
war, and others register the fact that the war is controversial, or hope
that it will soon end. But more of the novels try to sidestep the question
of the justice of the war and instead develop strategies for resolving the
conflict in ways that counter the international romance equals annexation paradigm. When international romance is consummated, but the
Mexican heroine returns to the United States with her new husband, for
instance, the novels may be suggesting that exceptional "white" Mexican women (and by extension, perhaps, the northern Mexican borderlands) can be incorporated into the nation, but that greater Mexico and
the mixed-race Mexican masses cannot be so easily assimilated. When
the heroines are only half-Mexican, or when international romance is
entirely repudiated, these stories reject the possibility of annexation more
forcefully. And often, the narratives end by indicating that the brothers
of the heroines of international romance remain at the forefront of the
struggles in Mexico. This may imply that elite Mexican men with political and commercial connections to U.S. American men should rule

Mexico, doubtless by taking U.S. interests to heart. Indeed, in some of these romances, the representations of U.S. merchants and especially merchants' sons, many of whom do not marry Mexican women, suggest that these novels may be advocating intimate economic relationships with Mexico rather than political or romantic ones. Although it would be difficult to argue in almost every case that the story-paper novels unequivocally endorse the war and the annexation of Mexico, in all of these narratives the boundaries of gender, race, and sexuality are central to debates over the politics of empire-building and the incorporation of "foreign" territories and peoples.

I suggested in the previous chapter that story-paper literature claimed to be neutral or independent and tried to appeal to a mass audience composed of multiple classes. Nonetheless, the political debates between Democrats and Whigs over the war and annexation resonate throughout the pages of these novels. Although Democrats advocated the annexation of all of Mexico, more of them wanted to take only the relatively sparsely inhabited parts of northern Mexico, especially California. And despite the fact that most of the Whigs voted for supplies and resources in support of the war, and even ran war hero Zachary Taylor as their presidential candidate in the election of 1848, many raised questions about the origin of the war, tried to devise strategies for ending it, and argued for a "No Territory" program. Indeed, Whiggish positions are implicitly referenced in the story papers more often than might be expected, not only when objections to annexation are voiced but also in the efforts to construct models of white Protestant manhood and fraternity that might serve as "mutualist" points of identification for U.S. American men of different classes. Such a conjunction of class, nativism, white manhood, and imperialism is especially significant in the work of Ned Buntline, whose infamous career as a purveyor of popular culture is the subject of chapter 5.

FIVE

From Imperial Adventure to Bowery B'hoys and Buffalo Bill

Ned Buntline, Nativism, and Class

Ned Buntline was surely one of the nineteenth century's most popular writers. His literary career spanned most of the second half of the nineteenth century, from the 1840s until his death in 1886, and during those years he produced dozens of mysteries-of-the-city and Western frontier novels. Buntline's significance as an innovator in these popular genres has sometimes been noted, but little has been said about the imperial adventure fiction that he wrote during the 1840s and 1850s. This chapter argues that Buntline's sensational literature about Mexico, Cuba, and an "empire of Popery" can tell us much about the intimate, volatile relationships among working-class culture, nativism, and empire in the mid–nineteenth century. As I suggested in the previous chapter, constructions of white Protestant manhood and fraternity figure significantly in Buntline's U.S.–Mexican War romances. In addition, plots about Cuban filibustering as male adventure emerge from within his mysteries-of-the-city novels about New York City and New Orleans, and fears of rival empires and anti-Catholic sentiments that were enflamed by the U.S.-Mexican War shape the nativist labor culture that he energetically promoted in his fiction and in his popular newspaper, *Ned Buntline's Own*. As in the other story-paper literature that we have considered, moreover, in Buntline's writing questions of empire are inseparable from issues of race, gender, and sexuality.

During the war years, Ned Buntline was one of the *Flag of Our Union*'s most popular writers, so much so that the publishers included a front-page biographical sketch, complete with a portrait of Ned with top hat and cane, in the 1 January 1848 issue. In addition to *The Volunteer*, Buntline published several pirate stories in the *Flag*, including *The Black Avenger of the Spanish Main: or, The Fiend of Blood*, which first appeared in the story paper on 10 July 1847, accompanied by a large picture of an ominous-looking pirate captioned "Death to the Spaniard!" A few months later, the first installment *of The Red Revenger, or, The Pirate King of the Floridas* was printed in the *Flag* ("Now for a rush! Another $100 Prize Tale" [6 November 1847]), to be followed in March of 1848 by *The Queen of the Sea; or, Our Lady of the Ocean*, which was set in seventeenth-century Panama. Other adventure stories that he wrote for the story-paper empire include *Matanzas; or, A Brother's Revenge. A Tale of Florida* (1848), a historical romance about power struggles between the Spanish and the French, and two romances about Peru, *The Last Days of Callao; or, The Doomed City of Sin!* (1847) and *The Virgin of the Sun: A Historical Romance of the Last Revolution in Peru* (1847).

Even before the U.S.–Mexican War years, Buntline scored his first successes as a professional writer by producing sea yarns that were sometimes loosely based on his own maritime experiences. Buntline signed up for the U.S. Navy in 1837, when he was sixteen, and during the next four years he fought in the Seminole War and sailed to various U.S., Caribbean, and Mexican ports.[1] After 1844, he co-edited a Pittsburgh magazine and later the *Western Literary Journal and Monthly Review*, a paper based first in Cincinnati and then Nashville, where he published a few Seminole War stories before moving to New York City to work as correspondent for the Philadelphia *Spirit of the Times*. In New York he was briefly embraced by that influential arbiter of genteel literary standards, the famous Whig Lewis Gaylord Clark, who published some of Buntline's stories in the *Knickerbocker* before dropping him. But before that happened, Buntline had already departed for Boston, where he quickly hooked up with Justin Jones and his story paper the *Star Spangled Banner* as well as with Gleason and Ballou at the *Flag of Our Union*. As a result, he produced a considerable number of romantic adventure novels with foreign settings, including two U.S.–Mexican War romances: *The Volunteer: or, The Maid of Monterey*, a hundred-dollar prize story that was serialized in the *Flag* and then reprinted as a pamphlet novel by Gleason in 1847; and *Magdalena, the Beautiful Mexican Maid*, which appeared in 1846.

Figure 8. Masthead of 1 January 1848 issue of the *Flag of Our Union*, with portrait of Ned Buntline and excerpt from Maturin Murray Ballou's *The Adventurer*. (Courtesy American Antiquarian Society)

By taking the U.S.-Mexican War as his subject, Buntline was dealing with nearly contemporary events, the outcome of which was still uncertain in August and September of 1847, when the *Flag* serialized *The Volunteer*. In October, the story was quickly published as a novelette, and since the war was still going on, the publishers suggested that it "might afford much interest to the gallant volunteers in Mexico, and their friends at home should send them something to wile [sic] away the hour of their night watches, in the interim of camp duty" (2 October 1847). Although Buntline and the paper were clearly trying to capitalize on the "state of feverish excitement" provoked by the war and although the novel champions the imperial manhood of the U.S. citizen-soldier, its position on the war and the question of the annexation of all or part of Mexico is more ambiguous, despite Buntline's efforts to use the conventions of romance to turn the invasion of Mexico into a chivalric U.S. rescue mission.[2]

From the beginning, the war is represented as, above all, a testing ground for U.S. manhood. When George's mother begs him not to enlist,

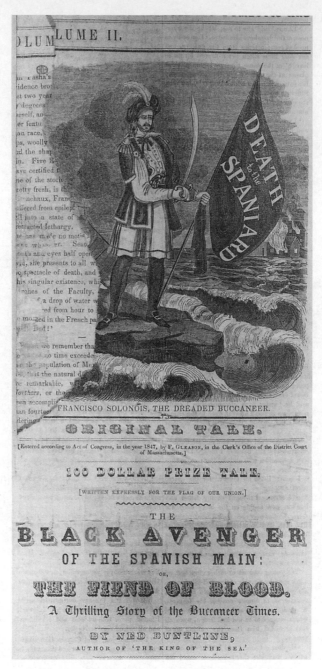

Figure 9.   Detail, "The Black Avenger of the Spanish
Main," from 10 July 1847 issue of the *Flag of Our Union*.
(Courtesy American Antiquarian Society)

he replies that the "call is for *men;* you would yourself blush if I were so unmanly as not to respond to the call!"[3] But the manly body of this "noble specimen of a back-woodsman" is represented in idealized terms even before he sets off for war: "He stood just six feet and one inch in height, was straight as one of his own forest maples, had a brow high, fair, and unfurrowed by care or dissipation, an eye blue as an Italian sky," as well as "limbs that developed muscle and strength which would in the days of Grecian splendor, have made him a favorite model for the sculptor's eye" (8). Blakey's status as an exemplary manly type clearly has much to do with his place of origin: that is, Rural Choice, Kentucky. Although Buntline had yet to write the urban melodramas that would help to make him even more famous, his urbanoid tendencies are fully on display when he borrows the following lines from Byron to describe Blakey's rural "class": "tall and strong, and swift of foot were they/Beyond the dwarfing cities' pale abortions.... No fashion made them apes of her distortions/Simple they were, not savage" (6). Although this Romantic privileging of the country over the city responds to the emergent industrial capitalism that was transforming Northeastern U.S. cities, it simultaneously stigmatizes the city as a feminizing space in which "fashion" holds sway and distinguishes a "simple" yet civilized yeoman masculinity from a "savage" state that is implicitly identified with foreign, nonwhite, or urban others.[4] So even though Buntline abjures the strategy of pairing an elite male hero with a lower-class Yankee vernacular sidekick (a strategy that, as we have seen, many other writers of war novels pursued), he still obscures class divisions in favor of an ideal of white, rural, "native" U.S. manhood.

The boundaries of an idealized masculinity are established in *The Volunteer* through contrast, as the heroic, chivalrous Blakey is opposed to Gorin, a rapacious Texas Ranger who burned down the house of the heroine's Mexican mother and Anglo-American father and tried to kill her and her brothers, thereby turning all of the remaining family members into guerrillas who fight for Mexico. By making the Texan Gorin into the villain in this story, Buntline displaces a critique of U.S. empire onto the republic of Texas, which he represents as a lawless world of crime and rule through force before the United States claimed it. He also decouples this rapacious masculinity from whiteness by describing Gorin as "one whose dark brow, coal-black eye and swarthy hue, made him much resemble the Mexican race" (22). At one point, Gorin even switches sides and fights for the Mexicans. But the treacherous and woman-hating ways of the dark Gorin, "that *thing* who calls himself a *man*" (45), only serve to make the blue-eyed Blakey's patriotic, chivalric masculinity all the more apparent. By positioning Blakey as the heroic defender of women, opposing him to the malevolent and ambiguously racialized Gorin, and rewarding him with the heroine's love, Buntline labors to depict the U.S. intervention in Mexico as something more than an opportunistic land grab. In other words, he strives to turn force/invasion into consent/marriage through a gendered, imperialist rhetoric of international romance.

The cross-dressed heroine Edwina Canales/Helen Vicars is a central figure in this attempted conversion. Her own transformation from male to female is also significant within the imperial plot. When Blakey first encounters her, she is dressed as a man and remains on the battlefield to fight U.S. forces even though the rest of her troops have fled. When she finally falls from her horse, Gorin tries to kill her, but Blakey prevents him. After this tenacious Mexican officer surrenders, Blakey observes that he "seemed to be but a young boy, his dress too was singular, and his appearance far more feminine than his actions would denote" (12). But once Blakey gets a closer look at the officer's "luxuriant and glossy curls," "delicate foot and hand," and "jet black eyes, so large, so dewy, and shaded by lashes of silken gloss," he quickly exclaims, "By heavens, you are a lady!" (12). Curious to know what "wrongs" induced her "to unsex [herself] and face the fearful perils of war" (12), he eventually learns that she was born in Mexican Texas and that her parents joined the rebellious Texans against Mexico but were murdered by Gorin and some of his henchman because she refused his attentions. She and her brothers escaped Gorin by fleeing to Mexico, where they adopted that nation's cause as their own. By the time Blakey hears this story, he is already in love with her— "in love with a foe!" (31). This causes a delay in the progress of their romance, since both of them are so patriotic, but by the end of the story Edwina has agreed to marry Blakey and to return with him to his "native land."

The heterosexual union between Blakey and Edwina/Helen, who has been converted from a masculine foe into a feminine love object, confirms Blakey's imperial masculinity and to a degree validates the U.S. presence in Mexico. Even though her brother initially feels that his sister, who comes from "one of the proudest stocks of Spain," should not marry "one of the Saxon blood" (70), he ultimately consents to the marriage, announcing, "We give you our dearest treasure, noble American—we know that you will guard and cherish her. You have won her by your prowess—take her, and God bless you!" (91). If as the defender of Mexico Edwina, despite her mixed U.S.-Mexican background, represents the nation, then in this scene, the fantasy of U.S. invasion as benevolent rescue climaxes with the guerrilla fighter "giving" his sister, as a sort of war trophy, to the U.S. volunteer in recognition of the latter's "prowess." The U.S. American's "noble" masculinity overrides differences of "blood" and status as the enmity between nations gives way to international romance and homosocial bonds between men. "No truce had been spoken of between them, yet neither he nor his men looked upon these Mexicans as enemies, nor did they regard him as a foe," Buntline writes near the end. "The circumstances under which they had met had made them friends" (89).

It is doubtful that this conclusion, however, signals a straightforwardly proannexationist position. For instead of remaining in Mexico, Blakey returns to Rural Choice with his bride, while the guerrilla Canales swears that he will go on fighting for Mexico after they depart. At the end, Buntline refers his readers to "the papers," in which "each new report from Mexico, brings accounts of his daring deeds" (100). He also warns his readers that General Urrea is still "in the field, and is one who while a blade is lifted against our flag, will still fling his banner to the breeze. Though an enemy, he is brave, skilful, and daring" (100). These passages imply that Blakey/the United States can "win" control of new areas (Edwina/northern Mexico) only with the consent and cooperation of a male Mexican elite, represented here by Canales and Urrea. But it is also unclear that Edwina stands in for the Mexican nation as a whole, or that the union between her and Blakey indicates the desirability of the annexation of Mexico. For it is important to recall that Edwina was born in Texas and is only half Mexican. She is even contrasted with General Urrea's daughter, Anita, who is said to be both "Castilian" and "Aztec" and who remains in Mexico to marry one of the Canales brothers. While for Buntline a creole Tejana can become a part of the U.S. family, the Mexican woman of Indian descent must stay where she is and be wedded to the Mexican guerrilla fighter, suggesting perhaps that the United States should not try to annex the whole of a more densely populated, "Indian" Mexico but should instead be content to take only the more sparsely settled northern borderlands. Although Buntline struggles to bind together heterodox international constituencies—in this case, the white rural settlers of Kentucky and the creole elite of Texas and Mexico—through a rhetoric of heterosexual union, the racial heterogeneity of Mexico seemingly makes him wary of endorsing the incorporation of all of Mexico into the United States.

What is more, images of U.S. intervention as rape rather than rescue repeatedly recur in the narrative, troubling the alignment of the villainous Gorin with the realm of brute force and of Blakey and the United States with a chivalric reverence for the principle of "consent." Buntline's novel opens on the fourth day of the attack on Monterrey, with U.S. troops "forcing their way through the walls of the houses, step by step, toward the heart of the city...through casements and lattices where never before was seen aught but flowers and smiling faces, now treading with armed and blood-stained heels over silken carpets, then crushing the flowers that had been reared and cherished by the fair hands of many a sweet southern girl" (7). The violent, sensational language of the opening paragraphs already figures the war as a rape in which U.S. soldiers force themselves upon the city of Monterrey, crushing the flower of southern girlhood as they brutally proceed. Just as it did for Lippard, the siege of Monterrey in particular causes problems of representation: how to romanticize this series of battles in which U.S. soldiers invaded Mexican homes, breaching walls between dwellings as they moved from one part of the city to the next, inevitably causing the injury and death of noncombatants as they proceeded? The violence of this opening series of scenes is never completely sublimated into romance, and throughout the narrative the U.S. presence in Mexico is repeatedly figured as an invasion rather than a righteous response to Mexican attacks on Texas and the United States. Toward the end of *The Volunteer,* Blakey even announces that this "will be the last war of *invasion* in which I shall ever participate. I would die for the *defence* of my country, but never again will I leave her borders to seek for glory!" (75). In passages such as this one, the fiction of the United States as chivalric defender of white Mexican womanhood cannot be sustained. And since the analogy between hero and nation also works in reverse, it could be argued that Blakey's heroic masculinity is compromised by the rapacious nationalist acts of wartime aggression that frame the story. This emphasis on the war as invasion also recalls the Whig redescription of the conflict with Mexico as a rapacious act of conquest.

And if international romance fails to fully resolve the contradictions and conflicts unleashed by the U.S.-Mexican War in *The Volunteer,* in *Magdalena, the Beautiful Mexican Maid,* the love plot itself has a tragic ending. Inspired by John Greenleaf Whittier's antiwar poem "The Angels of Buena Vista," which is incorporated into the text, the story is about a romance between Charles Brackett, a half "Castillian" Texas Ranger, and Magdalena Valdez, the daughter of a "Castillian noble" who lives on a hacienda in Mexico.[5] Brackett fights with special zeal against the Mexicans because the Mexican colonel Gustave Alfrede raped and killed his sister and mother back in Texas. This same Mexican officer is also trying to force a marriage to Magdalena, despite her repugnance for him, by pressuring her father, whose extreme "liberality" and mismanagement of his hacienda have caused him to become heavily indebted to Alfrede. Ultimately, the colonel threatens to make the whole family peons for life if Magdalena doesn't consent to marry him. Magdalena, however, quickly falls in love with Charles Brackett despite the fact that Mexico and the United States are at war: "I can almost forget that you are a foe!"—"Oh, *quite* forget, beautiful lady, for Americans are never foes to such as you. We oppose men like men; we meet the helpless with kindness."[6] At this point, the traditional closure of romance seems imminent, for it turns out that the two are cousins (Senor Valdez's lost sister was Brackett's mother) and are therefore "equal in birth" (50), so Senor Valdez consents to their union. But in place of the anticipated ending Buntline delivers a bleak conclusion: Brackett and Alfrede fatally wound each other at the battle of Buena Vista, and Magdalena kills herself when she finds their bodies on the field.

It could be argued that this tragic ending signifies the futility of war, which prevents the healing closure of international romance, and that the novel therefore suggests that imperialist U.S. policies are bloody and uselessly destructive. Such an interpretation of Buntline's purpose could be supported by Blakey's surprising insistence at the end of *The Volunteer* that the war "has been a sad one for both countries, one in which much noble blood has been lost, one which neither government can gain by!" (89). But in *Magdalena,* Buntline places more of the blame for the war on Mexico. Although the villain Gorin is a U.S. citizen in *The Volunteer,* in *Magdalena* the evil Alfrede is a Mexican creole, and the conflict between Brackett and Alfrede is said to result from Mexican war crimes in Texas rather than the atrocities committed by Texas rangers. Indeed, in *Magdalena,* Buntline goes so far as to commend the U.S. forces of occupation for refraining from committing "a single outrage upon the vanquished foe, even though there were men there whose relatives had been butchered in the 'Alamo,' or whose families had been robbed and murdered on the gory plains of Texas" (54). In these ways, Buntline suggests that the war is the result of the murderous excesses of Mexican troops in Texas, led by rapacious officers such as Alfrede. Such a reading is reinforced by Magdalena's fears at the end of the novel that if the Mexicans win, the family will be exposed to "rude and licentious men, who respect no law, and are governed by no principles" (76). All of this implies that Mexican men are unfit for republican government, a charge that was often made by those who opposed the annexation of Mexico. Here that "licentiousness," which is opposed to law and government, is identified with a rapacious Mexican masculinity that serves to define, by contrast, a heroic U.S.-American manhood.

But U.S.-American manhood, as embodied by Charles Brackett, is more oddly racialized in *Magdalena* than in *The Volunteer,* where it is represented by the "Saxon" Blakey. When Brackett is chosen to pass as a Mexican and spy on the enemy, a U.S. officer explains to General Taylor that Brackett is the perfect man for the job because, "as his mother was a Castillian, [he] is full as dark, but not quite so yellow as a real native. If he was stained with a shade of butternut color, and rigged up a la ranchero, he'll make as good-looking a Mexican as I ever drew lead on" (6). Although Brackett's patriotism is repeatedly praised and although his European descent is emphasized, the strange remarks about "color," along with Brackett's ability to easily pass as a Mexican, suggest a more ambiguous racial status.

On the one hand, it was extremely unusual that a non-Anglo man would be the romantic hero in such a novel; in *Magdalena* this is possible, it would seem, only because Brackett is part "Spanish" rather than mestizo or Indian. On the other hand, in a rare development, Brackett dies in the final chapter, preventing this international romance from engendering a future. Buntline's decision to give this novel a tragic ending suggests an unwillingness, in other words, to make this pair a model for a postwar relationship between the United States and Mexico. Instead, he implies that the war is basically a family squabble between "Spanish" Texans and Mexicans. Although Alfrede's rapaciousness and his use of debt as a way of controlling people anticipate Buntline's venomous descriptions of the wealthy "upper ten" in his urban melodramas, the vision of Mexico that is presented in this novel is generally negative, despite the idealized representation of Magdalena and her sister. Since Buntline blames the war on Mexican rapaciousness and even suggests that the seemingly benign Senor Valdez is incapable of managing his hacienda, it should not surprise us that in this novel he seems to want to keep Mexico at a distance rather than incorporate Mexicans, whether creole or Indian, into U.S.-America's future.[7]

These ambiguous representations of the U.S.-Mexican War do not, however, support the conclusion that Buntline was an ardent anti-imperialist, for he was always willing to promote the U.S. citizen-soldier, even if he expressed doubts about official U.S. foreign policy. During the U.S.-Mexican War years, we could say that Buntline's stance on the war was closer to that of the Whigs than the Democrats: he celebrated U.S. military victories and glorified military heroes but called the war an "invasion" of Mexico and refrained from endorsing the annexation of all of Mexico. But Buntline was never one to keep to a party line. Although his support for some Whig positions reflects the often intimate relationship between nativism and Whiggery in the 1840s and early 1850s, he switched political allegiances throughout his lifetime, and his most intense commitments were to the nativist political parties that flourished at midcentury. Biographer Jay Monaghan's assessment of Buntline's politics is perceptive: "The Buntlinites were poor people, suspicious of the Whigs" but opposed to the foreigners who were welcomed by the Democrats.[8] Or they could be described in Amy Bridges's terms, as members of the "old working classes" who responded to the threat of industrialization by scapegoating immigrants. Especially after he returned to New York City from Boston in late 1847, Buntline increasingly constructed himself as an advocate for this class through his authorship of mysteries-of-the-city literature and his flamboyant and hypervisible public persona.

In December of 1847, the first installment of Buntline's massive *Mysteries and Miseries of New York* appeared. Based on the pattern established by Eugène Sue in *Les Mystères de Paris* and imitated by countless others on both sides of the Atlantic, the novel exposed the city's mysteries, as Michael Denning puts it, "by telling tales of criminal underworlds, urban squalor, and elite luxury and decadence."[9] As part of that project, Buntline represented poor sewing girls persecuted by "fashionable young *gentlemen,* sons of the 'first families' "; a prostitute with a heart of gold; a clerk who is tempted to embezzle from his employer to support his gambling habit; and a dizzying array of other urban types.[10] In order to condemn urbanization, he also singled out for particular criticism spaces in which working-class blacks and whites mingled; included several representations of foreign-born criminals; and added an appendix that blamed immigrants for increases in urban crime. On the other hand, midway through the novel, he incorporated as one of the story's heroes the native-born Mose, the Bowery B'hoy, a character who was first introduced to the New York public in Benjamin Baker's play *A Glance at New York in 1848.*[11] In the months that followed, Buntline wrote a sequel to *Mysteries* called *Three Years After,* which Baker used as the basis for one of several more plays starring Mose. These plays were a resounding success, and Buntline's *Mysteries* was also incredibly popular, selling perhaps as many as 100,000 copies and ultimately inspiring the author to add *The B'hoys of New York* and *The G'hals of New York* to the list of sequels. Baker's plays and Buntline's novels were wildly popular in part because a significant sector of the New York population apparently recognized themselves in this representation. When the audience heard Mose's distinctive voice in *A Glance at New York,* one newspaper reported, it was "received with shouts of delight from the thousand originals of the pit."[12] As Buckley suggests, Mose was both "a fictional type arising within new forms of cultural production" and a social type that corresponded to " 'real' transformations in the social and cultural practices of the working classes during a crucial decade in their development."[13] Buntline played an important role in developing the Bowery B'hoy as a fictional type, and increasingly he came to think of himself as an advocate for the B'hoys as social types. For example, he started a story paper, *Ned Buntline's Own,* that featured serialized stories as well as muckraking, often scurrilous articles championing urban reform and nativist politics. And in May of 1849, on the morning of the day that he was arrested for fomenting the Astor Place theater riots, he was wearing, according to Buckley, "a tall 'Bowery B'hoy' hat."[14] That style of dress was particularly appropriate, since theater-going B'hoys were said to be the main participants in the riots. Posters that read: "WORKINGMEN, Shall AMERICANS OR ENGLISH RULE in this city?" had been displayed throughout the city on the day of the riot, and that evening Buntline and the B'hoys underlined their response to that question.[15] According to witnesses, Buntline started a fire "either with the view of destroying the building, or of giving color to the cry of fire," and "the mass congregated in Astor Place are pictured by some of the witnesses as inflamed to the highest pitch of excitement, and as heaving to and fro like the tumultuous waves of the ocean."[16] Although several other men were charged with participating in the riot, the judge who presided over the case decided that all of them showed signs of previous good character, "with the exception of the defendant Judson [Buntline]."[17] Consequently, Buntline was sentenced to one year of hard labor on Blackwell's Island. One sign of how far he had fallen was an article that appeared in the 13 October 1849 issue of the *Flag of Our Union,* which complained that Buntline's sentence was too light but exulted that this "notorious individual has at last been stamped with a legal brand as a villain for life."

Although Buntline's role as self-appointed advocate for the Bowery B'hoys in his public actions, journalism, and novels clearly indicates his significance in the mid-nineteenth-century popular culture of New York City, he never abandoned his earlier interest in U.S. empire. In *Mysteries and Miseries of New York,* issues of empire are relatively marginal, coming briefly into view, for example, when the gambler Henry Carlton vows to retire at fifty and "go to Mexico or South America, kick up a revolution, and found a kingdom for myself, as Aaron Burr intended to do" (part 3, 33); or when Buntline's narrator declares war against gambling dens and vows to "treat them worse than ever 'Rough and Ready' did the Mexicans" (part 3, 126); or when Carlton urges the embezzler Charley Meadows to "go into the interior of Cuba, change [his] name and buy a plantation" (part 4, 85). But in *The B'hoys of New York,* which was written after Buntline's conviction, a Cuban filibustering plot is central to the narrative. In this novel, Buntline's villain is the Spaniard Senor Alvorado, a smuggler and pirate who plans to amass millions of dollars in order to fund his plans to "strike for Revolution and the presidency of a *new* Republic!"[18] Even though his scheme to "accomplish the freedom of Cuba" is treated ambivalently by Buntline, Alvorado is at the same time blamed for a number of crimes. To name just a few of these, he rapes the seamstress Agnes Morton, the daughter of a merchant who killed himself after his business failed in the Panic of 1837, and Alvorado thereby causes her insanity and suicide; he pretends to get her recently unemployed brother, George, a job as a clerk for a Spanish merchant and then tries to have him killed while on a ship bound for Cuba; he betrays, robs, and kills a "good," Robin Hood–like, native-born pirate (who became a pirate only after killing the stepfather who murdered his mother and stole the fortune left to him by his father) and also accidentally murders the pirate's wife, whom he was trying to seduce; and in the dark conclusion, captioned "Read it and weep," his ship outruns George's, Alvorado escapes to Cuba, one of his mates shoots George in the head, and George's brains ooze out upon his new bride's snow-white dress. In visceral, sensational terms, then, Buntline constructs the Spaniard Alvorado as a foreign scapegoat for urban problems. In this way, Buntline brings together a variety of urban social types—the bankrupt merchant, the unemployed clerk, the orphan girl turned seamstress, the dispossessed and criminalized native New Yorker—and suggests that they are all victimized by the foreign pirate/revolutionary. This move recapitulates, on a symbolic level, nativist, "mutualist," cross-class alliances forged at the expense of immigrants and other foreign bodies, and it also recalls the representations of Spaniards and creoles as rapacious tyrants in story-paper novels about the U.S.-Mexican War.

But in this novel Buntline also suggests some of the many connections between New York City and Cuba at that moment, particularly the transnational schemes by New York merchants and Cuban expatriates to "liberate" Cuba from Spanish rule. After the signing of the Treaty of Guadalupe Hidalgo in 1848, many U.S. expansionists increasingly turned to Cuba as the next object of imperial interest. This time, Southern slaveholders were more enthusiastic because they believed that the incorporation of Cuba would involve the addition of one and possibly as many as three new slave states to the union. Many New York financiers and merchants also endorsed this project because Cuba was such an important trading partner, because many of them had close economic ties to Cuba's sugar planters, and because some New Yorkers even owned interests in Cuban plantations.[19] Although U.S. government officials considered different plans for convincing Spain to sell Cuba, others plotted more direct and aggressive military actions. For instance, in 1848 representatives of the Havana Club, a group of Cuban émigrés in New York, approached Mexican war hero General William Worth about leading an army to Cuba; he agreed to do it but then unexpectedly died of cholera in 1849.[20] Meanwhile, in July of 1848, Venezuelan-born Narciso Lopez founded the Junta Cubano, a New York group dedicated to organizing filibustering expeditions to take over the island. During the next three years, until his execution in Cuba in 1851, Lopez and his supporters would repeatedly try to mobilize support for these expeditions, especially in New York City, Washington, and New Orleans. According to historian Robert May, these efforts succeeded in bringing together a surprising variety of young men, for the "appeal of filibustering crossed class lines," drawing in "clerks, apprentices, and immigrants" as well as the sons of planters, merchants, and politicians.[21] Indeed, filibustering facilitated the sort of cross-class coalitions that the major political parties were also trying to consolidate.

Despite his representation of the Spaniard Alvorado as a villain in *The B'hoys of New York,* Buntline was also attracted to the project of Cuban filibustering. In 1851 he sold Cuban scrip that he claimed could be redeemed if Lopez's filibustering project succeeded, and he also delivered lectures on "Liberty in Cuba" and "Americanism at Home." Although Buntline's Mexican War fiction suggests that he had reservations about the annexation of all of Mexico, his greater enthusiasm for the cause of Cuban "freedom" could have been reinforced by his support for slavery; it may also have been affected by his marriage to Seberina Marin, whom he met in Cuba or Florida while he was a naval officer and who died in the mid-1840s.[22] The fact that Seberina was a Spanish creole from Florida or Cuba may well have encouraged Buntline to indulge in "Spanish fantasy" about international romance between U.S. men and Cuban women.

In *The B'hoys of New York,* for instance, the failed merchant's son George Morton wins the heart of Eugenia Dellarosa, the daughter of a wealthy Cuban. Although George worries that he is too poor to marry her, Eugenia assures him that "in America every honest man is a *king*— every freeman there equal to the highest born! I look upon you as a son of Washington; you are, at least, the king of my heart!" (135). When George reflects on the fact that his great-grandfather fought in the American Revolution, he suddenly feels better, for he realizes "that he was indeed equal to the highest born Grandee that ever wore a knightly order" (168). Although the novel ends tragically with George's death, this international romance figures Cuban wealth, represented in this case by Eugenia, as accessible even to nonelite U.S. men, as long as they are manly and patriotic, although the risks involved in attaining it may well be fatal.

If *The B'hoys of New York* registers Buntline's ambivalence about any attempts to "free" Cuba that might be led by Spanish creoles without the participation of U.S. Americans, *The Mysteries and Miseries of New Orleans*—a novel that Buntline first published in 1851, the year that Lopez was executed—contains a much more explicit endorsement of filibustering in Cuba, and it also traces connections between city and empire in the wake of the American 1848. By setting the opening scenes in New Orleans, Buntline in effect followed Lopez and his coconspirators from New York to that city, where they attracted a good deal of support from New Orleans merchants, both Whig and Democrat, who hoped to benefit from a more intimate trading partnership between Cuba and the United States—particularly by exporting wheat from the Mississippi Valley to Cuba.[23] New Orleans became Lopez's base of operations as he organized two more unsuccessful expeditions, including the final, fatal one. For the 1850 expedition, Lopez recruited privates by promising to match U.S. Army pay and to reward them with four thousand dollars in money or Cuban lands if the expedition were successful.[24] He also appealed to recruits by inviting them to show "to Cuba and the world, a signal example of all the virtues as well as all the valor of the American Citizen-Soldier."[25] Apparently these strategies worked, for Lopez had little trouble attracting soldiers. And according to the *New Orleans Delta,* three-fourths of those participating in the 1850 venture had previously fought for the United States in Mexico.[26]

Although the second half of *The Mysteries and Miseries of New Orleans* focuses on Lopez's final expedition to Cuba, the first half features a typical cluster of urban "crimes": an aristocratic libertine plots to seduce a virtuous *criolla,* a notorious pickpocket successfully bribes two immigrant policemen, and a young man's "passion for gambling" places him in the power of the villain Orrin Bird, who then seduces the young man's neglected wife, Fanny.[27] But this final subplot dominates the second half of the novel, which also opens up onto scenes of filibustering. When the young man, Charles Gardner, finds out about the seduction of his wife, he challenges Bird to a duel and kills him. At this point, Gardner worries that Bird's friends may try to avenge his murder, and so he looks "for some other sphere of action" (62). He doesn't have far to look, however, for a "new field of action was at that moment opening. Cuba and her wrongs was *[sic]* laid like a map before him. A land where the people were crushed by the despot's heel—a soil stained with the blood of those who had offered up their lives in freedom's causes, was before him, and knowing a few of those who, for 'God, Liberty, and Lopez,' would raise the banner and draw the steel, he volunteered" (62). This expedition partially repairs Gardner's damaged masculinity—Buntline assures the reader that each filibuster "was a *man*" (62)—and Gardner even manages to initiate an international romance with Guadalupe, the daughter of the Cuban hacienda owner Alvarez. But the expedition is ultimately foiled by the vengeful Fanny, who has vowed to punish Gardner for killing her paramour. In the long denouement, she follows him to Cuba, warns the authorities about his presence, writes a letter to Lopez convincing him to come to the island to support what she misrepresents as a widespread rebellion, and helps the Spanish rulers capture Lopez and his companions, who are then executed. Although this outcome makes Fanny the cause of the failed filibustering expedition that Buntline supports, the conclusion contains a surprising defense of her actions: "Man claims the right to avenge his own wrongs—and why not woman?" And at the end of the novel, Charles dies and Fanny boards a steamer bound for "the metropolis of the Empire State" where she will join, the narrator surmises, "the great whirlpool of society, which contains thousands of women of her stamp" (104).

It is likely that Buntline endorsed the filibustering expeditions of the mid-1850s, as opposed to the fictional Alvorado's schemes to make himself the president of a Cuban republic, because Lopez hoped to annex Cuba to the United States and because he recruited so many U.S. soldiers. The fact that Buntline favored the extension of slavery also must have contributed to his support for these ventures. Indeed, when the evil Spanish captain general learns of the filibusters' plans, he threatens to "free and let loose upon them the great horde of slaves which constitute the largest portion of our population" (73), thereby referencing the Spanish policy of playing upon the creoles' fears of race wars as a way to keep them in line.[28] Since Buntline aligns the U.S. Americans and the Spanish creoles against the villainous Spanish rulers and the "treacherous" slaves, he evidently means to place white supremacy, the protection of slavery, and U.S. expansionism in the Caribbean on the side of "liberation," and the emancipation of Cuban slaves on the side of "tyranny."

If Buntline's treatment of slavery and filibustering suggests that foreign policy cannot be adequately understood without considering U.S. domestic debates about the future of the "peculiar institution," the novel also reveals, more specifically, that the mysteries of the capitalist city were complexly entangled with questions of empire. Both *The B'hoys of New York* and *The Mysteries and Miseries of New Orleans* map multiple connections between city and empire as they retrace trade routes between New York, New Orleans, and Havana; follow the transnational networks of mid-nineteenth-century filibustering conspiracies; and focus on scenes of empire-building in the Americas as perilous but possibly redemptive sites where damaged urban masculinities might be rehabilitated and where urban class conflicts might give way to cross-class homosocial bonds between white brothers forged at the expense of people of color. All of this suggests not only that class formations and U.S. empire-building were inextricable in this period but also that issues of overseas empire emerge in the United States well before the 1890s, for the debates about the place of Cuba in U.S. foreign policy and the attempts of filibusters to "free" Cuba from Spain put such questions squarely on the agenda in the middle of the nineteenth century.

If Cuba is one important site where issues of empire become visible in Buntline's later work, it is by no means the only one. In *The Convict: or, The Conspirator's Victim,* a novel that was written while Buntline was imprisoned for leading the Astor Place riots, paranoid visions of "an *empire* of Popery" haunt the narrative.[29] This novel features a crime-busting author-hero of "Anglo-Norman descent" (6), Ernest Cramer, who is clearly modeled in part on Buntline himself. Cramer is victimized by Jesuits in league with the urban criminals that he exposes in his jour-

nalism, and the novel ultimately suggests that these conspirators plotted
the Astor Place riots as a way of ruining "Cramer's" reputation and
thereby neutralizing his opposition to their nefarious plans. As Cramer
describes his chosen "field for labor," he condenses a variety of urban
problems and blames them on foreigners and Catholics:

> The ill-paid artisan; the starving sewing girl; the wronged factory operatives,
> loaded down with oppression by monied monopolists; my dear country bur-
> dened with taxation to support paupers *imported* from foreign climes; labor
> rendered cheaper and more difficult to obtain by the beggarly competition of
> these foreign-born serfs; the blighting and dangerous influence of combined
> and secret associations of foreigners; the plot of a sect who design to make
> this country the stronghold and garden of Popery, and by electing their own
> members to public offices and power, to yet link their church with our Na-
> tional and State Governments; the gambling hells and dens of robbery and
> putridity in our cities; the prostitution of Justice; the barter and sale of all our
> dearest rights!—oh! in all *this,* is there not a field, glorious, even as it is a dan-
> gerous field for *ambition* to enter upon, for a bold and true-hearted lover of
> common humanity to labor in! (11–12)

In the course of the novel, Cramer articulates similar views in speeches
delivered before the Order of United American Mechanics, the Order of
United Americans, and the Daughters of America, three nativist organizations that Buntline supported. Articulating white egalitarian sentiments
to the nativist cause, he repeatedly worried that "a PAPAL EMPIRE"
will arise "on the ruins of this Republic" (243). But although Cramer
and his friend, Mexican War veteran Harry Whitmore, try to foil the
conspirators' plans to ruin him, at the end of the novel these plots succeed; Cramer is sent to jail as the tears roll down "many a manly cheek
of those sons of toil, who had left their work to come and learn the fate
of the 'friend of the working man'" (293).

During the 1850s, Buntline would continue to be deeply involved in
the project of conjoining working-class reform to nativist politics. The
pages of the newspaper that he edited, *Ned Buntline's Own,* were largely
devoted to promoting the nativist cause through stories, editorials, and
coverage of the activities of various nativist organizations. The Order of
United American Mechanics, which was one of Buntline's favorite
causes, attracted particularly large numbers of artisans and workingmen.
Founded in Philadelphia in 1845 and with chapters flourishing in New
York just a few years later, the order, according to Sean Wilentz, "barred
non-producers—merchants, professionals, financiers—as well as immigrants from their meetings," advocated temperance, and sought to reconcile small employers and workers within a "mutualist" vision of

America's future.[30] Buntline also promoted temperance, that notoriously anti-immigrant movement, though according to his biographer he sometimes showed up drunk at temperance rallies.[31] And he, too, embraced a mutualist politics that set "native"-born small producers against the new immigrant working classes, as his editorials make abundantly clear. In 1851, for instance, he reflected on the faces that he saw in an urban crowd as he complained about the decline of patriotism: "Occasionally the face of an American can be recognized whose mind is evidently grieved at the loss of patriotic spirits, but as the thousands hurry along, the blank face of Dutch and Irish, Italian, Hottentot, and Hindoo, tell but too plainly the change that a few brief years has brought forth in the character of our population, each day a day of servitude to labor in their efforts to destroy the American working classes."[32] Although he attacked all kinds of so-called foreigners, Buntline often singled out the Irish in his anti-immigrant tirades. Thus in 1853 he observed, "On Monday I saw a lot of men uniformed in green flags and etc. marching in our streets with a band at their head and muskets on their shoulders. Though they had *white* faces, I had an idea, that they were a company of [Bishop] Hughes' *black*-guards."[33] That this scapegoating of new immigrants for the problems of industrialization hampered the efforts of Buntline and other nativist labor advocates to effectively address such problems perhaps goes without saying.

But it should also be clear that issues of nativism and immigration open up onto issues of empire, and that therefore the nativist labor culture that Buntline represented must be placed in an international frame to be understood. Especially, the visions of Catholicism as a rival empire and the fears of Irish Catholic immigrants that nativist organizations of the 1850s exploited were intimately connected to the anti-Catholic sentiments and representations of imperial rivalries that circulated in the story papers during the U.S.-Mexican War. Representations of white, "native" Protestant manhood and fraternity, which were central to the ideological work of the story-paper empire, were also continuous with the nativist, mutualist constructions of manhood and fraternity that were promoted by groups such as the Order of United American Mechanics.

Buntline's complaint about "labor rendered cheaper and more difficult to obtain by the beggarly competition of these foreign-born serfs" also has important roots in the 1840s, not only because of intensified immigration and cross-class coalitions in behalf of the tariff which, it was promised, would protect workers and employers from the competition of foreign labor but also as a result of the representations of Mexican labor that emerged from travelers' accounts, soldiers' personal narratives, and war literature during this period. In Part 3, I will argue that ideas about free (white) labor were affected by the U.S.-Mexican War as I examine representations of Mexican peonage and other labor systems in the dime novels of A. J. H. Duganne and in writings associated with the labor and land reform movements of the mid–nineteenth century.

PART 3

Land, Labor, and Empire in the Dime Novel

SIX

The Contradictions of Anti-Imperialism

Slaves of the South—arise!
Clang ye your gyves to swell the cymbals' sound—
Lift your exulting eyes!
Lo! your white masters have new victims found—
Comrades ye have—in war's red bondage bound:
Ye shall hear answering cries,
Swelling your gasping sighs.

White slaves of Northern gold!
Build ye a Teocalli—where the foes
Of our ambition bold
May writhe beneath our Anglo-Saxon blows,
And shriek their curses in expiring throes—
Curses that shall be told
Till Eternity is old!

Destiny! Destiny!
Lo! 'tis our *mission* to pour out the tide
Of our heart-blood and die,
With foeman's corse stretched ghastly by our side;
Or live and trample him in vengeful pride:
This is our mission high—
Gospel of Liberty!

—A. J. H. Duganne,
"Manifest Destiny" (1855)

Who hath ordained that the Few should hoard
Their millions of useless gold?—
And rob the earth of its fruit and flowers,
While profitless soil they hold?
Who hath ordained that a parchment scroll
Shall fence round miles of lands,—
When millions of hands want acres—
And millions of acres want hands!

'Tis a glaring LIE on the face of day—
This robbery of men's rights!
'Tis a lie, that the word of the Lord disowns—
'Tis a curse that burns and blights!
And 'twill burn and blight till the people rise,
And swear, while they break their bands—
That the hands shall henceforth have acres,
And the acres henceforth have hands!

> —Duganne, "The Acres and the
> Hands," *The Iron Harp*

In A. J. H. Duganne's dime novel *The Peon Prince; or, The Yankee Knight-Errant. A Tale of Modern Mexico* (1861), the Yankee who appears in the subtitle is Putnam Pomfret, an "offshoot of that great Anglo-Saxon stock, whose footsteps track the paths of empire from the pine woods of Arastook to California cañons; from the wild swash of icy seas upon Labrador's beaches, to the swell of undulating waves in Pacific harbors."[1] A native of Vermont who comes to Vera Cruz to sell clocks to Mexicans, he is an example of what Alexander Saxton calls a *"natural Jacksonian...* vernacular character of lower-class status to whom is attributed class consciousness in the form of egalitarian values."[2] Like other popular comic vernacular characters such as the blackface minstrel and the Bowery B'hoy, or urban workingman, the Yankee speaks in a marked dialect, has jettisoned an older politics of deference, and frequently exemplifies, in Saxton's words, a "congruence between egalitarianism and the hard side of white racism."[3] But although other comic vernaculars continued to defend slavery until the outbreak of the Civil War, Saxton argues, throughout the 1850s the "Westernized Yankee drifted toward the Free Soil persuasion and by the end of that decade stood as a political foe to his own original siblings, the blackface minstrels."[4] For if blackface minstrelsy as a form of popular culture corresponded to a Jacksonian coalition that supported white egalitarianism and defended slavery, transformations in the Yankee character in the mid–nineteenth century responded to the formation of a new coalition—the Republican Party—which yoked white egalitarianism to ideologies of

Figure 10.   Cover of Augustine Joseph Hickey Duganne's
The Peon Prince. (Courtesy of the Hess Collection, University
of Minnesota Libraries)

Free Soil and free labor defined in opposition to the Southern world of
the plantation and chattel slavery.

The U.S.-Mexican War no doubt played an important role in the Yankee's "drift" toward Free Soil politics and the formation of this new coalition, for debates about the war, the annexation of new lands, and the
extension of slavery helped to polarize factions within both major political parties and ultimately facilitated the breakup of the party system

dominated by the Whigs and the Democrats. In the previous chapters, I suggested that opposition to the war and the annexation of new territories was perhaps strongest in New England, where a history of hostility to slavery and Southern interests, together with the strength of the Whig party and antebellum reform movements, combined to produce a good deal of opposition to the expansionist policies of Polk and the Democrats.[5] I also argued that story-paper literature of the late 1840s that expressed doubts about the war and annexation often featured pairings of elite romantic heroes and Yankee vernaculars. During the war years, then, mass cultural representations were already mobilizing the Yankee character against the post-Jacksonian Democratic coalition in ways that anticipated his more radical transformation and realignment with the Republican Party in the years to come. But this repositioning of the Yankee in the story papers was often motivated, as we have seen, by nativism and fears of national and racial contamination. And although the Republican Party of the early 1860s would for the most part abjure nativism in an effort to appeal to a broader coalition of white Northerners, white egalitarianism also limited its vision of a "free" society, despite some dissenting voices.

If, as Saxton argues, entrepreneurs in dime novel publishing "maintained a linkage to the Republican party comparable to that of the impresarios of blackface minstrelsy to the Jacksonian party," then it might be expected that the dime novels of the early 1860s would reflect the realignments of the post-1848 period.[6] One of the premises of Part 3 is that a reconstructed white egalitarianism, which was reshaped by internal and inter-American imperial encounters as well as the battle over slavery, was indeed central to the ideological work of dime novels during the Civil War years. Throughout Part 3 I suggest that the imperial encounter with Mexico and ideas about Mexican land policies and labor arrangements had formative effects upon ideologies of free land and free labor. But discussions of the Mexican hacienda and peonage also, as we shall see, raised questions about the Southern plantation and slavery, for writers who described these Mexican institutions often ended up comparing Mexican labor and land arrangements to Southern institutions, as well as to the Northern "free labor" system. The Wilmot Proviso, which would have banned slavery and other forms of "involuntary servitude" in any new lands acquired from Mexico, provoked many of these comparisons, and it also anticipated and contributed to the popularization of a Northern anti-imperialism that identified "southward" imperial expansion into Mexico, the Caribbean, and Central America with the U.S. South and with slavery extension.[7] Although, as we have already seen, it was widely believed that slavery could not thrive in Mexico during the late 1840s, many Southerners argued that slavery could be reintroduced there in the 1850s, and Southern interest in annexing more of Mexico as well as Cuba and Nicaragua meant that during this decade "manifest destiny became sectionalized," as historian Robert E. May puts it.[8] Even though filibustering expeditions and efforts to buy Cuba in the 1850s would continue to garner considerable support in New York City and in other parts of the North, after the debates about slavery extension that surrounded the Kansas-Nebraska Act of 1854, many Northerners, particularly those who were abandoning the Whigs and the Democrats to join the new Republican Party, would associate southward expansion with the Southern Slave Power's schemes to dominate national policy and to promote the strengthening of slavery. This rejection of Southern imperialism, however, was often motivated by white egalitarianism and fears of the incorporation of foreigners, nonwhites, and Catholics into the republic, as well as by a principled opposition to slavery.

In this chapter, I trace the prehistory of this sectionalization of Manifest Destiny in Northern antiwar literature published during the late 1840s. Despite the fact that many Southerners opposed the war and the annexation of large parts of Mexico, many New Englanders, especially, assumed even during these years that Southerners viewed the U.S.-Mexican War as an opportunity to fortify the institution of slavery. But although much of the Northern antiwar literature of the period focuses on the problem of slavery extension, ideologies of nativism and whiteness also shape a good deal of this literature. In chapter 8, I examine how these beliefs about empire, labor, and race were taken up and transformed by authors of dime novels in the early 1860s. In this chapter and in the next one, however, I also want to emphasize the possibilities and limits of a more radical version of this set of beliefs, a version that was promoted by some of the members of the land reform movement of the 1840s. Although most of the dime novel authors that I will discuss in chapter 8 emphasized a white egalitarianism that muted class differences among whites but stopped short of calling for a radical transformation of society, A.J.H. Duganne's writing was closely linked to labor and land reform movements that had significant ties to working-class communities. Assessing the significance of ideologies of nativism and white egalitarianism in the anti-imperialist literature produced by some of the land reformers, then, also helps us to understand how issues of empire affected reform and working-class cultures during these years.

Especially because of Duganne's long career as a popular writer and his involvement with the labor and land reform movements, his Yankee in Mexico provides an interesting point of departure for an analysis of race, labor, and empire in the dime novel during the early years of the Civil War. Born in Boston in 1823, Duganne first became famous as a popular poet, but after he moved to Philadelphia in the early 1840s he also began producing mysteries-of-the-city novels such as *The Knights of the Seal* (1845) and *The Daguerreotype Miniature; or, Life in the Empire City* (1846). These novels were urban melodramas in the tradition of Eugène Sue and George Lippard, who in fact dedicated the first edition of *The Quaker City* to Duganne. Like Lippard, Duganne also became involved with the land reform movement during these years, and much of his poetry was devoted to the promotion of that cause.

After the Panic of 1837, when the fledgling trade unions of the 1830s were destroyed by financial collapse and mass unemployment, many labor organizers turned to land reform as a solution for the problems that afflicted workers.[9] During the next decade, George Henry Evans used the newspapers he edited—including the *Radical,* the *Working Man's Advocate,* and *Young America*—to promote land reform as the key to realizing equality, solving the problem of nativism, and erasing class divisions in the United States, and these ideas spilled over into many other labor forums, including the National Industrial Congresses, which considered the ten-hour working day and land reform "the twin aims of all workingmen."[10] In 1844, Evans organized the National Reform Association to advance these principles.

Evans was influenced, as was the antebellum labor movement more generally, by Jeffersonian and Paineite agrarianism as well as by the more radical agrarian theories of Thomas Spence. Struck by the problems of poverty, unemployment, and exploitation in Northern cities, Evans decided that the "great evil" that caused this and almost every other social problem was the monopoly of the land.[11] Because Evans and his followers believed that "all men have a natural and inalienable right to life, and, of consequence, to...the use of land and the other material elements necessary to sustain life," they argued that policies governing the disposal of the public lands should be radically revised.[12] The basic principles of the National Reform Association were that the lands should not be sold to speculators but should rather be granted only to actual settlers; that limits should be set on the amount of land that anyone could acquire; that the right of occupancy should be transferable only to landless persons; and that the homestead should be exempt from execution for debt. By reforming the system in these ways, Evans hoped, lands could be preserved from speculators and other land monopolists and reserved for the "surplus" of workers in Northeastern cities who were competing for jobs and thereby driving down the price of labor. If land were available to every landless citizen, the reformers argued, then the Jeffersonian dream of a republic of small, independent, and virtuous producers might be realized.

During the 1840s, the land reform movement was a diverse coalition that included veterans of Jacksonian workingmen's organizations such as Evans, writers like Lippard and Duganne, and people of more Whiggish sympathies such as New York *Tribune* editor Horace Greeley. This movement became widely popular in part because its supporters successfully used a variety of cultural forms—including newspapers, almanacs, fairs, meetings, and songs—to promote it. Historian Jamie Bronstein points out that "the proliferation of print coincided with the attempt to create a land-reforming culture, an alternative political framework which included oral and participatory activities, and encompassed women and children along with men. Without access to publication this 'imagined community' of land reformers would never have been possible."[13] As Bronstein suggests, National Reform also "had its own poet, A. J. H. Duganne," whose poems "appeared in labor newspapers, in response to the clamorous requests of readers."[14] During the 1840s, Duganne's poem "The Acres and the Hands" appeared in *Young America* and in the *Voice of Industry,* a weekly paper that was at first published in Lowell, Massachusetts, and was for a while edited by factory operative Sarah Bagley.[15] In 1847 the poem was collected in *The Iron Harp,* a book of Duganne's poetry that included titles such as "The Song of Toil," "Earth-Sharing," "Our Mother Earth," "The Landless," "Who Owneth America's Soil," and "The Unsold Lands." Many of these poems were also reprinted in reform newspapers.

Although both Lippard and Duganne were involved with the land reform movement, however, they took different positions on the U.S.-Mexican War and the question of empire. While Lippard, as we have seen, linked land reform to the Democrats' program of U.S. expansionism, Duganne wrote a long poem called "Manifest Destiny" that echoed many of the Whig objections to the war that I outlined in the previous chapter. On the one hand, Duganne saw the war in Mexico as an aggressive act of "lust, and wrong, and crime—/Branding us to endless time." Comparing the United States to Rome, he warned that if the Roman empire fell, the fate of the rapidly expanding U.S. empire might not be any different. He also suggested that the masters of the "Slaves of the South" and the "White slaves of Northern gold" found "new victims...in war's red bondage bound," and he thereby connected Southern slaves to Northern white laborers and to Mexicans. What is more, he repeatedly lampooned the rhetoric of Manifest Destiny by contrasting the elevated language of mission with the bloody and destructive outcome of war. On the other hand, Duganne was heavily invested in the inviolability of national boundary lines and the distinctions between natives and foreigners. Defending the nation against "the invading hordes" would be a "glorious" task, he argued, but instead U.S. soldiers were the "foreign foeman" who stained their "patriot swords" by attacking those who were simply trying to defend their own homeland.[16] Like Buntline, Duganne aligned himself with the nativist movement, and during the 1850s he was an active member of the Know-Nothing Party in New York state.[17] His nativist beliefs are prominently displayed in his long poem "The True Republic," where to the problem of immigration he answers: "We cry aloud, with Monticello's sire: 'O that the Atlantic were a WALL OF FIRE!' "[18] So although Duganne's antiwar poem positions the United States as the invader of Mexico, it also implies that national boundaries must be respected because immigration and the mixing of peoples are dangerous. Despite his sympathy for the Mexican dead and wounded, moreover, he ended "Manifest Destiny" with a maudlin portrait of an orphaned U.S.-American child with "sunny Saxon hair" whose father was killed in Mexico.[19] This intensely anti-imperialist poem shows how difficult it can be to disentangle the antiwar arguments of many U.S. writers from ideas about the distinctness and preciousness of a "native" American "Anglo-Saxon" identity. For even as Duganne criticized the rhetoric of Anglo-Saxonism—as he seems to when he sarcastically commands the "white slaves of Northern gold" to build a Teocalli "where the foes/Of our ambition bold/May writhe beneath our Anglo-Saxon blows"—he compared the agents of U.S. empire to the ancient Aztecs whose rituals involving human sacrifice particularly horrified his contemporaries.[20] In other words, he raised the specter of racial degeneration as he condemned the U.S. presence in Mexico by suggesting that the actions of the U.S. expansionists were as barbarous as those of the ancient Aztecs.

In criticizing the war, Duganne was certainly not alone, especially among New Englanders. Although the scattered sentences that express Thoreau's objections to the war in his essay "Resistance to Civil Government" constitute probably the most famous example of literary dissent from this imperial enterprise, other famous New England writers such as Margaret Fuller and Ralph Waldo Emerson also opposed it. But even though those who argued against the war did so for many different reasons, notably including religious convictions as well as fears that it would invite the extension of slavery and increase the power of Southern interests within the Union, the racialist and sectarian beliefs that often underpinned antiannexationist sentiments among Whig and Democratic politicians also surfaced in many other antiwar writings. For as Matthew Frye Jacobson argues, throughout the nineteenth century it was often "not imperialism but *anti*-imperialism that rested upon the more virulently racialist logic of civilization, sovereignty, and self-government."[21] This does not mean, as Walter Michaels's work sometimes suggests, that anti-imperialism inevitably promoted a white supremacist, essentialist conception of national identity; anti-imperialisms are not reducible to such a formalist formula, and there are significant differences on issues of race, republicanism, nativism, and empire even among the anti-imperialists who deployed a rhetoric of Anglo-Saxonism.[22] But worries about contact with "degraded" nonwhite races or the incorporation of more foreigners and Catholics into the nation do indeed recur in much of the anti-imperialist literature that emerged from New England and other Northeastern sites during the 1840s; the language of racial and cultural contamination is especially pervasive. Thus while in the middle of his Editor's Address in the first issue of the *Massachusetts Quarterly Review*, Emerson quickly labeled the conflict in Mexico a "bad war," in his journal he predicted that "[t]he United States will conquer Mexico, but it will be as the man swallows the arsenic, which brings him down in turn. Mexico will poison us."[23] Although Emerson might well have meant to suggest that the debates over slavery extension that the war provoked might tear the Union apart, such a warning about Mexican "poison" is difficult to separate from the many anti-imperialist characterizations of the Mexican "enemy" as "degraded" and "corrupt."[24]

Sometimes dissenters invoked racial hierarchies to argue that the United States should take over the continent by peaceful rather than violent means. Even as the Boston Unitarian clergyman Theodore Parker opposed the war, for instance, he referred to the Mexicans as "a wretched people; wretched in their origin, history, and character."[25] Parker delivered several powerful antiwar speeches, and his bravery in loudly arguing against the war in many public forums, despite the racialist framework that he assumed, comes through especially clearly in a transcript of a speech given at Boston's Faneuil Hall on February 4, 1847, when soldiers tried to prevent him from speaking. (Their shouts are recorded in the transcript; as Parker denounced the war, the soldiers cried, "[K]ill him, kill him!" and flourished their bayonets.)[26] There are several searing passages in these speeches in which Parker compares the U.S. invasion of Mexico to England's "butchering" of Sikhs in India and seizure of lands in Ireland; or points to U.S. war crimes in Mexico; or sympathizes with "prostrate Mexico, robbed of more than half thy soil, that America may have more slaves; thy cities burned, thy children slain, the streets of thy capital trodden by the alien foot, but still smoking with thy children's blood."[27] Despite Parker's sympathy for Mexican losses, his anger at U.S. military expansion, and his many convincing arguments against the war, however, he also suggested that in "the general issue between this race and that, we are in the right. But in this special issue, and this particular war, it seems to me that we are wholly in the wrong; that our invasion of Mexico is as bad as the partition of Poland in the last century and in this." Although he agreed that the Anglo-Saxon race was probably destined to control the continent, he tried to persuade his audience that "this may be had fairly; with no injustice to anyone; by the steady advance of a superior race, with superior ideas and a better civilization; by commerce, trade, arts; by being better than Mexico, wiser, humaner, more free and manly."[28] So Parker opposed the use of military force, but he also affirmed many of the basic premises of racial Anglo-Saxonism and championed what Anders Stephanson calls "a new kind of thinking about destiny and empire, an empire of deterritorialized commerce."[29]

Similar contradictions appear in the antiwar literature of abolitionist poet James Russell Lowell. On the one hand, in the poems and letters that he published separately and then collected as *The Biglow Papers,* he developed a set of Yankee characters and deployed the Yankee dialect that was so popular in literature and on the stage in order to relentlessly lampoon the idea that the war was fought to extend the area of freedom. Adopting the persona of the Massachusetts Yankee Birdofredum Sawin, a private in the U.S. Army, for instance, Lowell writes:

> Afore I come away from hum I hed a strong persuasion
> That Mexicans wor n't human beans—an ourang outang nation,
> A sort o' folks a chap could kill an' never dream on't arter,
> No more 'n a feller'd dream o' pigs thet he hed hed to slarter:...
> But wen I jined I wor n't so wise ez thet air queen o'Sheby,

Fer, come to look at 'em, they aint much diff'rent from wut we be,
An' here we air ascrougin' em out o' thir own dominions,
Ashelterin' 'em, ez Caleb sez, under our eagle's pinions,
Wich means to take a feller up jest by the slack o' 's trowsis
An' walk him Spanish clean right out o' all his homes an' houses;
Wal, it doos seem a curus way, but then hooraw fer Jackson!
It must be right, fer Caleb sez it's reg'lar Anglosaxon.[30]

But although Lowell uses the Yankee persona to condemn the war and the dehumanization of Mexicans as well as to expose assertions of "anglosaxon" benevolence as a cover for thievery, another of these Yankee characters, the morally upright Hosea Biglow, also calls the Mexicans "poor half-Spanish drones" and views the contested area as "a grand gret cemetary / Fer the barthrights of our race."[31] And while it would be a mistake to identify Lowell's own positions entirely with those of his Yankee personae, Lowell would later write in a letter that "it is the manifest destiny of the English race to occupy this whole continent and to display there that practical understanding in matters of government and colonization which no other race has given such proof of possessing since the Romans."[32] This letter suggests that although Lowell despised the war and believed that it was fought to extend slavery, he also believed, like Parker, in a racial "destiny" that ultimately legitimated the control of the entire continent, though not through overtly violent means.

In his journalism during the war years, Frederick Douglass probably went further than any other U.S. commentator in condemning racial Anglo-Saxonism. In an editorial on the war published in January of 1848, as he catalogued some of the key words and phrases that circulated during the war years, he emphasized contradictions in the rhetoric of Manifest Destiny, most notably the contradiction between the abstract ideal of "free institutions" and a white supremacist pride in "Anglo-Saxon blood": "[The people] are worried, confused, and confounded, so that a general outcry is heard—'Vigorous prosecution of the war!'—'Mexico must be humbled!'—'Conquer a peace!'—'Indemnity!'—'War forced upon us!'—'National honor!'—'The whole of Mexico!'—'Our destiny!'—'This continent!'—'Anglo-Saxon blood!'—'More territory!'—'Free institutions!'—'Our country!'—till it seems indeed 'that justice has fled to brutish beasts, and men have lost their reason.'" [33] Douglass thereby tracked the formation in newspapers, political discourse, and everyday life of the language of U.S. Anglo-Saxon national identity that became more pervasive, as we have seen, during the war years. But Douglass made it clear to his readers that the republican ideal of freedom was fatally conjoined to a commitment to slavery and imperial aggression. After condemning the Whigs for weakly opposing Polk's expansionist designs, he blasted the Democrats for hypocritically using the language of freedom in order to deny freedom to people of color. "They annexed Texas under the plea of extending the area of freedom," Douglass charged. "They elected James K. Polk, the slaveholder, as the friend of freedom; and they have backed him up in his Presidential falsehoods. They have used their utmost endeavors to crush the right of speech, abridge the right of petition, and to perpetuate the enslavement of the colored people of this country." If this "war spirit" continued, Douglass warned, and if Mexico were conquered, if her people were "put under the iron arm of a military despotism, and reduced to a condition little better than that endured by the Saxons when vanquished by their Norman invaders," the United States would surely face "a terrible retribution." By identifying Mexicans with the freedom-loving Saxons to whom the expansionists often compared themselves, Douglass challenged the premise of racial Anglo-Saxonism that white Americans had a special talent for freedom. Instead, he suggested that the U.S. government was despotically repressing the freedom of Mexicans even as it crushed the democratic rights and perpetuated the enslavement of people of color at home.

Douglass was one of only a few antiwar writers who explicitly singled out the ideology of Anglo-Saxon national identity as a cause of this imperialist war, but he also voiced many of the other arguments used by war opponents during these years. For instance, he complained that the war was expensive, that "excessive demands are made on the national treasury" that might be better used for other purposes. He worried that democracy would be undermined when "[m]ilitary chieftains and heroes multiply," that the people would become accustomed to military hierarchies and authority and would forget the meaning of freedom. He connected such military, authoritarian values to the undermining of republican values when he denounced the "[g]rasping ambition, tyrannic usurpation, atrocious aggression, cruel and haughty pride [which] spread, and pervade the land." He extended his sympathy to the Mexicans as he graphically portrayed the horrors of war and unmasked so-called U.S. heroism: "The groans of slaughtered men, the screams of violated women, and the cries of orphan children, must bring no throb of pity from our national heart, but must rather serve as music to inspire our gallant troops to deeds of atrocious cruelty, lust, and blood." And he used a gendered, familial language of republicanism when he attacked "the present disgraceful, cruel, and iniquitous war with our sister republic." By feminizing Mexico and including "her" within the family of young republics, Douglass, like the Whig politicians that I discussed in chapter 4, depicted the war as a rapacious, incestuous violation of democratic consensual ideals rather than a chivalric rescue mission to extend democracy.

As he amplifies many of the antiwar arguments that were circulating during the war years, Douglass suggests that many of the soldiers who enlisted did so out of desperation or depravity rather than patriotism. Even though the penny press incessantly glorified the volunteer forces as virtuous citizen-soldiers inspired by love of their country, Douglass painted a very different picture of recruiters sweeping through rum shops and gambling houses, looking for "degraded men to vindicate the insulted honor of our Christian country." Although Douglass's emphasis on the degraded nature of these recruits stops short of explicitly linking that degradation to lower-class status, other war opponents more readily blamed poor and working-class men for much of the prowar sentiment. When Emerson criticized the political culture that supported the war, for instance, he observed: "We see that reckless and destructive fury which characterizes the lower classes of American society, and which is pampered by hundreds of profligate presses."[34] Other writers suggested that lower-class men enlisted in the war as an ill-advised way of achieving upward mobility. The popular author Grace Greenwood (Sara J. Clarke) opposed the war, for instance, by writing a story about a "poor, obscure boy" named Herbert Moore who volunteers to fight as a way of gaining "distinction" so that he can "stand on an equality" with his beloved, the wealthy Margaret Neale. Margaret herself, however, fiercely opposes this plan, emphatically denouncing the conflict with Mexico as "a war without one just cause, or one noble object; but waged against an unoffending people, in the rapacity of conquest, and for the extension and perpetuation of human slavery."[35] Like Douglass, Greenwood calls it a "most unholy war against a sister Republic" (106). Although in his heart Herbert also "utterly condemned the objects and conduct of the war," his fierce and fiery independence, which is here represented as an excessive and unfortunate masculine trait, prevents him from marrying Margaret anyway and being "lifted up" by her "dear arms" to a position he has "not earned" (103, 101). Herbert has to learn the hard way by experiencing the horrors of war and achieving none of its so-called honors that Margaret is right and that war service does not provide a legitimate means of rising above one's class. At the end of the story, when the disillusioned and sickly Herbert returns home, he therefore accedes to Margaret's "dominion" of "love" (118) and resolves to "put down forever that imperious and arrogant ruling spirit, pride, and to set my foot on that gilded form of selfishness called ambition" (117).

Emerson's linkage of the war to lower-class fury stoked by profligate presses and Greenwood's emphasis on a misguided ambition and desire for upward mobility among poor men raise the question: just what do we know about how poor and working-class people responded to the war? That is a difficult question to answer, however, in any simple way. Certainly many poor and working-class men signed up to fight in the war, but so, for instance, did many middle-class men and elites, for war service provided opportunities of fighting for a kind of "distinction" that was invaluable to future politicians. And if we turn to Emerson's "profligate presses" for evidence, the response to the war there is decidedly mixed. On the one hand, as Saxton suggests, mass-circulation daily newspapers such as the Baltimore *Sun,* the New York *Herald,* and the Philadelphia *Public Ledger* generally "applauded Polk's expansionist policies and supported the war to which those politics led."[36] Their mass circulations make it clear, however, that these papers were also read by many people who were not of the "lower classes," so although it can safely be assumed that many nonelite newspaper readers in Baltimore, New York, and Philadelphia supported the war, that support cannot be characterized as a uniquely or predominantly lower-class passion.

And yet, working-class advocates such as Philadelphia's George Lippard, as we have seen, as well as New York City's Mike Walsh and others defended the war. Walsh, a Protestant Irish immigrant, was a journalist and proslavery Democratic politician who during this period was, according to Sean Wilentz, "the one great political representative of the city's wage earners and struggling small producers," a man who managed "to bridge the gap between labor radicalism and Bowery republicanism that the unionists of the 1830s had never fully overcome." Wilentz suggests that out "of all the prominent local political figures of the early and mid-1840s, he spoke in an unvarnished language of class conflict, thrusting the labor theory of value into his listeners' faces, attaching the cause of the 'wage slaves' to that of the social democracy."[37] In his newspaper, the *Subterranean,* Walsh also championed the war against Mexico, claiming to be the first and perhaps "the only prominent man to advocate an extension of our form of government over *this* whole continent first, and then over the whole habitable globe as speedily as our means will admit." Although Walsh justified this aim by arguing that it was "the imperative duty of a democratic people to extend the blessings, or more correctly speaking, the rights, they enjoy, at every necessary sacrifice, to the whole human family," his description of Mexicans as "an undisciplined, effeminate and comparatively powerless people, whom we can at any time annihilate in a few months at pleasure" makes suspect his professions of benevolent intentions toward the globe's peoples.[38] Walsh's journalism during the war years also makes it evident that many of the Bowery B'hoys that he represented did indeed think of the war as a way of achieving a measure of class mobility in hard times. Perhaps nowhere is this clearer than in Walsh's account of a meeting in the Bowery led by the well-known "personator of negro characters" George Rice, which was devoted to raising a regiment of volunteers to fight in Mexico. Walsh quotes heavily from Rice's speech, which he renders in a Bowery B'hoy dialect, and he also includes the response of the crowd in parentheses. In Rice's conclusion, he addressed the crowd in the following terms:

> Fellow citizens! Or, if I may be allowed the expression, Compatriots in arms! You must all be aware of the great difficulty which exists among the *"boys"* at present of making, even by the sewerest application to business, anything like a nice stake. (marked sensation.) The truth of this here remark, fellow soldiers, is seen in the increasing brassiness of your *plugs*, in the dilapidated shabbiness of your general rig, and in the collapsed appearance of your stomachs, (breathless attention, followed by deep sighs)....Is such a state of affairs to be longer borne in silence by us—the most deserving and waluable portion of this community? (tremendous cries of no! never!) Shall we sit quietly, like an apple woman on a race ground, while there's one of the greatest chances ever known for making a stake, staring us in the wery face? (cries of no!)...Fellow citizens, shall it be said, or shall future ages be told that "old Rice" and the boys stood sucking their thumbs, for want of something more substantial to chawer upon, while Mexico, with her gold Jesuses, silver wash bowls, diamonds, and other little availables, are almost a calling on us to come and take 'em (tremendous cheering).

Following this appeal, according to Walsh, Rice "opened the roll list, which was filled up as fast as the names could be written."[39]

Although Rice made visceral appeals to the hunger and avarice of his New York auditors, many scholars have attributed working-class support for the war to a desire for more land to support the extension of an agrarian democracy that could mitigate the evils of "wage slavery" in Northeastern cities and the West. Walsh himself championed land reform principles; in 1844 his paper the *Subterranean* was even merged for a few months with Evans's *Working Man's Advocate,* though the merger ended in December after what Wilentz calls "a year of personal wrangling."[40] As I suggested in chapter 2, George Lippard's enthusiasm for the war had much to do with his utopian hopes for the fulfillment of the land reformers' project. Indeed, it is easy to see how arguments in favor of land reform could be deployed to justify U.S. expansion. The distinction between hard-working producers and idle nonproducers that supported the ideal of a redistribution of land, for instance, could also be used to defend the expropriation of land from Indians and Mexicans whose ideas about use, settlement, and property were different. In other words, this distinction helped to naturalize and even sanctify white forms of settlement and land use. The idea that defusing class conflict in Eastern cities depended upon the "safety valve" of free lands in the West would also seem to have required, as Frederick Jackson Turner argued a few decades later, an ever expanding frontier. Such an expanding frontier would in turn lead to the violent displacement of Indians and Mexicans. It is not surprising that Saxton sees this agrarian "line of thought" promoted by the National Reformers as the basis for much of the popular support for territorial expansion during this period.[41]

And yet, many land and labor reformers opposed U.S. expansion. Throughout the war years, the *Voice of Industry,* for instance, vigorously attacked the war and urged workers not to support it. During the first year of the conflict, at a time when enthusiasm for Polk's expansionist policies was at its zenith, *Voice* writers took a firm stand against them. On 15 May 1846, one writer argued that "Mexico is in a fair way to get soundly thrashed, simply because she will not lie still and quietly permit herself to be robbed of her rightful possessions. Our 'army of occupation' has not in fact *occupied* Texas, but has been pushed into the heart of a province of Mexico, and has threateningly pointed its cannon at the walls of one of its most important frontier cities." In June, another article noted that those "who take the pains to preserve all *anti-war papers* 'for future use' should be careful and keep a file of the Voice."[42] After detailing several moral and religious objections to the war, the writer concluded: "Fellow Reformers, are you ready to stand out now and be known as the uncompromising opposers of war in general, and of that piece of hellish iniquity, the present Mexican War in particular?" And at the end of the year, the *Voice* directed its remarks even more explicitly to workers: "Brother workingmen, at this time choose the lesser evil, and patronize that 'peculiar institution,' the prison, rather than pay a visit to that 'human slaughter house' and cripple manufactory in Mexico, to help sustain that 'very peculiar' institution of our *free and glorious Republic,* Negro Slavery." Arguing that a "clear conscience is better than all the glory that can be obtained by murdering our fellow beings in any war, much more such a thieving, abominable, unjust one as is the present," the writer repeated his or her advice to "Mechanics, Laborers, and everybody else, DON'T ENLIST."[43]

The reasons given in the land and labor reform press for opposing the war were various, ranging from moral and religious objections to political and economic considerations, but many of the concerns detailed in antiwar articles echo some of the republican ideals articulated by writers such as Douglass, Greenwood, and Parker. For example, some suggested that the war was an invasion of a sister republic and explained that those who refused to volunteer "understand that it is as wrong to invade the homes of others as it is to refuse to defend our own."[44] Others contended that the expansion of the military order required by the war effort imperiled republican ideals. In an article from the *Herald of Freedom* reprinted in Evans's *Young America* just before the war began, one journalist argued that governments viewed war as the remedy for the resistance of citizens and that war strengthened the authority of governments in ways that reinforced antirepublican hierarchies. "The hand of Government grows strong and its arm muscular with the exercise of battle. Its necessity becomes apparent, and manifest. Large armies show the need of subordination and command."[45] In an address of the Industrial Congress to the citizens of the United States on the subject of the war, the authors similarly suggested that the army "endangers your liberty, keeps from you the enjoyment of your just rights, is a chief item in the expense of government, corrupts the morals of the people, encourages idleness, is a gross departure from the principles on which our government was founded, destructive of the social equality that ought to exist between citizens of a Republic, by all the difference there is in the absolute authority of the Officer, and the slavish obedience of the soldier." Claiming that "the poor are mainly exposed to [war's] dangers, and receive few of its so-called honors," the representatives of the Industrial Congress advised workers "never to fight for despots to enslave you, or for territory which, without a change in our govermental [sic] policy, you will only be permitted to occupy as serfs or slaves."[46]

This address is only one of many contemporaneous examples in which the republican freedom of the working classes is defined in opposition to forms of unfree labor such as slavery. Such attitudes, as David Roediger and others have argued, often implied a distancing disdain for the slave, not an alliance with an oppressed fellow laborer.[47] As we shall see, white egalitarianism was the dominant note in the rhetoric of David Wilmot, the author of the famous antislavery extension proviso, and for many in the Free Soil movement, and later the Republican Party, that emerged from these debates over slavery. But although opposition to the extension of slavery could result from a fear of the proximity of slaves to white laborers, others connected the struggles of slaves and Northern workers. In an 1846 meeting of the New York Workingmen, for instance, those who attended demanded that Polk withdraw his troops and condemned the war as a plan to promote the interests of slaveholders, who live "in such luxurious idleness on the products of the workingmen."[48] And in a *Voice of Industry* editorial written in behalf of the "outraged working classes," for instance, one writer who argued that the "sole, open and secret motive for the war" was "*conquest for the extension of slavery*" also linked the antislavery struggle to labor reform and opposition to the war. "They are one movement applied to different latitudes," the writer declared. "The spirit which at the South opposes slave emancipation, opposes Labor Reform here at the North; and this accursed and infamous war is waged against the rights of the laboring classes indiscriminately."[49] By including slaves and Northern workers within the ranks of the laboring classes, this writer implicitly contested the rhetoric of Anglo-Saxon national unity and Manifest Destiny.

George Henry Evans, the leader of the land reform movement, tended to be wary about national expansion not so much because he believed that indigenous peoples or other governments might have prior claims, but rather because he believed that the United States already had enough land and that land speculators were likely to dominate in the new territories.[50] On the specific question of the annexation of Texas, the *Working Man's Advocate* argued that "Mexico can have no more claims upon Texas than Great Britain has upon the United States. The wrong is, that the Texians have taken with them to Texas the system of Land Plunder which had been imported here from Britain. The people of any part of the world have a right to go wherever there is uncultivated land and work it, as much as is necessary, for their own use; but they have no right to take more, either to *sell* it, or to *make other men work it for them*."[51] Evans was especially disturbed by the prospect that Texas might become a slave state, and he feared that speculators were already dividing up the new lands, which he felt should have been handed out to settlers. "The people of Texas had a right to propose to come under our government, and we had a right to accept their proposal," Evans suggested in *Young America,* "but they had no right to come in with a constitution tolerating slavery either white or black, by monopolizing land or bodies."[52] Evans applauded the Texans for disregarding what he called "the Monopoly Grants" of the Mexican government, but he bitterly concluded that "instead of establishing an Equal Right to the Soil, they merely substituted Texian for Mexican patroonery, and added Negro Slavery by way of *progress.*"[53] In this passage, Evans's object of attack is as much Mexico as it is the extension of slavery through the annexation of Texas. Although Evans also criticizes the United States, his attack on Mexican land policies and his defense of the Texans during these years of international conflict with Mexico echo the justifications for war used by land-hungry settlers and capitalists, who often characterized Mexican forms of property and ways of using the land as wasteful or unproductive.

Later, however, Evans began to explicitly and angrily denounce the war against Mexico. At the outset of an antiwar article published in November of 1846, he condemned the bad "conduct of the government in regard to the war upon Mexico for the extension of Land Monopoly and Slavery (for in no other light can it now be looked upon)." Focusing on the proposed sale of millions of acres of public lands, Evans demanded, "Is the war for the extension of Land Monopoly and Slavery, both wages and chattel, to be carried on at this cost? Are men sitting in their ease with fat salaries to send off poor lacklanders to be maimed and slayed for eight dollars a month, while their lands, and the lands and homes of their wives and children, are sold to the 'grasping speculators' in their absence?" After quoting a statement on the sorry condition of volunteers who were discharged in New Orleans, Evans advised Polk: "Better, by far, to stop the war at once, on the easiest terms you can, or even to back out. You are in the wrong!—The paltry dollars due to some of our rich capitalists might have been cause for non-intercourse, but could not authorize one mangled limb, much less all the slaughter that has been enacted. Those who were houseless and homeless in our midst far more demanded the protection of the Government than the speculators who could afford to send property out of the country."[54]

In this article, Evans opposed the war partly because he feared that any new lands acquired as a result would become the property of speculators rather than "lacklanders." He also suggested that the war was initiated in behalf of capitalists who had lost money by investing in Mexico, and he insisted that this was not enough of a reason to enact a "slaughter." Although he was outraged by the injuries and deaths that the war entailed, his focus was on U.S. losses and on those who "were houseless and homeless in our midst" rather than the losses suffered by Mexicans. Since, as we have seen, antiwar sentiment was often inseparable from national, racial, and religious antipathies, it is worth asking where Evans and the land reformers stood on such issues.

Although A. J. H. Duganne, the poet of National Reform, championed both nativist politics and changes in land policies, land reformers more often insisted that their program would make it possible to absorb many more immigrants into the nation. Evans argued, for example, that land reform would end the problem of nativism by encouraging immigrants to go West rather than compete in the labor markets of the East, so that "foreigners would be a benefit instead of an injury to the workingmen as well as to the country."[55] Evans criticized the members of the Native American movement for seeking to divide workers rather than looking to land reform to solve the problem of labor surpluses, and he made fun of "the selfish exclusiveness of the party assuming (rather ludicrously) the name of Native."[56] Instead of scapegoating immigrants, Evans suggested that foreign-born workers were the natural allies of native-born workers. In an article that appeared under the headline "To Native American Working Men," he contended that "almost the entire body of foreigners who come to this country are Working Men, who have been schooled by oppression into a keen and lively sense of Human Rights, and who, therefore, would always be found on the side [of] *Native* Working Men on all great questions of public policy."[57]

Although Evans welcomed new immigrants, his positions on race were more ambiguous. Sometimes Evans explicitly included blacks and American Indians within his definition of "the people" and argued that they also deserved to have a portion of land and a stake in the republic.[58] As Roediger has suggested, "Evans and his cothinkers did not argue for white supremacy—at times they bravely supported equal rights—but instead assumed that the position of white workers was central in any reform movement."[59] This "prioritizing of the struggles of whites" was especially evident when Evans argued against the phrase "free labor" and expanded the meaning of the word "slavery" to describe the situation of landless whites. In a fairly typical passage, he insisted that "there is slavery at home as well as at the South; White slavery as well as Black; slavery here in New York city; slavery all over the State, and, in fact, all over the United States. We had deceived ourselves by calling it by other names, but we have awakened out of the delusion."[60] Elsewhere he argued that those laborers who "are funnily enough called 'free' " are actually "compelled to work for what those who monopolize the soil choose to give them."[61] Evans's refusal of the term "free labor" and his preference for terms such as "white slavery" and "wage slavery" were typical of the antebellum labor movement. One the one hand, this refusal was an important critique of a liberal worldview that "idealized ownership of self and voluntary exchange between individuals who were formally equal and free."[62] But on the other hand, as Roediger suggests, many of those who used the phrase "white slavery" in particular "strongly supported the slavery of blacks."[63] Even though Evans generally agreed that chattel slavery must be abolished, he often suggested that the condition of white workers was just as bad as or even worse than that of black slaves, and he repeatedly contended that land reform was a more urgent issue than the abolition of slavery. For instance, in an article entitled "Slavery—Both Kinds" that appeared in *Young America* on 3 January 1846, Evans declared: "All our outcry about negro slavery will, as it should, pass for little or nothing so long as we neglect to provide inalienable homesteads for those who are now cut off from the soil and so rapidly accumulating in our cities and factories."

This prioritizing of whiteness also compromised Evans's defense of the land claims of North American Indians.[64] Evans opposed the war against the Seminoles in Florida, arguing that it was "a war of aggression on the part of the United States, evidently with the view of acquiring territory, without the shadow of reason or justice to support it."[65] In addition, he denounced the removal of the Cherokees from their lands in Georgia as a "costly, cruel, and unnecessary expatriation."[66] But he also wishfully maintained that the expulsion of the Indians from their lands "would have been entirely unnecessary but for land monopoly" and thereby failed to see how the movement of white settlers that he advocated also contributed to the displacement of the Indians.[67] A quotation on the masthead of his journals, which Evans attributed to the Sauk warrior Black Hawk, who fought a losing battle against the encroachments of settlers in Illinois and elsewhere, is a good example of this contradiction in Evans's thought: "My reason teaches me that *land cannot be sold.* The Great Spirit gave it to his children to live upon, and cultivate, as far as is necessary for their subsistence; and so long as they occupy and cultivate it, they have the right to the soil—but if they voluntarily leave it, then any other people have a right to settle upon it. Nothing can be sold, but such things as can be carried away."[68] Here Evans invoked a dead Sauk warrior who resisted the westward movement of white settlers in order to argue that the soil belonged to those who "cultivate" it and "settle upon it"—a view that was commonly endorsed by those who wanted to justify the dispossession of Indians by whites.

Generally, the land reformers held that if land monopolies were eliminated, whites and Indians would be able to coexist peacefully, because they believed that under those conditions there would be enough land for all. Evans himself usually ignored the possibility that ideas about property and land use might conflict. In an 1846 number of *Young America,* however, he explicitly addressed this problem. Writing about the dispute over Oregon, he asked: "Have a few natives, then, scattered over a large territory, a right to exclude all comers? Certainly not. If there is land more than is necessary for their use, others have a right to occupy it." Evans recognized that the key word, the one that could reopen the debate about the justice of white settlement, was "use." As he developed his argument, he even acknowledged that Indians and white settlers might have different ideas about what counted as use of the land. "But the natives want to hunt and fish, and the new comers want to cultivate," he suggested. "There is no difficulty here. The new comers want less ground than they would otherwise, and they have a right to take what is necessary for their use, where the natives have not a settlement, but no more." Here, Evans recognized incompatible ideas about land use only to override them with the optimistic explanation that farming required "less ground" than hunting and fishing. And although he seemed to accept the idea that hunting and fishing might constitute use of the land, the argument that whites could take up land where there was not an Indian "settlement" effectively defined land devoted to other purposes as waste, open to appropriation by white settlers who could "use" it. The position that hunting and fishing required more land than farming, which might conceivably limit the places where whites could settle were they to respect Indian claims, suddenly receded as Evans limited the sites of Indian land use to actual settlements. He concluded, however, that he had no doubt that "if land monopoly were prohibited, the native races would become cultivators of the soil."[69] The official National Reform Association position that there was enough land for all thus crucially depended on naturalizing white liberal conceptions of property and use and usually included such a Jeffersonian vision of Indian hunters converted into yeoman farmers peacefully and happily cultivating isolated plots of land.

But the very idea that "waste" land should belong to those who could use it depended on a racialized conception of property. In other words, ideas about what counted as use of the land were racialized through and through. As Cheryl Harris has argued, "[R]ights in property are contingent on, intertwined with, and conflated with race."[70] In this case, even though the land reformers deplored the dispossession of the Indians and sometimes cited Indian beliefs about the inalienability of the land as superior, they had trouble seeing uncultivated land as anything but waste. Harris suggests that such a set of beliefs justified conquest by embedding "the fact of white privilege into the very definition of property" (1721). "Only particular forms of possession—those that were characteristic of white settlement—would be recognized and legitimated" (1722), she writes. Despite the land reformers' sympathy for the Indians, then, their ideas about what counted as possession and use supported the claims of white settlers in the new territories. And such a linkage of legitimate property rights to white forms of settlement would also work to undermine Mexican land claims, for Mexican forms of property and ways of using the land would similarly seem wasteful, unproductive, or invisible from the perspective of land-hungry U.S.-American settlers and capitalists.[71]

And yet, although the National Reformers' ideas about land use generally supported the movement of white settlers into the West, a belief in the superiority of some Indian ideas about land prompted Evans to take an anti-imperialist position on the Indian uprisings in Yucatán in 1848. In part because of its distance from central Mexico and its closer proximity to Cuba and the United States, Yucatán had a tenuous and tempestuous relationship to Mexico in the postindependence years.[72] Yucatán separated from Mexico several times during this period, and in 1839 the rebel forces relied quite heavily on Indian soldiers to fight their battles. Meanwhile, after independence from Spain and especially in the 1840s, according to one historian, "the acquisition of private property was facilitated by legislation limiting the size of Indian *ejidos,* allowing for easy purchase of public lands, and rewarding soldiers with land grants in lieu of wages."[73] These incursions on Indian lands, which often facilitated the development of sugar plantations in the south, along with the arming of the Indians and the latter's resentment of onerous taxes, precipitated the rebellion known as the Caste War of 1847.[74]

In the summer of 1847, the Maya Indians rebelled against the creoles and quickly gained ground throughout the area. Because of the war with the United States, Mexico was not in a position to send forces to the area, and so in 1848 panicking creole elites appealed to several other nations, including the United States, for help. Many U.S. expansionists supported the annexation of Yucatán because of its proximity to Cuba and its potential importance for commerce and trade, and advocates of intervention represented the conflict as a battle of transnational whiteness against Indian savagery. Thus Polk's message to Congress invoked the Monroe Doctrine and recommended that means be placed at his disposal for the military occupation of Yucatán "in order to save the white population from destruction by the Indian race." And in letters from U.S. naval officers in Yucatán that were forwarded to Congress by the president, the writers frequently expressed sympathy for the whites and eagerly wished for the arrival of more U.S. troops to defend them. One writer even argued, "The war whoop of these ruthless Indians would have no terrors to those who have conquered the red men of our own territory."[75] In Congress, supporters of military occupation similarly described the conflict as a war between a transnational white civilization and Indian barbarism. Texas Democrat Sam Houston, for instance, argued that the whites "bear upon them the impress of civilization and brotherhood with ourselves," while the Indians, like those in Texas, were "of gigantic size, ferocious in their dispositions, loathsome in their habits, and rioted on human flesh."[76] Ardent expansionist and 1848 Democratic Party presidential nominee Lewis Cass, who suggested that the "Gulf of Mexico" must be "practically an American lake for the great purpose of security," agreed that the conflict was between "the white race" and "the colored race" and claimed that the naval officers as well as other sources spoke of the Indians "as we should speak, under similar circumstances, of our Indians."[77]

Some of the opponents of military occupation, on the other hand, argued that the Mexican Indians were citizens, not savages, and compared them to the French revolutionaries of 1848. Notably, Democratic senator Niles, who just a few months later would join the new antislavery Free Soil Party, claimed that because the Indians were Mexican citizens, the conflict in Yucatán was a civil war in which the United States had no right to interfere. Since the United States had applauded the efforts of the "sons of toil" to overthrow "the higher and aristocratic classes of their society" in France, he continued, it should also applaud this "revolutionary movement" in "another part of the world" instead of supporting the efforts of "the higher classes in another country to overthrow and even exterminate the lower classes."[78] In the House, Whig representative Joseph Root of Ohio, who was also about to join the Free Soilers, similarly feared that "we were sympathizing with the aristocracy of Yucatán" and were going to oppose "the democracy."

Although advocates of intervention described the conflict as a battle between creole civilization and savagery, Root instead viewed it as "a case
of the few opposing the many; of the aborigines of the country rising up
for their natural rights." Root also compared the French revolutionaries to the Mexican Indians, arguing that while "no doubt Louis Philippe
would have been very glad if we had sympathized on his side.... [W]ho
would have dared to propose that?" There was no reason at all to attack
the "native Yucatanese," he concluded, "unless, indeed, it was on account of their color."[79]

In the Senate, Niles's comparison of the Mexican Indians to the French
"sons of toil" was quickly attacked by his colleagues. Cass, for one, complained that when Niles compared the Indian rebels to the "workmen of
Paris," he "elevated" the Mexican Indians "much higher in the scale of
humanity than they now are, or, I am afraid, ever will be." Although Cass
conceded that "a false philanthropy may have given them the political
qualifications of citizens," he maintained that they were "utterly unprepared to exercise political power—as much so as our Indians, whose conduct they closely imitate in this war of extermination." Contemptuously
dismissing the comparison between French republicans and Mexican Indians, Cass played upon white fears of slave rebellion as he argued that
St. Domingo was instead "the exact prototype" of events in Yucatán.[80]
Just a few days later Southern Democrat John C. Calhoun, who opposed
intervention, nonetheless agreed with Cass that the conferral of political
rights on Mexican Indians had been a terrible mistake that should teach
the United States "a solemn lesson."[81] It is important to note, however,
that even the antislavery proto–Free Soiler Root invoked white egalitarian ideals. For even as Root argued that Mexican Indians were not savages
but citizens, he also maintained that the creoles in Yucatán "were about
equal to the Mexicans; and if there was anything under the face of heaven
meaner than a Mexican 'greaser,' he should like to know it." Root conceded that his "sympathies were, first, in favor of the white race; but those
who went on this ground must show him better samples of the white man
than these Spaniards before they would get up his sympathies very high."[82]
This example suggests that in the case of Yucatán, anti-imperialism could
also be motivated by a white egalitarian disdain for and rivalry with
"Spaniards" who, viewed through the lens of the Black Legend, were both
marginal whites and the decadent, "aristocratic" oppressors of Indians.

The debate between the two factions came to an unexpected end in
May of 1848 when news of a peace treaty between the creoles and Indians was reported to Congress, although that peace would soon be broken

and fighting would resume soon thereafter. In the *National Reform Almanac for 1849* (which also included two poems by Duganne), a short article argued for the "justice of the Indian demands" against the claims of the "white race" and described the short-lived peace treaty in laudatory terms that suggested parallels between the Indians' objectives and the projects of U.S. reformers. According to Evans, the treaty contained an article which said that lands should not be sold, that they "should remain unconveyed, *as a recourse for the subsistence of the people*"—an aim that sounded much like National Reform doctrine. Evans also reported that "after the land had been taken from the people, laws had been passed subjecting them to slavery where they had contracted debts," and so another provision of the treaty released debtors from manual service.[83] In the United States, the battle against imprisonment for debt had long been a working-class issue; in the same issue of the almanac, a report of the prospective measures endorsed by the 1848 Industrial Congress included the "Repeal of Laws for the Collection of Debts" (5). Evans added, in language that recalls that of Niles and Root, that these Indians constituted "the great body of the people of Yucatan" (41). And yet, he concluded, "United States troops, who had been engaged in the invasion of Mexico, have volunteered to the number of 800, to reconquer the people who have thus nobly vindicated their rights! These volunteers were lacklanders, who, for want of their rightful means of subsistence, have been induced to fight against the Mexicans for seven dollars a month, and now, being out of business, have been persuaded (probably without knowing or caring much about the merits of the contest) to fight in defence of the very system that had made them miserable *lacklanders!*" (42).

It is noteworthy that the *National Reform Almanac* described as "noble" a conflict that the imperialists denounced as a threat to white so-called civilization, that Evans argued against the rampant expansionist spirit that was quickly being redirected to Yucatán and Cuba as the war with Mexico drew to a close, and that he was eager to draw parallels between the struggles of whites and nonwhites rather than assigning them radically different places in the scale of humanity, as Cass did. Although Evans tried to map connections between the agrarian movements of Indians in Yucatán and white land reformers in the United States, he of course radically simplified complex relationships when he identified the "system" faced by the U.S. "lacklander" with the one that the Indians in Yucatán confronted. Indeed, he remained silent about the differences between these two struggles even though his own quotations from the treaty underlined them. For instance, whereas the third article of the treaty, from which Evans quoted, refers to and protects "Lands of Community and in Commons," the land reformers upheld, according to Jamie Bronstein, the "sanctity of private property" and "categorically refused to collectivize" it, even though they wanted to change the land laws radically, to limit the amount of land that any individual could own, and to make possible a more equitable distribution of land in the future.[84] This refusal, along with the belief that individual land ownership was the basis for economic and political independence, composed the liberal core of a program that was in other ways quite radical. Such a liberal set of beliefs about individual land ownership, however, helped to justify the dispossession of Indians in both the United States and Mexico: the Maya were, after all, responding in part to liberal land policies that threatened collectively held *ejido* lands. In other words, though land reformers such as Evans sympathized with Indians and criticized the government for unfairly expropriating their lands, the liberal conception of property that they endorsed also contributed to the displacement of Indians. What is more, this defense of the Indians against the creoles in Yucatán (the "descendants of the Spanish invaders") drew upon and reinforced the Black Legend, which made the Spanish the scapegoats for crimes that were committed by all of the European invaders.

But Evans's remarks on the uprising in Yucatán, as well as the reformers' responses to the war, at least make it clear that mid-nineteenth-century ideas about race, land, and labor must be placed in a global frame in order to be understood. I have argued that liberal and racialized conceptions of property limited the radicalism of the land reform project, and I have suggested that these beliefs about property were shaped by histories of both "westward" and "southward" expansion. But inter-American conflict and U.S. empire-building contributed to the racializing of ideologies of "free labor" as well as land. In *Racial Fault Lines,* Tomás Almaguer suggests that in postwar California nonwhites were associated with "unfree" labor systems that were supposedly threatening or degrading to whites. The U.S.-Mexican War no doubt played an important part in the dissemination of these kinds of ideas, for an emergent and racialized free labor ideology was prominently featured in debates over the Wilmot Proviso and in wartime representations of Mexican labor arrangements. During the 1850s, as the question of Manifest Destiny increasingly became sectionalized, issues of empire would continue to shape Northern Republican ideologies of race, land, and labor. In the next chapter, I explore comparisons of slavery, peonage, and free labor, as well as ideas about nonwhites and republican government, in Duganne's dime novel *The Peon Prince,* which was issued by Beadle and Company just as the Civil War broke out. Although it was published during the Civil War years, this novel and its sequel are set in Mexico during the 1840s: *The Peon Prince* takes place just before the U.S.-Mexican War begins, and the war provides the backdrop for much of the action in *Putnam Pomfret's Ward.* By reflecting on questions of race, labor, and land in the context of the U.S.-Mexican War, Duganne partly obscures the early 1860s context for these questions by displacing it, but his novels also reveal, I argue, the many connections between the late 1840s and the early 1860s, between debates over race, labor, and government in the U.S.-Mexican War and the Civil War eras, and between imperial expansion into "foreign" areas and "domestic" conflict in the post-1848 period.

SEVEN

The Hacienda, the Factory, and the Plantation

Thus a stranger, standing upon the table-land above the hacienda, might behold an illustration of the two extremes of Mexican existence. The mansion...was a perfect picture of rural luxury; while at a distance, the small gap of desert soil, crowded with miserable huts...denoted the absence of nearly all enjoyment, and the paralyzing effects of abject, unrequited servitude....The tenants...were now toiling in their master's fields, or in a factory which he had established upon the river some three miles from the hacienda. To this factory, a novel experiment at that time, the greater portion of the debtors who inhabited this village repaired at early dawn, there to toil till sunset, when, receiving their rations of food, they were permitted to return home to their miserable rest.

—Duganne, *The Peon Prince; or, The Yankee Knight-Errant. A Tale of Modern Mexico* (1861)

I want no stronger witness of the bald injustice of all servile labor than the contrast of a master dwelling in his palace and the servant in his hut; one reaping riches faster than his lavish hand can squander it; the other drudging hopelessly from birth to death, with all his toil appropriated by an "owner," and with even the offspring of his loins "sold off" to swell that owner's hoards.

—Duganne, *Camps and Prisons: Twenty Months in the Department of the Gulf* (1865)

Because Duganne's literary career bridged the transition from the labor newspapers, story papers, and periodical literature of the U.S.–Mexican War era to the dime novels of the Civil War years, his work is especially revelatory of the complex ways that race, empire, and labor and land reform were entangled from the 1840s through the 1860s, as the second "party system" broke down, the Republicans became the dominant party in the North, and the South seceded from the Union. During the 1850s, the Republicans gained support not only by appealing to Northern antislavery men who were fleeing both the Whig and Democratic parties but also by supporting a weaker version of the land reform platform that the National Reformers had advocated. Although the National Reformers had pushed for the reservation of public lands for landless actual settlers and for limitations on the amount of land that anyone could own, the Homestead Bill that was finally passed in 1862 granted settlers 160 acres of land after five years' residency but did nothing to limit the size of tracts acquired through purchase by others. And in the years that followed, Congress allocated massive land grants for railroads and other purposes, effectively foreclosing the National Reformers' dreams that the West would become a utopia for impoverished workers and small producers.[1] Moreover, while many of the land reformers insisted more vigorously on the material underpinnings of democratic freedoms and used the language of wage or white slavery more than the language of free labor, Republicans usually glorified free labor and tended to define it as freedom of contract and "the opportunity to achieve economic independence."[2] Still, by adopting the slogan of free soil, if not the more radical policies of the National Reformers, which they denounced as socialism or agrarianism, the Republicans appealed to a large body of urban workingmen and small farmers, many of whom viewed the Whigs as the party of the elite but did not endorse the alliance of the Democrats with Southern slaveholders. That this Republican hatred of slavery was quite compatible with a disdain for slaves and free blacks, however, is made clear by the frantic efforts of many Republicans to refute the Democrats' charges that the Republican program would mean equal social and political rights for black people.[3]

White egalitarian beliefs such as these influenced many of the efforts to keep slavery—and black people—out of the new territories. When Democrat (and future Free Soiler and Republican) David Wilmot of Pennsylvania, a war supporter, defended his famous amendment in Congress, he argued, "I would preserve to free white labor a fair country, a rich inheritance, where the sons of toil, of my own race and own color, can live without the disgrace which association with negro slavery brings upon free labor."[4] Although rhetorics of wage slavery and white slavery, which continued to be used by laborers in the late 1840s and 1850s, could suggest parallels, however problematic, between the labor of blacks and whites, such a language of free white labor, which became more pervasive during this period, depended upon the repudiation of such parallels. As free labor was identified with whiteness and nonwhites were identified with degraded, unfree labor, comparisons more often posited absolute racialized differences between labor systems.[5]

In Wilmot's famous speech, freedom is no abstract term; instead, it is emphatically and repeatedly identified with whiteness:

> Men of the North—Representatives of northern freemen, will you consummate such a deed of infamy and shame? I trust in God not. Oh! for the honor of the North—for the fair fame of our green hills and valleys, be firm in this crisis—be true to your country and your race. The white laborer of the North claims your service; he demands that you stand firm to his interests and his rights; that you preserve the future homes of his children, on the distant shores of the Pacific, from the degradation and dishonor of negro servitude. Where the negro slave labors, the free white man cannot labor by his side without sharing in his degradation and his disgrace.[6]

As Wilmot addressed his colleagues, the "Men of the North," he hailed them both as citizens of the Northern United States and as part of a "race" that he identified with freedom. Wilmot thereby echoed the language of U.S. racial Anglo-Saxonism, which claimed democratic institutions and the ideas of freedom and equality as the particular inheritance of whites.[7] "Shall we give up free territory, the inheritance of free labor? Must we yield this also?" Wilmot implored his audience. "Never, sir, never, until we ourselves are fit to be slaves....If we do, we are coward slaves, and deserve to have the manacles fastened upon our own limbs."

Despite the ban on other forms of involuntary servitude as well as slavery in Wilmot's original amendment, in this speech he said nothing about other kinds of coerced labor but instead emphasized an opposition between white freedom and black slavery.[8] In a good deal of U.S.–Mexican War literature, however, free labor and chattel slavery are also often compared to Mexican labor arrangements. In *Service Afloat and Ashore During the Mexican War* (1851), for instance, Lieutenant Raphael Semmes compared chattel slavery to Mexican peonage as he commented on the unequal division of property in Mexico. At first he described the propertyless "five-sixths of the eight millions of the country" as "laborers dependent from day to day upon their exertions for subsistence."[9] Although Semmes initially described this part of the nation as a class, however, in the analysis that followed he organized his account of these "dependent," propertyless laborers in racial terms: "They are not only separated by class but by race also, from the other one-sixth of the population; and there is no more sympathy or affinity between these two great fractions of the eight millions of Mexico, than there is between the slaves of the southern part of the United States and their masters—indeed, not so much" (17). Semmes attributed what he understood to be the greater "degradation" of the Mexican laborer to the pervasiveness of race mixing among blacks, Indians, and whites. And yet, Semmes also viewed Mexican labor arrangements as a sort of distorted mirror of the system of slavery in the U.S. South. For instance, he called debt peonage "a system of slavery," arguing that although peons were nominally freemen, "they are, in fact, reduced to a galling and life-long servitude" (249). In an implicit rebuke to the defenders of the Wilmot Proviso, he concluded:

> This is the boasted freedom of the Mexican soil, about which there has been so much senseless declamation in our congress, since the conclusion of the war. The well-fed and well-cared-for dependent of a southern estate, with us, is infinitely superior, in point both of physical and moral condition, to the *mozo* of the Mexican hacienda. The "hewers of wood and drawers of water" are slaves everywhere, as I have found; and whether the slave is so, *lege scripta,* or *lege necessitatis,* is, as the lawyers say, a distinction without a difference. (249–50)

Here, Semmes implicitly defends the extension of slavery and attacks the Wilmot Proviso by arguing that labor systems that are worse than slavery are already in place in Mexico. Although his vision of the laboring classes as "slaves everywhere" suggests that white Northern "free laborers" would not escape his contempt, his special focus on the "degraded" state of nonwhite laborers identifies the latter with a natural and necessary system of slavery against which white freedom may be measured.

According to one historian, the term "debt peonage" first appears in English in the mid–nineteenth century as a way of describing an array of labor arrangements.[10] Alan Knight has suggested that in the late colonial period and the early nineteenth century there were two forms of peonage: the first form was coercive, while the second, which Knight calls "traditional" peonage, "rested upon non-coercive foundations." Although "southern [Mexican] plantations" were the "great bastions" of classic, coercive debt peonage, he argues, "traditional" peonage, in which the worker was not necessarily tied to the hacienda by extra-economic coercion and in which debt did not always function as a bond, was more common, especially in northern Mexico.[11] By the twentieth century, of course, the term "peon" would become a sort of loose swear word, deployed by John Steinbeck, for instance, to disparage the Mexican workers with whom he contrasted Okie laborers during the Depression years.[12] Both the pejorative meanings of the term and its use to describe a wide variety of labor contexts, however, can be traced to the mid–nineteenth century, for journalists, soldiers, and other U.S. observers frequently invoked it when commenting upon Mexican society, and its meanings are inextricable from the imperial encounters that contributed to its production.[13]

Duganne's accounts of Mexico and of peonage in *The Peon Prince* and its sequel draw on these earlier forms of imperial knowledge, but they are also shaped by the events and concerns of the Civil War era. The dime novel was itself a new institution in 1861, although the pamphlet novels and story-paper fiction of the 1840s and 1850s provided many of the formulas, settings, and character-types used by the first dime novel authors. The story of how in 1860 Erastus and Irwin Beadle developed a format and a little later a distribution apparatus that turned the dime novel into one of the most successful forms of nineteenth-century mass culture has by now often been told. The introduction of these cheap novels, which were approximately one hundred pages long and which included sensational, eye-grabbing illustrations on the cover, was a landmark innovation in consumer culture that Bill Brown has suggestively compared to the chain-store system and the Five-and-Ten.[14] In an 1862 advertisement, Beadle and Company claimed that their novels were undoubtedly "the most popular series of books ever issued in this country," and in their catalogue Duganne was described as "one of our most popular writers."[15] The firm repeatedly issued a special page-long advertisement devoted to descriptions of each of Duganne's dime novels, a promotional tactic that they reserved for only a few of their most celebrated writers. In addition to his two dime novels about Mexico, Duganne also produced *Massasoit's Daughter; or, The French Captives* (1861), a story about conflicts between Indians and whites in New England, and *The King's Man: A Tale of South Carolina in Revolutionary Times* (1860).

As the titles and subject matter of these four stories suggest, the early dime novel included a variety of genres and focused on a range of time periods and settings. Philip Durham estimates that approximately three-quarters of Beadle's dime novels were about the frontier and that more than half were concerned with the trans-Mississippi West, but a catalogue published in the early 1860s also referred to numerous sea yarns, city novels, love stories, tales of the colonial period and the American Revolution, as well as historical romances about Mexico, Canada, and the Caribbean.[16] Although a staggering number of dime novels engaged issues of westward expansion and addressed white relations with North American Indians, Brown suggests that many early dime novel authors focused on earlier eras and older frontiers so as to "elide the political crisis provoked by the newer frontiers—the ultimately unmanageable question of slavery's expansion—while capitalizing on the irrepressible literary fascination with the Indian."[17] In the next chapter, I argue in more detail, by examining several dime novels that focus on contemporaneous frontiers, the question of slavery, and the Civil War, that the political crisis provoked by the debates over slavery was not entirely elided in the early dime novel, that on the contrary this crisis in fact returns to haunt many of these narratives. This concluding chapter of Part 3 opens up the discussion of popular sensational literature during the Civil War years by addressing the impact of multiple contemporaneous internal and inter-American conflicts—in the U.S. South, Minnesota, Cuba, Nicaragua, and Texas—on the early dime novel and on Northern Republican conceptions of race, land, labor, and empire. In this chapter, however, I look closely at Duganne's two dime novels about Mexico, reading them in relation to debates about the Wilmot Proviso, peonage and the hacienda, and race and republican government. I suggest that both of these novels strongly register a recent political crisis over a frontier—the war between the United States and Mexico—and indirectly refer to the North/South division over slavery.

As Brown suggests in the introduction to his recent anthology of dime novel Westerns, although the dime novel is "repeatedly cited to denote the sensationalist version of frontier adventure," the novels themselves often remain unread and are too often "reduced to a mere stereotype."[18] Especially because dime novels about Mexico and inter-American conflict have been underanalyzed in studies of this form of early mass culture, I want to consider in some detail these two popular examples of the "Mexico Western." Because they were among the most popular of Beadle's productions, Duganne's novels were some of the most widely circulated stories of the period, and they therefore offer important evidence about the significance of Mexico and inter-American relations in an emergent mass culture.

What is more, these novels and others like them helped to establish many of the formulas and themes that would be taken up by the movie Westerns of the twentieth century. Although it has become a truism that

Figure 11.   Cover of Augustine Joseph Hickey Duganne's
Putnam Pomfret's Ward. (Annenberg Rare Book and Manuscript Library, University of Pennsylvania)

dime novels were an important influence on movie Westerns, few scholars trace the relationships, based on a reading of the nineteenth-century
texts, between novels and movies. In contrast, in this chapter I argue that
Duganne's dime novels, as well as the story-paper fiction that preceded
them, helped to establish a new subgenre of mass entertainment that focused on Mexico as a space that was potentially like the United States—and
therefore not entirely "savage"—but that was still viewed as alien, largely
because of the mixtures of multiple "races" and the persistence of feudal and colonial institutions. These nineteenth-century representations

featured many of the paradigms and conventions that were later adapted in the filmic "Mexico Westerns" of the twentieth century which Richard Slotkin analyzes in *Gunfighter Nation,* including *The Treasure of the Sierra Madre* (1948), *Vera Cruz* (1954), and *The Magnificent Seven* (1960).[19] Slotkin defines the "Mexico Western" as "a subtype of the Western in which a group of American gunfighters crosses the border into Mexico during a time of social disruption or revolutionary crisis to help the peasants defeat an oppressive ruler, warlord, or bandit" (410). He argues that this plot-premise "mirrors the concrete themes and problematics of American engagement in the Third World, and its reflexivity mirrors the transformation of our domestic ideology and institutions in response to the exigencies of Cold War power politics" (410). Although Duganne's Yankee travels to Mexico in 1845 to sell clocks rather than to intervene in a revolutionary crisis, he quickly reveals his fighting skills when he is caught in the middle of a struggle between contending forces in a nation that is on the brink of war with the United States. And although Duganne's novels respond to the transformation of domestic ideology and institutions in the mid–nineteenth century rather than the Cold War era, they also take up issues that are central to the Mexico Westerns of the later era, including the problematics of U.S. involvement in Mexico and questions about race and republican self-government.

In the opening chapters of *The Peon Prince,* which take place in the autumn of 1845, an Italian bandit and a Mexican creole soldier vie for the love of Inez, the beautiful daughter of Murillo the Rich, a farmer. The soldier, Antonio La Vega, is a hotheaded and disdainful cavalry officer; the bandit chief Marani, on the other hand, disguises himself as a wealthy gentleman in order to win Inez's heart. Both are described as harboring unruly passions and both plan to kidnap Inez and force a marriage, though she is in love with Lorenzo, a poor artist. What follows is a series of capture-and-rescue episodes in which the Yankee, Putnam Pomfret, and the peon prince, Zumozin, are intimately involved. Ultimately, the Yankee and Zumozin join forces with a Mexican officer, Nunez, and a priest, Padre Herrata, to rescue Inez and expose the malfeasance of the alcalde and *hacendado* Juan Garcia, Zumozin's master, who had contrived to mislead Zumozin about his true identity and to steal the vast property left to him by his father. And in the sequel, which opens just as the U.S.-Mexican War is about to begin, the Yankee, Herrata, and Zumozin are reunited in order to prevent an unwilling woman—Teresa Glinton, who is from New Orleans and whose mother was a Mexican creole—from being married to an unscrupulous suitor, a dissipated libertine who is in the end revealed to be her half-brother, the product of an earlier forced marriage between Teresa's mother and another creole libertine. In this novel, Mexico is, on the one hand, a space of lawlessness, corruption, unstable government, and uncontrolled passions, but on the other hand, Duganne suggests that it might be redeemed and reformed through the combined agency of men such as Zumozin, Herrata, and Nunez, who believe in republican ideals and who are friends of the Yankee. In other words, Duganne is interested in Mexico as a space that might be remade in the image of the United States by a liberal coalition friendly to U.S. interests.[20]

Both of these narratives feature devices and motifs that are typical of the dime novel: disguise, the exposure of secret identities, violence, cliffhanging chapter endings, beautiful endangered virgins, an intense focus on muscular male bodies, and patriotism. They also incorporate many of the conventions of the story-paper international romances that I described in Part 2. By making one of the protagonists a Yankee, Duganne deployed in his novel a regional type that had long been popular in the theater and in cheap fiction, including the story-paper romances set during the U.S.-Mexican War. In the cheap fiction of the earlier period, Mexico was frequently represented as a land of lawlessness and forced marriage, where banditry prevailed over government and where a woman's consent was all too often considered irrelevant by an aristocratic patriarch or a rapacious villain enthralled to his passions. In the 1840s, these representations were deployed to explain the U.S. presence in Mexico even though many of these novels also implied that the annexation of all or part of Mexico was undesirable. As we have already seen, many wartime novels focused on a possible romance between a U.S. soldier and a Mexican woman in which the relationships between lovers suggested possible postwar relationships between nations. In Duganne's novels, however, international heterosexual romance is almost entirely displaced by international homosocial bonding, as the Yankee helps his allies foil the villains who threaten the women.

Like most of the story-paper Yankees in the war novels of the 1840s, Putnam Pomfret is seemingly ineligible for romance. Although the role of romantic hero was usually reserved for U.S. officers in these earlier stories, in Duganne's novels the Yankee is the only U.S. hero who plays a leading part, and international romance is largely foreclosed. This may follow from the changing circumstances of the early 1860s. The United States had pressured Mexico for more land and for transit rights across northern Mexico and the Isthmus of Tehuantepec throughout the 1850s, but by 1861 U.S. priorities were different. Since the United States was itself embroiled in the beginnings of a bloody and destructive civil war, concerns about the Monroe Doctrine and U.S. rivalries with European powers for influence in the Americas were subordinated to domestic concerns about the future of the Union and the international relations that might affect the outcome of the war. Insofar as international romance tests the possibility of an increasingly intimate relationship between the United States and Mexico, that possibility was therefore less desirable and less pressing during these years. But the shift from international romance to international homosocial bonding also responded to Duganne's own particular anti-imperialist and nativist beliefs, for fears of foreign influence and the perils of race-mixing probably would have made an emphasis on the "marriage" of nations unappealing to him anyway.

Many of these fears and beliefs are voiced by Duganne's Yankee. Although he joins forces with Officer Nunez, Padre Herrata, and Zumozin, his speech is full of racist invective against "greasers" and "Ingens." This casual racism is characteristic of the Yankee character type. As Saxton argues, earlier Yankee characters tended to accede to class hierarchies, but by the 1830s "the Yankee was opportunistically employing white racism to justify his shift from deference to egalitarianism."[21] Thus despite his relatively lowly origins and his status as a lower-class type, in *The Peon Prince* Putman Pomfret repeatedly asserts his superiority to the Mexicans on the basis of his race and national origin: "I cal'late you wont try to come Paddy over a live white man from the States," "I'm a free born citizen of the States," etc.[22] What is more, the affectionate references to him as "Our North American" (21), "our free American" (22), and "our Yankee" (32) all suggest that Duganne was constructing his Yankee as a point of identification for his Northern U.S. readers. But it is also important to note that the Yankee was rarely a completely positive character. As Francis Hodge observes in his wide-ranging study of Yankee theater, in many dialect comedies, "the Yankee is not often admirable or idealized; he belongs to a race of not-so-petty bargainers who win because they are more clever, more 'slick' than others."[23] The cleverness and "slickness" of Duganne's Yankee help him to defeat his Mexican foes, but these qualities, as well as his hyperbolic slangy speech, also make him more than slightly ridiculous.

And the Yankee is not the only hero in these novels, for Zumozin, Herrata, and Nunez also play significant roles. When we are first introduced to Zumozin, the Peon Prince of the title, "one of a great class of his countrymen" who toil "in the most abject and hopeless servitude"

(48), Duganne figures him as a Romantic hero, standing on the "highest ridge" of a "sublime" mountain, contemplating his evil fate. Zumozin toils in the "degrading" (91) position of a herd-boy on the hacienda of Juan Garcia, the corrupt alcalde, and dreams of freedom. He is also, however, the leader of one thousand Indians, whom he convenes as part of a ritual at the base of the ancient pyramids, where each swears "to be true to Aztlan" (105). Although at the end of *The Peon Prince* it is revealed that Zumozin's father was "an Italian grandee" and his mother an Indian princess, "chosen to be [his] bride out of all the dames of Spain's trans-Atlantic empire" (122), Zumozin repudiates wealth and "station," as well as Mexican "Society and the State," in order to "redeem and exalt the race of [his] mother—the race of Zumozin" (127). When we next meet him in *Putnam Pomfret's Ward*, his plans for the "improvement and elevation" of "the Indian population" are already well underway, and he hopes to unite "the scattered and dissimilar tribes, who owned a common country, into a warlike, disciplined nation, federated by a single object, the preservation of their own rude independence." To this, the Yankee replies that Zumozin should be president, and that the Indians "owned the land before any white feller ever set foot on 't."[24]

The main villain in *The Peon Prince* is the alcalde Garcia, "one of the largest landholders in that part of the country, as well as an extensive speculator in mines, and a man, likewise, who was reputed to exercise no little influence in political affairs at the capital" (74). While the Yankee and those Mexicans who are represented positively in this novel favor President Herrera, the moderate Mexican leader who wanted to negotiate instead of going to war with the United States over the annexation of Texas, Garcia is an ally of the anti–North American Paredes, a conservative who deposed Herrera and became president in January of 1846, just before the war started. But although U.S. interests clearly govern these distinctions between Mexican heroes and villains, Duganne also denounces the Mexican conservatives allied with Paredes by accusing them, through the figure of Garcia, of ruling through racial tyranny. Garcia hopes that a youth of royal blood "backed by European armies" will marry his niece and rule Mexico as its king; his desire to subvert the republic is rooted in his conviction that Mexico's "unquiet races can be ruled only with an iron scepter" (119).

The Mexican heroes who oppose this vision of Mexico's future are Zumozin, the radical priest Padre Herrata, and the army officer Captain Nunez. Herrata, "a patriot, in the highest sense of the word" (91), had been Zumozin's teacher, and from him Zumozin "imbibed a hatred of oppression in all its forms" (92). Nunez, on the other hand, at first seems to be Zumozin's rival for the affections of Garcia's niece. But the niece loves Nunez, and so Zumozin conquers his own desire for her and pledges a bond of brotherhood with Nunez. The homosocial bond between men is electric. As Zumozin promises to devote himself to his rival, Nunez draws Zumozin to his bosom: the "Serf clasped the soldier to his heart, and thus for a moment these two magnanimous men remained locked in each other's embrace. Strangers till this moment, one thrill of sympathy had united them. The magnetism of true souls had made them one" (83). At the end of the novel, Zumozin even resigns the wealth of Garcia, which should be his, along with the niece, to his "brother" (127) Nunez.

The magnetic homosocial bond between Herrata, Nunez, and Zumozin seems to be Duganne's way of imagining an interracial, cross-class alliance between Mexican creoles and Indians as an alternative to the rule of anti-U.S. conservatives such as Paredes. This U.S. interest in Mexican political divisions was no doubt reanimated by Mexico's own recent civil war. In response to the reform laws of the 1850s and the new liberal Constitution of 1857, which banned the corporate ownership of real estate and abolished judicial privileges for the army, the conservatives rebelled, dissolved Congress, deposed President Comonfort, and took power themselves.[25] During the three-year-long war that followed, Benito Juárez, an acculturated Zapotec Indian, radical liberal, and minister of justice under Comonfort, declared himself president and led the struggle against the conservatives from his base in Vera Cruz. On 6 April 1859 the United States officially recognized the Juárez regime, but U.S. leaders refused to provide any support for Juárez unless Mexico granted territorial concessions and transit rights to the United States. In late December the McLane-Ocampo Treaty was agreed upon, which granted the United States transit rights in return for two million dollars, but this treaty was rejected by the U.S. Senate shortly thereafter. Nonetheless, by late 1860 the liberals had won the war, and in June of 1861—two months after the U.S. Civil War began and Duganne's *The Peon Prince* was published—Juárez was officially declared president of Mexico. A few months later France invaded Mexico and another long struggle on the part of Juárez and his liberal government began. From 1862 through 1867, the years of the war against Maximilian's empire, Juárez appealed to Lincoln for support, stressing "the identity of constitutional principles shared by Mexico and the United States" as well as Mexico's opposition to slavery, but U.S. leaders, who were wary of upsetting France and sought to avoid foreign entanglements during the years of the U.S. Civil War, gave him "no direct support" (157). They never, however, recognized Maximilian's empire, either.[26]

Given this international context, Duganne must have expected that readers would have thought of Juárez when they read about the Indian Zumozin, the Yankee's choice for president of Mexico. As an embattled liberal government that was friendly toward the Republicans of the North, the Juárez regime would have been preferred by many Northerners to Maximilian, who was courted by the Confederacy. The trio of priest, officer, and Indian "noble" that is featured in these two dime novels, then, is Duganne's way of imagining a Mexican coalition, no doubt in part inspired by the Juárez coalition, composed of Indian leaders and liberal factions within the church and the army, which would be friendly to the United States.

Still, however, given the long history of U.S. debates about the ability of nonwhites to participate in republican government, such as those about the status of the Maya Indians in Yucatán that I discussed in the previous chapter, the place of Indians within this coalition would have been, to say the least, controversial. Proslavery politicians such as John C. Calhoun and Lewis Cass seized upon the Caste War in Yucatán to support their position that the Indians were unprepared to exercise political power.[27] Duganne must have had arguments such as these in mind when he pointed out that "many instances have occurred of pureblooded Indians attaining to high positions in the State, holding rank in civil and military affairs" (65). Although he suggested that these examples were exceptions, he argued that they served "but to exhibit more forcefully the injustice which creates social distinctions on account of the accident of birth." Duganne concluded that

> Mexico owed, probably, as much to the Indian and Mestizo portions of her citizens, during the struggle for independence, as to any other class. Guerrero, indeed, the first of her actual Presidents, and one of the bravest of her patriot commanders, was scarcely more a white than a negro in the quality of his blood. It is evident, therefore, that the inequality of political power is not the result of natural inferiority in the degraded classes, but rather the offspring of that injustice which repudiates all merit when opposed to prejudice. (65–66)

As Duganne argues against the "natural inferiority" of the "Indian and Mestizo" classes, the overlapping languages of class and race that he draws on lead him to break from the position, which was popular among many Northerners as well as Southerners, that nonwhites were unfit to exercise political rights in a democracy. After Vicente Guerrero, the liberal Mexican president and hero of the war for independence that Duganne refers to here, was deposed by conservative forces backed by "the great landowners, generals, clerics, and Spaniards resident in Mexico" in late 1829, he was executed, perhaps as a warning, Jan Bazant has argued, "to men considered as socially and ethnically inferior not to dare to dream of becoming president."[28] By linking his Indian hero Zumozin to Guerrero and implicitly to Juárez, Duganne criticizes the view, which was still shared by many whites on both sides of the border, that political rights and political leadership could be safely entrusted only to whites.

Of course, the attempted liberal incorporation of Indians into the Mexican nation-state also depended on racial hierarchies, hierarchies that are referenced in *The Peon Prince* by Zumozin's self-sacrifice, his sense of unworthiness, and his subordination to Nunez within the alliance. If Garcia's niece stands in for the Mexican nation, which Garcia wants to wed to a European prince, then Zumozin's self-sacrificing desire for her and Nunez's marriage to her suggest a political situation in which liberal creoles lead the nation while Indians are cast in supporting roles. Even this representation, however, is a much too cheery rendering of how creole rule and liberal policies actually affected Indian communities. For liberal land laws ultimately aimed at the privatization of all corporate lands, including communal lands held by Indians as well as church property. The attempted liberal shift from particularist forms of community to a universalist, nationalist one also erased the status of Indian, replacing it with the abstract identity of the citizen.[29] That this was a violent, incomplete process which provoked violent responses is evidenced by the large number of uprisings that occurred when liberals tried to enforce the new laws.[30] Even before he became president, Benito Juárez, for instance, found that the liberal policies that he advocated were objectionable to Indian communities in Oaxaca. But according to Jack Spicer, when Juárez, as governor of Oaxaca during the 1850s, suppressed the revolt of the Indians of Juchitan in the Isthmus of Tehuantepec, who were responding to the land provisions of the new reform laws, "he held that the existence of Indian communities based in the colonial system constituted a threat to the nation. They must be broken up at all costs, so that individual initiative and modern forms of representative government could prevail."[31]

So on the one hand, Duganne's representation of a liberal Mexican coalition that included a Mexican Indian leader was an important intervention in U.S. debates about whether nonwhites were now, or ever would be, fit to participate in republican government. In the United States, Indians had few political rights, and so to defend those rights, even elsewhere, and to advocate Indian political leadership, countered the view that only whites were capable of democratic self-rule. But liberal government was not the solution to the problem of Indian land loss. In fact, in Mexico, liberal policies often made things worse, for the privatization of property and attacks on corporate privileges, communal landholdings, and nonnational forms of community threatened the very existence of many Indian communities. Although Mexican liberals hoped that private, individual Indian land ownership would make Indians more "independent" and thereby do much to reverse the damage caused by colonial policies, the liberal emphasis on possessive individualism and private property did its own damage.[32] This was another version of the contradiction that U.S. land reformers such as George Henry Evans never successfully resolved: though they sometimes championed the claims of Indians against those of the federal government, the liberal conception of private property that they ultimately endorsed, despite their efforts to diffuse and equalize land ownership among a nation of small producers, was in violent competition with the ideas about collective property that many Indians assumed. And this liberal core of beliefs was very similar to the beliefs about individualism, property, and government that were held by many Mexican liberals. According to Rosaura Sánchez, early economic liberals in Mexico wanted to appropriate communal lands in order "to create small property owners and in that way develop a republic of small farmers."[33] The famous liberal and vice president of the Republic of Texas Lorenzo de Zavala was therefore not alone in idealizing what Charles Hale calls "the democracy of small property holders, artisans, and self-respecting laborers," for many Mexican liberals believed that the diffusion of land ownership among small producers rather than the large *hacendados* was critical to the success of Mexican democracy, despite the fact that liberal economic policies would often end up aggravating inequalities rather than mitigating them.[34]

Wanting Mexico to be remade in the image of the United States, Duganne could not see in his construction of a possible Mexican future what the land reformers also failed to understand in the U.S. context: the role that liberal forms of property and government played in deepening inequalities. This does not mean that there were not significant differences among different liberal positions: the land reformers' emphasis on the importance of the diffusion of land ownership and the material underpinnings of citizenship countered those aspects of an emerging free labor ideology that simply celebrated the laborer's juridical freedom to make a contract. As Eric Foner has argued, free labor ideology was "grounded in the precepts that free labor was economically and socially superior to slave labor and that the distinctive quality of Northern society was the opportunity it offered wage laborers to rise to property-owning independence."[35] Land reformers also championed the ideal of property-owning independence, but most did not believe that the ability to make a labor contract and to sell one's services in the market was a sufficient guarantee of that ideal. Therefore, like George Henry Evans, they often argued against the increasingly pervasive term "free labor" and referred to propertyless workers as "wage slaves."

The significance of this comparison between white Northern laborers and chattel slaves has been debated, as I have already suggested, by labor historians. Although David Roediger has argued that this comparison was intrinsically problematic and that those who deployed the wage slavery metaphor were often proslavery, Foner has suggested that despite its hyperbole and its use by some advocates of slavery, the rhetoric of wage slavery was also often used by artisans, factory workers, and others who opposed slavery, and he insists that it "suggested the superiority of a very different conception of labor relations than that embodied in contract thought."[36] Comparisons among peonage, chattel slavery, and Northern "free" labor were similarly fraught, in ways that both Roediger's and Foner's analysis helps us to understand.[37] When these different labor systems are viewed as like each other, the comparisons can indeed seem strained and hyperbolic: the forms of coercion and control that the "peon" and the slave were subjected to were dramatically different from those endured by the Northern white laborer. That peonage and slavery were racialized labor systems may also disappear from view when these three sets of labor relations are all described as forms of slavery. But arguments that insisted on the differences between free and unfree labor were also problematic. The opposition that David Wilmot, for instance, constructed between free labor and slave labor depended on a white egalitarian belief that nonwhites were degraded and that their presence threatened to degrade whites. On the other hand, abolitionists who emphasized a dichotomy between slave labor and free labor and idealized the latter sometimes helped "to legitimize the wage relationship," Foner suggests, "even as it was coming under bitter attack."[38] As Foner argues, it is important to understand how the refusal of the term "free labor" and the use of the wage slavery metaphor by antislavery labor advocates could function as an attack on chattel slavery as well as some aspects of economic liberalism. And yet, the fact that such comparisons were problematic both when they were made and when they were not made supports Roediger's claim that as "long as slavery thrived, any attempt to come to grips with wage labor tended to lapse into exaggerated metaphors or frantic denials of those metaphors."[39]

This double bind forged by the context of racialized labor relations also affected Duganne's discussions of peonage on a Mexican hacienda. Even the fact that Duganne represents peonage as quasi-ubiquitous in Mexico is already an exoticizing, othering move. According to John Tutino, during the postindependence period the "decline of silver mining and the weakness of commercial elites combined to threaten the power of the dominant class of central Mexico—the great families that during the late colonial era had integrated commercial, mining, and landed activities to rule the core regions of the colony."[40] In these circumstances, the hacienda became a less viable institution, and in many areas sharecropping and ranchero production expanded. Mexican liberals also almost universally attacked the hacienda in terms very similar to Duganne's, claiming that it was a feudal institution that encouraged dependency and impeded the formation of a class of smaller producers.[41] Finally, in his study of the hacienda during this period, D. A. Brading cites evidence that in the nineteenth century many workers avoided debt peonage; that in the northern province of San Luis Potosí resident peons were a relatively "privileged group within the work-force of the hacienda" who received wages as well as food rations; that tenants and sharecroppers were "more numerous and more deeply in debt"; and that debt was often more "of an inducement than a bond."[42] All of this suggests that we must examine as an ideological construction Duganne's representation of peonage as an institution "which prevails more or less throughout the whole of Mexico, and by which thousands are held in the most abject and hopeless servitude, sold and transferred with the land they cultivate or the mines they work" (48).

As Duganne describes debt peonage, he represents it as the antithesis of liberal modernity: it is feudal and the peon is a serf, but his degradation is worse than medieval. "It is not generally known that although slavery, as it exists in the United States, was long ago abolished in Mexico, there still remains in that unhappy land a system of serfdom immeasurably more degrading than the vassalage of the middle ages, and at best on a level with the worst forms of African bondage" (48). Like Raphael Semmes, although to different purposes, Duganne sees debt peonage as a kind of slavery, though slavery has been outlawed in Mexico; indeed, he views it as a form of compulsory labor equivalent to "the worst forms of African bondage" (48) in the United States. Juan Garcia, the owner of the hacienda, is, like a slaveowner, "master" of hundreds of people (90), and the hacienda itself is described in ways that recall contemporary descriptions of Southern plantations. What is more, his description of debt peonage as degrading recalls Wilmot's fears of the "degradation" of free white labor and the resulting efforts to exclude not only slavery but also black people from the lands acquired from Mexico. In other words, the representation of debt peonage as a state of paralyzing abjection and Duganne's description of the peon as a "ward" who is "entirely dependent upon his master" (49) resonate ominously with strains of republicanism and free labor ideology that identified such forms of unfree labor with degradation and dependence. For within republican thought, independence was identified with virtue and dependence was viewed with great suspicion. As Roediger suggests, republicanism had "long emphasized" that "weakness and servility made those most dependent a threat to the Republic, apt to be pawns of powerful and designing men." Although Republicanism could support attacks on social and economic arrangements that intensified forms of dependency, it could also suggest that those who long endured abject servitude might be undeserving of freedom and unfit for citizenship.[43] This helps to explain how ideas about Mexican debt peonage could and increasingly did, even in the twentieth century, support racist stereotypes of people of Mexican origin as naturally servile and as a threat to free white labor and the republic.

But Duganne also suggests parallels between Mexican peons and Northern laborers, so much so that these representations of peonage could be described in Eric Lott's terms as "displaced maps or representations of 'working-classness,'" with more sympathy for nonwhite laborers, despite the problems I've indicated, than can be found in the performances of blackface minstrelsy that Lott analyzes.[44] For as Duganne tries to represent debt peonage, he repeatedly adapts generic conventions from Eastern urban gothic fiction. First of all, as I suggested above, within urban reform literature it was not unusual for wage laborers to be described as serfs or slaves, so when Mexican peons are represented in these terms, comparisons between the two labor systems are not necessarily foreclosed. We have seen how writers such as Lippard relentlessly compared New York's "upper ten and lower million" by contrasting the mansions of the rich to the hovels of the poor. Duganne uses a similar rhetoric when he opposes the peons' "miserable huts" to their master's luxurious mansion to illustrate "the two extremes of Mexican existence" (90). Given the intensity of the debates in the United States over the abolition of imprisonment for debt, which had been considered an important working-class political issue in the years before the war, representations of debt peonage must have suggested resemblances between the predicament of some laborers in Northern U.S. cities and Mexico.[45] The bleak image of debtors who toil in the factory until sunset and then return home to their miserable rest cited at the beginning of this chapter would not be out of place in an urban gothic novel about the criminal excesses of capitalists in New York and Philadelphia or in an appeal for the ten-hour day.

Like early advocates of the working class in the United States, Duganne also invoked a distinction between producers and nonproducers by representing the nonwhite peoples of Mexico as a producer class, with Spanish colonizers and Mexican creole elites playing the role that Eastern capitalists occupied in urban reform literature. "While the Guadalupinoes [sic] and Creoles have enjoyed by turns the power and immunities of an aristocracy," Duganne argues, "the Aborigines, Mestizoes, Mulattoes, and Blacks, in all their various shades, have always, since the Conquest, occupied inferior grades of life, as 'hewers of wood and drawers of water'" (64). Duganne describes the Spanish colonizers as "petty tyrants, who, by monopoly, extortion and rapacity, amassed the wealth which properly belonged to those whose labor and struggles had opened the avenues to industry and commerce" (92)—the nonwhite laborers of Mexico. Monopoly, extortion, and rapacity were key words in the languages of class developed by white workers in Northeastern cities, who often opposed the productive labor of the working classes to the nonproductive idleness of the rich. Here, however, these languages of class are used to construct Spaniards and creole elites as an "aristocracy" that exploits the laboring classes and takes the wealth that "properly belongs" to the latter.

Even as Duganne deplores the cruel treatment of Mexico's nonwhite races and describes them as a class of producers, however, he also invokes the Black Legend, which held that the Spanish colonizers were more inhumane than other European colonizers in the Americas. Despite Duganne's opposition to the war and to U.S. empire-building, this position could fortify imperialist ideologies which suggested that U.S. expansion would bring liberty and enlightenment to the oppressed peoples of Mexico by displacing a tyrannical, largely Spanish ruling class. Such a set of beliefs could also reinforce the anti-Catholic nativism that

provoked riots in Northeastern cities and motivated the proliferation of
Spanish Catholic villains in Eastern urban gothic novels. Duganne's role
as a founder of the nativist Know-Nothing Party and one-term representative in the New York legislature shows how anti-imperialism and
sympathy for the nonwhite "producing classes" of Mexico could coexist with a U.S. political nativism that drew sharp distinctions between
so-called Americans and foreigners. What is more, Duganne's representations of the hacienda system and of peonage were quite similar to those
of many Mexican liberals. According to Brading, in the mid–nineteenth
century "a certain strain of radical indigenismo" attacked "the great estate as an illegal institution, with title deeds vitiated by the crime of the
Spanish Conquest and the subsequent seizure of Indian lands."[46] But
despite their identification with—or perhaps better, appropriation of—
Indian-ness in the service of nativist nation-building, these liberals also,
as I have suggested, attacked communal landholdings and tried to replace the status of "Indian" with that of the abstract citizen. This convergence between Duganne's position and that of the early Mexican
nation-builders reveals how liberal and white egalitarian assumptions
about race, property, and government could and did compromise even
radical republican positions that were relatively sympathetic to Indians.

The possibilities and limits of Duganne's position are also revealed
but in a different context—this time, he focuses on the plantation rather
than the hacienda—in *Camps and Prisons,* a personal narrative that he
published at the end of the Civil War. In 1862, one year after his two
dime novels about Mexico were issued, Duganne helped to raise a company of New York Volunteers to fight in the Civil War, and he became
the lieutenant colonel of the regiment. In the summer of 1863 he was
forced by circumstances to surrender to the Confederates in Louisiana,
and about half of his lengthy war memoir is about his time in prison.
But the first half concerns Duganne's travels through the South, as he
passes through New Orleans, "the empress city of the South," observes
ruined plantations, and comments on the differences between Northern
and Southern life.[47] Again and again, Northern Republican ideas about
land and labor provide the lens through which he interprets what he sees.
When he stops among the plantations of Bayou Lafourche in Louisiana,
for instance, he observes that half a century ago these lands

> promised comfort and competence to a hundred thousand white men, who,
> settling here, with skill and toil, might build up homes for free-born families.
> But speculating Capital came also to this treasury of cotton and sugar; and
> thereafter the curse of "adding field to field" laid grasp upon the future. So

up to our war-advent, the soil had been monopolized and swayed by Land-lordism, with its huge estates and negro-swarms, while ignoble "free labor" yielded acre after acre, and foot by foot, till it is now crowded back into the swamp bottoms, squalid and ague-stricken. (32)

At the beginning of this passage, Duganne's language recalls the white egalitarianism of the Wilmot Proviso, with its emphasis on the debase-ment of laboring white men who suffer because of the slave system; slav-ery is condemned, in "free labor" terms, because it leads to Landlordism and the monopoly of the soil, which in turn crowds free white laborers into the swamp bottoms. As Duganne proceeds, however, he focuses more closely on the black laborers who worked these plantations, and he adapts Republican free labor ideology to argue that the plantations should not be returned to their owners but that instead the former slaves should be armed and allowed to run them.

After walking down the road of a sugar plantation, "passing through miles of rotting cane, decadence of ungathered crops" (33), he reaches the quarters of the blacks and encounters Uncle Phil, a plantation-preacher and former slave and overseer's assistant on the estate. Phil takes him on a tour through the abandoned sawmill and sugar mill and demonstrates a knowledge of their workings that proves he could easily run a sugar-plantation himself. Meditating on the fact that thousands of such plantations have been "given over to destruction" while "the toil-ing people who had made them Edens of productiveness, were cast out on the highways" (36), Duganne imagines

> each broad plantation, with its vast machinery, confided to the hands which earned and paid for all the wide improvements. I fancy a "sugar-maker" like Uncle Phil still watching over every reservoir, and—backed by wise author-ity, assisted by selected men of science and of honesty—producing wealth for Government—large profits to the power that breaks his chain and gives him manhood in exchange for slavery. I see a grand militia, armed and drilled upon these green savannas; no longer chattel-souls, but conscious of their strength and numbers, marching to the cane and cotton-fields by tap of drum, and guarding bridge or railway line with ready rifles, and with surer knowl-edge of the ground than ever can be gained by Northern regiments. (37)

In this passage Duganne imagines the former slaves producing wartime profits for government; later, when he encounters field hands who have organized themselves into a "labor-phalanx" (62) to cultivate their old domain, he endorses this "free labor experiment" (63) and fantasizes about giving the men tools to work the land and guns to defend it: "I do not think a just or generous share in all the products of their toil would make them less desirous of protecting this fine country from the assaults of rebels. I dare surmise that these abandoned cane and cotton-fields would thrive as well beneath the willing hands of black-skinned soldiers, armed with rifles and supplied with ploughs, as ever they could thrive under reluctant toil of black-skinned Helots, with no interest in the land they cultivate" (65).

Duganne offers these suggestions as an alternative to the Union military policy in Louisiana, which was coordinated by two Massachusetts Republican congressmen: first by General Benjamin Butler, a former factory hand who, according to David Montgomery, had been a "Negro-baiting Buchanan [Democrat] right down to secession," and later by General Nathaniel Banks, who, like Duganne, had been affiliated with the Know-Nothings before the war and who was popular with Massachusetts workingmen.[48] In 1862, Butler began to require blacks to work for wages on the sugar estates of Unionist planters; his successor, Banks, "extended this labor system throughout occupied Louisiana."[49] Banks demanded that the former slaves sign yearly labor contracts or risk being arrested for vagrancy; he also initiated a pass system and did not allow workers to leave the estates without permission.[50] To many observers, this "compulsory system of free labor" looked a lot like slavery, and debates about the meaning of emancipation and free labor increasingly threatened to divide Republicans.[51]

For his part, in early 1863, Duganne criticized the "policy of conciliating planters" (38) and the "kid-glove fingering of slavery-issues, whereby the Louisiana of General Butler is to be made the Louisiana of General Banks" (37). He repeatedly attacked Banks's vagrancy laws and labor contracts by arguing, for instance, that the "great black human Force, whose life-long strength has been expended, for a hundred years, in servile toil, is reckoned in the 'labor-contracts' only as the 'stock,' whose service is to multiply the gains of capital" (68), and by complaining that Union soldiers were used "to awe the blacks and hold them closely to the 'labor contract'; to protect the 'planter's interests,' by hunting straggling recusants, and generally to act as 'overseers' in pay of Federal treasury" (51). He concluded that the labor policy of General Banks "practically enforces thraldom worse than former slavery" (48) and worried that such a policy might impede serious attempts "to solve the mighty labor-problem of our nation's future" (68). Duganne made it clear that he hoped that the great estates would not be given back to their "traitor owners" or transferred to "perjured agents of their late proprietors" (37) or to the Northern speculators that "hover, like so many vultures, in our army's rear" (38).

But even though he attacked the Banks labor system and viewed the black workers as a producer class who deserved a just share in the products of their toil, he never went so far as to imagine transferring the land to "the hands which earned and paid for all the wide improvements." Instead, he continued to imagine reconstructed Southern labor relations in paternalist terms, with black workers "backed by wise authority" producing for the government or, at best, receiving half of what they produced. But many freedmen wanted to grow subsistence crops on land of their own rather than working on plantations and producing for the market. And according to Eric Foner, at "the outer limits of Radical Republicanism, the idea of remaking Southern society produced a plan for national action to overturn the plantation system and provide the former slaves with homesteads."[52] Pennsylvania Republican Thaddeus Stevens was probably the most passionate advocate of this view in Congress; he suggested that lands be taken from the wealthiest Southerners so that each adult freedman could be given forty acres.[53] But that was not to be. Instead, in 1865, President Johnson initiated various policies that resulted in the return of most confiscated Southern lands to their former owners, bringing an end to hopes of making the diffusion of land ownership the material and economic basis of Reconstruction. The "debate over the land issue illuminated both divisions within Radical ranks and the limits of the Radical ideology," Foner argues. "Beyond equality, in other words, lay questions of class relations crucial to the freedmen and glimpsed in debates over confiscation, but lying beyond the purview of Radical Republicanism."[54]

Of course, "beyond equality" lay questions of race relations as well. In *Black Reconstruction,* W. E. B. Du Bois observes that the two great labor movements of the mid–nineteenth century, "Labor-Free Soil and Abolition, exhibited fundamental divergence instead of becoming one great party of free labor and free land" (21–22). Du Bois identifies the post-1848 battle for the West between opponents of slavery and Southern expansionists as an important chapter in this history. From the perspective of Southern champions of slavery, he suggests, the "foray into Mexico had opened an empire, but the availability of this land was partially spoiled by the loss of California to free labor." Throughout the 1850s, and notably during the controversy over slavery extension in Kansas and Nebraska, there "was a war," Du Bois argues, "to determine how far industry in the United States should be carried on under a system where the capitalist owns not only the nation's raw material, not only the land, but also the laborer himself; or whether the laborer was

going to maintain his personal freedom, and enforce it by growing political and economic independence based on widespread ownership of
land" (29). But although members of the westward-looking "Labor-Free
Soil" movement opposed the Southern "Slave Power," Du Bois argues
that the "abolition-democracy" was "stopped and inhibited by the doctrine of race, and the West, therefore, long stood against that democracy
of industry which might have emancipated labor in the United States,
because it did not admit to that democracy the American citizen of
Negro descent" (28).

As I have argued in this chapter and in the previous one, white egalitarianism limited the emancipatory vision of even the most radical of
the reformers who hoped that the widespread diffusion of Western lands
among small producers might provide a material basis for the political
and economic independence that was threatened by Northeastern industrialization. On the one hand, the racialized conception of property
assumed by the reformers was in violent competition with other ideas
about land held by Indians in the United States and Mexico, and it
thereby helped to legitimate the dispossession of the latter even though
some of the reformers sympathized with Indians. On the other hand, a
racialized conception of free labor and ideas about black "dependency"
also impeded the formation of "one great party of free labor and free
land" during the Civil War and Reconstruction. As Du Bois suggested,
"[To] have given each one of the million Negro free families a forty-acre
freehold would have made a basis of real democracy in the United States
that might easily have transformed the modern world" (602). Instead,
such a transformation was forestalled by widespread fears, which were
also harbored by many radical Republicans, that the confiscation of
Southern plantations and the redistribution of land to the freedmen
would threaten the sanctity of private property and discourage blacks
from laboring to earn money to purchase land.[55] Although the views of
radicals such as Duganne on questions of land, labor, race, and government represented a meaningful departure from dominant responses to
those questions, the white egalitarianism that often remained at the heart
of such views prevented the emergence of a truly democratic and interracial labor and land reform movement during those years.

Du Bois's analysis conjoins three episodes that are still too rarely considered together: U.S. empire-building in Mexico and the West, the formation of white labor movements, and the battle over slavery and the
Civil War. In other words, for Du Bois, "domestic" race, labor, and
land issues in the nineteenth century are inextricable from questions of

imperialism, hemispheric relations, and international capitalism. In the next chapter, I argue that such domestic and foreign issues are also complexly entangled in the Beadle's dime novels that were published just before and during the Civil War years. Although within the fields of U.S. history and literature the antebellum period marker often leads to the isolation of the Civil War and "domestic" conflict from post-1848 issues of imperial and neoimperial expansion into "foreign" areas, I examine the connections among domestic and foreign affairs, the struggle over slavery and the Civil War, and questions of empire in the early dime novel. I conclude that Northern ideas about labor, land, and race were shaped in important ways by mid-nineteenth-century debates about internal and inter-American empire-building as well as struggles over slavery.

EIGHT

The Dime Novel,
the Civil War, and Empire

Although issues of slavery, black/white race relations, and sectional division are central to Duganne's Civil War memoir, they hover ominously in the background of his two dime novel "Mexico Westerns." In the previous chapter, I suggested that Duganne's representations of peonage and the Mexican hacienda in *The Peon Prince* implicitly and explicitly reference domestic debates over slavery extension and over free and unfree labor. In *Putnam Pomfret's Ward,* which was published in October of 1861 and which is set during the U.S.-Mexican War, Duganne also takes up questions of empire, slavery, and the relationship between North and South, though he addresses some of these issues in muted and displaced ways. In this novel's opening, Charles Glinton, a young man from New Orleans, kills himself because he has just lost all of his money in a Mexican gambling den. The Yankee Putnam Pomfret arrives at the scene shortly after the suicide and decides to become involved in the case when he discovers that Glinton was a countryman. Glinton turns out to be the son of a Mexican woman and a New Orleans merchant who had worked as "a consignee of the Mexican and Indian traders."[1] After both of his parents died suddenly in New Orleans, young Glinton had been consumed by "an earnest desire to behold Mexico," his mother's "native land" (44), and so he had persuaded his sister, Teresa, to accompany him there. Although the Yankee Pomfret had never met the Southerner Glinton, when he learns that Glinton's sister is still in Mexico, he resolves to protect his "countrywoman" and to see her safely back to the United States.

Teresa is not entirely alone, however, for two slaves, Lucille and Hannibal, had also traveled to Mexico with the Glintons. In spite of Duganne's harsh criticisms of slavery in *Camps and Prisons,* in this novel the slaves are depicted as comical minor characters who are loyal and willing servants. And Duganne also presents a softened picture of the Southern slaveholder: when the Yankee itemizes Teresa's assets, he does not count the slaves as property, for "had they not been already emancipated by the Mexican laws," he knew they "would never be disposed of by their gentle mistress" (45). Nonetheless, even though Lucille and Hannibal have been freed by Mexican law, they happily accompany the Yankee and Teresa back to the United States and back into slavery.

By trying to minimize the significance of the sectional conflict over slavery and by emphasizing the common bonds of nationalism, Duganne, it could be argued, attempted to transcend or displace the actual division between North and South that culminated in the Civil War. In other words, the foreign setting and the focus on empire in this novel could be said to fortify, by contrast, a Unionist sentiment that overrides sectional differences. Duganne's representations of ludicrously happy slaves reinforce such an interpretation, as does the Yankee's intensely patriotic response to "the claim which he recognized as sacred above all things—the kindred of country recognized in a strange land" (21). Although this interpretation explains much that is at stake in the novel, however, other aspects of the plot underline the differences between Yankees and Southerners. The Southerner Charles Glinton is, after all, identified as closely with Mexico as with the United States, for his mother was Mexican and he is possessed by an intense desire to travel southward to Mexico, though this visit proves to be his downfall. Once he arrives, he is easily seduced into a life of dissipation and gambling—vices that are strongly associated in this narrative with a disturbingly foreign Mexico, which is represented as a space of lawlessness and reckless passions. So Duganne also suggests that the U.S. South is perilously close to, and perhaps already fatally entangled with, other exotic "southern" spaces such as Mexico. Duganne's anti-imperialist position on the U.S.-Mexican War was partly motivated, as we have seen, by a nativist desire to protect the nation from foreign influences, but in *Putnam Pomfret's Ward* the Southerner Glinton's Mexican mother, along with his father's inter-American commercial relations and the geographical proximity of New Orleans to Mexico, all seem to make him especially vulnerable to the "ruinous influence" (25) of Mexican gamesters. Indeed, the Mexican libertine who ultimately leads him astray turns out to be his own half-brother.

Although the first series of Beadle's dime novels issued in the early 1860s overlapped with the Civil War, Bill Brown suggests that the dime novel typically avoids references to that conflict and to the issue of slavery; instead, it projects "a unifying story of the West in the midst of the nation's actual North/South divide" and thereby effectively suppresses "racial tension and social crisis."[2] According to Brown, "the dime novel makes visible the ways in which the narration of the West aestheticizes the genocidal foundation of the nation, turning conquest into a literary enterprise that screens out other violent episodes in the nation's history."[3] In this chapter I will agree that dime novel authors often try to unify their white audience by constructing demonized representations of Indians, but I shall also argue that the North/South divide, the question of slavery, and black/white racial tensions are not entirely screened out in these novels; they often resurface, as they do in *Putnam Pomfret's Ward,* even as dime novel authors struggle to manage and contain them. And in some dime novels these issues are central. Metta Victor's *Maum Guinea* (1861), for instance, which was issued as a special Beadle double number, focused on slavery and Louisiana plantation life. According to legend, Lincoln compared it to *Uncle Tom's Cabin,* and it was reprinted and widely circulated in England, where it was said to have "had a powerful influence in aid of the Union cause at a time when a large part of the people of that country favored the recognition of the independence of the Southern Confederacy."[4] Victor also authored *The Unionist's Daughter: A Tale of the Rebellion in Tennessee* (1862), another double number that addressed near-contemporaneous events, in this case the violence directed at Unionists in Tennessee in the second half of 1861 and the winter of 1862, as well as the conflicts among slaves, secessionists, and Unionists that followed. And N. C. Iron, a local historian, wrote *The Two Guards* (1863), a novel about a slave who escapes from a New Orleans plantation and tries to build a free home in the Illinois wilderness. Along with heavy doses of romantic racialism, *The Two Guards* also includes a harsh representation of the Middle Passage, critical comments about the persistence of the illegal international slave trade in the Americas, and scathing depictions of Southern slaveholders. But even when early dime novels are not centrally about the North/South divide and the question of slavery, these issues sometimes emerge, often in displaced forms, to shape the plots of many of the novels.

They often resurface, moreover, within plots that are also about empire. And yet, many of these dime novels, which focus on an array of imperial encounters, call into question the explanatory power of the

Figure 12. "Caesar and Leo" illustration from N. C. Iron's
The Two Guards. (Special Collections and University
Archives, Rutgers University Libraries)

East/West axis as a heading under which to classify dime novels about
empire. For not only does the considerable significance of stories about
nineteenth-century Indian wars threaten to disappear within such a ca-
pacious construction of a U.S. West that effectively suppresses racial tension, but so also do the racial and imperial conflicts in dime novels about
the U.S.-Mexican borderlands, Mexico, the Caribbean, and Latin America. Few novels are set during the U.S.-Mexican War itself, but several
take place during the years of the Spanish conquest, and a massive number deal with disputes in the borderlands, especially Texas. Others are set
in nineteenth-century Mexico or South America, while still others focus

on Cuba and the Caribbean.[5] Although dime novels typically strive, as Brown argues, to reduce the historical and the social to the personal, racial conflicts and inter-American economic, political, and military relations ground the novels' very attempts to condense and manage such historical and social complexities. In order to address these complexities, however, we need to think about multiple racial formations and to place the U.S. "West" in a hemispheric frame.

Novels, for instance, that are set in the U.S.-Mexican borderlands often address race relations among white U.S. Americans, Indians, and people of Mexican origin as well as the history of international geopolitical conflict in that region, even as they try to legitimate U.S. control of the area. Rather than viewing these stories as simply internal to the U.S. "West," we might instead read them as discursive weapons in an ongoing battle to subsume incidents of border warfare, which suggest a different North/South axis—that of the Americas—within a linear national narrative.[6] Notably, John Emerald's *Cortina, the Scourge* (1872) retells the story of Juan Nepomuceno Cortina, the hero of numerous border ballads, who in 1859 defended a ranchero from abuse at the hands of Texas marshal Bob Shears. After shooting Shears in self-defense, Cortina retreated to his ranch; when attempted murder charges were filed against him, he and his supporters took over Brownsville, Texas, and held it for six months. According to historian David Montejano, during the series of conflicts that became known as the Cortina Wars, "Cortina defeated the Brownsville Rifles and Tobin's Rangers from San Antonio, maintaining control of the region until the U.S. army sent troops in December 1859," whereupon Cortina escaped across the border.[7] But before leaving for Mexico, he issued several proclamations to explain his actions, including one that set forth plans for a Texas secret society devoted to "the improvement of the unhappy condition of those Mexicans resident therein." This proclamation also included the following appeal:

> Mexicans! When the State of Texas began to receive the new organization which its sovereignty required as an integrant part of the Union, flocks of vampires, in the guise of men, came and scattered themselves in the settlements, without any capital except the corrupt heart and the most perverse intentions. Some, brimful of laws, pledged to us their protection against the attacks of the rest; others assembled in shadowy councils, attempted and excited the robbery and burning of the houses of our relatives on the other side of the river Bravo; while others, to the abusing of our unlimited confidence, when we intrusted them with our [land] titles, which secured the future of our families, refused to return them under false and frivolous pretexts; all, in

short, with a smile on their faces, giving the lie to that which their black en-
trails were meditating. Many of you have been robbed of your property, in-
carcerated, chased, murdered, and hunted like wild beasts, because your labor
was fruitful and because your industry excited the vile avarice which led them.
A voice infernal said, from the bottom of their soul, "kill them; the greater
will be our gain!" Ah! this does not finish the sketch of your situation.[8]

In his appeal, Cortina underlined as the cause of his rebellion the attacks
on the property and persons of Mexican Texans, which dramatically increased in the years following the Texas Revolution and the war between
the United States and Mexico. Montejano suggests that disbanded soldiers participated in raids on Mexican settlements, and the combination
of terror and legal machinations aimed at transferring land to the new-
comers caused many Texans of Mexican origin to flee the state, though
some elite Mexican Texans, especially those who had formed alliances
with Anglos, were able to hold on to their land.[9] But in the context of
the increasing dispossession of Mexican Texans and the pervasive climate of racial terror, Cortina's revolt became an important symbol for
people of Mexican origin of resistance to Anglo encroachments and to
the use of law and violence as tools for the subjugation of a people.

Emerald's *Cortina the Scourge* hardly does justice to this social bandit, but the novel does register the racial tensions and social crises that
scarred south Texas during these years. The opening paragraphs of the
story remind the reader that in 1859, Cortina, "a Mexican guerrilla, with
a band of Mexican adventurers, held possession of all that part of Texas
extending from the Rio Grande to the Nueces; and from the mouth of
the Rio Grande to Roma."[10] At the outset, Cortina is blamed for levy-
ing taxes upon the people, raiding, and, more ambiguously, displaying
"such desperate courage that the interior of the State of Texas became
alarmed" (10). After he kidnaps an Anglo girl, Mary Barton, the U.S.
heroes, who are positioned as the defenders of womanhood, pursue
Cortina and his gang. For the most part, the national and racial antagonisms that drive the plot are condensed and recast as a narrative about
gender and sexuality, where Anglos struggle to save the women who are
threatened by the Mexicans. An important subplot of the novel involves
the girlfriend of one of the white heroes, who had mysteriously disap-
peared years ago. It turns out that she had been seduced by a Mexican
who became a member of Cortina's gang, whereupon she disguised herself as a man and joined the band as well. This disguise enables some intense proto-lesbian scenes, complete with "impassioned, vehement
kisses" (91), between the disguised sweetheart and Cortina's daughter,

who doesn't know that she is a woman. And as the narrative increasingly focuses on the domestic life of Cortina and his associates, we also witness some other interesting reversals. When Mary Barton calls Cortina an outlaw, for instance, his daughter replies that he is not a criminal but a general who "is waging a war against the people who despoiled Mexico of her lands, killed her people and made her pay tribute to their treasury" (17). And as Cortina plans a "revolution of the Mexican states along the border" (54), he is represented, with some ambivalence, not as the agent of meaningless and sadistic violence but rather as a rebel with a cause, who plans to avenge Anglo crimes and to govern in such a way that the "rich will then give to the ranchero and the hauler of water" (74). Although in the conclusion, the cross-dresser is killed, the insurgent forces are defeated, and Cortina flees across the Mexican border, the novel emphasizes the violent history of recent race wars in the borderlands even as it struggles to contain and revise that history.

Novels about the U.S.-Mexican borderlands began to proliferate especially after the Civil War, when several authors started to produce stories about gold seekers in California and New Mexico, outlaws, U.S. traders in Mexico, the Alamo, the U.S.-Mexican War, Indian fighting in the Mexico-Texas border region, and a host of other topics. But issues of empire were central to the dime novel from the beginning, and during the Civil War years, questions of imperial expansion were difficult to separate from debates over slavery and Southern secession. In chapter 6, I suggested that although during the late 1840s Northern Democrats generally endorsed empire-building, after the debates over the extension of slavery and the Kansas-Nebraska Act of 1854, many Northerners viewed imperial expansion into Mexico, the Caribbean, and Nicaragua as a malign and specifically Southern project that threatened to extend the "Southern" boundaries of slavery. A split occurred in many popular representations of empire-building during the Civil War years: from a Northern Republican perspective, the "westward" movement of white settlers at the expense of Indians and people of Mexican origin was frequently viewed, especially in novels written by men, as a natural and preordained, if violent, process that confirmed free labor and white egalitarian ideals, while a "bad" imperialism was increasingly identified with the South and the project of "southward" expansion. In the rest of this chapter, I focus on three different visions of empire in Beadle's dime novels that were published during the early 1860s: first, representations of the U.S.-Dakota War of 1862 in Edward Ellis's 1864 novels *Indian Jim* and *The Hunter's Escape;* second, representations of race, land, and labor in several novels about the borderlands written by white women; and third, two novels that focus on empire in the "South," Metta Victor's *The Unionist's Daughter* (1862) and Mary Denison's *The Prisoner of La Vintresse* (1860). Instead of positioning the Indian Wars scenario as the ur-paradigm for other stories of empire in the early 1860s, I shall focus on their divergence: how Indian wars were recast as internal, domestic struggles, while "southward" expansion was identified by many Northerners during these years with imperialism as such. I also suggest that many white women writers of dime novels, as well as some of the men, emphasized a "middling" version of white egalitarianism: one that pulled back from a more radical leveling of social distinctions among whites in order to valorize a "middle" position defined in opposition to the idle luxury of foreign, slaveholding "aristocrats" as well as the passionate excesses of the lower classes.

IMPERIAL WHITE MANHOOD
AND THE U.S.-DAKOTA WAR (1862)

Although most scholars of the dime novel Western have suggested that its main focus was on conflicts between Indians and whites, few have registered how recent or even current—how "live"—many of these conflicts were. This may follow from the widely accepted premise that the earliest dime novels tell, in Brown's words, "a story of America's past," emphasizing in particular the colonial and postrevolutionary eras.[11] But although it is true that many dime novels feature conflicts that are historically remote, such as King Philip's War and other colonial-era encounters, many other narratives deal with much more recent events, such as the Seminole wars and Black Hawk's War; ongoing conflicts with Comanches and Apaches on the border between the United States and Mexico; and the uprisings of Dakota Indians in Minnesota in 1862, to name just a few examples. The claim that the dime novel projects a unifying story of the West in the midst of the nation's actual North/South divide elides the extent to which resistance on the part of various Indian tribes to the encroachments of white settlers persisted throughout the nineteenth century. The pervasiveness of this opposition to U.S. expansion reinforced an East/West divide that followed the movement of the frontier or borderlands, which surely helps to account for the intense and repeated efforts made by early dime novel authors to narrate, redescribe, or otherwise justify the dispossession and violent displacement of the natives.

Within two years of the war fought against the Dakota Indians in Minnesota, for instance, three dime novels were written about it, including Edward S. Ellis's *Indian Jim: A Tale of the Minnesota Massacre* (1864) and *The Hunter's Escape: A Tale of the North West in 1862* (1864), as well as Lieutenant-Colonel Hazleton's *The Silver Bugle; or, The Indian Maiden of St. Croix* (1864). The U.S.-Dakota War, which broke out three months after the Homestead Act was passed and just a few days before the Union army lost the second battle of Bull Run, was provoked by a host of Indian grievances: unpopular treaties through which most of the Dakota lands were transferred to the United States, late annuity payments, traders' exploitative practices, and whites' efforts to turn Indians into Christian farmers. Legal scholar Carol Chomsky suggests that although at one time the Dakota had inhabited large parts of the upper Midwest, between 1805 and 1858 most of their land had been ceded to the United States in exchange for annual cash payments, and by 1862 they retained "only a narrow strip of land—about one hundred twenty miles long and ten miles wide—along the Minnesota River in the southwestern part of Minnesota."[12]

The Dakota were split into factions: while about a quarter of the seven thousand Dakota had tried farming, wore Euro-American-style clothing, and had converted to Christianity, many of those who would make up the "war party" continued to try to live by hunting and resisted the adoption of white ideas about land, labor, clothing, and religion. By the 1860s, however, game became harder to find, in part because the Dakota were confined to such a small area. More and more settlers poured into the region, especially after Minnesota became a state in 1858, and they fenced off land and put further pressure on resources. Meanwhile, because of these pressures, the Dakota increasingly relied on government payments, which were frequently late. To make matters worse, "Indian agents as early as 1860 had adopted the practice of handing out annuity money and food only to Indians who showed some inclination to become farmers," and they also paid off traders for inflated claims of Indian debt before dividing what was left over among the Indians.[13] When in August of 1862, after a poor harvest that threatened many with starvation, Indians inquired about late annuity payments and asked traders for credit, trader Andrew J. Myrick replied, "So far as I am concerned, if they are hungry, let them eat grass."[14] Then, on 17 August, after a quarrel, four Indian hunters killed several white settlers near Acton. Soon thereafter a war party composed of the members of a hunters' lodge declared war on the whites, and in the next six weeks almost five hundred settlers were killed by the Indians. But the Dakotas failed to take the strongholds of Fort Ridgely and New Ulm; by mid-September an army of more than a thousand led by Colonel Henry H. Sibley arrived in the region; and by 26 September the fighting was over.[15]

Agents of the state immediately sought retribution. A military court tried almost 400 Indians, and 303 were judged guilty of participating in the uprising and sentenced to be hanged. When President Lincoln reviewed the trial transcripts, however, he decided that the available evidence justified hanging in thirty-nine cases. As a result, on 26 December at Mankato, Minnesota, thirty-eight men were hanged (one man was given a reprieve) in what was, according to Chomsky, "the largest mass execution in American history."[16] Chomsky reviews legal cases to support her argument that "the Dakota were a sovereign nation at war with the United States, and the men who fought the war were entitled to be treated as legitimate belligerents." Not surprisingly, however, the representatives of the state of Minnesota and the federal government didn't see it that way. Instead, the whites' tendency to view Indians as children, wards, and dependents—as people who were "other" and yet somehow internal to the white nation, as is suggested by Chief Justice Marshall's designation of them as "domestic dependent nations"—supported the decision to try the defendants for the civilian crimes of murder, rape, and robbery instead of viewing them as legitimate belligerents and therefore asking if they had broken "the customary rules of warfare."[17] What should rightfully have been understood as an international conflict was instead legally constructed as multiple conflicts between the state and individual subjects within it who had broken its laws.

When New Jersey schoolteacher Edward Ellis took up the subject of the U.S.-Dakota War in two dime novels published in 1864, he had already become famous as perhaps Beadle's most successful author. Ellis was promoted by the firm in an advertisement as "the best delineator of Border and Indian life now writing for the press," and his *Seth Jones; or, The Captives of the Frontier* (1860), which the ad bragged had "created a great sensation upon its first appearance," eventually sold almost 600,000 copies, in part because of an innovative advertising campaign.[18] Orville Victor, a Beadle's editor, once called it the perfect dime novel, and according to Christine Bold it established "the story of male heroism" as "the dominant dime novel formula."[19] In *Seth Jones*, male heroism is defined by white egalitarianism and Indian killing. Jones is a New Hampshire Yankee who encounters a pioneer named Alfred Haverland and his family in the borderlands of western New York sometime during the late eighteenth century. When Indians kidnap Haverland's daughter, Ina, what follows is a series of capture-and-rescue plots in which white "stratagem" and "wit" are pitted against the bodily prowess and fighting skills of the Indian: "When the Anglo-Saxon's body is pitted against that of the North American Indian, it sometimes yields; but when his mind takes the place of contestant, it *never* loses."[20] Still, even though the Mohawks are generally represented in the style of the classic Puritan captivity narrative, as savages ruled by "devilish passions" (214), the whites have to be able to imitate the Indians in order to defeat them, at least to the extent of incorporating their knowledge of the wilderness and their military tactics. Paradoxically, it is in part this very process of incorporating certain kinds of "Indian" wilderness skills that enables a leveling of social distinctions among whites. Although it turns out that Jones is really the gentleman Eugene Morton, who chose to impersonate a "Green Mountain Boy" in order to hide his true identity, throughout most of the novel his wilderness know-how and vernacular speech allow him to pass as a lower-class type, and class distinctions for the most part recede as Ellis instead emphasizes the common white manhood of his heroes.

Indian Jim, Ellis's first novel about the U.S.-Dakota War, also features an upper-class male hero whose elite class position is offset by his whiteness and his newly discovered ability to both "imitate" and kill Indians. This story is one of the many male "maturation" stories that were featured in dime novels; typically, according to Daryl Jones, such stories marry a romance plot to a sensational story of Western adventure.[21] These kinds of novels are pedagogical stories for boys that teach lessons about the forging of white egalitarian manhood at the expense of Indian "savages." In *Indian Jim,* Adolphus Halleck, a merchant's son and artist, travels to Minnesota to sketch pictures and to visit his cousin, Marian, who is herself visiting a family of settlers. Although Halleck is of upper-class origin, it is made clear to the reader that he is not a "'snob,' nor a 'spooney,' but possessed the sterling qualities of the true gentleman."[22] But Ellis also insists that this Easterner has a lot to learn about Indians. Throughout the first half of the novel, Halleck repeatedly voices the opinion, based on his reading of literature by Cooper and Longfellow, that Indians are noble savages who, "as a race, are high-souled, brave, and chivalrous; above even ourselves, in such qualities." Almost every other white character in the novel, however, refutes this opinion. Marian counters that "they are a treacherous, merciless, repulsive people, who are no more fit to live than tigers" (11), and she marvels that "any whites can bring themselves to live in the country" (11). She admits, though, that Christian Indians who "have laid aside their savage dress, manners, and customs" are "passable beings" (15). Young Will Brainerd, a recently discharged soldier who was wounded at the first battle of Bull Run, advises Halleck that "the legends that our forefathers have brought down to us are exemplified in these same Minnesota Indians" (31); Brainerd's father, Uncle John, warns that "those Minnesota savages, when their blood was up, were demons incarnate" (47); and even gentle Maggie, the Brainerd sister with whom Halleck quickly falls in love, tells him that "I once shared your views, but it required only a short residence here to dispel them. I am afraid there is little romance in this western life of ours" (22). In order to grow up and be a (white) man, Halleck has to learn that his cousin and the Brainerds are right about Indians.

Although this novel and its companion piece, *The Hunter's Escape*, catalogue many of the Dakotas' grievances (unfair treaties, late annuity payments, poor reservation lands, the outrageous claims of the traders), and although both include representations of an exceptional "good Indian," Christian Jim, both override these details by narrating the war as a horror story that reveals the "truth" of the Indian's "fallen nature."[23] Even though the author suggests that this "nature" may possibly be redeemed by conversion to Christianity, it erupts anew whenever the Indians "relapse into their former barbarism."[24] The war itself is explained as such a relapse—as a furious "tide of passion" (98)—and the lurid representations of "ghastly, swollen" white corpses "disfigured by all manner of mutilation" (80), which Halleck and young Brainerd repeatedly stumble across, are used to reinforce this explanation. When Indians trail and eventually attack Marian and the Brainerd family, who are trying to escape, even Halleck reluctantly has to accept this darker reading of the Indian's character. Meanwhile, each time that Halleck has to face an Indian foe, he surprisingly displays the skills of a "veteran woodsman" (68) and enjoys the "contest" more than his previous views of Indians might lead one to expect. The real turning point comes in the final chapter, when a war party captures the white women and one of the Indians stabs Maggie. "Infuriated beyond all measure, by the treacherous murder he had just witnessed, Halleck discharged his revolver directly into the breast of the savage; and after he had fallen, as rapidly as he could pull the trigger, dispatched the other five into the same dark bosom of sin and crime" (97). Transformed by his trials from a defender to a killer of Indians, Halleck also, it is implied, becomes a man in the process, one with a "realistic" view of Indians as well as masculine fighting skills that prove he is no "snob" or "spooney." At the end of the novel, the "once fashionable and frivolous" (100) Halleck fulfills a promise to Maggie that he will become a missionary and dedicate his life to the elevation and improvement of the "Indian character" (89); though "he almost faints at times in his efforts to 'crucify' the flesh" (100) as he tries to fulfill this promise.

Michael Rogin has suggested that in the nineteenth century whites imagined their relations to Indians on the model of a parent-child relationship. Although liberal culture claimed to eliminate "legitimate hierarchical authority and believed that 'manly independence' offered the only proper basis for relations among men," Indians were viewed as recalcitrant children who needed the paternal assistance of whites (particularly to help them break their communal ties to the land) in order to grow up.[25] "Relations with the Indians," according to Rogin, "permitted that domination over men forbidden but longed for in liberal society."[26] In *Indian Jim*, Adolphus Halleck becomes a (white) man first by killing and then by becoming a sort of missionary "father" to Indians. Indians are also aligned with the flesh that he has to crucify and the passions that he has to master, and they are thereby imagined as an interior part of the white male self, a part that must be controlled before adulthood can be attained. In both of these ways, whether Indians are figured as childish, dependent wards or as interior parts of a white male self, their status as members of a sovereign nation is ignored and erased.

Among white Northerners, then, the U.S.-Dakota War was widely understood as an internal conflict rather than an international one. This makes for an interesting comparison, for *Indian Jim* also contains several references to that other famous internal struggle that was taking place at the same time—that is, the Civil War. I have already suggested that Will Brainerd, the hardy young white settler, has just returned from that other theater of war when the novel opens. Although he was almost killed by Confederate soldiers at the first battle of Bull Run and has barely recovered from his wounds, he soon has to face another enemy—the Dakota Indians—in what he has come to think of as his home territory. "How sad it is," he remarks to Halleck after the Indians destroy the family homestead, "that, when we have met with such severe reverses in the South, we should now have this blow added also" (72). When soldiers wearing Union uniforms show up toward the end to help save the day—though they can't save Maggie—it soon becomes clear that they happened to be in Minnesota because they were collecting recruits to fight in the Civil War. What is more, when the captain decides to help Brainerd and Halleck hunt the Indians, he enlists the aid of Indian Jim, for he reasons that when we "wanted to hunt secesh or guerrillas down in Virginia, we managed to get hold of some of their contrabands to lead us to their holes. So, if we want to hunt red-skins, we must take a red-skin to guide us" (95). If this chain of reasoning suggests that secession-ists, contrabands, and "red-skins" are in some ways interchangeable, however, the paternalistic language of guardianship and the Christian rhetoric of mission that pervade these dime novels figure Indians as chil-dren and wards and align them with the body and the passions rather than according them either the status of renegade citizens or legitimate foreign belligerents.

WHITE WOMEN WRITERS AND THE BORDERLANDS

Although the story of white male heroism defined by imitating, killing, or becoming a father to Indians became an influential dime novel formula, it was not, as Christine Bold reminds us, the only one. Ann Stephens, one of the most popular female authors of the period, wrote the first dime novel, *Malaeska; The Indian Wife of the White Hunter,* a "woman-centered frontier narrative," as Bold puts it, which is set in colonial New York and which is about an Indian woman and the tragic fate of the child she has with a white man whom she marries but who dies soon thereafter.[27] Stephens, the daughter of a junior partner in a Connecticut woolen mill, was already very famous in 1860 when Beadle and Company paid her $250 for a revised and expanded version of the novel, which had previ-ously been published in 1839 in *The Ladies' Companion,* a magazine that she had also edited.[28] By choosing her novel as their first, Beadle and Company courted a certain respectability, despite the sensational subject matter, style, and emotional pitch of many of their offerings. A publisher's notice that appeared at the beginning of the first edition of *Malaeska* announced that the "novel chosen to begin the list, is a proof of the high standard which the publishers have adapted. It is one of the best stories ever written by a lady universally acknowledged to be the most brilliant authoress of America, and cannot fail to insure the success of the series, and amply sustain the reputation of the writer."[29]

Stephens went on to write several dime novels for the firm. *Myra: The Child of Adoption* (1860), the third dime novel published by Beadle, was based on the life of New Orleans heiress Myra Clark. Much of the novel takes place in Louisiana, but Stephens does not use that setting as an opportunity to criticize the institution of slavery. Since Stephens had published a famous reply to Victor Hugo defending the execution of John Brown by appealing to the sanctity of law, it is not particularly surprising that in *Myra* slaves are represented as "an ignorant and degraded class" and that one slave woman works as a spy for the white villain.[30] Three more of Stephens's novels—*Ahmo's Plot; or, The Governor's Indian Child* (1863), *Mahaska: The Indian Princess* (1863), and *The Indian Queen* (1864)—returned to the subject of Indian/white miscegenation. By setting these novels far in the Canadian past, Stephens effected a double displacement—both a temporal and a national shift—in order to address what was still a very controversial topic. When Stephens depicted more contemporaneous U.S. frontiers, as she did in two other dime novels, *Sybil Chase; or, The Valley Ranche. A Tale of California Life* (1861) and *Esther: A Story of the Oregon Trail* (1862), Indians and other nonwhites generally receded to the background and frequently occupied minor roles as servants. In *Esther,* the heroine falls for a wealthy Westerner, Claude La Clide, who has been masquerading as an Indian but who turns out to be a "white man" with an Indian grandmother. The climax occurs when La Clide is injured and is revealed to be "white": "Esther saw the white shoulder glowing from under the torn hunting shirt, and knew, with a thrill of joy, that the man whom she had taken so long for a Dakotah was of the same complexion as herself."[31] Although Stephens plays with the idea of romance between an Indian man and a white woman when La Clide is in "disguise," the opening premise of the novel is that Indians are a "people that have perished" (6); the denouement suggests that because Indians as a people have presumably vanished, a small amount of Indian blood can now safely be absorbed into whiteness.

On the other hand, in *Sybil Chase,* the "savage" frontier threatens to racialize the white heroine. Before moving to California, Sybil had fallen in love with the fiancé of her best friend and benefactor, and in a fit of pique wedded a gambler, Philip Yates, after the friend and her fiancé married in Cuba. But Yates turns out to be a bad man who is cruel to Sybil, disdains labor, and hires others to work his gold claim. California is represented as a savage space where dark passions erupt; the men who inhabit "the El Dorado of the New World" are wild and reckless lower-class types who indulge "every species of excess."[32] Sybil herself is no paragon of virtue, for she helps her gambler husband rob and cheat travelers of their wealth. Although there are no *Californios*—Californians of Mexican origin—in sight, Sybil herself undergoes a kind of "Spanish transformation" at several points in the novel, when she gives in to her passionate nature: her dress takes on "a Spanish effect" (14), she sings Spanish songs to her husband, and when she and her husband are threatened by a lynch mob she escapes by masquerading as "a Spanish sailor, her delicate skin dyed of a rich, dark brown, her golden hair concealed under a slouched hat, beneath which were visible short, thick curls of raven hair" (52). At the end of the novel her husband is lynched and Sybil Chase remains in the old house at the Valley Ranche, accompanied by an Indian servant.

Although in *Sybil Chase* Stephens paints a much bleaker picture of U.S. empire-building than Ellis does in his novels, this "dark" representation of the movement of U.S. settlers also aligns Spaniards and nonwhite peoples with the passions and implies that expansion may be undesirable because it threatens to turn white people into savages. In other words, Stephens suggests that the move outside the pale of white civilization and encounters with nonwhites in the borderlands may undermine free labor and white egalitarian ideals instead of confirming them: in *Sybil Chase* the gold mines attract a brutish class of whites who are tempted to make their living by stealing and speculating rather than by laboring. Still, in several of these novels and in *Malaeska*, Stephens does expose, as Bold argues, some of the costs of U.S. expansion; while Stephens's dime novels often reinforce racial and ethnic hierarchies along several different axes—black/white, Indian/white, and "Spanish"/white—she is much less celebratory of violent U.S. empire-building than is Ellis, for instance. Bold claims that despite the popularity of *Malaeska*, however, the even more massive success of Ellis's *Seth Jones* provoked a "paradigm shift" from "a centrally female to emphatically male Western." She suggests that in "direct contrast to *Malaeska*, *Seth Jones* and its imitators articulated the West in the optimistic, patriarchal terms of Manifest Destiny then in the ascendancy in public rhetoric."[33]

But this shift did not happen immediately, and as we shall see, some of the many female writers who produced dime novels also invoked "the optimistic, patriarchal terms of Manifest Destiny" to narrate the story of westward expansion. Although in the late 1860s the number of female-authored Beadle's dime novels dropped precipitously, during the Civil War years women were clearly among the most prominent and successful writers for the firm. Female authors such as Ann Stephens, Metta Victor, and Mary Denison were repeatedly featured in full-page advertisements issued by Beadle and Company to promote dime novels. These women, along with others, wrote about one-third of the Beadle's dime novels that were published from 1860 through 1865, and a significant number of those novels focused on empire and questions of U.S. expansion.

Along with Stephens, Metta Victor and her sister, Frances Fuller Barritt Victor, were especially famous for their Western romances. During their childhood and young adulthood, the Fullers moved westward several times, first from Rome, New York, to northern Pennsylvania, then to Wooster, Ohio, and finally to Michigan. Frances Fuller Barritt Victor wrote two dime novels for Beadle and Company and then many years later she moved to California with her naval engineer husband and contributed to the *Overland Monthly.* She wrote several books on the history and geography of the Northwest, became one of Hubert Howe Bancroft's staff writers, and produced several volumes for Bancroft's histories of the Western states.[34] In Victor's *East and West; or, The Beauty of Willard's Mill* (1862) as well as *Alicia Newcome, or, The Land Claim: A Tale of the Upper Missouri* (1862), the only real conflicts about expansion arise among whites. Although in many other dime novels, such as Ellis's *Indian Jim,* the violent displacement of the natives remains a live issue, *Alicia Newcome,* however, which takes place in Nebraska, opens with the assertion that the "Indian Territory had given way before the advancing hosts of civilization, and surveyors, speculators, locaters, squatters, traders, and adventurers gathered where the red-man had been, to found new States."[35] Later, the author notes approvingly that the "quiet beauty" of the area was no longer disturbed by the "coming and going of the Indian tribes who formerly traded there; these being removed to their 'reserves' by the Government" (55). For Victor, there is apparently little to regret about this violent history of removal and displacement, for she applauds "the new civilization" which brings with it "the best elements of health, wealth, and peace" (5). The dispute over land that is at the center of this novel does not involve conflicts between Indians and white settlers, as might be expected, but instead allows for the staging of a battle over property lines between white men. Although the novel reveals a good deal of anxiety about shifting class boundaries in the new settlements of the West, the author attempts to resolve the conflict by marrying the heroine—the product of what the author calls a "mesalliance" between the daughter of a noble English family and their gardener—to a young lawyer-pioneer who seems to represent middle-class republican "America." In this way, she valorizes a "middle" position defined in opposition to both a foreign, un-American nobility and an unprincipled, dangerous lower class. Her white egalitarianism is therefore decidedly of the middling variety,

which means that, like many of the other female authors of dime novels, she tried to level differences among whites by representing the
United States as a middle-class nation that honored (free) labor and republican virtues even in the new social formations of the West.

Fuller's sister, Metta, who married Beadle's editor Orville Victor, also
wrote approvingly of westward expansion and articulated a more cau-
tious and "middling" version of egalitarianism. The first two novels that
Metta Victor wrote for Beadle, as well as several others that she produced
during her career, were Westerns: *Alice Wilde: The Raftsman's Daughter*
(1860) was the fourth dime novel issued by Beadle, and *The Backwoods'
Bride. A Romance of Squatter Life* (1860) was number ten in the series.
Like her sister, Victor generally elides struggles over land between whites
and nonwhites and instead chooses to focus on conflicts between different groups of whites. In *The Backwoods' Bride,* the main conflict is between Harry Gardiner, a prosperous and handsome land speculator from
the East, and a group of Michigan squatters who have settled on lands that
Gardiner has purchased. Although the novel repeatedly reasserts Gardiner's
"rights" over and against the "assumed rights" of the squatters, there
is a certain amount of sympathy for the latter.[36] The heroine's father, the
poor settler Enoch Carter, comes West because he hopes that with "a
few years of labor" (17) he can make a better life for her, and he rearstic-
ulates land reform rhetoric and free labor ideals when he claims the land
as his own: "God made this earth to be free to all; and whoever takes
wild land, and clears it, and cultivates it, makes it his own—he's a right
to it. What right have these men that never did a day's work in their lives,
coming along and takin' the bread out of our mouths?" (18). Still,
though the novel gives space to two competing positions on property,
Victor ultimately upholds Gardiner's claims to the land but tries to me-
diate the conflict by marrying the wealthy land speculator to the squatter's daughter Susan. At the end of the novel, Gardiner gives all of the
lands back to the squatters (who are now referred to more generously as
"farmers"), who then decide to make him their candidate for Congress.
With this unlikely and fanciful conclusion, Victor espouses a certain
white egalitarianism—by marrying the lowly Western squatter's daughter to the wealthy Easterner—but she also affirms dominant liberal conceptions of property and reduces class conflict to an improper "envious
hatred" of the rich on the part of the "lower classes" (31). Indians, on
the other hand, are nowhere in sight in this novel, and this invisibility
means that the problem of white entitlement to the land is never raised
as such.

   In these two novels Victor for the most part removes nonwhites from the Western scene and thereby avoids confronting questions about either slavery or empire. But in some of her other dime novels, such as *The Two Hunters; or, The Cañon Camp. A Romance of the Santa Fé Trail* (1865), these questions reemerge. In *The Two Hunters,* Northerner Louis Grason, the son of an old and elite, if not fabulously wealthy, Knickerbocker family goes to St. Louis on business for his father and is quickly fascinated by the "mingled southern and western grace" of the society there.[37] Much to the dismay of his family, he is especially drawn to a young woman from New Orleans, the beautiful Mariquita Mora, whose Spanish mother is rumored to be "not the 'right kind of a woman'" (18). This rumor is based partly on speculation that she murdered her husband, and partly on the fact that her house "was a perfect Spanish Inquisition, whose victims were her colored people; that she had rooms and instruments of torture, where her slaves were 'punished'—not for their faults, but at the instigation of her caprice—even unto death; that so great was the terror in which her servants held her, they dared not complain to the authorities, who would be slow to espouse their cause against that of the rich Madame, while, in the mean time, the slightest sign of revolt on their part would be followed by such tortures as awed the boldest into abject silence" (18). (In a footnote, Victor claims that this character is based on an actual New Orleans woman who escaped to Cuba after her "numberless murders" of slaves incited the horror of the public.) Nonetheless, Grason falls in love with Mariquita, even though his aunt tells him the rumors about the mother and warns him that Southern girls have "careless, indolent southern habits" (20). And Mariquita agrees to marry him, but when Grason later sees her kiss her brother Pedro, he assumes that the brother is a lover and immediately leaves town and heads southwest in order to try to forget her. One year later, however, on the road to Santa Fe, he and his Yankee companion Buell encounter Pedro and Mariquita making their way toward some gold mines that Pedro has inherited in northern Mexico. They decide to join the party in order to better defend themselves against attacks by the Comanches, who are on the warpath because, in the words of a friendly Wichita Indian, they are "very mad at the white people" and have "torn up the papers sent them by the Great Father" (40). For a while Louis masquerades as a Wichita so that Mariquita will not recognize him, and, still believing Pedro to be Mariquita's lover, he enviously notes that the "Spaniard" was "as graceful, haughty, careless a specimen of southern beauty and chivalry as the young northerner ever had beheld" (40). But ultimately the truth emerges, the two lovers are reunited, and in the end they "return to the States, where the marriage of Louis and Mariquita could most properly be consummated" (100).

Like *The Backwoods' Bride*, *The Two Hunters* reveals a good degree of anxiety about the class boundaries that were threatened by new social formations in the borderlands. The lowly Connecticut Yankee and hunter Buell is paired with the blue-blood Grason, and they are able to meet on the common ground of imperial white manhood defined by their ability to both imitate and kill Indians. But the Yankee remains ineligible for romance, whereas the blue-blood is a romantic hero who can wed the wealthy "southern" heiress despite her mother's crimes. Although Mariquita's money seems to make up for her checkered family history and to make the match between herself and Grason roughly equal, a warning about the risks of cross-class marriages is embedded in Mariquita's history: her mother was an upstart peasant girl who married above her class and then murdered her husband. If the novel reasserts certain boundaries of class and status, however, it slightly revises emergent configurations of race as they are represented in the popular literature of the period. Although "Spanishness" was quasi-racialized in Stephens's *Sybil Chase*, and although to be "Mexican" was to be nonwhite in much of the Gold Rush and war-era literature of the mid–nineteenth century, Mariquita and Pedro are repeatedly described as white even though they are of Spanish descent and are frequently referred to as "Mexicans."[38] By calling the wealthy Moras white and wedding Mariquita to an elite Easterner, Victor pulls back from the egalitarianism that characterized so many of the early dime novels—since for Victor class distinctions between whites still matter tremendously—but she slightly expands the boundaries of whiteness to include subjects who would have been viewed as marginally white or as nonwhite in many other popular texts. If, as Saxton argues, the "hard side" of white racism often accompanied egalitarian rhetoric, then the reassertion of class boundaries in *The Two Hunters* may have supported the somewhat "softened" white racism that allows for the assimilation of the wealthy Mariquita into the white European American family.[39]

This white racism is only slightly softened, however, for the Moras are welcomed into the white family in no small part through the defining contrast of Victor's harshly racialized representations of Indians. Although the Moras are marked as "southern" types several times in the first half of the novel, it is only later, when the Yankee and Grason see them on the Santa Fe trail accompanied by Indians, that they begin to call the Moras both "whites" and "Mexicans" (28). Whereas the Wichitas in this novel are represented as friendly but cowardly and degraded, the Comanches are the stereotypical bloodthirsty marauders of white popular legend. According to Morris W. Foster, for those who "read the increasingly popular newspaper and dime novel accounts of life on the western frontier, Comanches became the scourge of the southern Plains, even though many of their raiding activities were covertly supported by Anglo traders, mostly based in Texas."[40] As Foster and others have suggested, such representations of the Comanches were used to justify the occupation of their lands and the deployment of military force in the borderlands. But these representations "masked the integral redistributive role that Comanches played in the political economy of the Great Plains and the American Southwest among various Euro-American interests during the eighteenth and nineteenth centuries."[41] Victor's novel, like many of the popular representations in this period, elides the Comanche-as-trader in order to isolate the image of the Comanche-as-raider that was often invoked to unify the white nation. Nor does the novel have anything to say about the federal efforts, beginning in the 1850s, to move Comanches north of the Red River in response to the persistent encroachments of white settlers and to confine them to reservations. Instead, Victor constructs the Comanches as a savage people outside of history, against whom a whiteness can be defined that embraces the lower-class Connecticut Yankee, the Knickerbocker whose family "associations were of the best" (15), and the rich creole Moras.

If Victor tries to eviscerate the recent history of imperial, international, and interracial rivalries and warfare in the borderlands, however, traces of those conflicts resurface in the novel. The very focus on the Southwestern transfrontera contact zone of the Santa Fe trail already brings into view, although from a skewed perspective, a space that exceeds the boundaries of the nation-state, one where U.S. whites, Mexicans, creoles, and different groups of Indians mingle and fight. In the nineteenth century the Comanche ranged across national boundary lines, raiding and trading in Texas, New Mexico, and in the Great Plains, as well as northern Mexico; the Comanchería did not respect, though it often took advantage of, the international border between Mexico and the United States.[42] And although it is unclear exactly when the novel takes place, when the Moras and the two white hunters travel together on the Santa Fe trail they are described as being outside the space of the U.S. nation, for Mariquita and Grason must return to the States so their marriage can be properly consummated. This could reference New Mexico's long post-1848 status as a territory, or it could indicate a pre-1848 time frame,

when the region was still a part of northern Mexico. Finally, New Orleans, the home of the Moras, is also a site that recalls multiple, overlapping national-imperial histories, although in this novel the Spanish presence there stands in for all the rest. In all of these ways, *The Two Hunters*
alludes to an international and inter-American context that cannot be adequately contained within a linear, "East/West" national narrative.

The novel also addresses the North/South sectional divide and the
battle over slavery, though the "South" takes on a variety of different
meanings in this text. The Moras are "southerners" in part because they
are from New Orleans, which is part of the Southern United States. But
they are also "southerners" because they are of Spanish, and therefore
of Southern European, descent. By drawing on the Black Legend—
Mariquita's mother is a slaveholder whose treatment of slaves is compared to the Spanish Inquisition—Victor is able to blame the horrors of
slavery on a "foreign" class of Southerners: it is also significant that
Pedro inherits from his Spanish father not only New Mexican gold mines
but also a Louisiana sugar plantation. At various times, though, the
Moras are associated not only with Spain and New Orleans but also
with Santa Fe and Mexico; they are called "Spaniards," "southerners,"
and "Mexicans," and those terms all become jumbled together in the
novel. This blurriness corresponds in part, I would argue, to Northern
fears, especially in the late 1850s and at the beginning of the Civil War,
of Southern expansion "southward" into the Caribbean, Mexico, and
Central America: everything "south" of the U.S. North was therefore,
from a Northern perspective, potentially part of a southern slave empire,
one that was also strongly identified by many Northerners with the history of Spanish imperialism in the Americas. But by 1865, the year that
The Two Hunters was published, Victor was apparently ready to wel-
come the "South" back into the national family, despite its history of
slavery and what is here represented as its almost foreign status: the marriage between the "northerner" Grason and the "southerner" Mariquita
is certainly suggestive of such a reconciliation.

THE NORTHERN NIGHTMARE OF A SOUTHERN EMPIRE

If in 1865 Victor was willing to imagine the reconciliation of North
and "South," however, just a few years earlier she emphasized the differences between sections by appealing to a nightmarish vision of the
South as an empire. In Victor's 1862 novel *The Unionist's Daughter:
A Tale of the Rebellion in Tennessee*, Eleanor Beaufort, the daughter of

a Tennessee plantation owner who remains loyal to the Union during the Civil War, shares his suffering when their neighbors and other Southern secessionists begin to persecute him. Although Eleanor has become engaged to their neighbor's son, Sinclair Le Vert, the elder Le Vert takes a leading role in the chain of events that leads to Walter Beaufort's imprisonment, escape, and eventual death at the hands of Confederate guerrillas, and he ultimately receives the largest share of Beaufort's confiscated estates. When near the beginning Mr. Le Vert visits Eleanor to try to persuade her to use her influence with her father in behalf of the secessionist cause, he tries to sway her by invoking a vision of "the magnificent promise of a Southern empire.... Glory will cover those who are first and foremost in achieving her empire. There is no telling what brilliant place your beauty and position may achieve for *you* in those elegant courts which *are to be*."[43] It turns out that Le Vert is a leader of the Knights of the Golden Circle, a secret society that actually existed in the South and that was organized in 1854 or 1855 in order to promote the project of a Southern slave empire that would include the U.S. South, Cuba, the West Indies, Mexico, Central America, and parts of South America.[44] Eventually this group was absorbed into the secessionist movement, but as Robert E. May suggests, this Southern dream of empire "was one of the first casualties of the Civil War."[45] Although early on many Southern leaders championed such an imperial project, once the war started pressures on resources and fears of antagonizing Europe quickly silenced the calls for empire. Still, in *The Unionist's Daughter* Victor's Southern villains often harbor such imperial ambitions. Another of Mr. Beaufort's persecutors argues that the "time has passed when republican sentiments can live at the South; we will be gentlemen and aristocrats, and rule our slaves as we please" (79). And a guerrilla leader who kidnaps Eleanor is characterized as "a reckless adventurer who had been one of Walker's right-hand men in his unlawful invasions, and who had taken advantage of the distracted condition of Tennessee to continue his old pursuits" (133).

By mentioning William Walker, who led several filibustering expeditions into Mexico and Central America and who seized control of Nicaragua from 1855 through early 1857 before being shot in Honduras in the fall of 1860, Victor alludes to a figure who had become an important symbol of the sectional divide between the South and the North on the question of imperial expansion southward.[46] Earlier in his life Walker had been a Free Soiler, but during his embattled Nicaraguan presidency he appealed to the U.S. South for support by reintroducing slavery in Nicaragua. In his memoir *The War in Nicaragua* (1860), Walker suggested that the reintroduction of slavery made his regime "the champions of the Southern States of the Union in the conflict truly styled 'irrepressible' between free and slave labor."[47] In defense of this theory of an irrepressible conflict between the Southern slaveocracy and what he called "the free labor democracy of the North," Walker recalled the recent history of debates over slavery in new states such as Kansas and Nebraska: "In 1856, the South began to perceive that all territory here-after acquired by the federal government would necessarily enure to the use and benefit of free labor. The immigrant from the free labor states moves easily and readily into the new territories; and the surplus of pop-ulation being greater at the North than at the South, the majority in any new territory would certainly be from the anti-slavery region."[48] In his memoir, Walker advised those in the free states that the only way to keep free laborers in the North from attacking "capital" and perhaps fo-menting a revolution was to safeguard the institution of slavery. But he also predicted that a "conflict of force" was about to take place between North and South, and he warned that in order to "avert the invasion which threatens the South, it is necessary for her to break through the barriers which now surround her on every side, and carry the war be-tween the two forms of labor beyond her own limits."[49] Walker con-cluded that the "true field for the exertion of slavery is in tropical America; there it finds the natural seat of its empire and thither it can spread if it will but make the effort, regardless of conflicts with adverse interests."[50]

Of course by 1862, the year that *The Unionist's Daughter* was pub-lished, Walker was dead and the Southern dream of a slave empire had faded. Nonetheless, Victor not only represents Southern secessionists as villains by attributing imperial ambitions to them, but she also invokes a female version of free labor ideals in order to characterize the North/South divide. Although despite her wealth Eleanor abhors "ab-solute and vacant idleness" (25), Marcia, the daughter of the imperial-ist Le Vert, is "magnificently indolent"; her "only idea of labor was that it made a slave of a human being" (25), and her ideas about politics are summed up by her horror that "Lincoln has split wood with his own hands; *mon ami,* just think what his wife must be!" (26). Although by birth Eleanor and her father belong to the "wealthy classes" who wel-come secession, fantasize about empire, and disdain labor, they eventu-ally join forces with the "party of the middle classes, mountaineers, and small farmers" (25) who support the Union. And if the broken engagement between Eleanor and the younger Le Vert represents the irrepressible conflict between Unionism and Southern secessionism, the romance between Eleanor and Captain Beverly Bell, a Tennessee Unionist military hero, signals her conversion to the Northern cause. Although Eleanor is "an aristocrat" and the daughter of a cotton planter while Bell's father is "only a Methodist parson," and although if "she were in her own home" he "could not even speak with her as an equal" (114), ultimately they marry in spite of Bell's reservations about the class disparity between them, as well as the fact that he has lost an arm fighting for the North. It is implied, moreover, that Eleanor has both learned and gained from her class "fall." When she meets the young Le Vert again toward the end of the novel, she is "astonished at her own mental growth since the time when she had thought this man her equal" (186). And in the conclusion, Eleanor goes to work as a music teacher in a female school in order to send her new husband to law school. Although she is often tired and discouraged, "she would not sacrifice the principles which have shed such luster upon her beauty and youth for a place beside Mrs. Jefferson Davis in that imaginary court which that lady has held in fancy for some time past" (214). In other words, Northern free labor and white egalitarian principles win out over the imperial and aristocratic values that Victor ascribes to the Southern Confederates.

While this white egalitarianism is of the "softer" kind that Saxton identifies with the "whiggish core" of the Republican Party—which means both that it is softer on racial questions and also that its egalitarianism is more muted than that espoused by Republicanism's Free Soil constituency—racial hierarchies are still fundamental to Victor's vision.[51] Even though Beaufort refuses to endorse the secessionist break with the Union, Eleanor repeatedly insists that her father is a "consistent and conscientious slaveholder" (17), and Pompey, a heroic and unbelievably loyal slave, even feels insulted when neighbors call Beaufort an abolitionist. Victor includes one brief scene in which Pompey and his wife hope that they will soon be delivered from bondage, but throughout much of the novel, Pompey seems more concerned for the welfare of the Beauforts than for that of his own family. At the end he follows Captain Bell and Eleanor to Cincinnati, where he "clings to them; does the rough work of the little household, the marketing, etc. and a good day's work as a blacksmith steadily besides" (214)—and even wants to give them his wages, though Eleanor tells him to save the money so that his family can come to join him in the North. So although *The Unionist's Daughter* looks ahead to a postslavery world, severely hierarchical and paternalist race and labor relations are still very much in place at the end, even if they have been reconstructed. What is more, in this novel suffering white Unionists for the most part replace slaves as objects of sympathy. As the friends of the Union are persecuted, they send up the cry "How long, oh Lord, how long?" (189); when Nashville is taken by the Northern armies, they rejoice at the "liberation" of their state from "bondage" (214); and Victor demonizes the Confederates by making much of reports that they whipped Unionist white women in Tennessee. It is as though the Unionists are the slaves, and meanwhile the actual slaves disappear from view or reappear only to serve as willing support systems for whites. In this text white people even claim the affect that would have been mobilized in behalf of the slave in slave narratives and other abolitionist literature.

If questions of empire resurface in Victor's dime novel about the Civil War, in Mary Andrews Denison's *The Prisoner of La Vintresse; or, The Fortunes of a Cuban Heiress* (1860), which was published by Beadle and Company before the war broke out, questions of race and slavery provoked by the impending North/South divide shape a plot that is otherwise about filibustering and international romance in Cuba and New York. Before she started writing for Beadle, Denison had already become famous as a contributor to the Boston-based story papers the *Olive Branch* and *Gleason's Literary Companion;* as editor of the *Lady's Enterprise;* and as the author of several novels, including *Gracie Amber* (1857), which was about a working-class girl's resistance to the seduction attempts of an aristocratic libertine, and *Old Hepsy* (1858), an antislavery novel that focused on the experiences of the daughter of a white woman and a black man.[52] Born in Cambridge, Massachusetts, a center of abolitionist sentiment, Denison married the Reverend Charles Wheeler Denison, who edited the *Emancipator,* which Albert Johannsen claimed was the first antislavery journal in New York.[53] She accompanied her husband to British Guiana in 1853 when he was appointed consul general there, and that may have encouraged her to write a novel about Cuba.[54]

By making the plot of her Cuban romance, *The Prisoner of La Vintresse,* turn on the imprisonment of a U.S. American who is charged with being a spy for the filibusters, Denison alluded to a subject that had been very much in the news during the previous decade. As I suggested in chapter 5, especially after 1848 various imperial projects centered on the acquisition of Cuba. Presidents Polk and Buchanan tried to buy Cuba in 1848 and 1859; and in 1854, during Pierce's administration, foreign ministers Pierre Soulé, James Buchanan, and John Mason coauthored the

Figure 13.   Illustration from Metta Victor's *The Unionist's
Daughter.* (Yale Collection of American Literature, Beinecke
Rare Book and Manuscript Library)

Ostend Manifesto, a dispatch to Secretary of State William Marcy that
condemned the "forced and unnatural connexion between Spain and
Cuba" and asserted that "Cuba is as necessary to the North American republic as any of its present members, and that it belongs naturally to the
great family of States of which the Union is the providential nursery."[55]
That this annexationist bid, bolstered by the barely veiled threat of war,
was conjoined to a defense of slavery was made clear by the authors' claim
that they would be unworthy of their gallant forefathers if they were to
"permit Cuba to be Africanized and become a second St. Domingo, with
all its attendant horrors, to the white race, and suffer the flames to enter
to our own neighboring shores, seriously to endanger or actually to con-
sume the fair fabric of our Union."[56] According to Philip Foner, when
the gist of this document was printed in the *New York Herald,* the "public reaction was so hostile that Pierce and Marcy did not dare to give
their full support to the designs on Cuba."[57] By then, the issue of slav-

ery extension had become so divisive that this transparent attempt to bully Spain into giving up Cuba was widely perceived by many Northerners as a plot to aggrandize the Southern slave power.[58]

Although the Republican national platform for 1856 scornfully called the Ostend Manifesto a "highwayman's plea" that "would bring shame and dishonor upon any government or people that gave it their sanction," during this decade many other U.S. Americans became involved in plots to invade and "liberate" Cuba.[59] In chapter 5 we saw how the New York nativist and working-class advocate Ned Buntline endorsed filibustering and incorporated Cuban filibustering plots into *The B'hoys of New York* and *The Mysteries and Miseries of New Orleans*. Buntline's novels as well as the existing historical evidence about filibustering expeditions suggest that in the late 1840s and early 1850s they attracted large numbers of both Southerners and Northerners, especially Northerners from New York City and other Northeastern port cities.[60] One model for this convergence of largely proslavery Northerners and Southerners was the Democratic Party, which appealed to a trans-sectional coalition of voters by yoking together white egalitarianism, the preservation of slavery, and expansion; but a diverse and irreducible set of material and economic interests, such as investments in Cuban plantations, shipping, trade, and finance also motivated these often trans-sectional ventures; and ideologies of imperial white manhood certainly played no small part.[61] As the issue of "southward" expansion became more and more a sectional question rather than one of party, however, filibustering, especially with respect to Cuba, became a more overtly proslavery and distinctively Southern enterprise. In 1849 the strongly proslavery Narciso López moved the base of his ill-fated filibustering expeditions from New York City to New Orleans in order to attract more support from influential Southerners; in 1853 and 1854 former Mississippi governor and U.S.–Mexican War hero John Quitman tried to organize another invasion of Cuba; and in 1856, Walker reinstated slavery in Nicaragua and made his infamous appeal to Southern slaveholders for support.[62] Each of these notorious filibustering expeditions was given a good deal of space in the newspapers and magazines of the decade, and each, along with the intensifying intraparty splits along sectional lines, contributed to the increasingly common perception that filibustering was a Southern project.

This does not mean, however, that all Northerners opposed the acquisition of Cuba. Northern Democrats such as John O'Sullivan and Mike Walsh, for example, were embroiled in Quitman's schemes to invade Cuba in the middle of the decade, and many others continued to

support proslavery expansion despite the defections of Free Soil Democrats to the new Republican Party.[63] But many of the Northerners who
opposed filibustering and annexation still supported various forms of
neocolonial control over Cuba. Luis Martínez-Fernández suggests that
during and after the Civil War, "a new brand of U.S. expansionism
gained pre-eminence. It did not seek the absorption of large territories
and their enslaved, dark-skinned populations; rather it sought bastions
for the protection of a commercial empire and eventually the establishment of enclaves for the extraction of raw materials and cultivation of
tropical staples."[64] In the 1850s, too, many Northerners who opposed
the addition of Cuba to the Union as a slave state nonetheless advocated
a U.S. commercial empire that depended on the protection of trade
routes, military bases, and markets. As Martínez-Fernández's remarks
suggest, however, race continued to be an important consideration for
both kinds of imperialists, for if the post-1865 champions of what
LaFeber has called the New Empire generally opposed the absorption of
large territories and populations of nonwhites, earlier debates about the
annexation of Cuba also repeatedly returned not only to the question of
the extension of slavery but also to white fears of a heterogeneous population of nonwhites in Cuba.

     In her dime novel, Denison returns to the conventions of the interna-
tional romances of 1846–1848 as she builds her plots around the threat
of a forced marriage, battles over consent, and inter-American love. The
heroine, Minerva, the Cuban heiress of the subtitle, is "partly of Spanish, partly of English blood," and this legacy means that she has "inherited some English tastes and traits" that Denison means for us to admire
at the expense of the "Spanish."[65] At the outset, her fiancé, Herman
Goreham protects her "with lover-like energy" (10) as he secures a seat
for her on a boat set to sail from Havana to New York City. But then he
goes ashore to retrieve some papers almost immediately afterward and
never returns. Later, we find out that Cuban authorities have arrested
Herman after Don Carlos, the lover that Minerva had spurned, accused
him of being a tool of the filibusters. It is unclear whether there is any
basis for these rumors; while Denison uses the filibustering charge and
the Cubans' subsequent treatment of Herman as proof of Spanish
tyranny, the narrative never directly refutes the accusation either. In any
case, Herman remains a prisoner for most of the rest of the novel, which
quickly shifts to the United States to follow the story of the Cuban heiress
in New York. Once in New York, Minerva tries to elude her Spanish
uncle, the General, "one of the grandees of Cuba," and his ward, Don

Carlos, "a fiery, passionate, and extremely elegant personage...possessing an immense fortune in sugar estates and slaves" (16).

Although the General has tried to force her to marry Don Carlos, she escapes to the Northern United States only to find the "Southern" General's agents, such as the evil Senor Velasquez, everywhere on the lookout for her as she negotiates the perils of the mysterious city, worries for the first time about money, dodges would-be lovers, dons a disguise, and ultimately contacts Herman's mother and hides out at the family farm near Saratoga. Next she is kidnapped by Senor Velasquez, who takes her on a ship bound for Havana but who suddenly dies on the way there. Before dying, however, he confesses his crimes and also reveals that Herman has been imprisoned in the jail at the slave quarters of the abandoned plantation La Vintresse. When she arrives in Cuba, Minerva hurries to La Vintresse and ensures that the emaciated, nearly dead Herman is attended to by a doctor and placed on a ship bound for the United States. Then, at the end of the novel, Minerva marries Herman and goes to live on the family farm, where "the pale son and his beautiful bride, make the home an Eden" (98).

Reading this novel as a post-1848 international romance, the marriage between Goreham and the Cuban heiress, who inherits a fortune built on "houses, lands, and ships" (24), would seem to figure a more intimate relationship, perhaps even some form of political union, between the United States and Cuba. According to the pattern established by the U.S.–Mexican War romances, the Spanish General, the guardian of the heiress, who ignores questions of desire and consent, represents a tyrannical Spanish ruling class that is unfairly trying to control the wealth of Cuba. The passionate, handsome, but evil-looking Don Carlos, who resembles the rapacious villains in the sensational literature of 1848, is also clearly marked as an inappropriate mate for the heiress, which suggests that the political union between Spain and Cuba is unnatural and undesirable. On the other hand, the "manly" Herman Goreham, who is accused of being a spy for the Yankee filibusters and a "dangerous enemy" (22) to the Cuban state, inherits the place of the U.S. soldier who romances the girl in the U.S.–Mexican War era story-paper fiction. The fact that the heiress is represented as white (largely due, it seems, to her British "blood") and that she ultimately goes to live on the family farm in New York may suggest that Cuba, too, might be incorporated into the United States, despite the fears of many U.S. whites that the Spanish "race," let alone large numbers of black and mixed-race people, could not easily be assimilated.[66]

But we must also attend to the anxieties about imperial policies that structure the novel, anxieties that also frequently shape the plots of the romances of 1848. Denison sometimes suggests, for instance, that intimate contact with foreign spaces and peoples may be dangerous and enervating; the strong, protecting U.S. American (or as Denison describes him, "the self-reliant, dignified man") is quickly transformed into a "pale, bowed down captive" (38) who must himself be rescued by the Cuban heiress. Although during this period, filibustering and imperial adventure were often identified, as they were for Buntline, with the reinforcement or enhancement of U.S. masculinity, here Denison implies that contact with the foreign actually threatens to weaken U.S. manhood. When Minerva rescues Herman, he is prostrate, weak, and wasted. "Language cannot convey an idea of his extreme emaciation" (95), Denison tells us. So even though "el Americano" Herman ends up married to the Cuban heiress, it is far from clear that the novel endorses territorial expansion. Indeed, as an abolitionist, Denison would most likely have been among those who feared that the annexation of Cuba would mean the addition of another slave state to the Union. This may help to explain why the scene of Herman's rescue is figured as the liberation of a slave: he is imprisoned, after all, in the jail of the slave quarters on an abandoned plantation, and in the illustration that accompanied the novel a severed chain lies in the foreground as the captive reaches out imploringly toward his rescuers and his black captor. This inverted representation implies that foreign entanglements threaten to turn white men into slaves even as it mobilizes antislavery sympathies in behalf of white men.

The "middling" version of white egalitarianism that frequently accompanied antislavery sentiments in dime novels written by women is also evident in *The Prisoner of La Vintresse*. The evil Spanish villains in this novel are, after all, fabulously wealthy slaveowning aristocrats. Their lavish, luxurious life, which is most explicitly lampooned when they visit Saratoga, is contrasted with the "plain" rural domesticity of the Gorehams. After the Cuban general has Minerva kidnapped, Herman's father confronts him, calls him a "rascally foreigner," and boasts that "we American citizens do not allow even Spanish dons to insult us with impunity." When the General asks whether he should call his slaves to show Goreham out, Herman's father threatens to pitch him and them out of the window and adds, "You had better take care how you insult a man who is king on his own soil" (87). By contrasting a passionate, evil, foreign, slaveowning class of Spanish aristocrats with a virtuous,

Figure 14. Illustration from Mary Denison's *The Prisoner of La Vintresse; or, The Fortunes of a Cuban Heiress*. (Courtesy of the Hess Collection, University of Minnesota Libraries)

domestic, white "middle" class of rural producers, Denison may mean to suggest that the existence of slavery in Cuba makes it an undesirable acquisition. For although Minerva herself is assimilable, she is of course half English. But she is an exception in a novel that mostly represents Cubans as disturbingly foreign, not quite white enough in the case of the Spaniards, and not white at all in most other cases. Minerva's whiteness is framed, for instance, through contrasts with nonwhite Cubans such as Bandola, the "Spanish," dark-skinned stewardess on board ship, who at one point says to the heiress: "How I wish I was white, senorita, and had a lover like [Herman]" (25). (At the end, the narrator suggests that "Bandola has never left her mistress, and probably never will" [98].) If this condescending representation of Bandola is of the romantic racialist stripe, however, Denison includes a much harsher depiction of the slave Jose, "a man as black in heart as in complexion" (95), who followed the General's orders and kept Herman a prisoner in La Vintresse. In all of these ways Denison racially "darkens" Cuba in ways that echo the various antislavery but still racially phobic objections to the annexation of Cuba.

And yet, the romance and marriage between Herman and the Cuban heiress suggests that some kind of intimacy between the United States and Cuba is desirable, even if that relationship does not take the form of territorial annexation. Denison's antislavery sentiments, combined with her representation of a racially darkened Cuba, suggest that her vision of the relationship between Cuba and the United States more closely conforms to that of the Northern commercial imperialists, for whom formal annexation and political incorporation were less important than the securing of trade routes and the maintaining of U.S. economic hegemony, if not political control, of the Caribbean. But although, as Martínez-Fernández suggests, Northern commercial interests mostly accepted the continuing existence of slavery and Spanish domination of Cuba as long as "Spain kept open the avenues of trade and maintained control of the slaves," Denison is more critical of the Spanish slaveowning class in Cuba.[67] Indeed, her representation of Cuba predicts the new, post–Civil War "northern based and abolitionist" brand of expansionism that continued to seek "the establishment of new bases to protect trade routes and the region's markets" but which, according to Martínez-Fernández, "completely transformed the rules of the game in the Spanish Caribbean."[68] That this new, abolitionist form of expansionism would also extend and support international, neocolonial racial hierarchies should come as no surprise given the anxiety about racialized constructions of the foreign that pervades Denison's dime novel.

In this chapter I have argued that issues of slavery and sectional division shape many of the dime novels of the Civil War period, and I have suggested that discussions of empire-building frequently provoke a consideration of these issues. But I have also tried to demonstrate that representations of empire and of the "West" in the dime novel Western must be placed in an inter-American frame and read in terms of multiple racial formations. Many scholars, especially in Chicana/o and Latina/o Studies, are currently doing work that might help us to attend to the entanglement of the "foreign" and the "domestic" in this fiction, rather than prematurely domesticating the space of the "West." In Border Matters, José David Saldívar argues for a "remapping" of American cultural studies that would respect "the materially hybrid and often recalcitrant quality of literary and (mass) cultural forms in the extended U.S.-Mexican borderlands."[69] And in a recent article called "From Borderlands to Borders: Empires, Nation-States, and the Peoples in Between in North American History," Jeremy Adelman and Stephen Aron call for more attention to the "power politics of territorial hegemony": "Absent the inter-imperial dimension of borderlands, the cross-cultural relations that defined frontiers take on a too simple face: 'Europe' blurs into a single element, and 'Indians' merge into a common front."[70] Both of these projects invite the rethinking of models of the "West" that isolate the U.S. nation-state from other imperial, national, and cultural histories.

In a similar vein, the work of other scholars suggests that we should rethink the relationships between "South" and "West," and that we might consider the "South" not just as the U.S. South but also as a trans-border contact and conflict zone encompassing Mexico, Cuba, the Caribbean, and other parts of the old Spanish empire in Central and South America. Such a model might build on the work of Joseph Roach, who has asked us to think about New Orleans as a circum-Atlantic space that opens up onto multiple imperial histories;[71] or José Limón's suggestion that both the U.S. South and greater Mexico have served as "peripheral" and "subordinated" yet "erotically and expressively valenced symbolic order[s]" for Northern capitalist modernity;[72] or Neil Foley's work on the "old South in the southwest," which explores how in "the ethno-racial borderlands of central Texas, the South, with its dyadic racial categories, first encountered the Southwest, where whiteness fractured along class lines and Mexicans moved in to fill the racial space between whiteness and blackness."[73] All of this work makes visible the imperial and transnational power relations, the diverse histories of migration, and the multiple racial formations that shape the spaces of the "South" and the "West." And if these models aid the analysis of issues of race, labor, land, and empire in the dime novel, in my final chapter I will suggest that they can also enhance our understanding of the inter-American significance of crime literature and the police gazette in the wake of the American 1848.

PART 4

Beyond 1848

NINE

Joaquín Murrieta
and Popular Culture

The events of 1846–1848 are a shadowy but important shaping presence in Joseph Badger's 1881 *Beadle's New York Dime Library* novel *Joaquin, the Terrible: The True History of the Three Bitter Blows that Changed an Honest Man to a Merciless Demon*. One of several Badger stories about the California social bandit Joaquín Murrieta, *Joaquin, the Terrible* features a villain, Don Manuel Camplido, who had served as a Mexican army officer in the "late war" and was infamous for his "arrant cowardice on the field of battle."[1] In California, Camplido conceals his Mexican origins, takes on a new name, John Vanderslice, and runs a gambling establishment called the Wheel of Fortune. Because he is angry with Murrieta for marrying Carmela, Camplido joins forces with another Mexican villain, Raymon Salcedo, who is trying to despoil the Murrietas of their California land grant, which was given to them "long before the Americans conquered the country" (3). Camplido, Salcedo, and their accomplice Dirty Dick mercilessly persecute Carmela, Joaquin, and his brother Carlos, who are in turn defended by an Irish-American worker named John Lynch. Despite Lynch's muscular assistance, however, "three bitter blows" fall on the Murrietas. As a result of the villains' schemes, Carlos is murdered and Joaquin is stripped and whipped until blood-red welts rise on his "white back" (28). After this humiliation, Joaquin, Carmela, and Lynch leave the area and give mining a try, but ugly Americans soon appear on the scene, saying that because they defeated Mexico in the war they deserve all of the gold. One of these

Americans is Camplido in disguise, and after they beat Murrieta and rape Carmela, Joaquin is finally transformed into a "merciless demon." The narrator concludes that although he is no "apologist for crime," he firmly believes that "not one man out of a hundred, who really possessed the *spirit of a man,* would have turned out any better than he, provided they were forced to pass through the same fiery ordeal, and were as innocent of wrong as was Joaquin Murieta when the blows began to fall" (29). In other words, Murrieta's fiery ordeal in the post-1848 period explains, if it does not justify, his subsequent career as an outlaw.

In its ambivalent sympathy for the bandit Murrieta, *Joaquin, the Terrible* effectively evokes what Michael Denning calls the "short period between 1877 and 1883" when dime novel outlaws such as the James Brothers and Deadwood Dick "defied the law and got away with it, escaping the moral universe of both genteel and sensational fiction."[2] Linking these dime novels to the 1873 depression and the labor struggles of the era, Denning persuasively argues that the dime novel outlaw was "both sufficiently distant from and implicated in the battles of labor and capital to offer a figure of those battles, a figure of vengeance and heroism."[3] In what follows, I emphasize how in the lands newly acquired from Mexico, and elsewhere too, transformations in law, labor, and capitalism were inseparable from mid-nineteenth-century struggles over race and empire. This was true, first of all, because both manual labor and land ownership were racialized categories. By the 1860s in California, according to one historian, the Californios had lost the "vast majority" of their land, and by 1880 "almost half" of the Californios and an "overwhelming majority" of other people of Mexican origin worked as laborers.[4] Similarly, between 1850 and 1900 in south and west Texas, the proportion of rural Mexicans who were ranch or farm owners was roughly cut in half, falling from about one-third to 16 percent, while the proportion of manual laborers rose from about one-third to two-thirds.[5] Since the attribution of whiteness to people of Mexican origin was connected to land ownership and class, increasing rates of landlessness and manual labor among Mexicans affected ideas about their racial status. On the other hand, although access to land and a better position in the racially segmented labor market often depended on claims to whiteness, the U.S.-Mexican War had laid a foundation, as we have already seen, for racializing Mexicans as nonwhite. Second, as Alexander Saxton and others have shown, racial issues played a significant role in the new working-class institutions of the West. But Tomás Almaguer notes that in California until the early twentieth century the relatively "small numbers and initial concentration in the most undesirable sectors of the new economy" of workers of Mexican origin "effectively militated against white working-class antagonism."[6] That antagonism was instead directed most intensely at Chinese workers, who became the target of the 1882 exclusion laws that were backed by the Workingmen's Party of California, the Knights of Labor, the National Labor Union, and the American Federation of Labor.[7] During the 1870s and the 1880s, then, transformations of labor and capitalism forever changed the lives of workers in both East and West, but as much of the popular sensational literature of the period suggests, battles of labor and capital were often battles over race and empire as well. This imbrication of race, empire, labor, and capitalism supports Denning's point that "frontier myths" are more directly related to "class conflicts than is usually thought."[8]

It is easy to imagine how the Joaquín Murrieta of Badger's 1881 novel could have served as a figure of vengeance and heroism for a wide audience of readers who were experiencing wrenching shifts in formations of race, labor, and capitalism during the last third of the nineteenth century. Originally a retainer on Santa Anna's estate, later a miner, and finally an outlaw who triumphed over his persecutors because of his bodily prowess, intelligence, and general derring-do before meeting a bloody death, Badger's Murrieta was a relatively humble figure who could credibly serve as a type of the heroic workingman. The alliance between Murrieta and the Irish-American worker John Lynch, a pairing between Mexican and Irishman that should be familiar by now to readers of this book, is also notable. On the one hand, this pairing supports Denning's argument that a working-class audience may have viewed Western outlaws as figures of class conflict. Lynch could even be seen as a stand-in for such a reader, and his bond with Murrieta, forged over and against more powerful oppressors, might be understood as a muted and displaced call for an alliance of workingmen in response to the forces that subordinate them. All of the historical and still active associations between the Irish and Mexicans, on the basis of religion as well as similar experiences of nativism, colonization, and migration, could be mobilized by depictions of such an alliance.[9] But this novel also strongly suggests that part of Murrieta's broad appeal lies in his whiteness, which it emphasizes. Indeed, the bond between Lynch and Murrieta could also be seen as an alliance between marginal whites. Despite the intensified, racialized patterns of labor and land ownership that became more firmly entrenched in the West during this period, perhaps more than three decades of distance from the war as well as the relatively small proportion of Mexican workers in California at this time combined to make it possible for a Mexican to be viewed as both a marginal white and a working-class hero.

On the other hand, the racial liminality of the wealthy villain Camplido is especially threatening, precisely because he is "white" enough to pass as a non-Mexican but is still irredeemably alien and monstrous. In this revisionist scenario, the duplicitous, nonproducing Mexicans Camplido and Salcedo are to blame for Mexican land loss and for the violence of the post-1848 years. And if Murrieta can be cast as a white working-class hero in part because whites and Mexicans were not yet competitors in the labor market, representations of other Mexicans in this novel—one villain is described, for instance, as "a heavy-set, low-browed fellow in whose veins there flowed more Indian than Spanish blood" (4)—suggestively predict how U.S.–Mexican War era depictions of Mexicans as evil, treacherous nonwhites would resurface in times of crisis. This would be especially true during periods of economic depression in the twentieth century after large numbers of immigrants came from Mexico to the United States.

Since 1853, the Murrieta story has circulated in an astonishing array of popular cultural forms, including California newspapers; John Rollin Ridge's 1854 novel *The Life and Adventures of Joaquín Murieta;* crime narratives serialized in police gazettes; dime novels; twentieth-century Western fiction; U.S. television shows and films; several Spanish-language *corridos* or ballads; plays in both English and Spanish, including one written by Pablo Neruda; and revisions published in Mexico, Spain, France, and Chile.[10] In *Roaring Camp,* her excellent study of the social world of the California Gold Rush, historian Susan Lee Johnson has written eloquently about how different versions of the Murrieta story illustrate "in microcosm some of the tensions between memory and history that characterize knowing the Gold Rush itself." Although both "English- and Spanish-language accounts," she suggests, have used "bandit narratives to make intelligible the events of 1853," representations produced by Murrieta's "familial, political, and intellectual heirs"— including oral narratives collected by Frank Latta as well as a substantial body of Chicano Studies scholarship—often "call into question traditions invented to explain and justify the imposition of Anglo American dominance in the diggings."[11] In his introduction to a recent reissue of a 1905 Spanish-language novel about Murrieta written by Ireneo Paz, literary scholar Luis Leal has also examined multiple versions of the story since 1854; he has suggested that all of them can be traced back to the John Rollin Ridge novel. In my conclusion, I move backward from the Beadle's dime novels of the 1880s to the 1850s, focusing especially on the sensational Murrieta crime story published in the *California Police Gazette* of 1859, and then I shift forward to the various accounts of Murrieta produced in both English and Spanish in the 1930s, during the years of the Great Depression. I argue that a discursive, inter-American battle over the meaning of the American 1848 is waged in this popular crime literature. Although the events of 1848 shape all of these versions, even the more sympathetic English-language accounts tend to uphold the ideal of the rule of law and to reproduce racialized stereotypes of Mexican savagery and lawlessness that can be traced to the U.S.–Mexican War era. Spanish-language *corridos* produced in the first half of the twentieth century, on the other hand, challenge this ideal as well as the attribution of a natural, racialized criminality to people of Mexican origin.

In this concluding chapter, I build on the argument, advanced throughout *American Sensations,* that U.S. racial economies and class relationships were fundamentally transformed by the U.S.-Mexican War and mid-nineteenth-century U.S. empire-building. In the previous chapters, I have suggested, among other things, that popular sensational writers with ties to working-class culture also wrote extensively about Mexico, the Americas, and the West; that popular representations of Mexicans during the war contributed significantly to the racialization of people of Mexican origin as nonwhite, but that representations of a minority of elite, usually landowning, "white" Mexicans also affected ideas about race; that U.S. imperialism provoked debates about the concept of an Anglo-Saxon national identity as well as discussions of nativism and free and unfree labor; and that all of these debates were variously intertwined with ideas about gender and sexuality. In this conclusion, I want to shift the discussion to a different context; that is, to the U.S. West and to the California Gold Rush, another important event marked by the American 1848. For if the war led to the remapping of national borders, the discovery of gold in California drew miners and other workers to the region from all over the world, but especially from Mexico, Hawaii, Chile, Peru, China, Ireland, Germany, France, the Eastern United States, and Australia.[12] While these shifts affected racial classifications in general, they dramatically influenced the racialization of former Mexican nationals and the construction of a transcontinental white national identity in particular.[13] Far from serving as a safety valve for class pressures, the newly acquired land in the West remained a battlefield where race and nationalism shaped class conflicts. These conflicts, as we have seen, sometimes erupted as nativism, often pitted white workers against people of color, and were always powerfully affected by the migratory movements of people across national boundaries and by the larger fields of hemispheric and global relations.

In what follows, I trace the interdependent histories of three developments: the popularization of a fictive transcontinental white national identity; the postwar reracialization of former Mexican nationals and other Spanish-speakers; and the articulation of a disjunctive, transnational, *mexicano* cultural nationalism that both responds to and challenges developments one and two. The different versions of the Murrieta story suggest, in other words, how whiteness took hold as a unifying national and transcontinental structure of feeling and how its parameters began to shift decisively in the postwar period to include previously despised groups of Europeans and to exclude many of the newly conquered peoples in the West.[14] Although these parameters varied in different places and circumstances and although they would continue to shift in response to changing conditions, still, as I have argued in this book in a variety of contexts, popular sensational literature established many of the patterns for thinking about issues of race, labor, empire, and national identity that would remain influential long after the war, the Gold Rush, and the remapping of national boundaries had become history.

And yet, many border ballads refuse such a remapping of the territory. Insisting that he is not a stranger (*extraño*), the Murrieta who tells his story in one of these *corridos* argues that "California is part of Mexico because God wanted it that way" ("De México es California/porque Díos así lo quizo"). Such a heroic narrative of resistance may in turn perform closures of its own: the sanctification of Mexican sovereignty elides the Spanish and Mexican subjugation of indigenous peoples, and Murrieta's insistence on his status as a "native" could imply a disdain for immigrants such as the Chinese workers who are persecuted by his gang in some of the English-language versions of the story. What is more, figuring resistance to U.S. power as a paradigmatically masculine feat best accomplished by the *corrido* hero with a pistol in his hand marginalizes female agency, as many feminist critics have suggested.[15]

But if the *corridos* paradoxically try to locate a national community in transregional and transnational movements of male workers, during and after the war a good deal of popular U.S. sensational literature labors to redefine and restrict a white national identity by identifying a community of people of Mexican origin and other Spanish-speakers with a "foreign" criminality.[16] Postwar sensational crime literature, especially, continues the work of wartime representations by racializing this community as essentially alien, in an early example of what Etienne Balibar calls "the immigrant complex": the "functioning of the category of *immigration* as a substitute for the notion of race and a solvent of 'class consciousness.'" This does not mean that pseudo-biological notions of race become irrelevant, but rather that they are supplemented by "culturalist" definitions of race which suggest that the differences between national cultures are natural and insurmountable but also perpetually endangered by the transnational movements and mixings of populations.[17] Although I would dispute the claim that the category of immigration dissolves class consciousness rather than strongly shaping the latter's multiple manifestations, Balibar's theory of the immigrant complex is suggestive for an analysis of racialized criminality in the post-1848 period. To explore the ways that national cultural differences are recast as the difference between legality and illegality in the wake of the war, I will now turn to the *California Police Gazette*'s sensational account of Murrieta's scandalous crimes and border crossings.

RACE WAR CRIMES

The criminal *fait divers*, by its everyday redundancy, makes acceptable the system of judicial and political supervisions that partition society; it recounts from day to day a sort of internal battle against the faceless enemy; in this war, it constitutes the daily bulletin of alarm or victory. The crime novel, which began to develop in the broadsheet and in mass-circulation literature, assumed an apparently opposite role. Above all, its function was to show that the delinquent belonged to an entirely different world, unrelated to familiar, everyday life.... The combination of the *fait divers* and the detective novel has produced for the last hundred years or more an enormous mass of "crime stories" in which delinquency appears both as very close and quite alien, a perpetual threat to everyday life, but extremely distant in its origin and motives, both everyday and exotic in the milieu in which it takes place.... In such a formidable delinquency, coming from so alien a clime, what illegality could recognize itself?
— Michel Foucault, *Discipline and Punish*

It is easy to recognize the basic outline of the *California Police Gazette*'s version of the Murrieta story in the pattern of the typical heroic border-*corrido*. As in the classic heroic *corrido,* in *The Life of Joaquin Murieta, the Brigand Chief of California* a man with a "very mild and peaceable disposition" turns into a criminal after being violently persecuted by white Americans and the regimes of law and lawlessness they bring with them.[18] But these two types of popular crime narrative show how complex and divided the international field of popular knowledge about crime and criminality was during this period. For although *corridos* take the part of the criminal and question the justice of U.S. law, the *Police Gazette* disseminates ambivalent representations of criminals but ultimately upholds the law by striving to make its victory over criminality seem natural, inevitable, and best for the safety of the public. That is, even though both types of popular crime narrative respond to what Michel Foucault calls "the desire to know and narrate how men have been able to rise against power" and "traverse the law," *corridos* attack the legitimacy of the new forms of power and law that the *Police Gazette* ends up defending.[19] As popular crime narratives, *corridos* and the *Police Gazette* are engaged in a discursive battle not over a generalized, abstract law or power as such, but over the violent transition from Mexican to U.S. law in the postwar period.

Even the title of the *California Police Gazette,* which was apparently modeled on the more successful and long-lived *National Police Gazette,* already implies a panoptic gaze leveled statewide, pulling together diverse incidents, crimes, and historical events into a field of visibility for the eye of police power.[20] Founded in 1845, the *National Police Gazette* was itself modeled on British police gazettes and "promised to publish descriptions of criminals and accounts of crime for the avowed purpose of revealing the identities of criminals and to supplement the work of the police."[21] During the U.S.-Mexican War the *National Police Gazette* even printed the names and descriptions of deserters from the U.S. ranks, and the War Department "thereupon authorized a large subscription for distribution among the soldiers."[22]

The *California Police Gazette,* a weekly four-page journal published in San Francisco that sold for twelve and a half cents per issue, or five dollars per year, was first issued in January 1859. The Murrieta story ran from 3 September to 5 November of that year and was subsequently reissued as a pamphlet novel.[23] In the same issues of the *California Police Gazette* that contained installments of the Murrieta story, readers could find news of California prison escapes; an editorial advocating that the state take over the management of prisons, using convict labor to

Figure 15. Cover of 1859 edition of *The Life of Joaquin Murrieta, the Brigand Chief of California.* (Courtesy of the Bancroft Library, University of California)

pay their costs; a story about the capture of 218 California Indians by a detachment of volunteers; and reprints of short crime stories from newspapers across the nation about the suicide of an unemployed former soldier, about a creature with the "form of a woman" and the head and arms of a pig, and about white people sold as slaves.[24] Each week, the paper ran a long profile of one in a series of "California Thieves," ending with a description of the criminal and speculations about his current whereabouts. Another weekly feature was the "City Police Court," a long column that listed the names, crimes, and often the race or nationality of those who had appeared before the San Francisco court that week. Although these features inspired a range of responses in its readers, the paper's main business is stated succinctly in an ad for a special edition of a *Pictorial California Police Gazette,* which promised "Portraits and Lives OF ABOUT FIFTY OF THE Most Notorious Thieves, Felons and Desperadoes in the State, many of whom are now at large!" along with portraits of judges and other state officials and views of the state prisons and jails. "This Pictorial SHOULD BE In the Hands of All," the ad states, "as by it many of the ESCAPED CONVICTS and DESPERADOES NOW AT LARGE Can be detected and brought to justice. It will also serve to put RESIDENTS OF THE REMOTE PORTIONS OF THE STATE UPON THEIR GUARD when visited by them."[25] Despite its sometimes ambivalent representations of criminals such as Murrieta, then, the *California Police Gazette* ultimately tried, in Foucault's words, to make "acceptable the system of judicial and political supervisions that partition society" by framing crime stories within a popular format that was strongly identified with the state and the police and that was devoted to helping citizens detect and capture criminals.

In the territories newly acquired from Mexico, however, making the "system of judicial and political supervisions" seem natural and right was both a more difficult and a more urgent task. Thus the *California Police Gazette* imports sensational racial stereotypes from the popular literature of the U.S.-Mexican War that help, on the one hand, to make a hero out of a representative of the state—namely, Harry Love, the California Ranger and former Mexican War soldier who leads the company of men who finally kill Murrieta—and, on the other, to racialize Mexicans by identifying them both as essentially foreign and as similar to so-called savage Indians. In this way, people of Mexican origin are represented as natural criminals, as part of what one contemporaneous writer called "the semi-barbarous hordes of Spanish America, whose whole history is that of revolution and disorder."[26]

The *California Police Gazette* makes crime both alien and familiar as it brings the story of the Sonoran bandit back into the homes of its readers. This version of the Murrieta crime narrative, which most of the Latin American versions seem to echo, follows Ridge's 1854 version closely, often word for word, but it mixes up the order of events, elides some passages and scenes, notably those that justify or excuse Murrieta's crimes, and adds new ones, especially flashbacks to the recent war, which most of the criminals and lawmen in this narrative are said to have fought in. War and crime are brought into an intimate and menacing relationship with each other as memories of war explode in the middle of different scenes. The *California Police Gazette* story is gorier and even more sensational than Ridge's, lingering over dripping blood, severed heads, and other body parts. It replaces Murrieta's mistress, Rosita, who survives a gang rape and a beating at the hands of lower-class "false" Americans in the Ridge version, with a first wife, Carmela, who is raped and killed, and a second wife who, dressed in male drag, often rides along with Murrieta and who survives to mourn his death. In both of these versions of the Murrieta story violence directed at women's bodies represents threats or violence to a larger community. In this and in innumerable other ways, Ridge's and the *Police Gazette*'s versions are part of an international field of popular sensational crime literature, one that includes broadsides about crimes and criminals; pamphlets supposedly based on criminal confessions; novels about the crimes of the rich and about capitalism as crime; detective fiction; an array of ballads and tales about bandits, rogues, and criminals; articles in daily and weekly newspapers; and mass-produced papers, like the *Police Gazette,* devoted to crime.[27]

Beginning in the 1850s, the story of Joaquín Murrieta began to circulate in a variety of such popular forms, but daily and weekly newspapers in California were one of its most important early sources. In January of 1853, California newspapers such as the *San Francisco Herald,* the *Calaveras Chronicle,* the *San Joaquin Republican,* and the *Sacramento Union* started carrying lurid articles about the crimes of a gang of "Mexican marauders" led by a Mexican named Joaquín.[28] These accounts placed "Joaquín" all over the state, attributing more crimes to him than he could possibly have committed.[29] Finally, in May, the California state legislature, unable to decide between the various Joaquíns that the newspapers had put into circulation, passed a bill authorizing a company composed mostly of former Mexican War combatants to capture "the party or gang of robbers commanded by the five Joaquíns, whose names are Joaquín Muriati, Joaquín Ocomorenia, Joaquín Valenzuela, Joaquín Botellier, and Joaquín Carillo."[30] This band of California Rangers narrowed the five Joaquíns down to one man, whom they killed, after which they cut off his head and preserved it in alcohol. Although many of the newspaper stories questioned whether this head belonged to the "real" Joaquín, it was publicly displayed, often along with affidavits and certificates testifying to its "identity," and promoted by posters, handbills, and advertisements in newspapers throughout northern California during the second half of the nineteenth century.

Newspapers, then, initially disseminated the story of Murrieta's criminality, spreading the news that the Mexican bandit's gang posed "a perpetual threat to everyday life" in the new state. But only a year later crime narratives about Murrieta were being published, including two that were serialized in relatively obscure weekly police gazettes and one novel, Ridge's *The Life and Adventures of Joaquín Murieta,* which appeared in San Francisco.[31] Although Ridge's story was published as a book instead of being serialized in a paper, his novel cannot be neatly separated from the daily and weekly newspaper accounts of Joaquín's crimes. Ridge's narrative is episodic, sometimes reading like a series of newspaper stories loosely pulled together, and many of the incidents he describes recall the contemporary newspaper reports that Ridge almost certainly read while he was living in Marysville and Yuba City, California, during those years. The narrative registers its place in this larger world of popular crime writing when Joaquín reads crime stories in the newspapers such as the Los Angeles *Star,* "which made a very free use of his own name in the account of these transactions and handled his character in no measured terms" (R, 30).

From the beginning of the narrative, Ridge also alludes to different types of crime literature, placing his novel within an international field of popular knowledge about crime by comparing Murrieta to the "renowned robbers of the Old or New World, who have preceded him" (R, 7). This body of crime literature about famous robbers not only "precedes" the crimes committed by Murrieta's gang but also actively inspires them. Reyes Feliz, for instance, "had read the wild romantic lives of the chivalrous robbers of Spain and Mexico until his enthusiastic spirit had become imbued with the same sentiments which actuated them" (R, 17). So Ridge repeatedly registers his awareness of a larger body of crime narratives set in Spain and Mexico as well as in England, France, and the United States that provide a framework within which his own text will inevitably be read.[32]

But if Ridge borrows from newspapers and other crime narratives, he is also interested in making distinctions within the field of crime literature. In other words, he wants to make it clear to readers that this novel transcends wild romance and cheap sensationalism, that it is not meant to imbue "enthusiastic spirits" with the same sentiments, and that his purpose is not to minister to "any depraved taste for the dark and horrible in human action" (R, 7). Thus at the outset he claims that rather than offering scenes of gratuitous violence to "depraved" readers, Murrieta's story is actually "a part of the most valuable history of the State" (R, 7). By using the genre of history to frame his crime narrative, Ridge aspires to a sort of literary respectability even as he tries to appeal to popular tastes.

Being recognized as an author was also important to Ridge, and so when the 1859 *California Police Gazette* version of the Murrieta story appeared, he accused the anonymous writer of plagiarism in the pages of the Marysville *Daily National Democrat,* which he was editing at that time.[33] Many years later, when a "third edition" of the novel, which the publishers claimed that Ridge had written, appeared shortly after his death in 1871, it included an author's preface that denounced the "crude interpolations, fictitious additions, and imperfectly designed distortions of the author's phraseology" in an earlier "spurious edition"—almost certainly the 1859 version—which, it claimed, had "circulated, to the infringement of the author's copyright and the damage of his literary credit."[34] For although Ridge worked as a journalist and newspaper editor in California for much of his life, he also had higher literary ambitions. During his lifetime in California he was fairly well known as a writer of romantic poetry, and even if in *Joaquin Murieta* he cynically worked within the conventions of the best-selling crime novel in hopes of making money, the novel still registers Ridge's concern with his "literary credit." For instance, he inserted one of his most famous poems, "Mount Shasta," into the narrative, and his language is often self-consciously literary as he includes romantic descriptions of nature, metaphysical ruminations about God and the universe, and moralizing assessments of the changes in Murrieta's character.

Much more than does the *Police Gazette,* Ridge makes Murrieta into a romantic hero by making him a rounder character. That is, although the *California Police Gazette* focuses on action and usually refrains from speculating about Murrieta's motives and feelings, Ridge gives him more of an interiority by giving us more information about his character. In the beginning, Ridge emphasizes "the nobility of soul" that Murrieta was forced to compromise when he became a criminal. According to Ridge, Murrieta's early criminal acts regrettably "shut him away forever from his peace of mind and purity of heart" (R, 14). Ridge suggests that Murrieta's criminality permanently stains him, but he also underlines the workings of Joaquín's conscience and his original moral superiority. In Ridge's text, Murrieta never entirely loses this moral responsiveness.

For instance, when he kills a young American named Allan Ruddle who tries to draw his pistol while Joaquín is robbing him, "Joaquin's conscience smote him for this deed, and he regretted the necessity of killing so honest and hard-working a man as Ruddle seemed to be" (R, 33). The *California Police Gazette* omits this glimpse into Joaquín's conscience, as well as many other similar passages that "would redeem with...refulgent light the darkness of his previous history and show him to aftertimes, not as a mere outlaw, committing petty depredations and robberies, but as a *hero* who has revenged his country's wrongs and washed out her disgrace in the blood of her enemies" (R, 80).

Passages like this one have led many to speculate that Ridge was projecting his own responses to racism as well as his feelings of victimization and desire for revenge onto Murrieta.[35] Ridge's family history is deeply implicated in the series of events that culminated in the removal of the Cherokee Indians from Georgia during the 1830s.[36] His relatively wealthy and prominent family initially fought removal but then acceded to it under pressure. That decision, however, was viewed as treachery by a faction of Cherokees led by John Ross. Members of this faction eventually murdered Ridge's father and grandfather in Arkansas, where they had relocated. Then in 1849, Ridge killed a man who had supposedly been sent by the Ross faction to provoke a fight with him. Ridge was forced to flee across the Missouri line and eventually to California, since he feared "that he would not receive a fair trial in the Cherokee Nation, which was controlled politically by Ross and his followers."[37] Although he dreamed of revenge for years, Ridge never returned to the Cherokee nation.

The resemblances between Murrieta's story and Ridge's are certainly striking. As Ridge's biographer, James Parins, suggests, "Joaquín himself must have fascinated Ridge. Here was a man who had tried to live peacefully despite wrongs inflicted on his family and friends. Joaquín's only crime at first was that he did not belong to the faction in power. Driven over the brink by his enemies, he had to react violently. This action forced him into exile, where his intelligence and courage let him revenge himself on his persecutors. He was admired by his own people and feared by his enemies. In many ways Joaquín's early history was much like that of the writer who was to immortalize him; his later career had to appeal to Ridge's deep thirst for revenge."[38] According to this logic, Ridge translates the battle between the Ross and the Ridge factions of the Cherokee nation into the conflict between Mexicans and "Americans" in the Murrieta story. Other critics have argued that Ridge was trying to compare the situation of the Cherokees in Georgia to that of the Mexicans in California. Karl Kroeber observes that the "Californians' treatment of the Mexicans parallels the Georgians' treatment of the Cherokee, whose expulsion was in part precipitated by a discovery of gold in their territory."[39] In either case, these arguments about projection all suggest that Ridge is exploring parallels between Indians and Mexicans in his novel, and that he is implicitly addressing "some of his concerns for his own race" by retelling Murrieta's crime story.[40]

It is certainly true that Ridge is intervening in a slippery field of racial classifications that are in flux during this period and that often conflate Mexicans and Indians. But although popular sensational writers often made "Indians" a monolithic category defined by "savagery," Ridge makes distinctions between different tribes on the basis of their distance from "savagery" and their success at adapting to "civilization."[41] Peter Christensen convincingly argues that Ridge believed in a hierarchy "in which some Native American tribes, such as the Cherokees, Aztecs, and Incas are seen as the superior representatives of their race."[42] Instead of aligning all Indians with all Mexicans, then, Ridge is more likely looking for resemblances between Cherokees as a superior type of Indian and Joaquín as the representative of a superior type of Mexican.

Internal hierarchies also stratify the category "Mexican" for Ridge. The editor's preface, probably composed by Ridge, suggests that Murrieta is an "exception" to the judgment that Mexicans are a people "who have so far degenerated as to have been called by many 'A Nation of Cowards'" (R, 4). Ridge's Murrieta is born "of respectable parents," can speak English fluently, and is so light skinned that he can successfully disguise himself as a red-haired, white North American. Fired "with enthusiastic admiration of the American character" (R, 8) until squatters jump his claim, rape his girlfriend, and whip him, Murrieta seems more like Ridge's example of a special type of Mexican who would be capable, in the absence of racism, of assimilating to American "civilization" than the representative of Mexicans as a conquered and outraged people. A few years later Ridge would even write editorials supporting filibustering expeditions into Nicaragua and Sonora, Mexico. According to Parins, Ridge advocated "annexing Sonora with or without Sonoran assent unless the Mexican government [could] maintain law and order."[43] Ridge also supported the claims of white settlers in California on Spanish and Mexican land grants, describing the conflict between the two as a struggle of "the masses against the aristocratic few who would rob and oppress them."[44] Given Ridge's views on these issues, it is difficult to believe that

he is defending the rights of Mexicans as a people over and against the
U.S. emigrants in *Joaquín Murieta,* or that the novel identifies Mexicans
with Indians in order to attack Manifest Destiny.

Instead, Ridge is championing the law and U.S. ideals but is claiming
that "prejudice of color" may lead to *"injustice to individuals"* (R, 158)
and the abrogation of law, which in turn engenders crimes such as Murrieta's. But if Ridge insists that Murrieta's story is a part of "the most
valuable history of the State" (R, 7), the *California Police Gazette* re-
stricts the meaning of Murrieta's example by making the latter only a
part of "the criminal history" (PG, 1) of California. And although Ridge
implies that the citizens of California need to think about how race prejudice turned Murrieta into a criminal, the *California Police Gazette*
makes Murrieta into an example of an innate, alien criminality.

The *California Police Gazette* version of the Murrieta story gives
crime a Mexican face, making it seem "very close" and yet still "quite
alien"—an enduring stereotype that resurfaces today ad nauseam in debates about immigration, welfare, and citizenship. Indeed, it is the very
combination of the "close" and the "alien" that makes the Mexican immigrant bandit seem especially threatening. Mexico is "close," first of
all, because it is geographically adjacent to the United States, sharing a
common border. In both Ridge's version and in the *Police Gazette,*
Joaquín and the members of his gang repeatedly cross and recross national boundary lines, mapping out transnational networks of migration
and illegal activity. The gang is continually reconstituted through the de-
partures and the arrivals of new members across the border, especially
from Sonora but also from Chile and Peru. Ridge suggests that the "ram-
ifications" of Murrieta's "organization" "are in Sonora, Lower California, and in this State" (R, 74), while the *California Police Gazette* notes
at the beginning that Murrieta's "powerful combination" was "steadily
increasing by arrivals from Lower California and Sonora" (PG, 8). In
both versions, Murrieta's gang is a sort of international army that both
recruits and deploys soldiers across national boundaries. Much of their
business involves moving stolen horses from the United States to Mexico. Again and again, the narratives expose secret connections between
Mexico and the United States, as when the wife of a "wealthy ranch
owner in Guadalajara, Mexico" travels to California to "urge [Joaquín]
on in his bloody warfare against the Americans" (PG, 105); or when
Murrieta repeatedly sends "remittances of money" to a "secret partner"
in the state of Sonora (R, 32). In these ways, the novels incessantly link
the cross-border movement of money and people to international crime

networks, thereby suggesting that the "closeness" of the United States to Mexico and the "openness" of adjacent national borders make the United States vulnerable to invasion by an alien race of lawless Mexicans who can easily move between nations.

This pattern of transnational movement is established in the beginning of the *California Police Gazette* version when Joaquín initially travels to San Francisco in 1848 to look for his brother Carlos, "who had long been living in California, and had obtained a grant of four leagues of land from one of those excessively generous governors who flourished about that time" (PG, 3). Not finding Carlos, Joaquín "retraced his steps homeward" (PG, 3) to Mexico. A year later, however, when a letter from his brother arrives that also brings news of the Gold Rush in California, Joaquín and his wife set out on the journey back to San Francisco. When they arrive, Carlos is about to leave for Mexico City, because his land has "been taken from him by the Americans, by means of forged papers" (PG, 3) and he needs to go to Mexico to "see the grantor himself, and so recover the land" (PG, 3). In the opening chapter of the novel, these actual and anticipated journeys across the border make national boundary lines seem porous and insecure, given the spatial proximity or "closeness" of Mexico to the United States. They also imaginatively link up northern Mexico and California, as the story of Joaquín's brother, who is a Sonoran, is identified with the history of the Californios, many of whom were forced to become involved in costly litigation over land grants. Carlos even plans to take "a young native Californian named Flores" (PG, 3) to Mexico with him to serve as a witness.

The journey into the heart of Mexico that Carlos proposes activates the memory of another system of political supervision, an older set of Mexican laws and institutions (the land grants of the "excessively generous" Mexican governors) that were in the process of being replaced by the U.S. political and legal system. But this transition did not happen seamlessly, and the older order continued to clash with the new. So the "Mexican period" still seemed close and yet alien to U.S. settlers in the sense that California had until very recently been a part of Mexico and so had been governed by other laws and institutions. Mexico's property law, for instance, continued to be a factor in land disputes throughout the second half of the nineteenth century, when white immigrants squatted on land owned by Mexicans and went to court (sometimes with forged papers) to challenge land grants made by the old regime.[45] After California became a state within the U.S. system, the Mexican period was increasingly represented with both fear and nostalgia as a superseded stage of history, as a time that was historically close and yet alien, already passing away in the face of Anglo-Saxon energy, institutions, and mastery of the "commercial principle." But as an earlier "stage" of California history, the period of Mexican rule continued to haunt, at times erupting from within that history to make national law and national boundary lines seem strange, new, and artificial rather than familiar, primordial, and natural.

For during the 1850s, U.S. boundaries, laws, and institutions were strange, new, artificial, unevenly in place, violently enforced, and violently abrogated. Instead of war giving way to peace and the rule of law, after 1848 war continued to be fought by other means as Spanish-speakers and other so-called foreigners confronted racist legislation, claim-jumping, vigilantism, and lynching at the hands of newly arrived immigrants from the Eastern United States, many of whom had fought on the U.S. side in the war. In San Francisco, for instance, the members of the nativist vigilante gang called the Hounds, who were especially fond of persecuting Spanish-speakers, were mostly "disbanded soldiers from the regiment of the New York Volunteers."[46] The war, in other words, was very recent, raw history that continued to shape the present as many of those who fought it reencountered each other in California.

The *California Police Gazette* tries to heal the wounds of war and to unify a heterogeneous society by defining a white American identity in opposition to what are constructed as the "savage" and therefore naturally criminal, essentially alien even if native, bodies of Mexicans, Latin Americans, and Californios within the state. This effort to stabilize differences responds to a crisis in the boundaries of whiteness and national identity in mid-nineteenth-century California. As we have seen, although the Treaty of Guadalupe Hidalgo guaranteed "all the rights of citizens" to Mexicans who chose to remain in the new territories and although the California state constitution defined Mexicans as "white" and declared them, as opposed to Indians, eligible for citizenship, these legal provisions were unevenly enforced during the postwar period. The big wave of immigration from Mexico and South America during the Gold Rush years, especially, upset the system of racial meanings and classifications that were initially proposed in California.[47] Leonard Pitt suggests that whether "from California, Chile, Peru, or Mexico, whether residents of twenty years standing or immigrants of one week, all of the Spanish-speaking were lumped together as 'interlopers and greasers.'... In essence then the Latin-American immigrants were a sort of catalyst whose presence caused the sudden and permanent dissolution of the social elements."[48] The precarious whiteness of certain Spanish-speakers did not simply dissolve into thin air, however. Rather, during the post-war period, the racialization of different groups of Spanish-speaking people was a problem addressed through legislation like the Foreign Miner's Tax and the Federal Land Law of 1851, through violence, and through popular representations such as the sensational crime literature I have been describing.

The racializations promoted by the Murrieta story must be understood in the context of what one historian has called "the great Sonoran migration of 1848–1856."[49] During these years, between ten and twenty thousand miners made the long journey across the desert and up the coast from Sonora to the goldfields of California, bringing with them superior mining skills as well as "hard feelings towards Americans developed when the latter invaded their homelands."[50] They were joined by five thousand miners from Latin America, most of them from Chile, in the year 1849 alone.[51] From the beginning, the Americans who were moving west in large numbers loudly voiced their resentment of "foreigners" in the mines; they believed that their recent victory in the war with Mexico entitled U.S. citizens and only U.S. citizens to claim the prodigious amounts of gold that had been discovered. In January of 1849, General Persifor S. Smith, whose ship had stopped at Panama on the way to California, where he would take command of the U.S. Army, issued a proclamation in response to this nativist hysteria, announcing his intention to fine and imprison "persons not citizens of the United States, who are flocking from all parts to search for and carry off gold belonging to the United States in California."[52] Xenophobic U.S. Americans violently turned foreigners away from Sutter's Mill in April, and other vigilantes drove Sonorans "out of the Tuolumne, Stanislaus, and Mokolumne River placers in the summer of 1849."[53] The Foreign Miner's Tax Law that was enacted in 1850 and that required all "foreigners" working in the mines to pay twenty dollars a month for a permit, was thus only one example among many of the ways that U.S. citizens quickly naturalized the new national boundary lines and, in Josiah Royce's words, "turned upon foreigners as a class, and especially upon Sonorans and South Americans."[54]

Despite the efforts of many Californios to distinguish themselves from the new immigrants, most Americans included them within this newly revised "class" of foreigners.[55] Although "local attachments and loyalties, class differences, and subtle variances in customs and language patterns" divided the different groups of Spanish speakers from each other, many white Americans saw no significant differences among them.[56]

In a discussion of the criminalization of Spanish-speakers during this period, Josiah Royce scathingly exposes the essentialist logic that supported the classification of these diverse groups of people as a race:

> It was, however, considered safe by an average lynching jury in those days to convict a "greaser" on very moderate evidence, if none better could be had. One could see his guilt so plainly written, we know, in his ugly, swarthy face, before the trial began. Therefore the life of a Spanish-American in the mines in the early days, if frequently profitable, was apt to be a little disagreeable. It served him right, of course. He had no business, as an alien, to come to the land that God had given us. And if he was a native Californian, a born "greaser," then so much the worse for him. He was so much the more our born foe; we hated his whole degenerate, thieving, land-owning, lazy, and discontented race.[57]

The "denial, or flattening, of differences within a particular racially defined group," which Michael Omi and Howard Winant identify as a key feature of racial essentialism, can be seen in the pejorative epithet "greaser" that collapses the differences between the "native Californian" and the "alien" Mexicans, Chileans, and Peruvians.[58] The more neutral but still homogenizing term "Spanish-American" that Royce chooses in order to distinguish himself from the nativist vigilantes also covers over differences between those who had elected to become U.S. citizens, those who became citizens by default under the terms of the treaty, those who retained other national or regional allegiances and never hoped to become citizens, and those who were excluded from citizenship because they were considered Indian or mestizo. And even though the nativists assumed that all "greasers" were "aliens," even the qualifier "native" failed to protect the Californios from those who found a natural criminality, common to the native and alien alike, inscribed on their "swarthy" faces. Indeed, their (similarly problematic) claim to "native" status made them even more of a threat to the white settlers who coveted their land; it is not surprising that Royce added "land-owning" to the long list of racist adjectives that the white nativists used to vilify the "native" Californians.

Of course, many Californios were still legally considered white and were therefore in a much better position than the Chinese, blacks, and Indians, who were absolutely excluded from citizenship on the basis of their race, as well as many other people of Mexican origin. But racial categories were swiftly being re-created, reinhabited, transformed, and destroyed during the 1850s.[59] In practice, access to white privilege was, as I have already suggested, always severely stratified by class. As Tomás

Almaguer suggests, although the land-owning elite Californios were often considered white, assimilable, and worthy of intermarriage with other kinds of white people, working-class people of Mexican origin were "often denied their legal rights by being categorized as Indians."[60] Even members of the elite, however, could lose their white privilege if they were dark skinned. Almaguer tells the story of Manuel Dominguez, who had served as a delegate to the California State Constitutional Convention of 1849 but was barred from testifying in a San Francisco courtroom in 1857 because the judge ruled that he was an Indian. In the wake of the war and with the increasing dispossession and proletarianization of the Californio ranchero class and the influx of new immigrants, the hold on whiteness of any of these Spanish-speakers became increasingly tenuous as, more and more, they were all lumped together.

The *California Police Gazette* version of the Murrieta story exploits this ambiguous racial status but ultimately labors to unify and racialize these diverse groups by identifying them with an innate, savage criminality. As we have seen, the novel initially focuses on postwar injustices inflicted on different groups of Spanish-speakers, linking these injuries together only to override them in favor of a crime narrative that justifies state-sponsored violence. I have suggested that the story of Joaquín's brother, Carlos, whose Mexican land grant is taken away from him "by means of forged papers," recalls the fate of the Californios, who were displaced during the postwar period through fraud, the complicated and costly Land Law of 1851, and frivolous lawsuits.[61] The ensuing scene— in which Joaquín is prevented from working the mines on the Stanislaus River by a group of "lawless and desperate" men—typifies a long, bloody history of Anglo claim-jumping and violence inflicted on Sonoran miners during the Gold Rush. Finally, the existence of an extensive, hidden network of Californios, Mexicans, and Latin Americans who help Joaquín avenge his injuries implies that all of these groups have suffered similar injustices. The opening frame, then, suggests that Joaquín's injuries are representative of wrongs suffered by Californios, Sonorans, and Latin Americans as a group, and that the criminality of the group is to some degree a legitimate or at least understandable response to these postwar injuries. If the novel's opening emphasizes the constructedness of Joaquín's criminality, however, the narrative ultimately overrides this explanation in favor of one that suggests that this criminality is rooted in the dark recesses of his nature—a "savage" impulse that takes him outside the pale of white civility.

This redrawing of boundaries around whiteness depends upon the importation of stereotypes from U.S.–Mexican War era sensational literature that define U.S. Anglo-Saxon heroism by opposing it to Mexican "savagery." One flashback in particular, which fleshes out Captain Love's U.S.-Mexican War encounter with a "hideous-looking fellow, half Indian, half Mexican," suggestively indicates the larger project of this version of the Murrieta story. Echoing Ridge's language, the *California Police Gazette* sets up Love as a point of identification for its readers early on by characterizing him as a "hardy pioneer" who "during the Mexican war had performed valuable service as an express rider, carrying dispatches from one military post to another, over the wildest and most dangerous parts of Mexico" (PG, 14). But the *Police Gazette* embroiders with lurid and telling details a scene that Ridge only hints at as it interjects a long description of Love's victory over a band of guerrillas led by a "half Indian, half Mexican" warrior. The threat represented by this mestizo soldier, "whose face was marked with a deep scar across his right cheek...urging his animal on with such savage fury, that its sides were covered with gore" (PG, 15), haunts the narrative, which opposes white representatives of the racial state to "savage," lawless Mexicans by reinserting both within the theater of the recent war.[62]

The novel repeatedly describes the gang's crimes as the continuation of war by other means. At night, the members of Murrieta's gang sit around the campfire remembering the war by telling gory, sensational stories about the battles they fought with "the guerrilla chief and priest, padre Jurata [sic]" (PG, 8)—a character loosely based on the famous Mexican fighting priest, Padre Jarauta. The brutal Three-Fingered Jack, in particular, who is closely identified with Jarauta and who lost his fingers while fighting the war, is a character straight out of U.S.–Mexican War era pulp fiction. A long story about Jarauta in combat, "sheathing his dripping blade in the bodies of the dead as well as the living, and in a perfect frenzy of excitement severing the neck-joints and casting the gaping heads into the rushing water" (PG, 21), is framed by multiple accounts of Jack's murderous abandon. Indeed, when one of the bandits suggests that Jack "takes rather too much delight in drawing blood," another replies, "Not half so much as old Padre Jurata whom some of us had for a leader in Mexico" (PG, 20). As Jack satisfies "his brutal disposition" by "discharging three loads from his revolver into the head" of a corpse, tortures Chinese miners, and exults in "the luxurious feast of blood" (PG, 23), the *Police Gazette* implies that Mexican "savagery" has migrated from the battlefields of the U.S.-Mexican War to the California goldfields.

If early on the novel suggests that Joaquín is an "exceptional" Mexican who is *made* into a criminal by un-American Americans, by the end it identifies him with the essentially depraved and bloodthirsty Jack. Even in the opening chapters of the novel, however, Joaquín is more brutal than in Ridge's version. For instance, Joaquín's first vengeful murder, which is briefly described after the fact by Ridge, becomes a full-blown, bloody scene in *The Life of Joaquin Murieta, the Brigand Chief of California*. Joaquín's eyes glare "with the fury of an enraged tiger" and his body seems to "quiver with excitement" as he plunges his knife again and again "into the body, until the latter was almost hacked to pieces, for the demon of revenge possessed the soul of Joaquin and urged him to excess" (PG, 6). And when Joaquín and his gang later meet up with the men who killed Carmela, Joaquín, who has intermittently tried to control Jack's sadistic behavior, commands him to exercise his "natural propensity," an order that encourages Jack to disembowel them and cut out their hearts. As the narrative proceeds, Joaquín's desire for revenge is thus figured, more and more, as savage, innate, and out of control, as something that links him to the utterly savage Jack, who indiscriminately hacks people to pieces because his "heart to its very core is black with evil" (PG, 29). In this way, the wild, brutal Jack is figured as Joaquín's inner "truth": Jack is an indispensable part of Joaquín's organization that Joaquín cannot control, and ultimately does not want to control, as long as the "demon of revenge" spawned by postwar California possesses him.

By identifying Joaquín's gang and the extended network of people who support them with an innate, savage criminality linked to the U.S.-Mexican War, the narrative implicitly redraws the boundary lines around the white nation, collapsing the differences between diverse peoples of Mexican origin and other Spanish-speakers, whether they are "natives" or "foreigners," and classifying them as an inassimilable body within the nation-state. When, after a day of adventure, the bandits sit around the fire singing a song called "Our Home Is Mexico," which they claim was "a favorite with the padre Jurata" (PG, 64), this vision of an insurgent alien nation within the white republic is even supported by a cultural nationalist anthem, albeit one that is sung to the tune of "The Maid of Monterey." In this fantasy of postwar cultural hybridity, the *California Police Gazette* has Joaquín's men proclaim their eternal allegiance to Mexico (the novel includes a full set of lyrics) to the tune of a song that is about "south of the border" romance. Although the novel's representation of this musical interlude says a lot more about the work of postwar national fantasy than it does about Mexican culture, the *Gazette* does get one thing right when it insists upon the importance of music in disseminating a nationalist sentiment across borders and in defiance of official national jurisdictions.[63] This transnational national sentiment transmitted by *mexicano* songs is the subject of the next part of this chapter.

JOAQUÍN MURRIETA AND THE CHICANA/O COUNTERCULTURES OF MODERNITY

Joaquín Murrieta has been an important and pervasive symbol of resistance for people of Mexican origin in the United States in diverse forms of twentieth-century cultural production, from barrio murals to Rodolfo "Corky" Gonzales's nationalist epic poem "I Am Joaquín" to versions of the Murrieta *corrido* sung by Los Madrugadores, Lalo Guerrero, and Lydia Mendoza, among many others.[64] Stories about Murrieta's severed head, which was exhibited in mining camps throughout California, seem to have stimulated many Chicana/o responses, including Luis Valdez's play *The Shrunken Head of Pancho Villa*, Richard Rodriguez's essay "The Head of Joaquín Murrieta," and Cherríe Moraga's *Heroes and Saints*. Moraga's play, which focuses on a woman who is born without a body because of her mother's exposure to pesticides in the fields of the Central Valley, might be read as a radical revision of the many male-authored accounts of displacement and loss provoked by Murrieta's head.[65] Rodriguez's essay offers one such account, albeit one which is unusual in that it ultimately recoils from rather than celebrates Murrieta as a symbol of the larger community. Rodriguez writes in a half-satirical, half-serious way about his travels around the state with a Jesuit priest named Alberto Huerta in search of the head, which he describes as a symbol of California's violent, gothic past. But the more Huerta urges Rodriguez to help him pursue various leads and thereby calls him "to come to terms with California," the more Rodriguez anxiously "pull[s] back" in order to return to "the California of Fillmore Street, of blond women and Nautilus-educated advertising executives, this California of pastels and pasta salad…where I live."[66] These very different examples suggest that whether the myth of Murrieta as symbol of a larger Chicano community has been enthusiastically endorsed, implicitly criticized and imaginatively transformed, or nervously relegated to a dead past, many Chicana/o cultural producers have felt compelled to come to terms with it.

Literary critics who write about Murrieta often privilege Ridge's novel as an authoritative text, implicitly distinguishing it from the subliterary newspaper accounts that preceded it in the 1850s as well as from the mass cultural texts, such as the *California Police Gazette* and the dime novels, that followed it. I have suggested that such an analysis elides a larger, violently divided inter-American field of popular knowledge about crime that responded to and helped to reshape class and racial formations in the wake of the American 1848. But if the low or mass-cultural world of cheap sensational literature and the crime gazette constitutes one important part of that field, the ballads and legends produced by diasporic *corrido* communities are surely another. In this concluding section, I want to do two things: first, to argue that *corridos* and other forms of cultural production by people of Mexican origin are an important part of the story of post-1848 U.S. popular culture; and second, to show how Murrieta and the American 1848 returned to haunt the 1930s, an era characterized by economic hard times, nativism, and the deportation and repatriation of Mexicans. The uncanny return of the Murrieta story during the years of the Great Depression suggests its relevance for more historically proximate as well as ongoing debates about law, labor, race, crime, and nationalism in the United States.

Neither the *Police Gazette* nor the *corrido* version of the Murrieta story can be attributed to an individual author, as Ridge's novel can, and that may be one of the reasons, aside from the fascinating set of issues that his text raises, that many discussions of Murrieta focus only on Ridge. The "author" of the *California Police Gazette* is unknown, but the text's close relationship to Ridge's novel, to the newspaper stories, and to the conventions of U.S.–Mexican War era cheap fiction make traditional notions of individual authorship untenable anyway. On the other hand, *corridos* also challenge such notions of authorship because they are extremely formulaic, influenced substantially by oral traditions, and because their producers are usually anonymous; rather than reflecting the views of an individual author, *corridos* offer, in Ramón Saldívar's words, "a heightened, reflexive analysis of the mutual values and orientations of the collective."[67] In the case of the Murrieta *corrido,* we could go even further, for its migratory movements call into question notions of a stable, unitary community. The formulaic nature of the *corrido,* as well as its sensational, body-grabbing qualities, doubtless facilitated its transmission across widely dispersed sites. As José Limón suggests, "The sheer music, the strict predictable measured poetics, the Spanish language of the *corrido*" and its "strong sensory quality" may well have "constituted a point of resistance" to U.S. capitalist modernity at "the level of form."[68]

Because *corridos* are usually transmitted orally, it is difficult to confidently fix their point of origin. Luis Leal has suggested that the Murrieta *corridos* are based on a song about Indian warfare from nineteenth-century Zacatecas that gives the date of the events it describes as 1853, and he concludes that there was probably an earlier prototype for both *corridos* that is lost today.[69] According to Víctor Sánchez, a member of the group that first recorded it in 1934, "The *corrido* was written before I was born; it is from the last century. I heard it as a child in Mexico, sung during the time of the Revolution, and later in Arizona."[70] As this sensational crime story moves across regional and international boundary lines, it exposes the violence of U.S. empire-building and incessantly registers shifts in racial and national boundaries, thereby foregrounding the historical contingency of changing definitions of the native and the alien.

The *corrido* recorded during the 1930s must be understood in relation to the virulent nativism of the period and to the English-language versions of the story that were issued during those years. Novels such as Ernest Klette's *The Crimson Trail of Joaquin Murieta* (1928), Dane Coolidge's *Gringo Gold* (1939), and especially Walter Noble Burns's *The Robin Hood of El Dorado* (1932), which inspired the 1936 Hollywood movie, look back upon an earlier era of immigration and state formation and try to exorcise the ghosts of race wars past, or rather to suggest that racial injustice and the violence of conquest are part of the dead past, which has given way to the rule of law. They also labor to make the post-1848 boundary line between the United States and Mexico seem natural and right by representing Spanish-speakers and especially people of Mexican origin as outlaws who threaten the state, in part because they easily move between nations. But the dead past is reanimated, the border becomes uncanny, and the alien and the native become hopelessly entangled in these narratives, which invoke ghosts that they cannot possibly lay to rest. To follow the ghosts in these Murrieta narratives means, then, as Avery Gordon puts it, to be startled into a recognition of the animating force of "what seems dead, but is nonetheless alive," to confront "whatever organized violence has repressed and in the process formed into a past, a history, remaining nonetheless alive and accessible to encounter."[71] For as debates over nativism and immigration grew more heated during the Depression years and as the 1930s began to uncannily resemble Murrieta's California, the ghosts of California's so-called past clamored noisily in the present, troubling claims that acts of racist injustice had been superseded by democracy and the rule of law.

More than a million Mexican immigrants crossed the border and resettled in the United States between 1890 and 1920.[72] As David Gutiérrez suggests, "Mexican immigrants filled a wide variety of occupations, ranging from agricultural labor, mine work, and railroad construction and maintenance, to common day labor on innumerable construction sites throughout the Southwest." In California, workers of Mexican origin made up almost 17 percent of unskilled construction workers and almost 75 percent of the state's farm labor force.[73] During prosperous times the immigrants were welcomed by California agribusiness and other employers and were more or less uneasily tolerated by most white workers, who generally benefited from their better position within the racially segmented labor market. But after the stock market crash of 1929 and the onset of the Great Depression, Mexican workers became convenient scapegoats for white nativists. The American Federation of Labor, the Veterans of Foreign Wars, and the American Legion, to name just three groups, supported the Immigration Service's intensified efforts to deport so-called illegal and undesirable Mexican immigrants, and between 1930 and 1939 Mexicans constituted "46.3 percent of all of the people deported from the United States"[74] During the early 1930s, U.S. Secretary of Labor William Doak specifically targeted labor organizers and strikers for deportation, and Southern California in particular became "the focal point of the deportation frenzy."[75] Also, in August of 1931, the California state legislature passed the Alien Labor Act, which made it illegal for companies to hire aliens for public works projects such as construction of highways, schools, and government office buildings— a policy which often meant that workers who "looked" Mexican were presumed to be illegal aliens.[76] Finally, repatriation programs were established that, according to Camille Guerin-Gonzales, "made no effort to distinguish between immigrants and U.S. born Mexicans and, in fact, set numerical goals that included both groups."[77] In all of these ways, nativists insisted that people of Mexican origin were fundamentally alien despite the promise of abstract equality enshrined in the rhetoric of liberal democracy.

For many writers, this context made the Murrieta story newly relevant. For instance, in Walter Noble Burns's 1932 novel *The Robin Hood of El Dorado*, racial injustice is deplored, but it is also relegated to the dead past, represented as part of an older age of terror and lawlessness that has been superseded by "the era of law and order."[78] In the early chapters of the novel, as Burns rehearses the racist acts of white nativist terrorism that turned Murrieta into a criminal, he explains that nativists contravened the Constitution and the laws of the United States:

> As California had fallen into American hands as spoils of war, the American miners were imbued with the idea that the gold of California was rightfully theirs and theirs only. But as selfishly human as the idea may have been, it was legally without justification. According to the constitution and the laws of the United States, Mexicans and all other foreigners had as much right to mine in California as Americans themselves. But the legality of the position of the Mexicans had no effect in mitigating American hostility towards them. The feeling between the two races grew more and more embittered. (44)

Here Burns extends some sympathy to the Mexican immigrant who is treated unfairly by the U.S. Americans. But as we shall see, he also mitigates this criticism of the nativists by calling their behavior "selfishly human," and he justifies state intervention after Murrieta becomes an outlaw.

In Murrieta's California, according to Burns, the "law was a dead letter. Citizens were helpless and dared not defend themselves. The marauders came and went as free as the winds with reckless bravado but they left no clews behind. Their trails were red with blood but from the scenes of their crimes they vanished like phantoms" (129). Inevitably, then, in Burns's account, law must be enforced by the state, which as he imagines it rightfully unleashes its "crushing power" to end what he sees as Joaquín's reign of terror. In Burns's narrative of state formation, an age of lawlessness and terror must give way to an age of law. As he puts it in the novel's concluding chapters, the "age of law was dawning in 1853. For more than three years, the state had endured Joaquin Murrieta's reign of rapine and devastation. Now the Days of the Terror were drawing to a close. The state had grown weary of the red nightmare; and the weariness of the state was a menace of death. Heretofore communities, countrysides, counties, had fought Murrieta. For the first time he was to feel the crushing power of the state as a state" (256). Here Burns animates the state, endowing it with a kind of moral agency as it awakens from the "red nightmare" and crushes resistance. For Burns, the death of the Mexican immigrant outlaw coincides with the dawn of a new age. "As the outlaw died, the sun rose over the distant Sierras, and plains and mountains were bathed in the radiance of the morning. For California, a new era came with the sunrise—an era of law and order" (275). By concluding in this way, Burns suggests that the ghosts that haunted Murrieta, and the legally unjustified acts of nativist terrorism that provoked him, have been safely quarantined in the past, so that now they are no more than part of a "tale told in the twilight or a song sung to a guitar" (304).

If Burns labors to make the age of lawlessness and racial terror part of the dead past, however, there are several places in the text where his allusions to the present open up a wider, contemporaneous frame of reference for the Murrieta story. For instance, even as he tries to distance this story from his own time by making it, in the opening frame, a sort of gothic story told by an old-timer, a second-generation forty-niner who mourns the death of the old mining towns like a "mourner standin' by an open grave," he still yokes the past to the present as he comments on the fate of the succeeding generations of white Californians: "The Forty-Niners dipped up a fortune casual-like from some nameless creek in a tin washpan," the old-timer suggests, "but their children have had to scratch mighty hard for a livin'" (1). Here, this reference to economic hard times and perhaps to agricultural labor almost, but not quite, brings into view the scenes of nativist terrorism, labor competition, and white supremacist retrenching that were taking place in California during the early 1930s. Instead, this context eerily looms on the margins of Burns's story, only to be repressed by a temporal shift of the setting back to the California of the 1850s that Burns tries to place securely in the past.

Issues of law and racial terror are also significant in the 1936 MGM film *The Robin Hood of El Dorado,* but the movie's position on these issues was shaped by the requirements of Hollywood's new Production Code, which was energetically enforced after 1934.[79] Concerned that gangster films and other outlaw stories might make crime seem more attractive during this period of crisis, the code mandated that "the presentation must not throw sympathy with the criminal as against the law, nor with the crime as against those who must punish it." Furthermore, "Law and justice must not by the treatment they receive from criminals be made to seem wrong or ridiculous." Identifying banditry as one type of a "class" of "*sin* which by its nature *attracts,*" the writers of the code concluded that this class "needs real care in handling, as the response of human natures to their appeal is obvious." Sounding something like Burns in their appeal to a narrative of development and state formation, they even suggested that while in "lands and ages of less developed civilization and moral principles, revenge may sometimes be presented," in "modern times" it "shall not be justified." On the other hand, although its authors tried to ban any criticism of the law, the code also stated that the "just rights, history, and feelings of any nation are entitled to consideration and respectful treatment."[80] This self-regulation on the part of the motion picture industry was partly motivated by market considerations. As Helen Delpar suggests, "More American films than ever before were shown in Mexico after World War I, when they displaced European productions, which had predominated before the war." And during the 1920s, she claims, Mexican officials had frequently objected to "the usual portrayal of Mexicans in motion pictures" as "a bandit or a sneak," as one official put it.[81] For all of these reasons, Production Code czar Joe Breen closely scrutinized representations of law and banditry in *The Robin Hood of El Dorado*. After reviewing the film, Breen required that the filmmakers eliminate the word "greaser" from the movie because of its "definite offensiveness to the Mexican government and people." Troubled by the number of killings in the film, he also suggested that instead of emphasizing a "spirit of revenge" they should focus on Murrieta's wish to bring his persecutors "to justice."[82]

Even though Breen and the forces behind the Production Code pressured the filmmakers to de-emphasize revenge as a motive and to idealize legal justice, it is still easy to imagine that many moviegoers would have viewed Murrieta as a figure of vengeance and heroism during the Depression era. As C. L. R. James argues, popular representations of crime during this period often respond to the "bitterness, the violence, the brutality, the sadism simmering in the population, the desire to revenge themselves with their own hands, to get some release for what society had done to them since 1929," and surely that helps to explain the appeal of the Murrieta story for a mass audience.[83] While some versions of the story position him as part of a wealthy Mexican family, this one makes him a humbler figure who falls in love with the daughter of a rich landowner only to be banished from the region after the U.S. takeover in 1848. Later, after enduring a series of humiliations that includes a public whipping, he joins a group of Mexican outlaws who attack upper-class *hacendados* as well as Americanos. The *New York Times* film critic found the film to be "a brutally frank indictment of American injustice, greed and cowardice in the years of the California gold rush," and Murrieta's Robin Hood–like robbing of the rich of both groups might well have seemed like justice to those who were experiencing the devastating effects of the Depression.[84] The star of the movie was Warner Baxter, a matinee idol during the silent film era who successfully made the transition to talkies and who was one of the most popular actors of the 1930s. Baxter had previously played a wide range of both nonwhite and iconically white roles, from the tragic Indian

Alessandro in the 1928 *Ramona* and the Cisco Kid to Jay Gatsby. But although the casting of a big star as Murrieta probably contributed to the latter's appeal and although Breen had eliminated the references to "greasers" and was eager to avoid offending Mexicans, the film still contrasts a relatively whitened Murrieta with the murderous Three-Fingered Jack, and it also ultimately attempts to "throw sympathy" against the Mexican criminals and with U.S. law. Toward the end of the movie, one of the gang's robberies inadvertently causes the death of a young bride-to-be; her bereaved fiancé forms a posse to pursue the gang, and Murrieta is tracked down and killed by the posse. The denouement champions the rule of law, in other words, by insisting that breaking the law inevitably leads to horrible if unintended consequences. In the end, then, the film followed the Production Code injunction that although in "lands and ages of less developed civilization and moral principles," revenge that flouted the law might be understandable, in "modern times" it could not be justified.

Both the novel and the movie versions of *The Robin Hood of El Dorado* try to uphold the ideal of the rule of law by rigorously distinguishing an earlier, "less developed" postwar California from a contemporaneous modernity. Novelist Walter Noble Burns's efforts to use a narrative of development to separate an age of terror from an age of law fail in part, as we have seen, because the 1930s context keeps resurfacing on the margins of his text, but also because his revision of the story, like the movie version, shows how law and racial terror frequently accompanied rather than worked against each other. In other words, the law to which both novel and film appealed often supported nativism and white supremacy.

This point is made even more forcefully in the Joaquín Murrieta *corrido,* "a song sung to a guitar," which is also a product of 1930s California, a time when laws often enabled racial terror rather than prohibiting it. Luis Leal suggests that the earliest, most complete surviving version of the Murrieta *corrido* was recorded in 1934 in Los Angeles by Los Hermanos Sánchez y Linares, otherwise known as Los Madrugadores, or the Early Risers. According to Chris Strachwitz, Los Madrugadores "were one of the first groups to make an impact via Spanish language radio as well as via recordings in the Los Angeles area during the early thirties." Jesús and Víctor Sánchez, the original members of the group, grew up in Sonora, Mexico, where their father worked as a miner. When the two were teenagers, the family came to the United States as contract laborers, and eventually Jesús and Víctor worked in the fields in the Fresno area. In 1930 the brothers went to Los Angeles, and for several years they, along with Pedro González, developed an extremely successful radio program that aired from 4:00 to 6:00 in the morning "because it was cheaper to buy air time and it was the time when farm workers got up to go to work." The radio show mixed music and community activism, as González, its host, provided important job information to laborers and spoke out against the mass deportations of both "native" and "alien" Spanish-speakers that were taking place in Los Angeles.[85] In 1934, the same year that Los Madrugadores recorded the Joaquín Murrieta *corrido,* González was sent to San Quentin on trumped-up statutory rape charges.[86] If as "an exceptionally flexible musical genre," in George Sánchez's words, the *corrido*'s "relation to the working-class Mexican immigrant audience in Los Angeles" was "critical to its continued popularity," then the story of the unjust treatment and criminalization of a Mexican immigrant in the United States must have taken on new and tragic resonances for that working-class audience during these years of intensified nativism and forced repatriation, especially in light of González's harsh experiences with the law.[87]

But although the version of the Murrieta *corrido* recorded by Los Madrugadores in 1934 undoubtedly responded to the particular conjunction of postrevolution immigration, Anglo-American nativism, and *mexicano* cultural nationalism in Los Angeles, it also continued to transmit countermemories of the American 1848. For while a fictive, precariously unified white national identity was reformulated in the cheap sensational literature that was moving west along with the Americans who were rushing for gold and land, the U.S.-Mexican War also provoked other forms of national fantasy in the *décimas, corridos,* and other songs that accompanied the Spanish-speaking people who were migrating north to California during the postwar period. Although the apex of the heroic *corrido* tradition comes, according to Américo Paredes, during the Mexican Revolution, the post–U.S.–Mexican War era marks a crucial transitional time for Mexican folk music, as songs about the war, in particular, relied more upon narrative and thereby became more *corrido*-like. Paredes argues, for example, that "*décimas* about Jarauta, the fighting priest who was a guerrilla against Scott's forces and who was executed because he refused to recognize the Treaty of Guadalupe, are more purely narrative than most others of their time. Jarauta himself is cast in the pattern of the *corrido* hero."[88] We last encountered Jarauta, you will recall, in Ridge's novel and in the *California Police Gazette,* where he was instead cast in the role of the bloodthirsty, savage leader of many of the members of Murrieta's band during the U.S.-Mexican War. If in the English-language versions the evil Padre Jarauta prefigures the monstrous Three-Fingered Jack, whose viciousness justifies the imposition of U.S. laws despite Murrieta's appeal, Paredes implies that the *décimas* underline the injustice of U.S. law by celebrating Jarauta's doomed resistance to it.

María Herrera-Sobek and other *corrido* scholars have suggested that there was a "renaissance" in *corrido* production during the middle of the nineteenth century, when ballads dealing with conflicts between Anglos and Mexicans began to proliferate.[89] These songs helped to disseminate an uneven, contradictory national sentiment. As Paredes puts it, the "blaze stirred up by the daily conflict" between Mexicans and Anglo-Americans meant that a "nationalist feeling" arose in the borderlands before one was strongly and widely articulated in greater Mexico. Although "Mexican nationalist feeling does not define itself until the last third of the nineteenth century," Paredes argues, in "the northern frontiers, however, and in the parts of the United States recently taken from Mexico, nationalism begins to be felt toward the end of the 1830s, if we may take the folklore of these regions as an indication."[90] In the face of a conquest that was often figured as the dismemberment of Mexico, the postwar producers of *décimas* and *corridos* struggled to remember a truncated national body, reasserting its integrity by constructing a nationalist sentiment that was in many ways a defensive response to Anglo-American racism and the violence of U.S. nation-building.

I am arguing that, despite their different relationships to literacy, orality, and national languages, *corridos* and sensational crime literature such as the English-language Murrieta novels are intersecting, hybrid forms. But this hybridity does not magically dissolve differences or reconcile warring interpretations of the conquest and its consequences. Instead, the cultural syncretism of these popular texts forces us to confront the unequal power relations and the larger sphere of inter-American conflict that mutually shaped them.[91]

As popular forms, *corridos* and U.S. sensational literature might initially seem to belong to incommensurate worlds. *Corridos* are, after all, closely linked to oral traditions, while sensationalism signals the emergence of a U.S. mass culture marked by industrialized modes of cultural production and enabled by improvements in literacy rates, changes in print technology, and the development of transportation networks. This does not mean, however, that *corridos* were produced by a thoroughly premodern folk or that sensational literature is simply the corrupted, debased result of the incursions of capital into the sphere of popular culture, because there are many folkloric motifs and patterns in sensational literature and many links between *corridos,* the spread of print capitalism, and the uneven modernization of social space. Although they were inevitably transformed as they moved from one context to another, *corridos* were frequently printed as broadsides or in newspapers, for instance, and they are sometimes based on newspaper stories;[92] their dissemination was facilitated by the growth of railroad networks throughout Mexico and the United States in the last quarter of the nineteenth century;[93] and they often register the dislocating effects of U.S.-capitalist restructuring. For even though some *corridos* were produced and performed by people who had lived in the border regions for years and were now being encroached upon by Anglo immigrants, *corrido* communities from at least the mid–nineteenth century on have more often been multiple and heterogeneous; marked by displacements and movements; stratified by differences of gender, generation, and regional origin; and composed of both immigrants and "natives." Indeed, we might say that *corridos* constitute, in James Clifford's words, a "traveling culture," a popular form in motion, for they were frequently disseminated by migrant workers such as cowboys, railroad hands, and miners and they are often about labor migration and, more generally, movement between regions and nations.[94]

For instance, "Kiansis I," one of the earliest extant *corridos,* memorializes the experiences of Mexican vaqueros who drove cattle from Texas to Kansas during the 1860s and 1870s, recording the perils of the long journey and celebrating the superior skills of the vaqueros. Although "Kiansis I" opposes "Americanos" working the trail to the "*mexicanos*" who outperform them, it is unclear whether the *mexicanos* are Texas-Mexicans, Mexicans who came to Texas to work as cowboys, or workers who came to Texas from other parts of the United States. In other words, the "*mexicano*" community that the *corrido* invokes cannot be neatly circumscribed within a fixed space outside the migratory trajectory of the cattle drive. Similarly, "Los reenganchados a Kansas," a *corrido* from a later period, follows the movements of Mexican workers who cross into the United States and are sent as contract laborers on a train to Kansas City.[95] Far from reflecting a premodern, fixed folk community, the *corrido* focuses on the rapid movements of the train and the journey from El Paso, Texas, where many of the agencies recruiting Mexican labor were located, through Oklahoma to the railroad yards of Kansas City. If, as Paul Gilroy argues, the ship is a crucial conduit for the "early politics and poetics of the black Atlantic world," then the train has surely been a crucial vehicle for the migratory meanings of community mobilized by the *corrido*. It is worth repeating, however, that not all forms of movement and displacement are the same. While U.S. settlers and sensational popular cultures moving west after 1848 tried to naturalize the new national boundaries and to assert a white U.S.-American identity, the workers moving from south to north—say, from Sonora, Mexico, to Sonora, California—in the wake of the war and in the face of brutal U.S. racism in many instances articulated a kind of disjunctive transnational nationalism that overflows, as Gilroy puts it, "the containers that the modern nation state provides."[96]

But if *corridos* and sensational literature mark different routes through modernity, both exemplify the ways that modern nationalisms have, as Cynthia Enloe suggests, "typically sprung from masculinized memory, masculinized humiliation, and masculinized hope."[97] Sensational U.S.–Mexican War literature and postwar crime narratives most often focus on violent encounters between men; nation-building is represented as a patrilineal enterprise; and women are usually figured as the spoils of war or as mediators whose bodies facilitate or threaten national unity. Susan Lee Johnson has argued that in the post-1848 state-building period, "persistent stories of Gold Rush violence and vengeance hark back to an earlier ethic, not yet archaic, in the 1850s, under which rape, lynching, and whipping took on meaning as affronts to male honor."[98] Similarly, nineteenth-century *corridos* frequently valorize a violent masculine hero who steadfastly resists U.S. expansion and depredation, avenging a series of humiliations.[99]

In the version of the Murrieta *corrido* recorded by Los Madrugadores, for instance, cowardly Americans murder his brother and kill Joaquín's wife, Carmelita, after making her suffer ("Carmelita tan hermosa / Cómo la hicieron sufrir"). The *corrido* omits the third humiliation that is presented as decisive in the English-language texts: the public whipping that Murrieta is forced to endure at the hands of the Americans. In the *corrido,* the violence done to Carmelita seems to stand in for the physical punishment that Murrieta himself withstands in the other versions, for the outrage done to his wife is the occasion ("Vengo a vengar a mi esposa") for his transformation into a Robin Hood–style social bandit who robs from the rich, takes his hat off to the humble and poor, and is called a bandit only because U.S. laws are so unjust. The writer of the *California Police Gazette* version, who suggests that Murrieta's wife, Carmela, is "ravished" and then killed, is more explicit about her suffering than the *corrido* is, or than Ridge is about Rosita's fate (in his version she is raped but not killed). Despite their differences, however, all three versions still figure violence to the woman's body as the ultimate outrage that prefigures or stands in for, depending on the version, violence done to Murrieta's own body and to the larger community. By making the woman a victim rather than an actor in this drama, and by provoking nationalist affect through a patriarchal narrative of rape, masculine humiliation, and violent homosocial revenge, the *corrido,* like Ridge and the *Police Gazette,* identifies masculinity with resistance and makes emasculation and the violated female body the signs of conquest. Thus all three versions appeal to gender differences in order to stabilize the ruptures of a violent, migratory inter-American modernity.

It could be argued that the Murrieta *corrido* evokes, in Julie Skurski's words, "ideas of undisputed origins, original creation, and sustained tradition" in order to suggest that people of Mexican origin "share an original identity which can be liberated or restored through the rejection of colonialism's pervasive influence."[100] In other words, in response to U.S. imperialism, the *corrido* strives to make Murrieta the bearer of an originary, authentic "Mexican" identity, reasserting the wholeness and reintegration of the Mexican nation as a way of dealing with the trauma of the war and the losses imposed by the treaty. What is more, by naturalizing the connection between the soil and the Mexican nation ("I'm neither a Chilean nor a stranger on this soil which I tread. California is part of Mexico because God wanted it that way"), the *corrido* constructs a national sentiment that conceals its own constructedness.[101] An insistence on the integrity of the Mexican national body despite the ruptures of war is also signaled by the *corrido*'s conclusion, which omits any mention of the severed head, so important in Ridge's and the *Police Gazette* texts, in favor of a first-person assertion of Murrieta's *mexicano* identity ("Yo soy ese Mexicano/de nombre Joaquín Murrieta").

But if the *corridos* circulate a cultural nationalism that may seem to be formally equivalent to the white nativist nationalisms of 1850s and 1930s California promoted in the crime gazette and the sensational novel, the different relationships that these nationalisms have to the U.S. nation-state significantly affect their meanings. In other words, while nationalisms as such may be inherently exclusionary, the different material and political histories of U.S. and Chicano nationalisms suggest that their identity can be affirmed only at the cost of an extremely high level of abstraction. Although the nationalism of the migrants who called themselves Anglo-Saxon usually supported the white supremacist U.S. state, the nationalist sentiments invoked by the members of *corrido* communities were both at odds with official U.S. nationalism and at a distance from and irreducible to an emergent nationalism associated with the Mexican nation-state. Thus although the *corridos* can support exclusionary forms of nationalism, they also disseminate memories of another America and thereby challenge narratives of U.S. national identity that require the interiorization and naturalization of the external borders of the state.[102] For the process of internalizing national boundaries allows only some of us to, as Balibar suggests, "inhabit the space of the state as a place where we have always been—and always will be—'at home.' "[103]

Even when the *corridos* seek to disseminate exclusionary national sentiments, they underline the impossibility of a unitary national identity as they incessantly register the disruptions, displacements, and movements that provide the unstable ground for asserting it. The very fact that we can only guess about the *corrido*'s origins and that we have no access to a complete, unfragmented, certifiably nineteenth-century Murrieta *corrido* suggests that the folk tradition that transmits national identity is in this case manifestly synthetic, unavoidably responding to capitalist modernity even when resisting it. As Víctor Sánchez remembers, "We had many requests for this *corrido,* at parties, and then after we began to sing it on the radio, people would send us cards to the station and ask that we record it so they could have the disc. Felipe Valdéz Leal added three or four verses to make it fit both sides of the record—I don't remember which ones but possibly the one about coming from Hermosillo."[104] In other words, the national sentiment preserved in the Murrieta *corrido* was not only disseminated through mass cultural media such as records and the radio but was also decisively shaped by these cultural technologies, since additions were made so it would "fit" the record. Finally, the transregional and often transnational trajectories of those who have performed this *corrido*—from Zacatecas to Sonora, from Sonora to Arizona, from Sonora–Arizona to California, and maybe back again, to name just a few possible routes—problematize any appeal to the idea of a static, unfragmented national community. These singers, musicians, field laborers, miners, and other workers have preserved memories of the American 1848 and of a postwar crisis in the racial state that continues to haunt the U.S. "home" in an age of law and racial terror that has not ended.

CODA: BEYOND 1848

I began writing about race, labor, U.S. politics, popular culture, and the American 1848 in the early 1990s, a time when nativist retrenching made strikingly apparent the resemblances between the post-1848 period and my own. During the 1990s Californians debated and then passed the anti-immigrant Proposition 187, which would have made undocumented immigrants ineligible for public social services, health care, and education; Proposition 227, which virtually eliminated bilingual education in California; a "three strikes" law that contributed to the ongoing and disproportionate criminalization and imprisonment of brown and black people; and Proposition 209, which invoked the ideal of colorblindness to dismantle affirmative action and other policies of racial redress. As I wrote the early drafts of this chapter on Joaquín Murrieta, it was clear that the interconnections among law, nativism, and class and racial hierarchies that I traced from the 1840s to the 1930s continued to significantly affect U.S. culture and politics.

Today in the year 2001, some things have changed, but much remains the same. In a departure from its overtly anti-immigrant platform in the previous presidential election, in 2000 the Republican Party presented as a candidate a former Texas governor and scion of a wealthy oil family who made overt and widely publicized efforts to win over Latino voters, an effort that included Spanish-language radio and television ads. Meanwhile, George W. Bush's Mexican-American nephew, George Prescott Bush, frequently made public appearances to support his uncle, appearances that underlined the Bush family's own international romance, the marriage between a Mexican woman, Columba, and the candidate's brother, Jeb. The rhetoric of international romance also appeared in speeches in which Bush asked voters to imagine the relationship between Mexico and the United States on the model of the family, as when he called for a "special relationship" with Mexico in which differences would be "differences among family, not rivals." For the most part, this familial vision of what one press release called "A United Western Hemisphere" meant "uplift" through NAFTA and applying "the power of the markets to the needs of the poor."[105] Similarly, Democrat Al Gore aired a thirty-second television ad in which he spoke in Spanish "throughout the entire spot," as the Gore-Lieberman 2000 website proudly proclaimed. In his appeal to Latino voters, Gore also invoked the family, insisting that "in America, words like *familia, communidad, opportunidad,* and *educacion* are not just *palabras*—they are the values that guide our lives."[106] Like Bush, he strongly endorsed NAFTA, claiming that it had deepened neighborly, inter-American ties.

On the other hand, Reform Party candidate Pat Buchanan focused on the similarities between Gore and Bush on these issues and took a much more overtly nativist position. Articles posted on Buchanan's campaign website suggested that both Bush and Gore favored a "U.S. merger with Mexico"; that a vote for Bush meant a "vote for essentially making Mexico a 51st state"; and that the Democrats were seeking a new base in illegal immigration. Opening a policy statement called "Trouble in the Neighborhood" with the history of the 1836 Texas-Mexico conflict, the U.S.-Mexican War, and the cession of the Southwest and California to "America," Buchanan promised voters that although "Mexican irredentism" was "alive and well," he intended to fight it, for "we cannot allow to rise within our country a nation within a nation where Spanish is the language and anti-Americanism the ideology, while U.S. taxpayers pay for its schools and services as it swells inexorably towards the Nuevo Aztlan of the Chicano activists' dreams." Sounding a lot like the anti-imperialist nativists of the 1840s and 1850s, in a book published in 2000 Buchanan called for "a republic, not an empire": "We are not imperialists; we are not interventionists; we are not hegemonists; and we are not isolationists. We simply believe in America, first, last, and always."[107]

After George W. Bush was officially awarded the presidency in a contest decided by the narrowest of margins, news exit polls showed that 63 percent of Latinos had voted for Gore, although Bush did much better among Cuban Americans, most importantly in Florida, the state where the election was ultimately decided.[108] Probably because of the use of the "butterfly ballot" in Florida's heavily Democratic West Palm Beach County, Buchanan picked up a surprising number of critical votes there but received only a small percentage of the national popular vote. The controversies that broke out in the wake of the Florida election, however, contradicted the rhetoric of racial inclusion, based on the model of the family, used by the candidates for the two major political parties. In addition to the disputes about the butterfly ballot, outmoded machines for counting the votes in many areas, and the intervention of the Supreme Court, large numbers of African and Haitian Americans claimed to have been "denied access to polling booths, intimidated, harassed, and even threatened when they attempted to vote."[109] After the election, Kweisi Mfume, the president of the National Association for the Advancement of Colored People, charged that there was "evidence of massive voter disenfranchisement of people of color during the presidential election.

The election in Florida was conducted in a manner which was unfair, illegal, immoral and undemocratic."[110]

Despite the ongoing conflicts about the election and the legitimacy of
the official results in Florida, Buchanan's poor showing may at least suggest to some that the popular appeal of nativism has finally waned. It
should be noted, however, that even as Bush and Gore deployed the rhetoric of international romance with its emphasis on family ties, they also
continued to insist upon the importance of policing the U.S.-Mexico border. During the campaign Bush championed projects such as El Paso's
"Operation Hold the Line," and in his "Century of the Americas" speech
he promised to expand patrols to "make our borders something more
than lines on a map." Similarly, Gore praised the "openness" of America but also continued to worry about stemming "the flow of illegal immigrants to America": "We must have secure borders and strong border
control. We must return illegal aliens to their homes, especially criminal
aliens." This double emphasis should remind us of the international romances of the mid–nineteenth century that simultaneously promoted
closer economic ties between the United States and the other Americas
and expressed fears about threats to national boundaries and the incorporation of alien, especially nonwhite, people into the United States. Although the rhetoric of international romance and family is ostensibly
more welcoming than that of nativism, it has often been used to legitimate or even to deepen dramatically unequal power relations. At the
same time, it should be remembered that a rhetoric of inter-American
romance has long coexisted with an exclusionary emphasis on border
control and the policing of aliens. Both were prominently featured in the
sensational literature of the American 1848, a moment that continues to
haunt the present.

Notes

CHAPTER 1. INTRODUCTION

1. For two different accounts of this incident, see Jay Monaghan, *The Great Rascal: The Life and Adventures of Ned Buntline* (New York: Bonanza, 1951), 3–33; and Don Russell, *The Lives and Legends of Buffalo Bill* (Norman: University of Oklahoma Press, 1960), 149–61. Although Russell claims that "nothing in the Buffalo Bill legend has been more exaggerated than Ned Buntline's part in it" (150), Buntline's novels and plays about Buffalo Bill certainly contributed to the construction of the legend.

Peter Buckley's unpublished 1984 doctoral dissertation, "To the Opera House: Culture and Society in New York City, 1820–1860" (State University of New York at Stony Brook, 1984), is still the best source for information on Buntline. See also Buckley, "The Case against Ned Buntline: The 'Words, Signs, and Gestures' of Popular Authorship," *Prospects* 13 (1988): 249–72.

2. Richard Slotkin, *Gunfighter Nation: The Myth of the Frontier in Twentieth-Century America* (Norman: University of Oklahoma Press, 1998), 87.

3. Ibid., 83, 86.

4. On Bowery B'hoys and G'hals, see Buckley, "To the Opera House," 294–409; Eric Lott, *Love and Theft: Blackface Minstrelsy and the American Working Class* (New York: Oxford University Press, 1993), 81–88, 154, 160, 201, 207–8; Christine Stansell, *City of Women: Sex and Class in New York, 1789–1860* (Urbana: University of Illinois Press, 1987), 89–101; and Sean Wilentz, *Chants Democratic: New York City and the Rise of the American Working Class, 1788–1850* (New York: Oxford University Press, 1984), 300–301.

5. Lawrence Levine, *Highbrow/Lowbrow: The Emergence of Cultural Hierarchy in America* (Cambridge: Harvard University Press, 1988), 68. Levine discusses the Astor Place riot as a symptom of an emerging high/low split within the public sphere and, more specifically, within the sphere of culture. For more

on the Astor Place riot, see also Peter Buckley, "To the Opera House"; David Grimsted, *Melodrama Unveiled: American Theater and Culture, 1800–1850* (Chicago: University of Chicago Press, 1968), 68–74; Lott, *Love and Theft*, 9, 65, 66–67, 81, 85, 88, 106; and Eric Moody, *The Astor Place Riot* (Bloomington: Indiana University Press, 1958).

6. Lott, *Love and Theft*, 66, 67.

7. In *Culture and Imperialism* (New York: Knopf, 1993), Edward Said defines imperialism as "the practice, the theory, and the attitudes of a dominating metropolitan center ruling a distant territory" and colonialism as "the implanting of settlements on distant territory" (9). Although I might quibble with the use of the term "distant," and though it's sometimes difficult to separate the two rigorously, I generally agree with Said's definitions of imperialism as territorial expansion and colonialism as (re)settlement. For some reflections on what the terms "imperialism" and "colonialism" might mean in a specifically U.S. context, see Jenny Sharpe, "Is the United States Postcolonial? Transnationalism, Immigration, and Race," *Diaspora* 4, no. 2 (1995): 181–99 (thanks to David Kazanjian for bringing this article to my attention); Eva Cherniavsky, "Subaltern Studies in a U.S. Frame," *boundary 2* 23, no. 2 (1996): 85–110; Arnold Krupat, "Postcoloniality and Native American Literature," *Yale Journal of Criticism* 7, no. 1 (1994): 163–80; Gilbert Joseph, Catherine Legrand, and Ricardo Salvatore, *Close Encounters of Empire: Writing the Cultural History of U.S.–Latin American Relations* (Durham: Duke University Press, 1998); Amy Kaplan and Donald Pease, eds., *Cultures of United States Imperialism* (Durham: Duke University Press, 1993); and Said, *Culture and Imperialism*, 8–9, 282–96. See also the articles collected in the special issue "Imperialism—A Useful Category of Historical Analysis?" of *Radical History Review* 57 (1993): 1–84.

8. Michael Denning, *Mechanic Accents: Dime Novels and Working-Class Culture in America*, rev. ed. (1987; London and New York: Verso, 1998), 13, 85.

9. For an excellent discussion of the relationship between city and empire in some of the popular literature of the nineteenth century, see Richard Slotkin, *The Fatal Environment: The Myth of the Frontier in the Age of Industrialization, 1800–1890* (Middletown, Conn.: Wesleyan University Press, 1985). Slotkin suggests that "literary mythology" tries to mask "the internal social conflicts of the Metropolis by projecting class war outward into racial war on the borders" (51–52).

10. David Potter, *The Impending Crisis, 1848–1861* (New York: Harper and Row, 1976), 16–17.

11. Michael Paul Rogin, *Subversive Genealogy: The Politics and Art of Herman Melville* (New York: Knopf, 1983), 103. Hereafter cited in text.

12. Scholars in Chicano and Latino Studies have addressed the significance of 1848 in a number of different ways. During the 1970s, the "internal colonialism" model was widely influential. For more on the internal colonialism model, see Michael Omi and Howard Winant, *Racial Formation in the United States: From the 1960s to the 1990s,* rev. ed. (New York: Routledge, 1994), 36–47. As Omi and Winant explain, the "internal colonialism" analogy emerged in the late 1960s and early 1970s and was especially popular among "radical nationalist movements" that "rejected reform-oriented politics" and

preferred "to link their struggles with those of such national liberation movements as the Vietnamese, Algerian, or Chinese revolutions" (44). Theories of internal colonialism "attempted the synthesis of different aspects of racial oppression: economic, political, and cultural, through the invocation of a colonial model" (45). While Omi and Winant credit this model for emphasizing the significance of race as well as for understanding racial dynamics as "global and epochal in character" (37), they argue that it is "a politically and not analytically grounded analogy" (46).

For examples of the internal colonialism model in Chicano Studies, see Rodolfo Acuña, *Occupied America: A History of Chicanos,* 4th ed. (1972; New York: Longman, 2000); Mario Barrera et al., "The Barrio as Internal Colony," in *People and Politics in Urban Society,* ed. Harlan Hahn (Beverly Hills, Calif.: Sage Publications, 1972); and Barrera, *Race and Class in the Southwest: A Theory of Racial Inequality* (Notre Dame: University of Notre Dame Press, 1979). For a critique of that model, see Tomás Almaguer, "Ideological Distortions and Recent Chicano Historiography: The Internal Colonialism Model and Chicano Historical Interpretation," *Aztlan* 18, no. 1 (spring 1987): 7–28. Almaguer identified five problems with this model. First, he argued that it gave "insufficient attention to both the significance of internal class stratification within the Mexican population before and after the United States–Mexico war" (11). He suggested that some historians who invoked this model, moreover, were silent about the "ranchero elite's treatment of the Indian population" (12). Second, he emphasized that "both Spain and later Mexico retained territorial claim to the Southwest on the basis of their imposition or perpetuation of a colonial system predicated on their ruthless exploitation of the truly indigenous Indian population" (14). Third, he argued that because some Mexicans were defined as white and accorded citizenship status, they were not "subordinated to the same inferior legal-political status accorded others in classic colonial situations or to blacks and Indians at this historical juncture elsewhere in the United States" (15). Fourth, he pointed to the "profound differences" that existed among the experiences of different racial minorities (16). And finally, he suggested that there was a "major discontinuity between the nineteenth- and early twentieth-century Chicano experiences," since by the twentieth century the "ranchero class" had lost their land and new waves of immigrants experienced the "rapid proletarianization of the Mexican population" (24).

Clearly Almaguer was responding to a different moment (1987) in Chicano Studies, a moment when the "internal colonialism" model needed to be reconsidered. Since he wrote this essay, several significant books in the field of Chicano/Latino Studies have made 1848 an important period marker while remaining sensitive to the problems and questions that he describes. See Almaguer, *Racial Fault Lines: The Historical Origins of White Supremacy in California* (Berkeley: University of California Press, 1994); Neil Foley, *The White Scourge: Mexicans, Blacks, and Poor Whites in Texas Cotton Culture* (Berkeley: University of California Press, 1997); David G. Gutiérrez, *Walls and Mirrors: Mexican Americans, Mexican Immigrants, and the Politics of Ethnicity* (Berkeley: University of California Press, 1995); David Montejano, *Anglos and Mexicans in the Making of Texas, 1836–1986* (Austin: University of Texas Press, 1987); and

Rosaura Sánchez, *Telling Identities: The Californio Testimonios* (Minneapolis: University of Minnesota Press, 1995).

13. José David Saldívar, *Border Matters: Remapping American Cultural Studies* (Berkeley: University of California Press, 1997), 177.

14. Susan Lee Johnson's outstanding social history of the California Gold Rush was published just as I was finishing the final revision of this manuscript. *Roaring Camp* should become the standard work on the subject. For some insightful remarks about the Gold Rush and 1848, see Johnson, *Roaring Camp: The Social World of the California Gold Rush* (New York: W. W. Norton and Company, 2000), 79–81, 95. See also Malcolm Rohrbough, *Days of Gold: The California Gold Rush and the American Nation* (Berkeley: University of California Press, 1997), 216–29; Almaguer, *Racial Fault Lines*, 26–29; and Jay Monaghan, *Chile, Peru, and the California Gold Rush of 1849* (Berkeley: University of California Press, 1973).

15. Donald C. Biggs, *Conquer and Colonize* (San Rafael, Calif.: Presidio, 1977).

16. On the participation of Mexican War veterans in the Caste War and on this conflict in general, see Gilbert Joseph, "The United States, Feuding Elites, and Rural Revolt in Yucatán, 1836–1915," in *Rural Revolt in Mexico: U.S. Intervention and the Domain of Subaltern Politics,* ed. Daniel Nugent (Durham: Duke University Press, 1998), 178–91. See also Joseph, "From Caste War to Class War: The Historiography of Modern Yucatán," *Hispanic American Historical Review* 65, no. 1 (1985): 111–34; and Nelson Reed, *The Caste War of Yucatan* (Stanford: Stanford University Press, 1964). On filibustering during this period, see Luis Martínez-Fernández, *Torn between Empires: Economy, Society, and Patterns of Political Thought in the Hispanic Caribbean, 1840–1878* (Athens: University of Georgia Press, 1994), esp. 23; Tom Chaffin, *Fatal Glory: Narciso Lopez and the First Clandestine U.S. War against Cuba* (Charlottesville: University Press of Virginia, 1996); Charles Brown, *Agents of Manifest Destiny: The Lives and Times of the Filibusters* (Chapel Hill: University of North Carolina Press, 1980); and Robert E. May, "Young American Males and Filibustering in the Age of Manifest Destiny: The United States Army as a Cultural Mirror," *Journal of American History* 78, no. 3 (December 1991): 863.

17. See Martínez-Fernández, *Torn between Empires.* Martínez-Fernández suggests that the "year 1848 stands out as a significant watershed in the course of international rivalries in the Hispanic Caribbean. Up to that point the policy of the United States in the region had been defensive. That year, however, the United States began to put forth a much more aggressive policy, particularly toward Cuba" (20). See also Reginald Horsman, *Race and Manifest Destiny: The Origins of American Racial Anglo-Saxonism* (Cambridge: Harvard University Press, 1981), 272–97.

18. See Richard Slotkin, *Regeneration through Violence: The Mythology of the American Frontier, 1600–1860* (Middletown, Conn.: Wesleyan University Press, 1973); Horsman, *Race and Manifest Destiny,* 189–207; Dee Brown, *Bury My Heart at Wounded Knee: An Indian History of the American West* (New York: Henry Holt, 1970), 1–12; Brian Dippie, *The Vanishing American: White Attitudes and U.S. Indian Policy* (Middletown, Conn.: Wesleyan University Press,

1982); Lucy Maddox, *Removals: Nineteenth-Century American Literature and the Politics of Indian Affairs* (New York: Oxford University Press, 1991); Michael Paul Rogin, *Fathers and Children: Andrew Jackson and the Subjugation of the American Indian* (New York: Knopf, 1975); Almaguer, *Racial Fault Lines*, 150–170.

19. Brown, *Bury My Heart at Wounded Knee*, 13–102; Carol Chomsky, "The United States–Dakota War Trials: A Study in Military Injustice," *Stanford Law Review* 43, no. 1 (November 1990): 13–98; Gary Anderson and Alan Woolworth, eds., *Through Dakota Eyes: Narrative Accounts of the Minnesota Indian War of 1812* (St. Paul: Minnesota Historical Society Press, 1988); and Roy W. Meyer, *History of the Santee Sioux: United States Indian Policy on Trial*, rev. ed. (Lincoln: University of Nebraska Press, 1993).

20. Walter LaFeber, *The Cambridge History of Foreign Relations: The American Search for Opportunity, 1865–1913*, vol. 2 (New York: Cambridge, 1993), 53–54. LaFeber suggests that by the late 1880s the U.S. military had consolidated white power over the entire country, "and in the late 1890s white Americans were using this continental empire as a base from which to create a new empire of commerce and insular possessions in the Caribbean and across the Pacific Ocean." As Amy Kaplan ably explains, during the 1890s "politicians, intellectuals, and businessmen on both sides of the debate were redefining national power as disembodied—that is, divorced from contiguous territorial expansion." According to Kaplan, "[w]ith the end of continental expansion, national power was no longer measured by the settlement and incorporation of new territory consolidated by a united state, but by the extension of vaster yet less tangible networks of international markets and political influence." Amy Kaplan, "Romancing the Empire: The Embodiment of American Masculinity in the Popular Historical Novel of the 1890s," *American Literary History* 2, no. 4 (winter 1990): 662.

21. LaFeber, *The New Empire: An Interpretation of American Expansion, 1860–1898* (1963; Ithaca: Cornell University Press, 1998), xxxii. Hereafter cited in text.

22. Charles Vevier, "American Continentalism: An Idea of Expansion, 1845–1910," *American Historical Review* 65, no. 2 (1960): 323. When in the late nineteenth century anti-imperialists argued against the acquisition of lands "disconnected" from the continent, they sometimes implied that earlier expansion had been a natural and organic process; not imperialism at all but, as Albert Weinberg put it in a different context, "the irresistible movement of American population into undeveloped land" that was contiguous. Albert Weinberg, *Manifest Destiny: A Study of Nationalist Expansionism in American History* (Gloucester, Mass.: Peter Smith, 1948), 198.

23. Amy Kaplan, "'Left Alone with America: The Absence of Empire in the Study of American Culture," in *Cultures of United States Imperialism*, ed. Kaplan and Pease (Durham: Duke University Press, 1993), 17.

24. Richard Stott, *Workers in the Metropolis: Class, Ethnicity, and Youth in Antebellum New York City* (Ithaca: Cornell University Press, 1990), 3.

25. Kerby Miller, *Emigrants and Exiles: Ireland and the Irish Exodus to North America* (New York: Oxford University Press, 1985), 280, 291.

26. Bruce Levine, *The Spirit of 1848: German Immigrants, Labor Conflict, and the Coming of the Civil War* (Urbana: University of Illinois Press, 1992), 1–82. According to Levine, almost "60,000 Germans arrived per year during the latter half of the 1840s" (15).

27. David Henkin, *City Reading: Written Words and Public Spaces in Antebellum New York* (New York: Columbia University Press, 1998), 30. See also Amy Bridges, *A City in the Republic: Antebellum New York and the Origins of Machine Politics* (Cambridge: Cambridge University Press, 1984), 39.

28. Bruce Laurie, *Working People of Philadelphia, 1800–1850* (Philadelphia: Temple University Press, 1980), 29.

29. Oscar Handlin, *Boston's Immigrants: A Study of Acculturation* (Cambridge: Harvard University Press, 1959), 74–75; and Bridges, *City in the Republic,* 58.

30. Allan Pred, *Urban Growth and City-Systems in the United States, 1840–1860* (Cambridge: Harvard University Press, 1980), 4.

31. Henkin, *City Reading,* 107; Charles Sellers, *The Market Revolution: Jacksonian America, 1815–1846* (New York: Oxford University Press, 1991), 369–72; Ronald Zboray, *A Fictive People: Antebellum Economic Development and the American Reading Public* (New York: Oxford University Press, 1993); Zboray, "Antebellum Reading and the Ironies of Technological Innovation," in *Reading in America: Literature and Social History,* ed. Cathy N. Davidson (Baltimore: Johns Hopkins University Press, 1989), 182–91; and Alexander Saxton, *The Rise and Fall of the White Republic: Class Politics and Mass Culture in Nineteenth-Century America* (London and New York: Verso, 1990), 95–105.

32. Saxton, *Rise and Fall,* 95–101; and Henkin, *City Reading,* 105.

33. Sellers, *Market Revolution,* 370.

34. Bridges, *City in the Republic,* 21; Sellers, *Market Revolution,* 40–44.

35. Zboray, *Fictive People,* 55–82. Sellers notes that in the 1840s, "the United States almost trebled its railway network to 8,879 miles" (392).

36. Ibid., 75.

37. Henkin, *City Reading,* 105–6.

38. Pred, *Urban Growth,* 4.

39. Wilentz, *Chants Democratic,* 107.

40. Ibid., 114–16.

41. Ibid., 299.

42. Laurie, *Working People,* 10.

43. Ibid., 29–30.

44. Handlin, *Boston's Immigrants,* 74–75; Bridges, *City in the Republic,* 58. According to Handlin, the ready-made clothing industry, sugar refining, iron works, and shipbuilding were particularly affected (77–78).

45. Lott, *Love and Theft,* 4, 11. Lott's work is a good example of how a good deal of excellent American Studies scholarship still subsumes all other meanings and consequences of the events of 1848 within a national narrative of slavery and freedom. He argues, for instance, that "the minstrel show provided the soundtrack for the American 1848" (210), revealing "the political unconscious of Manifest Destiny" (203). The "racial repressed" that Lott uncovers, however, has little to do with U.S. imperialism, Mexico, immigrant workers, or interna-

tional conflict. Instead, Lott focuses on "the sectional conflict western emigration not only failed to dispel but—in reopening the question of whether the occupied land would be slave or free—actually revivified" (170). As a result, his brilliant analysis of the relationship between the formation of U.S. working-class whiteness and fantasies of blackness elides the important relationships between whiteness, blackness, and other racializations as they were elaborated during and after the U.S.-Mexican War in the borderlands and in the gold mines of California. Lott's analysis shows how the international dimensions of the U.S.-Mexican War and the nonbinary race relations that it affected tend to disappear within national narratives that isolate domestic, sectional conflict from a larger global framework.

46. Noel Ignatiev, *How the Irish Became White* (New York: Routledge, 1995), 1.

47. Ibid., 76, 96.

48. Charles Bergquist, *Labor and the Course of American Democracy: U.S. History in Latin American Perspective* (London and New York: Verso, 1996), 45–78.

49. Saxton, *Rise and Fall,* 1.

50. Ibid., 10.

51. For the later nineteenth century, see Saxton's outstanding study *The Indispensable Enemy: Labor and the Anti-Chinese Movement in California* (1971; Berkeley: University of California Press, 1995).

52. "Race and the House of Labor," in *The Great Fear: Race in the Mind of America,* ed. Gary B. Nash and Richard Weiss (New York: Holt, Rinehart, and Winston, 1970), 98.

53. Dale Steinhauer, "The Immigrant Soldier in the Regular Army during the Mexican War," in *Papers of the Second Palo Alto Conference,* ed. H. Joseph, A. Knopp, and D. Murphy (Brownsville, Tex.: U.S. Department of the Interior, 1997), 66. According to Steinhauer, one-quarter were Irish and 1 in 7 was of German birth.

54. Robert Ryal Miller, *Shamrock and Sword: The Saint Patrick's Battalion in the U.S.-Mexican War* (Norman: University of Oklahoma Press, 1989), 23.

55. On nativist riots during the 1840s and 1850s, see David Grimsted, *American Mobbing, 1828–1861: Toward Civil War* (New York: Oxford University Press, 1998), 218–45.

56. Miller, *Shamrock and Sword,* 163.

57. Amy Bridges, "Becoming American: The Working Classes of the United States before the Civil War," in *Working-Class Formation: Nineteenth-Century Patterns in Western Europe and the United States,* ed. I. Katznelson and A. Zolberg (Princeton: Princeton University Press, 1986), 186. Bridges suggests that the "threatened but as yet unproletarianized crafts . . . were at the heart of that movement, in organizations like the Order of United American Mechanics, and temperance activity was also strongly associated with nativism." See also Laurie, *Working People,* 174–76; and Wilentz, *Chants Democratic,* 323–25.

58. Bruce Laurie, " 'Nothing on Compulsion': Life Styles of Philadelphia Artisans, 1820–1850," *Labor History* 15 (1974): 250. Cited in Bridges, *City in the Republic,* 96.

59. Michael Hogan, *The Irish Soldiers of Mexico* (Guadalajara: Fondo Editorial Universitario, 1997), 136–42.

60. Jenny Franchot, *Roads to Rome: The Antebellum Protestant Encounter with Catholicism* (Berkeley: University of California Press, 1994), 100, 109; David H. Bennett, *The Party of Fear: From Nativist Movements to the New Right in American History* (Chapel Hill: University of North Carolina Press, 1988), 40.

61. Matthew Frye Jacobson, *Whiteness of a Different Color: European Immigrants and the Alchemy of Race* (Cambridge: Harvard University Press, 1998), 204.

62. Ibid., 214.

63. Thomas Hietala, *Manifest Design: Anxious Aggrandizement in Late Jacksonian America* (Ithaca: Cornell University Press, 1985), 97.

64. Saxton, *Rise and Fall,* 102.

65. I understand the process of racialization in Michael Omi's and Howard Winant's terms, as "occurring through a linkage between structure and representation. Racial *projects* do the ideological 'work' of making these links. *A racial project is simultaneously an interpretation, representation, or explanation of racial dynamics, and an effort to reorganize and redistribute resources along particular racial lines.* Racial projects connect what race *means* in a particular discursive practice and the ways in which both social structures and everyday experiences are racially *organized,* based upon that meaning." See Omi and Winant, *Racial Formation,* 56.

66. Almaguer, *Racial Fault Lines,* 13.

67. Denning, *Mechanic Accents,* 86, 87.

68. John Fuller, *The Movement for the Acquisition of All Mexico, 1846–1848* (Baltimore: Johns Hopkins University Press, 1936), 129–30, 162–63; Horsman, *Race and Manifest Destiny,* 175–85; John H. Schroeder, *Mr. Polk's War: American Opposition and Dissent, 1846–1848* (Madison: University of Wisconsin Press, 1973), 35–39; and Anders Stephanson, *Manifest Destiny: American Expansion and the Empire of Right* (New York: Hill and Wang, 1995), 49–55.

69. Fuller, *Movement,* 85–87, 111–14, 130; Horsman, *Race and Manifest Destiny,* 241; Stephanson, *Manifest Destiny,* 48.

70. Fuller, *Movement,* 51–52, 82–83, 87–89, 109–10, 114–16, 130, 161–62; Stephanson, *Manifest Destiny,* 48.

71. Fuller, *Movement,* 35–36, 53–57, 106–9; Stephanson, *Manifest Destiny,* 48–49.

72. Michael Holt, *The Rise and Fall of the American Whig Party: Jacksonian Politics and the Onset of the Civil War* (New York: Oxford University Press, 1999), 248–58; Horsman, *Race and Manifest Destiny,* 237–40; Schroeder, *Mr. Polk's War,* 6–7, 28–32, 72–78, 129–30.

73. Horsman, *Race and Manifest Destiny,* 237.

74. *Democratic Review,* August 1847, 101; Stephanson, *Manifest Destiny,* 46–47. In 1845, O'Sullivan declared that it was the manifest destiny of the United States "to overspread the continent allotted by Providence for the free development of our yearly multiplying millions" (*Democratic Review,* 17 [1845], 5).

75. For an excellent discussion of the contradictions in O'Sullivan's and other literary Young Americans' use of the concept of Manifest Destiny, see Priscilla Wald, *Constituting Americans: Cultural Anxiety and Narrative Form* (Durham: Duke University Press, 1995), 105–6. As Wald observes, O'Sullivan's collaborators at the *Review,* such as Evert Duyckinck, "did not share his politics" (109). She also suggests that while " 'the continent' of Manifest Destiny rhetoric helped to image and ground coherence" (113), still, "conflicts exacerbated by expansion consistently troubled assertions of national coherence" (115).

76. Ned Buntline, *The Volunteer: or, The Maid of Monterey. A Tale of the Mexican War* (Boston: F. Gleason, 1847), 75. Hereafter cited in text. In the 1850s, however, he would promote filibustering expeditions to take over Cuba, in part because of his proslavery allegiances; this imperial enterprise was supported by proslavery Southerners who wanted to expand that institution. See Monaghan, *The Great Rascal,* 194.

77. Jamie Bronstein, *Land Reform and Working-Class Experience in Britain and the United States, 1800–1862* (Stanford: Stanford University Press, 1999), 146.

78. A. J. H. Duganne, *The Poetical Works of Augustine Duganne* (Philadelphia: Parry and McMillan, 1855), 231; "Augustine Joseph Hickey Duganne," in *Dictionary of American Biography,* vol. 3, ed. Johnson and Malone (New York: Scribner's, 1937), 492.

79. See Denning, *Mechanic Accents,* 85–117; David Reynolds, *Beneath the American Renaissance: The Subversive Imagination in the Age of Emerson and Melville* (Cambridge: Harvard University Press, 1988); Reynolds, ed., *George Lippard, Prophet of Protest: Writings of an American Radical, 1822–1854* (New York: Peter Lang, 1986); Reynolds, "Introduction," in *The Quaker City; or, The Monks of Monk Hall* by George Lippard (Amherst: University of Massachusetts Press, 1995), vii–xliv.

80. *Nineteenth Century,* vol. 2, 187.

81. See Denning, *Mechanic Accents,* 112–14.

82. Shelley Streeby, "Haunted Houses: George Lippard, Nathaniel Hawthorne, and Middle-Class America," *Criticism* 38, no. 3 (1996): 450–58.

83. Denning, *Mechanic Accents,* 87.

84. Christine Bold, *Selling the Wild West: Popular Western Fiction, 1860–1960* (Bloomington: Indiana University Press, 1987), 2. See also Denning, *Mechanic Accents,* 20: "In the early years, successful dime novelists like George Lippard, T. S. Arthur, and Ned Buntline were able to begin their own story papers. But the tendency of the industry was to shift from selling an 'author' who was a free laborer, to selling a 'character,' a trademark whose stories could be written by a host of anonymous hack writers and whose celebrity could be protected in court."

85. Bold, *Wild West,* 3.

86. This method has been inspired in particular by the work of Saxton and Denning. In his afterword to the 1998 edition of *Mechanic Accents,* Denning suggests: "The possibility for oppositional or alternative readings of cultural commodities, whether books or other media, depends finally on the cultivation, organization, and mobilization of audiences by oppositional subcultures and so-

cial movements: a history of reading must be accompanied by a history and reconstruction of those movements and cultures" (264).

87. Néstor García Canclini, *Hybrid Cultures: Strategies for Entering and Leaving Modernity,* trans. Christopher L. Chiappari and Silvia L. López (Minneapolis: University of Minnesota Press, 1995), 146. See also Canclini, *Transforming Modernity: Popular Culture in Mexico,* trans. Lidia Lozano (Austin: University of Texas, 1993), 22: "In short, popular cultures are the product of unequal appropriation of cultural capital, the people's own reflections about their living conditions, and conflict-ridden interaction with hegemonic sectors."

88. Canclini, *Hybrid Cultures,* 4. On this point, see also Stuart Hall, "What Is This Black in Black Popular Culture?" in *Black Popular Culture,* ed. Gina Dent (Seattle: Bay Press, 1992), 24–33; George Lipsitz, *Time Passages: Collective Memory and American Popular Culture* (Minneapolis: University of Minnesota Press, 1990); Denning, *Mechanic Accents,* 26, 60; Lott, *Love and Theft,* 17–18.

89. See John Beverley, *Subalternity and Representation: Arguments in Cultural Theory* (Durham: Duke University Press, 1999), 109. Beverley observes that the "left" critique of Cultural Studies "takes the form, generally, of a return to the Frankfurt School." See also Denning, *Mechanic Accents,* 260–61.

90. Michael Paul Rogin, *Blackface, White Noise: Jewish Immigrants in the Hollywood Melting Pot* (Berkeley: University of California Press, 1996), 47.

91. Richard Brodhead, *Cultures of Letters: Scenes of Reading and Writing in Nineteenth-Century America* (Chicago: University of Chicago Press, 1993), 79.

92. Reynolds, *Beneath the American Renaissance,* 171.

93. Ibid., 183.

94. Denning, *Mechanic Accents,* 29.

95. Ibid., 10–11. See also his first four chapters on the production of and audiences for sensational literature, 1–61.

96. Zboray, "Ironies," 195–96.

97. Ann Cvetkovich, *Mixed Feelings: Feminism, Mass Culture, and Victorian Sensationalism* (New Brunswick, N.J.: Rutgers University Press, 1992), 15. For more on European and especially French versions of sensation literature, see Denning, *Mechanic Accents,* 86–85, 103–5; and Peter Brooks, *Reading for the Plot: Design and Intention in Narrative* (New York: Vintage, 1985), 143–70.

98. The phrase "sensationalized body genres" is Rogin's; see *Blackface,* 30.

99. Tom Gunning, "The Horror of Opacity: The Melodrama of Sensation in the Plays of André de Lorde," in *Melodrama: Stage, Picture, Screen,* ed. Jacky Bratton, Jim Cook, and Christine Gledhill (London: British Film Institute, 1994), 51–52.

100. Tom Gunning, "An Aesthetic of Astonishment: Early Film and the (In)Credulous Spectator," in *Viewing Positions: Ways of Seeing Film,* ed. Linda Williams (New Brunswick, N.J.: Rutgers University Press, 1995), 125.

101. Ibid., 121–24.

102. The literature on sentimentalism is immense. For some other important discussions of sentimentalism, see Ann Douglas, *The Feminization of American Culture* (1977; New York: Anchor-Doubleday 1988); Jane Tompkins, *Sensational Designs: The Cultural Work of American Fiction* (New York: Oxford University Press, 1985); Phil Fisher, *Hard Facts: Setting and Form in the American Novel*

(New York: Oxford University Press, 1985); Karen Sanchez-Eppler, *Touching Liberty: Abolition, Feminism, and the Politics of the Body* (Berkeley: University of California Press, 1993); Shirley Samuels, "Introduction," in *The Culture of Sentiment: Race, Gender, and Sentimentality in Nineteenth-Century America* (New York: Oxford University Press, 1992), 3–8; Laura Wexler, "Tender Violence: Literary Eavesdropping, Domestic Fiction, and Educational Reform," in *The Culture of Sentiment,* 9–38; Lauren Berlant, "Pax Americana: The Case of Show Boat," in *Cultural Institutions of the Novel,* ed. D. Lynch and W. Warner (Durham: Duke University Press, 1996), 417; Berlant, "Poor Eliza," *American Literature* 70, no. 3 (September 1998): 636; Berlant, "The Subject of True Feeling: Pain, Privacy, and Politics," in *Cultural Pluralism, Identity Politics, and the Law,* ed. A. Sarat and T. Kearns (Ann Arbor: University of Michigan Press, 1999), 49–84; June Howard, "What Is Sentimentality?" *American Literary History* 11, no. 1 (spring 1999): 63–81; Bruce Burgett, *Sentimental Bodies: Sex, Gender, and Citizenship in the Early Republic* (Princeton: Princeton University Press, 1998); Elizabeth Barnes, *States of Sympathy: Seduction and Democracy in the American Novel* (New York: Columbia University Press, 1997); Julia Stern, *The Plight of Feeling: Sympathy and Dissent in the Early American Novel* (Chicago: University of Chicago Press, 1998); and Mary Chapman and Glenn Hendler, "Introduction," in *Sentimental Men: Masculinity and the Politics of Affect in American Culture* (Berkeley: University of California Press, 1999), 1–16.

Barnes suggests that sentimental literature aims at the "successful conversion of the material body into the immaterial soul" (12); Samuels identifies the "move outside or beyond the boundaries of a gendered or racialized body" (5) as characteristic of sentimentalism; and Sanchez-Eppler notes that sentimental texts often betray a horror of embodiment and respond by reasserting a "Christian and sentimental vision of noncorporeal freedom and personhood" (48).

103. Jonathan Elmer, *Reading at the Social Limit: Affect, Mass Culture, Edgar Allan Poe* (Stanford: Stanford University Press, 1995), 102, 107.

104. Thanks are due to George Lipsitz for his ideas on this point. From a variety of perspectives, a number of scholars have focused on the opposition between liberal constructions of abstract citizenship, on the one hand, and the particularities of persons and the material histories of different kinds of bodies, on the other. See, for instance, Lisa Lowe, *Immigrant Acts: On Asian American Cultural Politics* (Durham: Duke University Press, 1996); Lauren Berlant, "National Brands/National Body: Imitation of Life," in *Comparative American Identities: Race, Sex, and Nationality in the Modern Text,* ed. Hortense Spillers (New York: Routledge, 1991); and Michael Warner, "The Mass Public and the Mass Subject," in *Habermas and the Public Sphere,* ed. Craig Calhoun (Cambridge: MIT Press, 1992), 377–401. Lowe critically engages Marxist theory in order to emphasize how the liberal citizen-subject is "defined by the negation of the material conditions of work and the inequalities of the property system" and is thereby split off "from the unrepresentable histories of situated embodiment that contradict the abstract form of citizenship" (2). Drawing on the work of Carole Pateman and other feminist critics of liberal contract theory, Berlant has argued that "white male privilege has been veiled by the rhetoric of the bodiless citizen, the generic 'person' whose political identity is a priori because it is, in theory,

non-corporeal" (112). And Warner suggests that in the "bourgeois public sphere" a "principle of negativity" mandated that "the validity of what you say in public bears a negative relation to your person"; he observes that "the rhetorical strategy of personal abstraction" implied "a utopian universality" that theoretically allowed people "to transcend the given realities of their bodies and their status" but that it was also "a major source of domination," since "such unmarked self-abstraction" was a "differential resource" (382) available primarily to those who were white, propertied, and male. That is, as Berlant puts it, "surplus corporeality" weighs heavily on those "hyperembodied" subjects who do not have the privilege of suppressing their bodies in a culture where "public embodiment is itself a sign of inadequacy to proper citizenship" (114). In mid-nineteenth-century sensational literature, uncanny bodies are deeply marked by the particularities of race, class, and gender, and these particularities signal what was exiled from liberal constructions of the disembodied citizen-subject: the material histories of situated embodiment, labor, and property that return to haunt.

I do not mean to suggest that there exists a prediscursive, "natural" body that sensational literature somehow liberates through spectacular acts of representation. As Foucault has taught us, there is no prepolitical body that can ground a politics; bodies are constructed through discourse; discourses on the body may operate as disciplinary mechanisms; and the proliferation of discourses on the body was characteristic of a nineteenth-century regime of power that worked in part by investing bodies with meaning. Popular sensational literature may itself be seen as such a disciplinary mechanism insofar as it essentializes bodies even as it helps to construct them. This is perhaps most obvious with respect to race and gender. Sensational literature works as a mechanism of racialization when it represents raced bodies as "something objective and fixed, a biological datum" [Omi and Winant, *Racial Formation,* 55]; it functions as a mechanism of gendering when it constructs women's bodies as essentially and especially vulnerable to extremes of passion and feeling. But this literature may also register the contradictions between the liberal ideal of abstraction and the material and embodied histories and knowledges that this ideal excludes but nonetheless presumes and exploits. These histories and knowledges are not primordial, natural, or preideological; they must be placed within histories of shifts in larger structures such as the organization of labor, the rise of body-transforming institutions such as the prison and the factory, urbanization, and the intensification of U.S. imperial and inter-American contact and conflict.

See also Michel Foucault, *Discipline and Punish: The Birth of the Prison,* trans. Alan Sheridan (New York: Vintage, 1979); and *The History of Sexuality: An Introduction,* vol. 1, trans. Robert Hurley (New York: Vintage, 1990). For readings of Foucault in relation to the British Victorian sensation novel of the 1860s, see Cvetkovich, *Mixed Feelings,* esp. 30–32; and D. A. Miller, *The Novel and the Police* (Berkeley: University of California Press, 1988).

105. Rogin, *Blackface,* 52.

106. For a quick summary of how during these years "the culture of sentiment became less directly identified with public virtue and benevolence and more associated with women's moral, nurturing role in the private sphere of the bourgeois family," see Chapman and Hendler, *Sentimental Men,* 3.

107. Lippard, *The Quaker City*, 305.

108. Reynolds, "Introduction," *The Quaker City*, xxii.

109. Amy Kaplan, "Manifest Domesticity," *American Literature* 70, no. 3 (September 1998): 600–601.

110. Louisa May Alcott, "Pauline's Passion and Punishment," in *Louisa May Alcott Unmasked: Collected Thrillers*, ed. Madeleine Stern (Boston: Northeastern University Press, 1995), 3–4. Hereafter cited in text.

111. Brodhead, *Cultures of Letters*, 101.

CHAPTER 2. GEORGE LIPPARD'S 1848

1. George Lippard, *New York: Its Upper Ten and Lower Million* (1853; Upper Saddle River, N.J.: Literature House/Gregg Press, 1970), 284. Hereafter citations will appear in the text. This scenario is obviously informed by an agrarian theory of Western lands as a sort of "safety valve" that could mitigate class tensions in the East. For one of the classic American Studies discussions of this theory, see Henry Nash Smith, "The Garden as Safety Valve," in *Virgin Land: The American West as Symbol and Myth* (New York: Vintage, 1950), 234–45. See also Frederick Jackson Turner, *Rereading Frederick Jackson Turner: 'The Significance of the Frontier in American History' and Other Essays*, ed. John Mack Faragher (New York: Holt, 1994). For persuasive evidence that the safety valve never worked, see Fred A. Shannon, "A Post Mortem on the Labor Safety-Valve Theory," *Agricultural History* 19 (January 1945): 31–37. For a helpful discussion of the links between land reform activism and U.S. working-class history, see William F. Deverell, "To Loosen the Safety Valve: Eastern Workers and Western Lands," *Western Historical Quarterly* 19 (August 1988): 269–85. For recent work that confronts and complicates the Turnerian premises upon which twentieth-century versions of the safety valve theory are based, see Clyde A. Milner, II, ed., *A New Significance: Re-Envisioning the History of the American West* (New York: Oxford University Press, 1996). For an analysis of Turner's work in relation to his historical context and to other work in American Studies, see David W. Noble, *The End of American History: Democracy, Capitalism, and the Metaphor of Two Worlds in Anglo-American Historical Writing, 1880–1990* (Minneapolis: University of Minnesota Press, 1995).

2. On the print revolution, see Michael Denning, *Mechanic Accents: Dime Novels and Working-Class Culture in America* (1987; London and New York: Verso, 1998), 10–11, 85–117, and throughout; Robert Johannsen, *To the Halls of the Montezumas: The Mexican War in the American Imagination* (New York: Oxford University Press, 1985), 16–20, 175–79; and Alexander Saxton, *The Rise and Fall of the White Republic: Class Politics and Mass Culture in Nineteenth-Century America* (London and New York: Verso, 1990), 95–108, 321–47.

3. See Johannsen, *Halls*, 45–67; and Reginald Horsman, *Race and Manifest Destiny: The Origins of American Racial Anglo-Saxonism* (Cambridge: Harvard University Press, 1981), 208–71. Horsman argues that in "confronting the Mexicans the Americans clearly formulated the idea of themselves as an Anglo-Saxon race. The use of Anglo-Saxon in a racial sense, somewhat rare in the political ar-

guments of the early 1830s, increased rapidly later in the decade and became commonplace by the mid-1840s" (208–9).

4. For popular representations of Mexico as a "false nation," see Gene Brack, *Mexico Views Manifest Destiny, 1821–1846: An Essay on the Origins of the Mexican War* (Albuquerque: University of New Mexico Press, 1975). On the nation as imagined community, see Benedict Anderson, *Imagined Communities: Reflections on the Origin and Spread of Nationalism,* rev. ed. (London and New York: Verso Press, 1991). According to Anderson, the spread of print capitalism is an indispensable precondition for the rise of modern nationalisms. Because of the conjunction of the print revolution and the war, the late 1840s represent a key moment in the formation of modern U.S. nationalism. On nationalism as "fictive ethnicity," see Etienne Balibar, "The Nation Form," in *Race, Nation, Class: Ambiguous Identities,* trans. Chris Turner (London and New York: Verso, 1991), 96–100. Balibar suggests that "[f]ictive ethnicity is not purely and simply identical with the ideal nation which is the object of patriotism, but it is indispensable to it, for, without it, the nation would appear precisely as an idea or an arbitrary abstraction; patriotism's appeal would be addressed to no one. It is fictive ethnicity which makes it possible for the expression of a preexisting unity to be seen in the state, and continually to measure the state against its 'historic mission' in the service of the nation and, as a consequence, to idealize politics" (96).

5. See Priscilla Wald's reading of Freud's 1919 essay "The Uncanny" in *Constituting Americans: Cultural Anxiety and Narrative Form* (Durham: Duke University Press, 1995), 5–7. Wald notes that Freud's essay was written "while the national boundaries of Europe were being redrawn" (5); links together discussions of nationalism and Freud's meditations on "the anxiety designated by the German *unheimlich* (literally, not homely or homelike)" (5); and argues that "the uncanny sends us home to the discovery that 'home' is not what or where we think it is and that we, by extension, are not who or what we think we are" (7). I find her remarks particularly useful in thinking about the popularization of nationalism and the eruption of uncanny American sensations in the wake of the war with Mexico and the redrawing of national boundaries that followed it.

6. Richard Slotkin, *The Fatal Environment: The Myth of the Frontier in the Age of Industrialization, 1800–1890* (Middletown, Conn.: Wesleyan University Press, 1985), 192. See also Arthur Pettit, *Images of the Mexican American in Fiction and Film* (College Station: Texas A&M University Press, 1980), 3–79; Norman D. Smith, "Mexican Stereotypes on Fictional Battlefields: or Dime Novels of the Mexican War," *Journal of Popular Culture* 13 (spring 1980): 526–40; Johannsen, *Halls,* 186–202.

7. Denning, *Mechanic Accents,* 87. David Reynolds considers Lippard to be "the most militantly radical novelist of the pre-Civil War period." See Reynolds, *Beneath the American Renaissance: The Subversive Imagination in the Age of Emerson and Melville* (Cambridge: Harvard University Press, 1988), 205. For other studies of Lippard as an urban writer, see Gary Ashwill, "The Mysteries of Capitalism in George Lippard's City Novels," *ESQ* 40, no. 4 (1994): 293–317; Heyward Ehrlich, "The 'Mysteries' of Philadelphia: Lippard's Quaker City and 'Urban' Gothic," *ESQ* 18, no. 1 (1972): 50–65; J. V. Ridgely, "George Lippard's

The Quaker City: The World of the American Porno-Gothic," *Studies in the Literary Imagination* 7, no. 1 (spring 1974): 77–94; Slotkin, *Fatal Environment,* 151–58; Larzer Ziff, *Literary Democracy: The Declaration of Cultural Independence in America* (New York: Viking, 1981), 87–107; Janis Stout, *Sodoms in Eden: The City in American Fiction before 1860* (Westport, Conn.: Greenwood, 1976), 50–54; Adrienne Siegel, *The Image of the American City in Popular Literature, 1820–1870* (Port Washington, N.Y.: Kennikat, 1981), 78–79; Dana D. Nelson, *National Manhood: Capitalist Citizenship and the Imagined Fraternity of White Men* (Durham: Duke University Press, 1998), 135–37, 143–61; and Christopher Newfield, *The Emerson Effect: Individualism and Submission in America* (Chicago: University of Chicago Press, 1996), 95–96.

8. Pierre Bourdieu, *The Field of Cultural Production,* ed. Randal Johnson (New York: Columbia University Press, 1993), 195.

9. David Reynolds, *George Lippard, Prophet of Protest: Writings of an American Radical, 1822–1854* (New York: Peter Lang, 1986), 9. See also the account of Lippard's trajectory in Denning, *Mechanic Accents,* 88–89.

10. Denning, *Mechanic Accents,* 87.

11. For some insightful remarks about the significance of Philadelphia's violently divided public sphere for Lippard's work, see Noel Ignatiev, *How the Irish Became White* (New York: Routledge, 1995), 124, 128, 144, 149, 156.

12. *Quaker City* weekly, 30 December 1848. Hereafter, citations will appear in text.

13. Jamie Bronstein, *Land Reform and Working-Class Experience in Britain and the United States, 1800–1862* (Stanford: Stanford University Press, 1999), 241.

14. Nelson, *National Manhood,* 151.

15. Bruce Burgett, *Sentimental Bodies: Sex, Gender, and Citizenship in the Early Republic* (Princeton: Princeton University Press, 1998), 15.

16. I have learned much from Nelson's reading of Lippard's *The Quaker City* in *National Manhood.* Her suggestions that questions of civic order are mapped across female bodies and that Lippard fears the threat of "unregulated social mixing" (146) are insightful, and they help to explain part of what is at stake in a good deal of the literature that he produced. But the isolation of *The Quaker City* from the larger body of Lippard's work, especially his journalism, speeches, and post-1845 literature, threatens to makes invisible his activism in labor and land reform movements and other radical democratic associations. This activity complicates Nelson's claims that Lippard's work is symptomatic of "anxieties generated with the middle classes' move toward professionalization" (137). Lippard would have especially resented being aligned with the middle classes. "In every age, the classes improperly styled by this title," Lippard argued in *The Quaker City* weekly, "have been the veriest lick-spittles of Power" (2 June 1849).

17. In *Fatal Environment,* Slotkin argues that Mexico became "a darkened mirror in which Americans saw the features of their own culture and society in obscure and exaggerated forms. The divisions of class and race, the political divisions between entrepreneurs and Jacksonian workingmen and paternalists, were reproduced in the depiction of Mexico, making that nation an unwilling

testing ground for the definition and resolution of *Yanqui* ideological issues"
(174). See also 179.

18. On U.S. responses to the European revolutions of 1848, see Larry J.
Reynolds, *European Revolutions and the American Literary Renaissance* (New
Haven: Yale University Press, 1988).

19. George Lippard, *The White Banner* (Philadelphia: George Lippard,
1851), 52. Hereafter citations will appear in text. A shorter, slightly different
version of *Adonai* was serialized in the *Quaker City* weekly, beginning 30 December 1848 and ending 29 September 1849, under the title *The Entranced; or,
The Wanderer of Eighteen Centuries*. The analysis that follows draws on both of
these versions.

20. On the repression of the revolution in France, see Roger Price, ed., *Revolution and Reaction: 1848 and the Second French Republic* (London: Croom
Helm, 1975); and John Merriman, *The Agony of the Republic: The Repression
of the Left in Revolutionary France, 1848–1851* (New Haven: Yale University
Press, 1978).

21. As Adonai listens to the debate on the floor, one senator argues that the
Declaration's premise that "all men are born free and equal" is an "error," since
"[t]here must be classes in this world; there must be castes; there must be rich and
poor" (51–52). Another suggests that "Commerce and Manufactures" are "the
great ideas of America," and that the Constitution is meaningless unless they are
fostered and protected "even at the expense of nine-tenths of the People, and by
robbing nine-tenths of the fruits of their Labor" (52).

22. "The Imprisoned Jesus" and "The Carpenter's Son," in *Nineteenth Century* 1, no. 1 (January 1848): 80, 286.

23. For more on Lippard's representations of the human Jesus, see David
Reynolds, *Faith in Fiction: The Emergence of Religious Literature in America*
(Cambridge: Harvard University Press, 1981), 137–38, 188, 194.

Lippard's interest in uncanny bodies probably derived in part from a Pennsylvania Quaker tradition that had splintered in the first half of the nineteenth
century over disagreements about the importance of the earthliness (as opposed
to the remote and disembodied divinity) of Jesus and the relationship between the
accumulation of capital and spiritual virtue. See Robert Doherty, *The Hicksite
Separation: A Sociological Analysis of Religious Schism in Early Nineteenth Century America* (New Brunswick, N.J.: Rutgers University Press, 1967), 31; Bliss
Forbush, *Elias Hicks: Quaker Liberal* (New York: Columbia University Press,
1956); Thomas D. Hamm, *The Transformation of American Quakerism: Orthodox Friends, 1800–1907* (Bloomington: Indiana University Press, 1988), 16;
and H. Larry Ingle, *Quakers in Conflict: The Hicksite Reformation* (Knoxville:
University of Tennessee Press, 1986). In 1827 the Philadelphia Yearly Meeting of
Friends had split into two factions. According to Doherty, Orthodox Pennsylvania leaders tended to be wealthy men who believed that elites should guide the
general membership and that "secular success might well be used as a guide to
one's spiritual progress" (31). On the other hand, the Hicksite Quakers that the
Orthodox opposed were, Thomas Hamm suggests, a more "motley group"
composed of "artisans displaced by an industrial economy, farmers with heavy
mortgages, extreme conservatives fearful of innovation, and liberals opposed to

intolerance" (16). Although the Hicksite movement was undoubtedly, as Doherty suggests, a heterogeneous response to Orthodoxy, many of its adherents were hostile to commercial values and some, following Hicks, conceived of Jesus as a kind of Everyman rather than as a unique vessel of Divinity.

24. See also David Reynolds, *George Lippard*, 89.

25. Bruce Laurie, *Working People of Philadelphia, 1800–1850* (Philadelphia: Temple University Press, 1980), 35.

26. He argued that when Calvin's theology was reduced to political economy, "you have this result: The poor, the laboring, the unfortunate, are the castaways, damned in this world, beneath the hoof of oppression and destined to damnation in the next, beneath the frown of God—the Rich, the powerful, the successful, who coin their riches, power, and success, out of the last dregs of human woe, are the ELECT destined to hold the wealth, the power and fame of this world, and to enjoy the eternal happiness of the next" (134).

27. Laurie, *Working People*, 37, 39.

28. Lippard was raised by evangelical Methodists, and his ideas about the importance of the body were also inspired by a Pennsylvania German communitarian tradition which, he argued, had tried to address "the great problem, which divides the world—Can education and mental progress be conjoined with hard-handed Toil?" (*The Quaker City*, 19 May 1849). Lippard was especially fascinated by the early immigrant socialists who had founded religious colonies such as Ephrata and Johannes Kelpius's "The Woman of the Wilderness" along the Wissahikon River in Pennsylvania. See David Reynolds, *George Lippard*, 104–13. See also David Reynolds, *Faith in Fiction*, 187–96.

29. Laurie, *Working People*, 150.

30. George Lippard, *The Quaker City; or, The Monks of Monk Hall*, ed. David Reynolds (Amherst: University of Massachusetts Press, 1995), 262. On the Kensington and Southwark riots, see Michael Feldberg, *The Philadelphia Riots of 1844: A Study of Ethnic Conflict* (Westport, Conn.: Greenwood, 1975), ix. See also David Montgomery, "The Shuttle and the Cross: Weavers and Artisans in the Kensington Riots of 1844," in *Workers in the Industrial Revolution*, ed. Peter Stearns and David Walkowitz (New Brunswick, N.J.: Transaction, 1984), 44–74.

31. See also Denning, *Mechanic Accents*, 114–15.

32. I am thinking here of Sacvan Bercovitch's analysis of "the myth of America" in *The Puritan Origins of the American Self* (New Haven: Yale University Press, 1975).

33. David Roediger, *The Wages of Whiteness: Race and the Making of the American Working Class* (London and New York: Verso, 1991), 80.

34. See Louis Hartz, *The Liberal Tradition in America: An Interpretation of American Political Thought since the Revolution* (New York: Harcourt, Brace, Jovanovich, 1983).

35. George Lippard, *Legends of Mexico* (Philadelphia: T. B. Peterson, 1847), 11, 12. Hereafter citations will appear parenthetically in the text.

36. Johannsen, *Halls*, 16.

37. See Cecil Robinson, *The View from Chapultepec: Mexican Writers on the Mexican-American War*, ed. and trans. Cecil Robinson (Tucson: University of Ari-

zona Press, 1989), 24; Rodolfo Acuña, *Occupied America: A History of Chicanos,* 4th ed. (1972; New York: Longman, 2000), 48; and David J. Weber, *The Mexican Frontier, 1821–1846: The American Southwest under Mexico* (Albuquerque: University of New Mexico Press, 1982), 274.

38. Johannsen, *Halls,* 8.

39. Anderson, *Imagined Communities,* 35. Hereafter cited in text.

40. For more on the significance of the telegraph in the history of electronic mass media, see George Lipsitz, *Time Passages: Collective Memory and American Popular Culture* (Minneapolis: University of Minnesota Press, 1990), 6–7.

41. Horsman, *Race and Manifest Destiny,* 208, 251.

42. Horsman explains that "Anglo-Saxon" was an ambiguous and flexible adjective that "was often used in the 1840s to describe the white people of the United States in contrast to blacks, Indians, Mexicans, Spaniards, or Asiatics" (4). But the race scientist Josiah Nott, for instance, classified the Celts with the "dark-skinned" races that he deemed inferior to the Anglo-Saxons. Many nativists would have agreed. See Horsman, *Race and Manifest Destiny,* 4, 131. See also Matthew Frye Jacobson, *Whiteness of a Different Color: European Immigrants and the Alchemy of Race* (Cambridge: Harvard University Press, 1998), 206.

43. For an analysis of American millennialism and the idea of Manifest Destiny, see Ernest Tuveson, *Redeemer Nation: The Idea of America's Millennial Role* (Chicago: University of Chicago Press, 1968), 91–136. For an argument about the significance of Puritan millennialism, see Sacvan Bercovitch, *Rites of Assent: Transformations in the Symbolic Construction of America* (New York: Routledge, 1993), 32–37.

44. On war opposition, see John M. Schroeder, *Mr. Polk's War: American Opposition and Dissent, 1846–1848* (Madison: University of Wisconsin Press, 1973); and Frederick Merk, *Manifest Destiny and Mission in American History* (Cambridge: Harvard University Press, 1963), 89–106.

45. *The Life and Writings of Thomas Paine,* vol. 3, ed. Daniel Edwin Wheeler (New York: Vincente Parke and Company, 1908), 111. For a discussion of Paine's *Crisis* papers, see Eric Foner, *Tom Paine and Revolutionary America* (New York: Oxford University Press, 1976), 139–142.

46. Slotkin, *Fatal Environment,* 175–80.

47. Jenny Franchot, *Roads to Rome: The Antebellum Protestant Encounter with Catholicism* (Berkeley: University of California Press, 1994), 35–82; David Levin, *History as Romantic Art* (New York: Harcourt, Brace, and Jovanovich, 1959); John P. McWilliams, *The American Epic: Transforming a Genre, 1770–1860* (Cambridge: Cambridge University Press, 1989), 158–86; and Eric Wertheimer, *Imagined Empires: Incas, Aztecs, and the New World of American Literature, 1771–1876* (Cambridge: Cambridge University Press, 1999), 128–31.

48. Johannsen, *Halls,* 30, 146, 150, 156–57, 180, 245–48.

49. J. G. A. Pocock, *The Machiavellian Moment: Florentine Political Thought and the Atlantic Republican Tradition* (Princeton: Princeton University Press, 1975), 510.

50. "Cole's Pictures," *Journal of Commerce,* Archives of American Art, Reel D6, frame 337. Quoted in Angela Miller, *The Empire of the Eye: Landscape*

Representation and American Cultural Politics, 1825–1875 (Ithaca: Cornell University Press, 1993), 23.

51. Miller, *The Empire of the Eye,* 34. Cole's is a cyclical-providential view of history, as opposed to a redemptive history. For the distinction between the two, see Sacvan Bercovitch, *The Puritan Origins of the American Self,* 137–46. For an argument about the persistence of an "apprehension of doom" about the "haunting course of empire" in Jacksonian America based on the cyclical-providential view of history, see Perry Miller, "The Romantic Dilemma in American Nationalism and the Concept of Nature," in *Nature's Nation* (Cambridge: Harvard University Press, 1967), 206–7. I am arguing that a tension between a redemptive and a cyclical-providential view of history haunts Lippard's War literature.

52. On the Black Legend, see Roberto Fernández Retamar, "Against the Black Legend," in *Caliban and Other Essays,* trans. Edward Baker (Minneapolis: University of Minnesota Press, 1989), 56–73; Charles Gibson, ed., *The Black Legend: Anti-Spanish Attitudes in the Old World and the New* (New York: Alfred A. Knopf, 1971); David Gutiérrez, "Significant to Whom? Mexican Americans and the History of the American West," in Milner, *A New Significance,* 68; Raymund Paredes, "The Origins of Anti-Mexican Sentiment in the United States," in *New Directions in Chicano Scholarship,* ed. Ricardo Romo and Raymund Paredes (La Jolla: University of California, San Diego, 1978), 139–65; and David J. Weber, *The Spanish Frontier in North America* (New Haven: Yale University Press, 1992), 335–41. Fernández Retamar argues that although the "crimes" of the Spanish conquerors were indeed "monstrous," "the nascent bourgeoisie of other metropolises who created the Black Legend" did so "not, of course, for the benefit of those peoples martyred by the Spanish conquest but rather to cover up their own rapacity.... To give a name to this common cause—the cause of world exploitation, genocide, pillage, and horror—they dusted off the terms 'Western' and 'Western culture,' according to them the very essence of human splendor. This White Legend of the 'civilized' West is the reverse of the original, and it has no other purpose or value" (60). For an excellent account of how "these and other constructions of a Spanish other led inexorably to the Enlightenment's exclusion of Spain from the realm of the civilized and even to the U.S. hostile takeover of Spain's empire at the end of the last century" as well as to U.S. ideologies of Manifest Destiny, see George Mariscal, "The Role of Spain in Contemporary Race Theory," *Arizona Journal of Hispanic Cultural Studies* 2 (1998): 7–22.

53. Although Prescott, according to John P. McWilliams, Jr., assumed "the formidable task of acknowledging Spanish cruelties while upholding Spanish heroism" (174), his contemporaries were more likely to emphasize the cruelties even as they paradoxically described the U.S.-Mexican War as a sort of re-enactment of the Spanish conquest. "Drawn to the Spanish subject as a critical precursor," McWilliams writes, "American writers were thus prone to distance themselves from the very analogy their words suggest" (162).

54. For sobering reflections on "the precariousness of empathy and the thin line between witness and spectator" in the context of a discussion of the nineteenth-century emphasis on "the spectacular character of black suffering," see Saidiya Hartman, *Scenes of Subjection: Terror, Slavery, and Self-Making in*

Nineteenth Century America (New York: Oxford University Press, 1997), 19 and throughout.

55. On the incorporation of Europeans as white ethnics through racial exclusion, see esp. Roediger, *The Wages of Whiteness,* 133–63; and *Towards the Abolition of Whiteness: Essays on Race, Politics, and Working-Class History* (London and New York: Verso, 1994), 181–98; Theodore Allen, *The Invention of the White Race: Racial Oppression and Social Control,* vol. 1 (London and New York: Verso, 1994); Noel Ignatiev, *How the Irish Became White* (New York: Routledge, 1995); and Michael Paul Rogin, *Blackface, White Noise: Jewish Immigrants in the Hollywood Melting Pot* (Berkeley: University of California Press, 1996).

56. In response to an earlier version of this essay, George Mariscal pointed out that Arista is constructed as a racialized "oriental" figure in ways that might respond to race scientists' ideas about the Spanish as a mongrel race with African/Arab characteristics. See also Johannsen, *Halls,* 199.

57. Lippard seemed to regret this later. In the 5 May 1849 issue of the *Quaker City* weekly, he solicits letters from private soldiers for a book called *The Real Heroes of the Mexican War.* "It will picture the deeds of every man who distinguished himself, and not confine itself to a mere eulogy of those titled persons, whose greatness too often consists, solely in their rank and official position."

58. This is a good example of what Dana D. Nelson has identified as the process whereby "national manhood substitutes itself for nascently radical, local democratic practices, energies, and imaginings, not replacing local manhoods so much as enlisting them for and orienting them toward a unified, homogeneous national ideal" (x).

59. On the cult of the "Vanishing American," especially with regard to Cooper's work, see Lora Romero, *Home Fronts: Domesticity and Its Critics in the Antebellum United States* (Durham: Duke University Press, 1997), 35–51.

60. Horsman, *Race and Manifest Destiny,* 210.

61. *Democratic Review* 21 (November 1947): 388–90.

62. For an analysis of these and other stereotypes of women of Mexican origin in California, see Antonia Castañeda, "The Political Economy of Nineteenth Century Stereotypes of Californianas," in *Between Borders: Essays in Mexicana/Chicana History,* ed. Adelaida del Castillo (Encino, Calif.: Floricanto, 1990), 213–36. On the construction of Californiana women in Anglo-American discourses and in testimonios, see Rosaura Sánchez, *Telling Identities: The Californio Testimonios* (Minneapolis: University of Minnesota Press, 1995): 198–227.

63. For an important analysis of Chicana critiques of consensual paradigms, see Carl Gutiérrez-Jones, *Rethinking the Borderlands: Between Chicano Culture and Legal Discourse* (Berkeley: University of California Press, 1995): 103–22.

64. Johannsen, *Halls,* 91.

65. Bill Brown, *The Material Unconscious: American Amusement, Stephen Crane, and the Economies of Play* (Cambridge: Harvard University Press, 1996), 125, 127, 129. See also Amy Kaplan, "The Spectacle of War in Crane's Revi-

sion of History," in *New Essays on the* Red Badge of Courage, ed. Lee Clark Mitchell (New York: Cambridge University Press, 1986), 77–108; and Alan Trachtenberg, "Albums of War," in *Reading American Photographs: Images as History, Matthew Brady to Walker Evans* (New York: Hill and Wang, 1989), 71–118.

66. Johannsen, *Halls,* 221.

67. William H. Prescott, *History of the Conquest of Mexico* (New York: Modern Library, 1998), 362, 365, 366.

68. Ramon Alcaraz et al., *The Other Side: or, Notes for the History of the War Between Mexico and the United States,* trans. Albert C. Ramsey (1850; New York: Burt Franklin, 1970), 80.

69. "Third Day" is reproduced in Martha Sandweiss, Rick Stewart, and Ben Huseman, *Eyewitness to War: Prints and Daguerreotypes of the Mexican War, 1846–1848* (Washington, D.C.: Smithsonian Institution Press, 1989), 29. For more on other popular prints of the encounter at Monterrey, see 14–15, 29–30, 115–31. Thanks to Nicole Tonkovich for calling my attention to this book. See also Ronnie C. Tyler, *The Mexican War: A Lithographic Record* (Austin: Texas State Historical Society, 1973).

70. For two examples, see Sandweiss et al., *Eyewitness to War,* 115–19.

71. Alcaraz et al., *The Other Side,* 32.

72. This literature is described by Eric Sundquist, "The Literature of Expansion and Race," in *The Cambridge History of American Literature, Volume 2,* ed. Sacvan Bercovitch (Cambridge: Cambridge University Press, 1995), 154–55.

73. David J. Weber, *The Mexican Frontier, 1821–1846: The American Southwest under Mexico* (Albuquerque: University of New Mexico Press, 1982), 162–63. See also Neil Foley, *The White Scourge: Mexicans, Blacks, and Poor Whites in Texas Cotton Culture* (Berkeley: University of California Press, 1997), 17–19; and Terry G. Jordan, *German Seed in Texas Soil: Immigrant Farmers in Nineteenth-Century Texas* (Austin: University of Texas Press, 1966), 31–59.

74. A good deal of promotional literature, usually produced by those with financial investments in colonization projects, was aimed at potential German immigrants. In 1845, for instance, Johann H. S. Schulz called Texas the paradise of North America; another German writer claimed that Texas soil was "among the most fertile in the world" (cited in Jordan, *German Seed in Texas Soil,* 40). During this period, tens of thousands of German immigrants came to Texas. Some of these colonists were connected to a German overseas colonization society; others settled on *empresario* grants; and still others were part of a short-lived utopian communal settlement founded by German intellectuals.

75. George Lippard, *'Bel of Prairie Eden: A Romance of Mexico* (Boston: Hotchkiss and Co., 1848), 20. Hereafter citations will appear in the text.

76. Teresa Goddu, *Gothic America: Narrative, History, and Nation* (New York: Columbia University Press, 1997), 5.

77. Amy Kaplan, " 'Left Alone with America': The Absence of Empire in the Study of American Culture," in *Cultures of United States Imperialism,* ed. Kaplan and Donald Pease (Durham: Duke University Press, 1993), 14–15.

CHAPTER 3. THE STORY-PAPER EMPIRE

1. On the significance in the mid-nineteenth-century United States of "a male homosociality that consists of submission to superiors," see Christopher Newfield, *The Emerson Effect: Individualism and Submission in America* (Chicago: University of Chicago Press, 1996), 2 and throughout.

2. For the most comprehensive study of late-nineteenth-century U.S. ideologies of manhood and empire, see Gail Bederman, *Manliness and Civilization: A Cultural History of Gender and Race in the United States, 1880–1917* (Chicago: University of Chicago Press, 1995). See also Amy Kaplan, "Romancing the Empire: The Embodiment of American Masculinity in the Popular Historical Novel of the 1890s," *American Literary History* 2, no. 4 (winter 1990): 659–89. Most studies of manhood and empire in the first half of the nineteenth century focus on conflicts with U.S. Indians. For two especially interesting examples, see Dana D. Nelson, *National Manhood: Capitalist Citizenship and the Imagined Fraternity of White Men* (Durham: Duke University Press, 1998), 61–101; and Michael Paul Rogin, *Fathers and Children: Andrew Jackson and the Subjugation of the American Indian* (New York: Knopf, 1975), esp. 251–79. In her recent book about the Southern Mines in California during the mid-nineteenth century, Susan Lee Johnson provides an excellent analysis of how ideologies of racialized manhood in California were reconstructed in response to the Gold Rush. See *Roaring Camp: The Social World of the California Gold Rush* (New York: W. W. Norton and Company, 2000). See also Johnson's "'A Memory Sweet to Soldiers': The Significance of Gender," in *A New Significance: Re-Envisioning the History of the American West,* ed. Clyde A. Milner II (New York: Oxford University Press, 1996), 255–78; and Carroll Smith-Rosenberg's groundbreaking essay "Davy Crockett as Trickster: Pornography, Liminality, and Symbolic Inversion in Victorian America," in *Disorderly Conduct: Visions of Gender in Victorian America* (New York: Knopf, 1985), 90–108. See also Cynthia Enloe's chapter "Nationalism and Masculinity," in *Bananas, Beaches, and Bases: Making Feminist Sense of International Politics* (Berkeley: University of California Press, 1990), 42–64.

3. On women's involvement in the war, see Elizabeth Salas, *Soldaderas in the Mexican Military: Myth and History* (Austin: University of Texas Press, 1990), 29–33; Robert Johannsen, *To the Halls of the Montezumas: The Mexican War in the American Imagination* (New York: Oxford University Press, 1985), 136–38; and Linda Vance, "Women and the Mexican War," *Papers of the Second Palo Alto Conference,* ed. H. Joseph, A. Knopp, and D. Murphy (Brownsville, Tex.: U.S. Department of the Interior, 1997), 51–56.

4. Frances Calderón de la Barca, *Life in Mexico* (Berkeley: University of California Press, 1982), 433–34. Cited in Salas, *Soldaderas,* 30.

5. John Greenleaf Whittier, *The Poetical Works of John Greenleaf Whittier,* vol. 1 (New York: AMS Press, 1969), 116. See also Johannsen, *Halls,* 216–17. For a critique of the Mexican nationalist image of the *soldadera* as the carrier of "a fatal load of abnegation, silent suffering, stoicism, and stubborn veneration for their men," see Carlos Monsiváis, *Mexican Postcards,* ed. and trans. John Kraniauskas (London and New York: Verso, 1997), 6. On debates among Chicanas and

Chicanos about the significance of the *soldadera* figure, see Salas, *Soldaderas,* 15–19. According to Salas, "[S]ome women object to soldadera imagery and consider the symbol to be an albatross around the neck.... Other Chicanas think that soldadera imagery is a powerful legacy and a flexible enough symbol to empower Mexican women for many generations to come" (122). See also Silvia Marina Arrom, *The Women of Mexico City,* 1790–1857 (Stanford: Stanford University Press, 1985), 32–38.

6. On the prevalence in imperial discourse of "sexual and gendered metaphors" that feminize the colonies, see Ann Laura Stoler, *Race and the Education of Desire: Foucault's History of Sexuality and the Colonial Order of Things* (Durham: Duke University Press, 1995), 174. See also Anne McClintock, " 'No Longer in a Future Heaven': Nationalism, Gender, and Race," in *Becoming National: A Reader,* ed. Geoff Eley and Ronald Suny (New York: Oxford University Press, 1996), 260–84; and Caren Caplan, Norma Alarcón, and Minoo Moallem, eds., *Between Women and Nation: Nationalisms, Transnational Feminisms, and the State* (Durham: Duke University Press, 1999). On nineteenth-century representations of Mexico and Cuba as white women, see Michael Hunt, *Ideology and U.S. Foreign Policy* (New Haven: Yale University Press, 1987), 59–61.

7. See also Amy Kaplan, "Manifest Domesticity," *American Literature* 70, no. 3 (September 1998): 585: "In debates about the annexation of Texas and later Mexico, both sides represented the new territories as women to be married to the U.S."

8. On the "rhetorical relationship between heterosexual passion and hegemonic states" in the nineteenth-century Latin American context, see Doris Sommer, *Foundational Fictions: The National Romances of Latin America* (Berkeley: University of California Press, 1991), 31 and throughout. I call such conceptions of heterosexuality "emergent" because medical and legal narratives of homosexual and heterosexual identity do not begin to proliferate until at least the last third of the nineteenth century. See Eve Kosofsky Sedgwick, *Epistemology of the Closet* (Berkeley: University of California Press, 1990), 2 and throughout. See also Michel Foucault, *The History of Sexuality: An Introduction,* vol. 1, trans. Robert Hurley (New York: Pantheon, 1978); Jonathan Katz, "The Invention of Heterosexuality," *Socialist Review* 20 (1990): 17–34; and " 'Homosexuality' and 'Heterosexuality': Questioning the Terms" and "Coming to Terms: Conceptualizing Men's Erotic and Affectional Relations with Men in the United States, 1820–1892," in *A Queer World: The Center for Lesbian and Gay Studies Reader,* ed. Martin Duberman (New York: New York University Press, 1997), 177–80, 216–35; John D'Emilio and Estelle B. Freedmen, *Intimate Matters: A History of Sexuality in America,* 2d ed. (Chicago: University of Chicago Press, 1997), 121; George Chauncey, Jr. "From Sexual Inversion to Homosexuality: Medicine and the Changing Conceptualization of Female Deviance," *Salmagundi,* nos. 58–59 (fall 1982–winter 1983): 114–46; Siobhan Somerville, *Queering the Color Line: Race and the Invention of Homosexuality in American Culture* (Durham: Duke University Press, 2000); and Charles Rosenberg, "Sexuality, Class and Role in 19th-Century America," *American Quarterly* 25, no. 2 (May 1973): 131–53. On sexuality in mid-nineteenth-century New York,

see Timothy Gilfoyle, *City of Eros: New York City, Prostitution, and the Commercialization of Sex, 1790–1920* (New York: W. W. Norton, 1992), 17–178. On the emergence of homosexual subcultures in the 1840s, see 135–38, 141.

9. Sedgwick, *Epistemology,* 1. See also David Potter, *The Impending Crisis, 1848–1861* (New York: Harper and Row, 1976).

10. Stoler, *Race and the Education of Desire,* 175.

11. For a suggestive analysis of race and norms of manhood and sexuality during the Civil War, see Christopher Looby, "'As Thoroughly Black as the Most Faithful Philanthropist Could Desire': Erotics of Race in Higginson's *Army Life in a Black Regiment,*" in *Race and the Subject of Masculinities,* ed. Harry Stecopoulos and Michael Uebel (Durham: Duke University Press, 1997), 71–115.

12. Stoler, *Race and the Education of Desire,* 176.

13. On O'Sullivan and Young America, see Perry Miller, *The Raven and the Whale: The War of Words and Wits in the Era of Poe and Melville* (New York: Harcourt, Brace and World, 1956); Priscilla Wald, *Constituting Americans: Cultural Anxiety and Narrative Form* (Durham: Duke University Press, 1995), 106–26; and Edward Widmer, *Young America: The Flowering of Democracy in New York City* (New York: Oxford University Press, 1999).

14. Henry Nash Smith, *Virgin Land: The American West as Symbol and Myth* (New York: Vintage, 1950), 95–96. See also Ralph Admari, "Ballou, the Father of the Dime Novel," *American Book Collector* 4, no. 34 (September–October 1933): 121–29; Peter Benson, "Maturin Murray Ballou" and "Gleason's Publishing Hall," in *Publishers for Mass Entertainment in Nineteenth-Century America,* ed. Madeleine Hall (Boston: G. K. Hall and Co., 1980), 27–35, 137–45; and Mary Noel, *Villains Galore: The Heyday of the Popular Story Weekly* (New York: Macmillan, 1954), 18–55.

15. Alexander Saxton, *The Rise and Fall of the White Republic: Class Politics and Mass Culture in Nineteenth-Century America* (London and New York: Verso, 1990). On the Whigs, see Michael F. Holt, *The Rise and Fall of the American Whig Party: Jacksonian Politics and the Onset of the Civil War* (New York: Oxford University Press, 1999); and Daniel Howe, *The Political Culture of the American Whigs* (Chicago: University of Chicago Press, 1979). On the Democrats, see Jean Baker, *Affairs of Party: The Political Culture of Northern Democrats in the Mid–Nineteenth Century* (Ithaca: Cornell University Press, 1983). On nativist organizations, see Ray Allen Billington, *The Protestant Crusade, 1800–1860: A Study of the Origins of American Nativism* (Chicago: Quadrangle, 1964); Dale Knobel, *"America for the Americans": The Nativist Movement in the United States* (New York: Twayne Publishers, 1996), 1–154; and Louis Scisco, *Political Nativism in New York State* (New York: Columbia University Press, 1901). See also *Essays on Antebellum American Politics, 1840–1860,* ed. Stephen Maizlish and John Kushma (College Station: Texas A&M University Press, 1982).

16. Linda Williams, "Melodrama Revised," in *Refiguring American Film Genres: History and Theory,* ed. Nick Browne (Berkeley: University of California Press, 1998), 75. I am adapting Sommer's category "international romance" as she elaborates it in *Foundational Fictions.*

17. See the *Flag of Our Union,* 25 March 1848; see also Noel, *Villains Galore,* 33.

18. *Flag of Our Union,* 24 July 1847. Hereafter, citations appear in text.

19. *Flag of the Free,* 26 April 1849. But it also attacked the "radicalism of the present day" as a "spirit of Fourierism" that "strikes boldly at the rights of individual property" (16 January, 1847).

20. Admari, "Ballou," 122.

21. On literacy rates, see Michael Denning, *Mechanic Accents: Dime Novels and Working-Class Culture in America* (1987; London and New York: Verso, 1998), 30–31.

22. Benson, "Gleason's Publishing Hall," 140.

23. For a suggestive analysis of the complex relationship between capitalism and ideas about adventure, see Michael Nerlich, *Ideology of Adventure: Studies in Modern Consciousness, 1100–1750,* vol. 1, trans. Ruth Crowley (Minneapolis: University of Minnesota Press, 1987).

24. Wald, *Constituting Americans,* 109, 114.

25. Admari, "Ballou," 122.

26. See Admari, "Ballou"; and Benson, "Maturin Murray Ballou."

27. For more on Averill, see Smith, *Virgin Land,* 94, 96–98, 106, 111, 126.

28. Quoted in Benson, "Gleason's Publishing Hall," 141.

29. Johannsen, *Halls,* 186–87.

30. Richard Brodhead, *Cultures of Letters: Scenes of Reading and Writing in Nineteenth-Century America* (Chicago: University of Chicago Press, 1993), 79. It is also true, as I suggested in the introduction, that there were many male sentimentalists. See Mary Chapman and Glenn Hendler, eds., *Sentimental Men: Masculinity and the Politics of Affect in American Culture* (Berkeley: University of California Press, 1999).

31. I agree with Denning that the "assumption of a universal middle-class culture" has too often "paralyzed serious thinking about class and culture" (259). The relationship between a working-class audience and the often middle-class values promoted by mass-produced literature, which was also read by members of other classes, is a question that must be investigated in particular contexts rather than a formula that can be assumed to make the former disappear within the latter.

32. Brodhead, *Cultures of Letters,* 79.

33. Kaplan, "Manifest Domesticity," 583, 584. For more on domesticity in a global context, see the collection *Burning Down the House: Recycling Domesticity,* ed. Rosemary George (Boulder: Westview, 1998), especially George's excellent introductory essay, "Recycling: Long Routes to and from Domestic Fixes," 1–20.

34. Daniel Cohen, "Introduction," in *The Female Marine and Related Works: Narratives of Cross-Dressing and Urban Vice in America's Early Republic* (Amherst: University of Massachusetts Press, 1997), 20. Examples include the cross-dressed military maids featured in ballads, pamphlets, broadsides, and other literature about the Revolutionary War, the War of 1812, the Mexican War, and the Civil War; the dime-novel Amazons of the second half of the nineteenth century that Henry Nash Smith in *Virgin Land* read as a disturbing sign of an increase of sensationalism in U.S. culture; and the cross-dressed picaras

who are featured in many different types of story-paper literature, from mysteries-of-the-city novels to pirate tales such as Ballou's *Fanny Campbell*. In other words, U.S. readers have long enjoyed stories that play with the theatricality of gender. Besides the many novels that include cross-dressers, the story papers sometimes printed brief stories about "passing women." During the late 1840s, for instance, the *Flag of Our Union* carried a news item about a woman who cross-dressed, married another woman, and passed as a man for years in Paris, France (16 October 1847), as well as a story about Hungarian women who enlisted in the army (9 June 1849). For an excellent analysis of cross-dressing in dime novels, see Nicole Tonkovich, "Guardian Angels and Missing Mothers: Race and Domesticity in *Winona* and *Deadwood Dick on Deck*," *Western American Literature* 32, no. 3 (fall 1997): 240–64. For an analysis of Mexican *soldaderas* in *corridos*, see María Herrera-Sobek, "The Soldier Archetype," in *The Mexican Corrido: A Feminist Analysis* (Bloomington: Indiana University Press, 1990), 84–116. On cross-dressing in the Civil War period, see Elizabeth Young, *Disarming the Nation: Women's Writing and the American Civil War* (Chicago: University of Chicago Press, 1999), esp. 149–94. Young suggests that Loreta Velazquez's *The Woman in Battle* should be read as a picaresque novel. On the female picaresque in the early national period, see Cathy Davidson, *Revolution and the Word: The Rise of the Novel in America* (New York: Oxford University Press, 1986), 179–92. See also Dianne Dugaw, *Warrior Women and Popular Balladry, 1650–1850* (Chicago: University of Chicago Press, 1989); and Julie Wheelwright, *Amazons and Military Maids: Women Who Dressed as Men in Pursuit of Life, Liberty, and Happiness* (London: Pandora, 1989).

35. Davidson, *Revolution*, 185; Young, *Disarming*, 156.

36. The "Rio Grande" marked the contested boundary between Mexico and the United States that had sparked the war of 1846–1848, and "Aroostook" indicated a conflict, which nearly became a war, between the United States and England over the U.S.-Canadian border a few years earlier.

37. See also the *Flag of the Free*, 10 June 1848.

38. Kirby Miller, *Emigrants and Exiles: Ireland and the Irish Exodus to North America* (New York: Oxford University Press, 1985); David Roediger, *The Wages of Whiteness: Race and the Making of the American Working Class* (London and New York: Verso, 1991), 144–47. See also Theodore Allen, *The Invention of the White Race*. Vol. 1, *Racial Oppression and Social Control* (London and New York: Verso, 1994); Oscar Handlin, *Boston's Immigrants: A Study in Acculturation* (Cambridge: Harvard University Press, 1959); and Noel Ignatiev, *How the Irish Became White* (New York: Routledge, 1995).

39. William J. Orr and Robert Ryal Miller, "Introduction," in Frederick Zeh, *An Immigrant Soldier in the Mexican War*, ed. Orr and Miller, trans. Orr (College Station: Texas A&M University Press, 1995), xviii. See also Sister Blanche Marie McEniry, *American Catholics in the War with Mexico* (Washington D.C.: Catholic University of America, 1937). On Irish soldiers who fought for Mexico, see Michael Hogan, *The Irish Soldiers of Mexico* (Guadalajara: Fondo Editorial Universitario, 1997); Robert Ryal Miller, *Shamrock and Sword: The Saint Patrick's Battalion in the U.S.-Mexican War* (Norman: University of Oklahoma

Press, 1989); and Dennis Wynn, *The San Patricio Soldiers: Mexico's Foreign Legion* (El Paso: Texas Western Press, 1984).

40. Denning, *Mechanic Accents*, 10–11.

41. Ibid., 15–16.

42. Sommer, *Foundational Fictions*, 6, 14.

43. For a useful summary of these transformations, see Charles Sellers, *The Market Revolution: Jacksonian America, 1815–1846* (New York: Oxford University Press, 1991).

44. Saxton, *Rise and Fall*, 132.

45. Amy Bridges, *A City in the Republic: Antebellum New York and the Origins of Machine Politics* (Cambridge: Cambridge University Press, 1984), 2, 93, 96, 154.

CHAPTER 4. FOREIGN BODIES AND
INTERNATIONAL RACE ROMANCE

1. See "Treaty of Guadalupe Hidalgo," in *U.S.-Mexico Borderlands: Historical and Contemporary Perspectives*, ed. Oscar J. Martinez (Wilmington, Del.: Scholarly Resources, 1996), 26.

2. Neil Foley, *The White Scourge: Mexicans, Blacks, and Poor Whites in Texas Cotton Culture* (Berkeley: University of California Press, 1997), 13, 15.

3. I take the phrase "irresistible romance" from Doris Sommer, *Foundational Fictions: The National Romances of Latin America* (Berkeley: University of California Press, 1991).

4. Thomas Bangs Thorpe, *The Taylor Anecdote Book: Anecdotes and Letters of Zachary Taylor* (New York: D. Appleton and Company, 1848), 42.

5. Dale Knobel, *Paddy and the Republic: Ethnicity and Nationality in Antebellum America* (Middletown, Conn.: Wesleyan University Press, 1986), 60–62, 90–95.

6. Cited in Sister Blanche Marie McEniry, *American Catholics in the War with Mexico* (Washington D.C.: Catholic University of America, 1937), 126.

7. [Luther Giddings]. *Sketches of the Campaign in Northern Mexico by an Officer of the First Regiment of Ohio Volunteers* (New York: George P. Putnam and Co., 1853), viii.

8. See Noel Ignatiev, *How the Irish Became White* (New York: Routledge, 1995), 162: "Nativism had subsided with the outbreak of the Mexican War, but it rose up again in the mid-1850s with the sudden appearance of the Know-Nothing Movement." Studies of nativism in the mid–nineteenth century include Ray Allen Billington, *The Protestant Crusade, 1800–1860: A Study of the Origins of American Nativism* (1938; Chicago: Quadrangle, 1964); Jenny Franchot, *Roads to Rome: The Antebellum Protestant Encounter with Catholicism* (Berkeley: University of California Press, 1994); and Dale Knobel, *"America for the Americans": The Nativist Movement in the United States* (New York: Twayne Publishers, 1996).

9. Charles Averill, *The Mexican Ranchero: or, The Maid of the Chapparal. A Romance of the Mexican War* (Boston: F. Gleason, 1847), 91–92. Hereafter cited in text.

10. David Roediger, *The Wages of Whiteness* (London and New York: Verso, 1991), 141.

11. Ibid., 133–63. For more on the Irish and whiteness, see Ignatiev, *How the Irish Became White;* Theodore Allen, *The Invention of the White Race.* Vol. 1, *Racial Oppression and Social Control* (London and New York: Verso, 1994); Michael Paul Rogin, *Blackface, White Noise: Jewish Immigrants in the Hollywood Melting Pot* (Berkeley: University of California Press, 1996), 56–58; Eric Lott, *Love and Theft: Blackface Minstrelsy and the American Working Class* (New York: Oxford University Press, 1993), 71, 75, 94–96, 148–49, 237; Matthew Frye Jacobson, *Whiteness of a Different Color* (Cambridge: Harvard University Press, 1998), 4, 5, 13, 15–19, 38, 41, 46, 48–56, 68, 70, 159; Foley, *The White Scourge,* 97–98.

12. T. B. Thorpe, *Our Army on the Rio Grande* (Philadelphia: Carey and Hart, 1846), 132. See also Thorpe, *Our Army at Monterey* (Philadelphia: Carey and Hart, 1847), 96; John Kenly, *Memoirs of a Maryland Volunteer* (Philadelphia: J. B. Lippincott, 1873), 299; Richard McSherry, *El Puchero: or, A Mixed Dish from Mexico* (Philadelphia: Lippincott, Grambo, 1850), 90.

13. See Jacobson, *Whiteness,* 38.

14. Dale Steinhauer, "The Immigrant Soldier in the Regular Army during the Mexican War," in *Papers of the Second Palo Alto Conference,* ed. H. Joseph, A. Knopp, and D. Murphy (Brownsville, Tex.: U.S. Department of the Interior, 1997); and Robert Ryal Miller, "Introduction," in Frederick Zeh, *An Immigrant Soldier in the Mexican War,* ed. Orr and Miller, trans. Orr (College Station: Texas A&M University Press, 1995). On the U.S. Army during the war, see James McCaffrey, *Army of Manifest Destiny: The American Soldier in the Mexican War, 1846–1848* (New York: New York University Press, 1992); and Richard Winders, *Mr. Polk's Army: The American Military Experience in the Mexican War* (College Station: Texas A&M University Press, 1997). On war mobilization and the idealization of the volunteer, see Robert Johannsen, *To the Halls of the Montezumas: The Mexican War in the American Imagination* (New York: Oxford University Press, 1985), 21–67.

15. Franchot, *Roads to Rome,* 100, 109; David H. Bennett, *The Party of Fear: From Nativist Movements to the New Right in American History* (Chapel Hill: University of North Carolina Press, 1988), 40.

16. *Congressional Globe,* 30th Congress, 1st session, Appendix, 100.

17. Zeh, *Immigrant Soldier in the Mexican War,* 4.

18. Ibid., 4, 5.

19. When Zeh criticizes his fellow soldiers for vandalizing a Catholic church, for instance, he adds: "[In] this land which is as lovely as it is wretched, there is not the slightest trace [of Christian civilization], notwithstanding all the anxious devotion to ritual" (48).

20. Ibid., 79.

21. Ibid., 55.

22. Michael Hogan, *The Irish Soldiers of Mexico* (Guadalajara: Fondo Editorial Universitario, 1997), 41, 112. Other studies of the San Patricios include Robert Ryal Miller's *Shamrock and Sword: The Saint Patrick's Battalion in the*

U.S.-Mexican War (Norman: University of Oklahoma, 1989); and Dennis Wynn's *The San Patricio Soldiers: Mexico's Foreign Legion* (El Paso: Texas Western Press, 1984). See also Mark Day's excellent documentary *The San Patricios: The Tragic Story of the St. Patrick's Battalion* (Vista, Calif.: San Patricio Productions, 1996); and Ignatiev, *How the Irish Became White,* 161.

23. For fascinating examples of how war can intensify social antagonisms in ways that encourage imaginative and actual alliances with the national so-called enemy, see George Lipsitz, *The Possessive Investment in Whiteness: How White People Profit from Identity Politics* (Philadelphia: Temple University Press, 1998), 184–210; and George Mariscal, "*Aztlán in Vietnam: Chicano and Chicana Experiences of the War* (Berkeley: University of California Press, 1999), 36–46, 84–96, 126–32, 168–69, 242–43.

24. Hogan, *Irish Soldiers,* 92.

25. Ibid., 160.

26. George Davis, *Autobiography of the Late Col. Geo. T.M. Davis* (New York: Published by his legal representatives, 1891), 227–28.

27. Raphael Semmes, *Service Afloat and Ashore During the Mexican War* (Cincinnati: W.H. Moore, 1851), 428.

28. Many soldiers' personal narratives and histories include anecdotes about the San Patricios, often noting their spectacular punishment and execution. See, for instance, Samuel Chamberlain, *My Confession* (New York: Harper and Brothers, 1956), 228: "The execution of the last number was attended with unusual and unwarrantable acts of cruelty.... Colonel Harney, on account of the proficiency he had acquired as an executioner in hanging Seminoles in Florida, was selected to carry out the sentence."

29. Daniel Ullmann, "The Course of Empire: An Oration Delivered Before the Order of United Americans" (New York: William B. Weiss, 1856), 5. Hereafter cited in text. For more on Ullmann, see Jacobson, *Whiteness,* 70–72.

30. See also Amy Kaplan, "Manifest Domesticity," *American Literature* 70, no. 3 (September 1998): 585.

31. *Congressional Globe,* 29th Congress, 2d Session, 109.

32. Ibid., Appendix, 301; and 30th Congress, 1st Session, 120. Most of the Whigs, on the other hand, adopted a "No Territory" position in order to stop "an immoral war of aggression by making its prolongation pointless," as well as to sidestep the sectional controversies provoked by the Wilmot Proviso, which stipulated that slavery and other forms of involuntary servitude should be outlawed in any territory acquired from Mexico. See Michael Holt, *The Rise and Fall of the American Whig Party: Jacksonian Politics and the Onset of the Civil War* (New York: Oxford University Press, 1999), 253.

33. Robert J.C. Young, *Colonial Desire: Hybridity in Theory, Culture and Race* (New York: Routledge, 1995), 9.

34. *Congressional Globe,* 29th Congress, 2d Session, 301. According to historian Reginald Horsman, "[T]he Whig press constantly reiterated its fears of racial amalgamation." See Horsman, *Race and Manifest Destiny: The Origins of American Racial Anglo-Saxonism* (Cambridge: Harvard University Press, 1981), 238–39.

35. *Congressional Globe,* 29th Congress, 2d Session, 516. R.M.T. Hunter went even further: "I do not want their people.... But I have many reasons for desiring to acquire a portion of their territory contiguous to us which is so nearly unoccupied that the influence of these people could not be sensibly felt, as a political element in our system." See ibid., 30th Congress, 1st Session, Appendix, 276.

36. Ibid., 30th Congress, 1st Session, Appendix, 273.

37. Ibid., 29th Congress, 2d Session, Appendix, 132.

38. Ibid., 29th Congress, 2d Session, Appendix, 218.

39. Ibid., 29th Congress, 2d Session, Appendix, 278.

40. The following novels were read for this chapter: *The Prisoner of Perote: A Tale of American Valor and Mexican Love* (Boston: F. Gleason, 1848); Arthur Armstrong's *The Mariner of the Mines: or, The Maid of the Monastery* (Boston: F. Gleason, n.d.); Charles Averill's *The Secret Service Ship, or, The Fall of San Juan D'Ulloa* (Boston: F. Gleason, 1848) and *The Mexican Ranchero: or, The Maid of the Chapparal* (1847); Buntline's *Magdalena, the Beautiful Mexican Maid* (New York: Williams Brothers, 1847) and *The Volunteer: or, The Maid of Monterey* (Boston: F. Gleason, 1847); Alice Cleveland's *Lucy Morley: or, The Young Officer* (Boston: F. Gleason, 1846); Newton Curtis's *The Hunted Chief: or, The Female Ranchero* (New York: Williams Brothers, 1847), *The Vidette, a Tale of the Mexican War* (New York: Williams Brothers, 1848), and *The Prairie Guide: or, The Rose of the Rio Grande* (New York: Williams Brothers, 1847); Robert Greeley's *Arthur Woodleigh, A Romance of the Battle Field in Mexico* (New York: William B. Smith, 1847); Harry Halyard's four novelettes, *The Mexican Spy: or, The Bride of Buena Vista* (Boston: F. Gleason, 1848), *The Ocean Monarch: or, The Ranger of the Gulf* (Boston: F. Gleason, 1848), *The Heroine of Tampico: or, Wildfire the Wanderer* (Boston: F. Gleason, 1847), and *The Chieftain of Churubusco, or, The Spectre of the Cathedral* (Boston: F. Gleason, 1848); J.H. Ingraham's *The Texan Ranger: or, The Maid of Matamoras* (New York: Williams Brothers, 1847); and Harry Hazel's [Justin Jones], *Inez, the Beautiful: or, Love on the Rio Grande* (Boston: Justin Jones, 1846). Citations from each will be cited parenthetically in the text.

41. Antonia Castañeda, "The Political Economy of Nineteenth Century Stereotypes of Californianas," in *Between Borders: Essays on Mexicana/Chicana History,* ed. Adelaida del Castillo (Encino, Calif.: Floricanto Press, 1990), 220, 225. See also Castañeda, "Engendering the History of Alta California, 1769–1848: Gender, Sexuality, and the Family," in *Contested Eden: California before the Gold Rush,* ed. Ramón Gutiérrez and Richard Orsi (Berkeley: University of California Press, 1998), 230–59; Tomás Almaguer, *Racial Fault Lines: The Historical Origins of White Supremacy in California* (Berkeley: University of California Press, 1994), 46, 57–62; Rosaura Sánchez, *Telling Identities: The Californio Testimonios* (Minneapolis: University of Minnesota Press, 1995), 188–267; David Montejano, *Anglos and Mexicans in the Making of Texas, 1836–1986* (Austin: University of Texas Press, 1987), 37, 49.

42. Castañeda, "Political Economy," 220, 223.

43. On the disruptive effects of female masculinities, see Judith Halberstam, *Female Masculinity* (Durham: Duke University Press, 1998).

44. See also Elizabeth Young, *Disarming the Nation: Women's Writing and the American Civil War* (Chicago: University of Chicago Press, 1999), 167–70. Young argues that in Loreta Velazquez's *The Woman in Battle*, a Civil War–era text about cross-dressing, "military masquerade" provides "a symbolic frame for the representation of male homoeroticism"; she also observes that "the homosocial world of the military afforded new opportunities for the expression and representation of homoerotic desire" (169).

45. For a brief discussion of how the "demasculinization of colonized men and the hypermasculinity of European males represent principle assertions of white supremacy," see Ann Laura Stoler, "Carnal Knowledge and Imperial Power: Gender, Race, and Morality in Colonial Asia," in *Feminism and History*, ed. Joan Wallach Scott (New York: Oxford University Press, 1996), 215.

46. Young, *Colonial Desire*, 109.

47. See also José Limón, *American Encounters: Greater Mexico, the United States, and the Erotics of Culture* (Boston: Beacon Press, 1998), 136–37.

48. Alexander Saxton, *The Rise and Fall of the White Republic: Class Politics and Mass Culture in Nineteenth-Century America* (London and New York: Verso, 1990), 249.

49. Ibid., 337, 201.

50. Ibid., 184.

51. Ibid., 113.

52. Ibid., 184–85.

53. Amy Bridges, *A City in the Republic: Antebellum New York and the Origins of Machine Politics* (Cambridge: Cambridge University Press, 1984), 154.

54. Saxton, *Rise and Fall*, 119.

55. Ibid., 338.

56. On marriage contracts in the United States during this period, see Amy Dru Stanley, *From Bondage to Contract: Wage Labor, Marriage, and the Market in the Age of Slave Emancipation* (Cambridge: Cambridge University Press, 1998), 175–217. See also Norma Basch, *In the Eyes of the Law: Women, Marriage, and Property in Nineteenth-Century New York* (Ithaca: Cornell University Press, 1982).

57. *Congressional Globe*, 30th Congress, 1st Session, Appendix, 87.

58. Ibid., 29th Congress, 2nd Session, Appendix, 232.

59. Carole Pateman, *The Disorder of Women: Democracy, Feminism, and Political Theory* (Stanford: Stanford University Press, 1989), 83.

60. Carl Gutiérrez-Jones, *Rethinking the Borderlands: Between Chicano Culture and Legal Discourse* (Berkeley: University of California Press, 1995), 44.

61. See Lott, *Love and Theft*; Rogin, *Blackface*, 19–44; and Alexander Saxton, "Blackface Minstrelsy, Vernacular Comics, and the Politics of Slavery in the North," in *The Meaning of Slavery in the North*, ed. David Roediger and Martin Blatt (New York: Garland, 1998), 157–75.

62. Lott, *Love and Theft*, 194.

63. Michael Holt, *The Political Crisis of the 1850's* (New York: John Wiley and Sons, 1978), 42–43.

64. Michael Paul Rogin, *Subversive Genealogy: The Politics and Art of Herman Melville* (New York: Alfred E. Knopf, 1983), 106.

65. *Congressional Globe,* 30th Congress, 1st Session, Appendix, 262.

66. Ibid., 349.

67. Ibid., 87.

68. See Lucy Maddox, *Removals: Nineteenth-Century American Literature and the Politics of Indian Affairs* (New York: Oxford University Press, 1991), 3–49.

69. *Congressional Globe,* 30th Congress, 1st Session, Appendix, 197.

CHAPTER 5. FROM IMPERIAL ADVENTURE TO BOWERY B'HOYS AND BUFFALO BILL

1. Peter Buckley, "The Case against Ned Buntline: The 'Words, Signs, and Gestures' of Popular Authorship," *Prospects* 13 (1988): 256; and Jay Monaghan, *The Great Rascal: The Life and Adventures of Ned Buntline* (New York: Bonanza: 1951), 48, 55. The information about Buntline's literary career in the 1840s is drawn from these two sources.

2. On popular romances of the 1890s and the recasting of the Spanish-Cuban-American War as a "rescue mission for American manhood," see Amy Kaplan, "Romancing the Empire: American Masculinity in the Popular Historical Novel of the 1890s," *American Literary History* 2, no. 4 (winter 1990): 659–90.

3. Ned Buntline, *The Volunteer: or, The Maid of Monterey* (Boston: F. Gleason, 1847), 9. Hereafter cited in text.

4. On the Romantic privileging of the country over the city as a response to industrialization, see Raymond Williams, *Culture and Society, 1780–1950* (New York: Columbia University Press, 1983).

5. On Whittier's antiwar poetry, see Robert Johannsen, *To the Halls of the Montezumas: The Mexican War in the American Imagination* (New York: Oxford, 1985), 215–17.

6. Ned Buntline, *Magdalena, the Beautiful Mexican Maid: A Story of Buena Vista* (New York: Williams Brothers, 1846), 33. Hereafter cited in text.

7. On the stereotype of men of Mexican origin as "idle squanderers," see Tomás Almaguer, *Racial Fault Lines: The Historical Origins of White Supremacy in California* (Berkeley: University of California Press, 1994), 51–53.

8. Monaghan, *The Great Rascal,* 150.

9. Michael Denning, *Mechanic Accents: Dime Novels and Working-Class Culture in America* (1987; London and New York: Verso, 1998), 85.

10. Ned Buntline, *The Mysteries and Miseries of New York: A Story of Real Life* (New York: Berford and Co., 1848), part 1, 11. Hereafter cited in text.

11. Buntline, *Mysteries and Miseries,* part 5, 14–15.

12. *Albion,* 19 February 1848; cited in Peter Buckley, "To the Opera House: Culture and Society in New York City, 1820–1860," unpublished doctoral dissertation, State University of New York at Stony Brook, 1984, 389.

13. Buckley, "To the Opera House," 298–99.

14. Buckley, "The Case against Ned Buntline," 251.

15. Monaghan, *The Great Rascal,* 175.

16. Scrapbook Volume G, Charles Patrick Daly Papers, New York Public Library.

17. Ibid.

18. Ned Buntline, *The B'hoys of New York: A Sequel to the Mysteries and Miseries of New York* (New York: Dick and Fitzgerald, n.d.), 72. Hereafter cited in text.

19. Tom Chaffin, *Fatal Glory: Narciso Lopez and the First Clandestine U.S. War against Cuba* (Charlottesville: University Press of Virginia, 1996), 49–50.

20. Charles Brown, *Agents of Manifest Destiny: The Lives and Times of the Filibusters* (Chapel Hill: University of North Carolina Press, 1980), 45–47.

21. Robert E. May, "Young American Males and Filibustering in the Age of Manifest Destiny: The United States Army as a Cultural Mirror," *Journal of American History* 78, no. 3 (December 1991): 863.

22. Monaghan, *The Great Rascal,* 194. Former employee Thomas Paterson, who wrote a scathing and vindictive biography of Buntline, argued that "[h]is own account is, that being in Havana, he made the acquaintance of Don Manuel de Candelario, who had a daughter called Dona Seberina, living in the palace of her aunt, the Countess Escudera, and that he no sooner appeared in his sailor's toggery, and combed red-rusty hair, than Duchess and Countess prostrated themselves before him." He was rumored to have abandoned her when she became ill and was also said to be having an affair with a married woman in Nashville while Dona Seberina was still alive. Since in the course of his lifetime he was charged with bigamy and was married several times, it would not be surprising if this were true. See Thomas Paterson, *The Private Life, Public Career, and Real Character of that Odious Rascal NED BUNTLINE!!* (New York: Thomas Paterson, 1849), 7.

23. Chaffin, *Fatal Glory,* 93–98.

24. Ibid., 99.

25. Ibid., 110.

26. Ibid., 109–10.

27. Buntline, *The Mysteries and Miseries of New Orleans* (New York: Akarman and Ormsby, 1851), 24. Hereafter citations appear in text.

28. Luis Martínez-Fernández, *Torn between Empires: Economy, Society, and Patterns of Political Thought in the Hispanic Caribbean, 1840–1878* (Athens: University of Georgia Press, 1994), 26–27. See also Gerald Poyo, *"With All and For the Good of All": The Emergence of Popular Nationalism in the Cuban Communities of the United States, 1848–1898* (Durham: Duke University Press, 1989), 7.

29. Ned Buntline, *The Convict: or, The Conspirator's Victim* (1851; New York: Dick and Fitzgerald, 1863), 22. Hereafter citations appear in text.

30. Sean Wilentz, *Chants Democratic: New York City and the Rise of the American Working Class, 1788–1850* (New York: Oxford University Press, 1984), 344. See also Bruce Laurie, *Working People of Philadelphia, 1800–1850* (Philadelphia: Temple University Press, 1980), 174–77.

31. Monaghan, *The Great Rascal,* 165.

32. *Ned Buntline's Own,* 8 February 1851.

33. Ibid., 27 August 1853.

CHAPTER 6. THE CONTRADICTIONS OF ANTI-IMPERIALISM

1. A.J.H. Duganne, *The Peon Prince; or, The Yankee Knight-Errant. A Tale of Modern Mexico* (New York: Beadle, 1861), 20.

2. Alexander Saxton, *The Rise and Fall of the White Republic: Class Politics and Mass Culture in Nineteenth-Century America* (London and New York: Verso, 1990), 186.

3. Ibid., 200.

4. Alexander Saxton, "Blackface Minstrelsy, Vernacular Comics, and the Politics of Slavery in the North," in *The Meaning of Slavery in the North,* ed. David Roediger and Martin Blatt (New York: Garland, 1998), 166.

5. John H. Schroeder, *Mr. Polk's War: American Opposition and Dissent, 1846–1848* (Madison: University of Wisconsin Press, 1973), 35–38.

6. Saxton, *Rise and Fall,* 322.

7. On the Wilmot Proviso, see Eric Foner, "The Wilmot Proviso Revisited," *Journal of American History* 56 (1969): 262–79; and Foner, *Free Soil, Free Labor, Free Men: The Ideology of the Republican Party before the Civil War* (1970; New York: Oxford University Press, 1995), 60, 83, 106, 116, 164, 188, 190, 267, 309, 314. Wilmot's proposed amendment stated that "there shall be neither slavery nor involuntary servitude in any territory on the continent of America which shall hereafter be acquired by or annexed to the United States." See *Congressional Globe,* 29th Congress, 2d Session, Appendix, 318.

8. Robert E. May, *The Southern Dream of a Caribbean Empire, 1854–1861* (Baton Rouge: Louisiana State University Press, 1973), 21, 136, and throughout.

9. See Sean Wilentz, *Chants Democratic: New York City and the Rise of the American Working Class, 1788–1850* (New York: Oxford University Press, 1984). According to Wilentz, by "the mid-1840s, land reform had captured the imagination of almost every labor radical still active in New York" (336).

10. Helene Zahler, *Eastern Workingmen and National Land Policy, 1829–1862* (New York: Columbia University Press, 1941), 67. On the land reform movements in Britain and the United States during this period, see Jamie Bronstein's excellent study, *Land Reform and Working-Class Experience in Britain and the United States, 1800–1862* (Stanford: Stanford University Press, 1999). For more on Evans, see David Roediger, *The Wages of Whiteness: Race and the Making of the American Working Class* (London and New York: Verso, 1991), 71, 77–80, 110; John Jentz, "Artisans, Evangelicals, and the City: A Social History of Abolition and Land Reform in Jacksonian New York," unpublished doctoral dissertation, City University of New York, 1977; Saxton, *Rise and Fall,* 96, 102, 103, 206–7; Eric Lott, *Love and Theft: Blackface Minstrelsy and the American Working Class* (New York: Oxford University Press, 1993), 129, 132, 155, 202.

11. *Working Man's Advocate* [hereafter *WMA*], 16 March 1844.

12. Ibid., 10 May 1845.

13. Bronstein, *Land Reform,* 128. For a comprehensive discussion of these cultural forms, see chapter 5, "Making Working Class-Activism: Anglo-American Organizational Strategies," 112–59.

14. Ibid., 146.

15. See the *Voice of Industry,* 14 April 1848. On Bagley as editor of the *Voice,* see Madeleine Stern, ed., *We the Women: Career Firsts of Nineteenth-Century America* (New York: Schulte Publishing Company, 1963), 85–86.

16. A. J. H. Duganne, *The Poetical Works of Augustine Duganne* (Philadelphia: Parry and McMillan, 1855), 226, 229.

17. Louis Scisco, *Political Nativism in New York State* (New York: Columbia University Press, 1901), 240.

18. Duganne, *Poetical Works,* 97.

19. Ibid., 233.

20. Ibid., 229.

21. Matthew Frye Jacobson, *Whiteness of a Different Color: European Immigrants and the Alchemy of Race* (Cambridge: Harvard University Press, 1998), 210.

22. Walter Benn Michaels, "Anti-Imperial Americanism," in *Cultures of United States Imperialism,* ed. Amy Kaplan and Donald Pease (Durham: Duke University Press, 1993), 365–91; and Michaels, *Our America: Nativism, Modernism, and Pluralism* (Durham: Duke University Press, 1995).

23. *Massachusetts Quarterly Review* 1, no. 1 (December 1847); and *Miscellaneous Notebooks of Ralph Waldo Emerson,* vol. 9 (1843–1847). Edited by Ralph Orth and Alfred Ferguson (Cambridge: Harvard University Press, 1971), 430–31. For a more detailed consideration of Emerson's positions on such questions, see John Q. Anderson, "Emerson on Texas and the Mexican War," *Western Humanities Review* 13, no. 2 (spring 1959): 191–99.

24. See Robert Johannsen, *To the Halls of the Montezumas: The Mexican War in the American Imagination* (New York: Oxford University Press, 1985), 277–78.

25. *Sermons on War* by Theodore Parker (reprinted from volume 4 of the 1863 edition of *The Collected Works of Theodore Parker,* ed. Frances P. Cobbe), with a new introduction by Alice Kessler Harris (New York: Garland, 1973), 23. On Parker's opposition to the war, see also Johannsen, *Halls,* 278.

26. Ibid., 37.

27. Ibid., 26, 54, 62, 73.

28. Ibid., 24.

29. Anders Stephanson, *Manifest Destiny: American Expansionism and the Empire of Right* (New York: Hill and Wang, 1995), 56.

30. Robert Russell Lowell, *The Biglow Papers* (London: J. C. Hotten, 1865), 44–45.

31. Ibid., 30, 28.

32. Cited in Johannsen, *Halls,* 218.

33. *North Star,* 21 January 1848. All of the Douglass quotations that follow are from this source.

34. *Massachusetts Quarterly Review* 1, no. 1 (December 1847).

35. Grace Greenwood, *Greenwood Leaves: A Collection of Sketches and Letters.* 2d ser. (Boston: Ticknor, Reed, and Fields, 1852), 100–101. Hereafter citations will appear in text.

36. Saxton, *Rise and Fall,* 102.

37. Wilentz, *Chants Democratic*, 334–35. For more on Walsh, see Robert Ernst, "The One and Only Mike Walsh," *New-York Historical Society Quarterly* 26 (1952), 43–65; Noel Ignatiev, *How the Irish Became White* (New York: Routledge, 1995), 77–79; David Roediger, *The Wages of Whiteness*, 75, 77, 80; and Wilentz, *Chants Democratic*, 327–35, 340, 342, 356–57, 359, and 389.

38. *Subterranean*, 6 June 1847.

39. Ibid., 16 May 1846.

40. Wilentz, *Chants Democratic*, 340. See also Bronstein, *Land Reform*, 164.

41. Saxton, *Rise and Fall*, 103.

42. *Voice of Industry*, 12 June 1846.

43. Ibid., 11 December 1846.

44. Ibid., 9 January 1847.

45. Cited in *Young America*, 6 September 1845. Hereafter YA.

46. Cited in *Voice of Industry*, 25 June 1847.

47. Roediger, *The Wages of Whiteness*, 65–66.

48. Philip Foner, *History of the Labor Movement in the United States*, vol. 1 (New York: International Publishers, 1947), 278.

49. *Voice of Industry*, 26 November 1847.

50. See also Roediger, *The Wages of Whiteness*, 80.

51. *WMA*, 22 March 1845.

52. *YA*, 27 December 1845.

53. Ibid., 26 July 1845.

54. Ibid., cited in the *Voice of Industry*, 27 November 1846.

55. *YA*, 2 April 1845.

56. *WMA*, 11 May 1844.

57. Ibid., 15 June 1844.

58. He argued, for instance, that just as the United States owed the Indians land "in return for that of which they had been robbed," so did "blacks have the same right, in lieu of that from which they have been stolen away." See *WMA*, 15 November 1845.

59. Roediger, *The Wages of Whiteness*, 79.

60. *YA*, 26 April 1845.

61. *WMA*, 22 March 1845.

62. Amy Dru Stanley, *From Bondage to Contract: Wage Labor, Marriage, and the Market in the Age of Slave Emancipation* (Cambridge: Cambridge University Press, 1998), x.

63. Roediger, *The Wages of Whiteness*, 74. For a discussion of the history of the use of the terms "white slavery" and "wage slavery" in the antebellum labor movement, see Roediger's entire chapter "White Slaves, Wage Slaves, and Free White Labor," 65–92. For a discussion of Evans's role in these discussions, see 77–80.

64. See also ibid., 78–80.

65. *Radical*, November 1841, 165.

66. *YA*, 27 December 1845.

67. Ibid., 6 December 1845.

68. Ibid., December 27, 1845.

69. Ibid., January 10, 1846.

70. Cheryl Harris, "Whiteness as Property," *Harvard Law Review* 106, no. 8 (June 1993): 1714. Hereafter cited in text.

71. See, for instance, Reginald Horsman, *Race and Manifest Destiny: The Origins of American Racial Anglo-Saxonism* (Cambridge: Harvard University Press, 1981), 210.

72. Gilbert Joseph, "The United States, Feuding Elites, and Rural Revolt in Yucatán, 1836–1915," in *Rural Revolt in Mexico: U.S. Intervention and the Domain of Subaltern Politics,* ed. Daniel Nugent (Durham: Duke University Press, 1998), 176.

73. Robert W. Patch, "Decolonization, the Agrarian Problem, and the Origins of the Caste War, 1812–1857," in *Land, Labor, and Capital in Modern Yucatán: Essays in Regional History and Political Economy,* ed. Jeffrey T. Brannon and Gilbert M. Joseph (Tuscaloosa: University of Alabama Press, 1991), 52.

74. The account that follows is drawn from Joseph's article as well as from Nelson Reed, *The Caste War of Yucatan* (Stanford: Stanford University Press, 1964).

75. 30th Congress, 1st Session, Senate Executive Document 45. In Brantz Mayer, *Mexican Miscellanies,* vol. 11, no. 14, Bancroft Library, University of California, Berkeley.

76. *Congressional Globe,* 30th Congress, 1st Session, Appendix, 604.

77. Ibid., 616, 618.

78. Ibid., 612.

79. Ibid., 712.

80. Ibid., 618–19.

81. Ibid., 633.

82. Ibid., 712.

83. *National Reform Almanac for 1849* (New York: Young America, 1849), 41. Hereafter cited in text.

84. Bronstein, *Land Reform,* 33.

CHAPTER 7. THE HACIENDA, THE FACTORY, AND THE PLANTATION

1. For more on the Republican appropriation of National Reform issues, see Helene Zahler, *Eastern Workingmen and National Land Policy, 1829–1862* (New York: Columbia University Press, 1941), 175–201.

2. Eric Foner, *Free Soil, Free Labor, Free Men: The Ideology of the Republican Party before the Civil War* (1970; New York: Oxford University Press, 1995), xxvi.

3. See Eugene H. Berwanger, *The Frontier against Slavery: Western Anti-Negro Prejudice and the Slavery Extension Controversy* (Urbana: University of Illinois Press, 1967), 123, 129–31, 134–37.

4. *Congressional Globe,* 29th Congress, 2d Session, Appendix, 317.

5. Foner, *Free Soil,* xxvii. See also Tomás Almaguer, *Racial Fault Lines: The Historical Origins of White Supremacy in California* (Berkeley: University of California Press, 1994), 5–6, 12–15, 33–37, 51, 69–70, 153–54; David Roediger, *The Wages of Whiteness* (London and New York: Verso, 1991), 47, 81,

85–87, 175; Bernard Mandel, *Labor, Free and Slave: Workingmen and the Anti-slavery Movement in the United States* (New York: Associated Authors, 1955); and Jonathan Glickstein, *Concepts of Free Labor in Antebellum America* (New Haven: Yale University Press, 1991).

6. *Congressional Globe,* 29th Congress, 2d Session, Appendix, 317.

7. See Reginald Horsman, *Race and Manifest Destiny: The Origins of American Racial Anglo-Saxonism* (Cambridge: Harvard University Press, 1981).

8. *Congressional Globe,* 29th Congress, 2d Session, Appendix, 315. For a discussion of the myriad "halfway houses of semifree labor" in the antebellum period, see Foner, *Free Soil,* xxvii–xxviii. Foner notes that the "West, imagined (and often experienced) by white laborers as a land of economic independence, simultaneously harbored indentured Indian labor, Mexican-American peonage, and work under long-term contracts for Chinese immigrants" (xxvii). See also Howard Lamar, "From Bondage to Contract: Ethnic Labor in the American West," in *The Countryside in the Age of Capitalist Transformation: Essays in the Social History of Rural America,* ed. Steven Hahn and Jonathan Prude (Chapel Hill: University of North Carolina Press, 1985), 293–326; and Alexander Saxton, *The Indispensable Enemy: Labor and the Anti-Chinese Movement in California* (1971; Berkeley: University of California Press, 1995).

9. Raphael Semmes, *Service Afloat and Ashore During the Mexican War* (Cincinnati: W. H. Moore, 1851), 17. Hereafter cited in text.

10. Arnold J. Bauer, "Rural Workers in Spanish America: Problems of Peonage and Oppression," *Hispanic American Historical Review* 59, no. 1 (January 1979): 34–63. See also Alan Knight, "Mexican Peonage: What Was It and Why Was It?" *Journal of Latin American Studies* 18 (May 1986): 41–72; Eric Van Young, *Hacienda and Market in Eighteenth-Century Mexico: The Rural Economy of the Guadalajara Region, 1675–1820* (Berkeley: University of California Press, 1981), 236–69; Charles Gibson, *The Aztecs under Spanish Rule: A History of the Indians of the Valley of Mexico, 1519–1810* (Stanford: Stanford University Press, 1964), 220–56; Magnus Morner, "The Spanish American Hacienda: A Survey of Recent Research and Debate," *Hispanic American Historical Review* 53, no. 2 (May 1973): 183–216; D. A. Brading, *Haciendas and Ranchos in the Mexican Bajio, León 1780–1860* (Cambridge: Cambridge University Press, 1978), 3–4, 9–10, 25–26, 35–38, 76–77, 97–100, 196–99); Francois Chevalier, "The North Mexican Hacienda: Eighteenth and Nineteenth Centuries," in *The New World Looks at Its History,* ed. Archibald Lewis and Thomas McGann (Austin: University of Texas Press, 1963), 95–107; Harry Cross, "Living Standards in Rural Nineteenth-Century Mexico: Zacatecas, 1820–1880," *Journal of Latin American Studies* 10 (1978): 1–19; John Tutino, "Life and Labor on North Mexican Haciendas: The Querétaro-San Luis Potosí Region, 1775–1810," in *El Trabajo y los Trabajadores en la Historia de México,* ed. Elsa Frost, Michael Meyer, and Josefina Vázquez (Tucson: University of Arizona Press, 1979), 339–78.

11. Knight, "Mexican Peonage," 42, 45–46.

12. John Steinbeck, *The Harvest Gypsies: On the Road to the Grapes of Wrath* (1936; Berkeley: Heyday Books, 1988), 52–57. Steinbeck deplores the treatment of foreign labor but still claims that white laborers have too much

"pride and self-respect" to "accept the role of field peon" (57) that he suggests Mexicans accepted.

13. See also *The Rough and Ready Annual, or Military Souvenir* (New York: Appleton, 1848), 194; and Richard McSherry, *El Puchero; or, A Mixed Dish from Mexico* (Philadelphia: Lippincott, Grambo, 1850), 144.

14. Bill Brown, *Reading the West: An Anthology of Dime Westerns* (Boston: Bedford, 1997), 14.

15. Advertisement in Mary Denison, *Tim Bumble's Charge* (New York: Beadle, 1862); Catalogue of Beadle's Dime Novels in N.C. Iron, *The Two Guards* (New York: Beadle, 1863).

16. Philip Durham, "Introduction," in *Seth Jones and Deadwood Dick on Deck,* ed. Durham (New York: Odyssey, 1966), ix. This estimate is based on Durham's study of 1,531 Beadle's titles.

For more on dime novel genres see Michael Denning, *Mechanic Accents: Dime Novels and Working-Class Culture in America,* rev. ed. (1987; London: Verso, 1998). Denning rightly points out that "Beadle and Adams, though important, did not entirely dominate sensational fiction" (15). Although in this study I consider other forms of popular literature such as the story paper, my analysis of the dime novel after 1860 is largely based on Beadle's fiction. But even though in this book I do not analyze post-1860 dime novels published by firms other than Beadle's, my research suggests that other publishers similarly issued an extensive array of novels about the border, Mexico, and the Americas.

17. Brown, *Reading the West,* 167.

18. Ibid., v.

19. Richard Slotkin, *Gunfighter Nation: The Myth of the Frontier in Twentieth-Century America* (1992; Norman: University of Oklahoma Press, 1998), 405–40. Hereafter cited in text.

20. Slotkin argues that the "'Mexico' of counterinsurgency films is a potentially 'Americanizable' land" (410).

21. Alexander Saxton, *The Rise and Fall of the White Republic: Class Politics and Mass Culture in Nineteenth-Century America* (London and New York: Verso, 1990), 186

22. A.J.H. Duganne, *The Peon Prince; or, The Yankee Knight-Errant. A Tale of Modern Mexico* (New York: Beadle, 1861), 22, 85. Hereafter cited in text.

23. Francis Hodge, *Yankee Theatre: The Image of America on the Stage, 1825–1850* (Austin: University of Texas Press, 1964), 4.

24. A.J.H. Duganne, *Putnam Pomfret's Ward; or, A Vermonter's Adventures in Mexico* (New York: Beadle, 1861), 54, 55, 57.

25. Jan Bazant, "From Independence to the Liberal Republic, 1821–1867," in *Mexico since Independence,* ed. Leslie Bethell (New York: Cambridge University Press, 1991), 36–38.

26. Brian Hamnett, *Juárez* (London: Longman, 1994), 154, 157. The information in this paragraph is based on Hamnett and Bazant. See also Richard Sinkin, *The Mexican Reform, 1855–1876: A Study in Liberal Nation-Building* (Austin: Institute of Latin American Studies, 1979); and Laurens Perry, *Juárez and Diaz: Machine Politics in Mexico* (DeKalb: Northern Illinois University Press, 1978).

27. *Congressional Globe,* 30th Congress, 1st Session, Appendix, 613–20, 630–33.

28. Bazant, "From Independence to the Liberal Republic," 12.

29. Ana Maria Alonso, *Thread of Blood: Colonialism, Revolution, and Gender on Mexico's Northern Frontier* (Tucson: University of Arizona Press, 1997), 120–26. See also Charles A. Hale, *Mexican Liberalism in the Age of Mora, 1821–1853* (New Haven: Yale University Press, 1968), 222–46; Rosaura Sánchez, *Telling Identities: The Californio Testimonios* (Minneapolis: University of Minnesota Press, 1995), 96–141.

30. John M. Hart, "The 1840s Southwestern Mexico Peasants' War: Conflict in a Transitional Society," in *Riot, Rebellion, and Revolution: Rural Social Conflict in Mexico,* ed. Friedrich Katz (Princeton: Princeton University Press, 1988), 249–68; Leticia Reina, "The Sierra Gorda Peasant Rebellion, 1847–1850," in *Riot, Rebellion, and Revolution,* 269–94; John Kicza, "Introduction," in *The Indian in Latin American History: Resistance, Resilience, and Acculturation* (Wilmington, Del.: Scholarly Resources, 1993), xxi–xxii; Jack Spicer, *Cycles of Conquest: The Impact of Spain, Mexico, and the United States on the Indians of the Southwest, 1533–1960* (Tucson: University of Arizona Press, 1962), 334–42; John Tutino, *From Insurrection to Revolution in Mexico: Social Bases of Agrarian Violence* (Princeton: Princeton University Press, 1986), 242–64; Paul Vanderwood, *Disorder and Progress: Bandits, Police, and Mexican Development* (Wilmington, Del.: Scholarly Resources, 1992), 35–38. But see also Dawn Fogle Deaton, "The Decade of Revolt: Peasant Rebellion in Jalisco, Mexico, 1855–1864" and Michael Ducey, "Liberal Theory and Peasant Practice: Land and Power in Northern Veracruz, Mexico, 1826–1900," in *Liberals, the Church, and Indian Peasants: Corporate Lands and the Challenge of Reform in Nineteenth-Century Spanish America,* ed. Robert Jackson (Albuquerque: University of New Mexico Press, 1997), 37–93. Ducey argues that "a wide gap often separated the objectives of the liberal legislation and the manner in which local officials and villagers enforced the laws," and that it was "only in the late nineteenth century that the liberal property regime became a system for the widespread expropriation of peasant producers" (65).

31. Spicer, *Cycles of Conquest,* 338.

32. Hale, *Mexican Liberalism,* 221, 237–39.

33. Sánchez, *Telling Identities,* 127.

34. Hale, *Mexican Liberalism,* 200; Brading, *Haciendas and Ranchos,* 2.

35. Foner, *Free Soil,* ix.

36. Ibid., xix. See also Roediger, *The Wages of Whiteness,* 43–92.

37. See also Barry Goldberg, "Slavery, Race, and the Languages of Class: 'Wage Slaves' and White 'Niggers,'" *New Politics* 1, no. 3 (summer 1991): 65–83.

38. Foner, *Free Soil,* xxi–xxii.

39. Roediger, *The Wages of Whiteness,* 87.

40. Tutino, *From Insurrection to Revolution,* 224.

41. Brading, *Haciendas and Ranchos,* 2–3.

42. Ibid., 5, 9.

43. Roediger, *The Wages of Whiteness*, 35, 66. Roediger argues that republicanism "suggested that long acceptance of slavery betokened weakness, degradation, and an unfitness for freedom. The Black population symbolized that degradation" (66).

44. Eric Lott, *Love and Theft: Blackface Minstrelsy and the American Working Class* (New York: Oxford University Press, 1993), 68.

45. See Walter Hugins, *Jacksonian Democracy and the Working Class: A Study of the New York Workingmen's Movement, 1829–1837* (Stanford: Stanford University Press, 1960), 27, 33, 108, 138, 145, 146.

46. Brading, *Haciendas and Ranchos*, 2.

47. A. J. H. Duganne, *Camps and Prisons: Twenty Months in the Department of the Gulf* (New York: J. P. Robens, 1865), 15. Hereafter cited in text.

48. David Montgomery, *Beyond Equality: Labor and the Radical Republicans, 1862–1872* (New York: Alfred E. Knopf, 1967), 75; Ronald Formisano, *The Transformation of Political Culture: Massachusetts Parties, 1790s–1840s* (New York: Oxford University Press, 1983), 286, 340.

49. Eric Foner, *Reconstruction: America's Unfinished Revolution, 1863–1877* (New York: Harper and Row, 1988), 55.

50. Ibid., 55. W. E. B. Du Bois, *Black Reconstruction in America, 1860–1880*. (New York: Russell and Russell, 1935), 68. Hereafter cited in text.

51. Foner, *Reconstruction*, 56, 60. See also Rebecca Scott, "Defining the Boundaries of Freedom in the World of Cane: Cuba, Brazil, and Louisiana after Emancipation," *American Historical Review* 99, no. 1 (February 1994): 70–102.

52. Foner, *Reconstruction*, 235.

53. Ibid.

54. Ibid., 237.

55. Ibid., 236–39.

CHAPTER 8. THE DIME NOVEL, THE CIVIL WAR, AND EMPIRE

1. A. J. H. Duganne, *Putnam Pomfret's Ward; or, A Vermonter's Adventures in Mexico* (New York: Beadle, 1861), 45. Hereafter cited in text.

2. Bill Brown, *Reading the West: An Anthology of Dime Westerns* (Boston: Bedford, 1997), 32, 31.

3. Ibid., 31.

4. Charles Harvey, "The Dime Novel in American Life," *Atlantic Monthly* 100 (July 1907): 39, 43.

5. See the many titles on these topics from the first Beadle's series in Albert Johannsen, *The House of Beadle and Adams and Its Dime and Nickel Novels: The Story of a Vanished Literature*, vol. 1 (Norman: University of Oklahoma Press, 1950), 92–99. There are even more examples from later years.

6. José David Saldívar, *Border Matters: Remapping American Cultural Studies* (Berkeley: University of California Press, 1997), 1–14, 159–83.

7. David Montejano, *Anglos and Mexicans in the Making of Texas, 1836–1986* (Austin: University of Texas Press, 1987), 33.

8. U.S. Congress, House, *Difficulties on the Southwestern Frontier,* H. Exec. Doc. 52, 36th Congress, 1st Session, 2 April 1860, 80–81. Cited in *U.S.-Mexico Borderlands: Historical and Contemporary Perspectives,* ed. Oscar J. Martinez (Wilmington, Del.: Scholarly Resources, 1996), 75–76. See also Montejano, *Anglos and Mexicans,* 32.

9. Montejano, *Anglos and Mexicans,* 26–32.

10. John Emerald, *Cortina, the Scourge; or, The Lost Diamond* (New York: Beadle and Adams, 1872), 9. Hereafter cited in text.

11. Brown, *Reading the West,* 5.

12. Carol Chomsky, "The United States–Dakota War Trials: A Study in Military Injustice," *Stanford Law Review* 43, no. 1 (November 1990): 15.

13. Gary Anderson and Alan Woolworth, eds. *Through Dakota Eyes: Narrative Accounts of the Minnesota Indian War of 1862* (St. Paul: Minnesota Historical Society Press, 1988), 12; Chomsky, "The United States–Dakota War Trials," 17.

14. Quoted in Roy W. Meyer, *History of the Santee Sioux: United States Indian Policy on Trial,* rev. ed. (Lincoln: University of Nebraska Press, 1993), 114.

15. The account in this paragraph is largely drawn from Chomsky's article and the *Through Dakota Eyes* collection.

16. Chomsky, "The United States–Dakota War Trials," 13. See also David Nichols, *Lincoln and the Indians: Civil War Policy and Politics* (Columbia: University of Missouri Press, 1978), 65–118.

17. Chomsky, "The United States–Dakota War Trials," 15.

18. Daryl Jones, *The Dime Novel Western* (Bowling Green, Ohio: Popular Press, 1978), 8.

19. Christine Bold, "Malaeska's Revenge; or, The Dime Novel Tradition in Popular Fiction," in *Wanted Dead or Alive: The American West in Popular Culture,* ed. Richard Aquila (Urbana: University of Illinois Press, 1996), 23. See also Bold, *Selling the Wild West: Popular Western Fiction, 1860 to 1960* (Bloomington: Indiana University Press, 1987), 1–36.

20. Edward Ellis, "Seth Jones; or the Captives of the Frontier," in Brown, *Reading the West,* 188–89, 198. Hereafter cited in text.

21. Jones, *Dime Novel Western,* 149.

22. Edward Ellis, *Indian Jim: A Tale of the Minnesota Massacre* (New York: Beadle, 1864), 10. Hereafter cited in text.

23. Edward Ellis, *The Hunter's Escape: A Tale of the North West in 1862* (New York: Beadle, 1864), 38.

24. Ellis, *Hunter's Escape,* 13.

25. Michael Paul Rogin, *Ronald Reagan, the Movie and Other Episodes in Political Demonology* (Berkeley: University of California Press, 1987), 151. See also Rogin, *Fathers and Children: Andrew Jackson and the Subjugation of the American Indian* (New York: Knopf, 1975).

26. Rogin, *Ronald Reagan, the Movie,* 162.

27. Bold, "Malaeska's Revenge," 23.

28. Stephens was also an editor for several other magazines during the course of her career, including the *Portland Magazine, Graham's Magazine, The Ladies' World, Peterson's Ladies National Magazine,* and *Mrs. Stephens Illustrated New Monthly,* and she had also written several very successful novels, perhaps most

notably the urban melodramas *Fashion and Famine* (1854) and *The Old Homestead* (1855). For interesting readings of these two novels, as well as Stephens's *Mary Derwent,* see Nina Baym, *Woman's Fiction: A Guide to Novels by and about Women in America, 1820–1870* (Ithaca: Cornell University Press, 1978), 181–88. See also Brown, *Reading the West,* 53–55; Paola Gemme, "Legacy Profile: Ann Sophia Winterbotham Stephens," *Legacy* 12, no. 1 (1995): 47–55; Gemme, "Rewriting the Indian Tale: Science, Politics, and the Evolution of Ann S. Stephens's Indian Romances," *Prospects* 19 (1994): 376–87; and Madeleine Stern, *We the Women: Career Firsts of Nineteenth-Century America* (New York: Schulte, 1963), 29–54.

29. "Malaeska," in Brown, *Reading the West,* 57.

30. Ann Stephens, *Myra: The Child of Adoption. A Romance of Real Life* (New York: Beadle, 1860), 11; Stern, *We the Women,* 49.

31. Ann Stephens, *Esther: A Story of the Oregon Trail* (New York: Beadle, 1862), 121. Hereafter cited in text.

32. Ann Stephens, *Sybil Chase; or, The Valley Ranche. A Tale of California Life* (New York: Beadle, 1861), 43. Hereafter cited in text.

33. Bold, "Malaeska's Revenge," 24.

34. Albert Johannsen, *The House of Beadle and Adams,* vol. 2 (Norman: University of Oklahoma Press, 1950), 29–30. For more on the sisters and their dime novels, see Henry Nash Smith, *Virgin Land: The American West as Symbol and Myth* (New York: Vintage, 1950), 264–68.

35. Frances Fuller Barritt Victor, *Alicia Newcome, or, The Land Claim: A Tale of the Upper Missouri* (New York: Beadle, 1862), 5. Hereafter cited in text.

36. Metta Victor, *The Backwoods' Bride. A Romance of Squatter Life* (New York: Beadle, 1860), 14. Hereafter cited in text.

37. Metta Victor, *The Two Hunters; or The Cañon Camp. A Romance of the Santa Fé Trail* (New York: Beadle, 1865), 15. Hereafter cited in text.

38. See Neil Foley, *The White Scourge: Mexicans, Blacks, and Poor Whites in Texas Cotton Culture* (Berkeley: University of California Press, 1997), 19–24; and Tomás Almaguer, *Racial Fault Lines: The Historical Origins of White Supremacy in California* (Berkeley: University of California Press, 1994), esp. 46.

39. Alexander Saxton, *The Rise and Fall of the White Republic: Class Politics and Mass Culture in Nineteenth-Century America* (London and New York: Verso, 1990), 149.

40. Morris W. Foster, *Being Comanche: A Social History of the American Indian Community* (Tucson: University of Arizona Press, 1991), 46.

41. Foster, *Being Comanche,* 47.

42. See Curtis Marez, "Signifying Spain, Becoming Comanche, Making Mexicans: Indian Captivity and the History of Chicana/o Popular Performance," *American Quarterly* 53, no. 2 (2001): 267–307. According to Foster, the new borderline between the United States and Mexico actually "worked to the advantage of Comanche bands" because "Mexican authorities could not pursue Comanche raiders into Texan and U.S. territory" (45). The phrase "transfrontera contact zone" is José David Saldívar's. See Saldívar, *Border Matters,* 13.

43. Metta Victor, *The Unionist's Daughter: A Tale of the Rebellion in Tennessee* (New York: Beadle, 1862), 18. Hereafter cited in text.

44. Robert E. May, *The Southern Dream of a Caribbean Empire, 1854–1861* (Baton Rouge: Louisiana State University Press, 1973), 149.

45. May, *Southern Dream,* 247.

46. For more on Walker, see Charles Brown, *Agents of Manifest Destiny: The Lives and Times of the Filibusters* (Chapel Hill: University of North Carolina Press, 1980), 174–218, 266–457; May, *Southern Dream,* 77–135; Richard Slotkin, *The Fatal Environment: The Myth of the Frontier in the Age of Industrialization, 1800–1890* (Middletown, Conn.: Wesleyan University Press, 1985), 242–61; William O. Scroggs, *Filibusters and Financiers: The Story of William Walker and His Associates* (New York: Macmillan, 1918).

47. William Walker, *The War in Nicaragua* (Mobile, Ala.: S.H. Goetzel and Co., 1860), 263.

48. Ibid., 263–64, 265.

49. Ibid., 265, 266.

50. Ibid., 280.

51. Saxton, *Rise and Fall,* 261–62.

52. For biographical information on Denison, see Johannsen, *House of Beadle and Adams,* vol. 2, 79. For quick readings of a few of Denison's 1850s novels, see Baym, *Woman's Fiction,* 270–72.

53. Johannsen, *House of Beadle and Adams,* vol. 2, 79.

54. *The Prisoner of La Vintresse* was the second novel that she wrote for Beadle; she also authored Beadle's Dime Novel no. 6, *Chip: The Cave-Child* (1860), which was about the daughter of a Delaware Indian woman and a Frenchman in Pennsylvania; *Florida; or, The Iron Will* (1861), a drama of big-city life among the elite; *Ruth Margerie: A Romance of the Revolt of 1689* (1862), a story of the Puritans; *Tim Bumble's Charge* (1862), which features a "comical" Irishman; *The Mad Hunter* (1863), a New York murder mystery; and a novel about the American Revolution, *Captain Molly* (1856).

55. James Buchanan et al., "The Ostend Conference," in *What Happened in Cuba? A Documentary History,* ed. Robert Smith (New York: Twayne Publishers, 1963), 65.

56. Buchanan et al., "The Ostend Conference," 67.

57. Philip Foner, *A History of Cuba and Its Relations with the United States,* vol. 2 (New York: International Publishers, 1963), 101.

58. May, *Southern Dream,* 75, 76.

59. "Republican National Platform, 1856," in *What Happened in Cuba?,* 75.

60. For more on filibustering's place in American social history, both North and South, see Robert E. May, "Young American Males and Filibustering in the Age of Manifest Destiny: The United States Army as a Cultural Mirror," *Journal of American History* 78, no. 3 (December 1991): 857–86.

61. On the first, see Saxton, *Rise and Fall,* 141–54. On the material interests, see Luis Martínez-Fernández, *Torn between Empires: Economy, Society, and Patterns of Political Thought in the Hispanic Caribbean, 1840–1878* (Athens: University of Georgia Press, 1994), 24.

62. On López, see May, *Southern Dream,* 26–27.

63. Ibid., 52.

64. Martínez-Fernández, *Torn between Empires,* 167–68.

65. Mary Denison, *The Prisoner of La Vintresse; or, The Fortunes of a Cuban Heiress* (New York: Beadle, 1860), 16, 40. Hereafter cited in text.

66. Reginald Horsman, *Race and Manifest Destiny: The Origins of American Racial Anglo-Saxonism* (Cambridge: Harvard University Press, 1981), 281–83.

67. Martínez-Fernández, *Torn between Empires*, 227.

68. Ibid., 228.

69. Saldívar, *Border Matters*, 5.

70. Jeremy Adelman and Stephen Aron, "From Borderlands to Borders: Empires, Nation-States, and the Peoples in Between in North American History," *American Historical Review* 86, no. 1 (June 1999): 815.

71. Joseph Roach, *Cities of the Dead: Circum-Atlantic Performance* (New York: Columbia University Press, 1996). See also Kirsten Silva Gruesz's "New Orleans: Capital of the Nineteenth Century" in her book *Ambassadors of Culture: The Transamerican Origins of Latino Writing* (Princeton: Princeton University Press, 2001).

72. José Limón, *American Encounters: Greater Mexico, the United States, and the Erotics of Culture* (Boston: Beacon Press, 1998), 7–33.

73. Foley, *White Scourge*, 15, 17.

CHAPTER 9. JOAQUÍN MURRIETA AND POPULAR CULTURE

1. Joseph Badger, Jr., *Joaquin the Terrible: The True History of the Three Bitter Blows that Changed an Honest Man to a Merciless Demon*, Beadle's New York Dime Library 13, no. 165 (21 December 1881): 6. Hereafter cited in text.

2. Michael Denning, *Mechanic Accents: Dime Novels and Working-Class Culture in America*, rev. ed. (1987; London and New York: Verso, 1998), 160.

3. Ibid., 166.

4. Lisbeth Haas, *Conquests and Historical Identities in California, 1769–1936* (Berkeley: University of California Press, 1995), 2, 69.

5. David Montejano, *Anglos and Mexicans in the Making of Texas, 1836–1986* (Austin: University of Texas Press, 1987), 73.

6. Tomás Almaguer, *Racial Fault Lines: The Historical Origins of White Supremacy in California* (Berkeley: University of California Press, 1994), 72.

7. Alexander Saxton, *The Rise and Fall of the White Republic: Class Politics and Mass Culture in Nineteenth-Century America* (London and New York: Verso, 1990), 303.

8. Denning, *Mechanic Accents*, 165.

9. See chapter 4.

10. See John Rollin Ridge, *The Life and Adventures of Joaquín Murieta, the Celebrated California Bandit* (1854; Norman: University of Oklahoma Press, 1955); and the *California Police Gazette* version of the story, which was published under the title *The Life of Joaquín Murieta, the Brigand Chief of California* (1932; Fresno, Calif.: Valley Publishers, 1969). The latter includes a bibliography listing some of the different versions of the Murrieta story (117–20). For some of the *corrido* versions, see Luis Leal, "El Corrido de Joaquín Murrieta: Origen y difusión," *Mexican Studies/Estudios Mexicanos* 11, no. 1 (winter 1995): 18–23; and liner notes, "Joaquín Murrieta," *Corridos & Tragedias de la*

Frontera, Mexican-American Border Music, vols. 6 and 7, Arhoolie Records 7019/720, 38–40. See also Luis Leal, "Introduccíon," in *Vida Y Aventuras del Más Célebre Bandido Sonorense Joaquín Murrieta,* by Ireneo Paz (Houston: Arte Público, 1999), 1–95. In this introduction, Leal exhaustively catalogues the many different forms of the story, including fiction, poetry, music, film, and history.

Many of the Spanish-language versions, including a novel published in Los Angeles in 1919, seem to be based on the *California Police Gazette* adaptation. See *Joaquin Murieta, the Brigand Chief of California,* x. Subsequent citations from the two novels appear in parentheses in the text. Citations from the *Police Gazette* version are preceded by PG, and those from the Ridge version are preceded by R. All quotations from the Murrieta *corrido,* whether in Spanish or in English translation, are from the Arhoolie Records liner notes, and will also appear parenthetically in the text.

11. Susan Lee Johnson, *Roaring Camp: The Social World of the California Gold Rush* (New York: W.W. Norton, 2000), 28, 48, 50. This study appeared just as I was finishing my revision of the manuscript.

12. Malcolm Rohrbough, *Days of Gold: The California Gold Rush and the American Nation* (Berkeley: University of California Press, 1997), 216–29. See also Almaguer, *Racial Fault Lines,* 26–29; Jay Monaghan, *Chile, Peru, and the California Gold Rush of 1849* (Berkeley: University of California Press, 1973); Alexander Saxton, "Mines and Railroads," in *The Indispensable Enemy: Labor and the Anti-Chinese Movement in California* (1971; Berkeley: University of California Press, 1995), 46–66; and Johnson, *Roaring Camp,* 57–95.

13. On the reconstruction of whiteness in this period, see Reginald Horsman, *Race and Manifest Destiny: The Origins of American Racial Anglo-Saxonism* (Cambridge: Harvard University Press, 1981); Noel Ignatiev, *How the Irish Became White* (New York: Routledge, 1995); Eric Lott, *Love and Theft: Blackface Minstrelsy and the American Working Class* (New York: Oxford University Press, 1993); David Roediger, *The Wages of Whiteness: Race and the Making of the American Working Class* (London and New York: Verso, 1991); and Saxton, *Rise and Fall.*

14. On "structures of feeling," see Raymond Williams, *Marxism and Literature* (New York: Oxford University Press, 1977), 133–34.

15. See JoAnn Pavletich and Margot Gayle Backus, "With His Pistol in *Her* Hand: Rearticulating the Corrido Narrative in Helena María Viramontes' 'Neighbors,'" *Cultural Critique* 27 (spring 1994): 127–52; Rosa Linda Fregoso and Angie Chabram, "Chicana/o Cultural Representations: Reframing Alternative Critical Discourses," *Cultural Studies* 4, no. 3: 208; Angie Chabram-Dernersesian, "I Throw Punches for My Race, but I Don't Want to Be a Man: Writing Us—Chica-nos (Girl, Us)/Chicanas—into the Movement Script," in *Cultural Studies,* ed. Lawrence Grossberg, Cary Nelson, and Paula Treichler (New York: Routledge, 1992), 81–95. For an analysis of female soldiers in *corridos,* see María Herrera-Sobek, *The Mexican Corrido: A Feminist Analysis* (Bloomington: Indiana University Press, 1990), 84–116.

16. See Carl Gutiérrez-Jones, *Rethinking the Borderlands: Between Chicano Culture and Legal Discourse* (Berkeley: University of California Press, 1995).

Gutiérrez-Jones's important study of the "process by which Chicanos have become institutionally and popularly associated with criminality" (1) has significantly influenced my argument about the construction of a post–Mexican War racialized criminality.

17. Etienne Balibar, "Is There a Neo-Racism?" in Balibar and Immanuel Wallerstein, *Race, Nation, Class: Ambiguous Identities,* trans. Chris Turner (London and New York: Verso, 1991), 20. Balibar further defines the immigrant complex as "a racism whose dominant theme is not biological heredity but the insurmountability of cultural differences, a racism which, at first sight, does not postulate the superiority of certain groups or peoples in relation to others but 'only' the harmfulness of abolishing frontiers, the incompatibility of life-styles and traditions" (21).

18. On the epic heroic *corrido,* see José Limón, *Mexican Ballads, Chicano Poems: History and Influence in Mexican-American Social Poetry* (Berkeley: University of California Press, 1992), 16–77; John McDowell, "The Corrido of Greater Mexico as Discourse, Music, and Event," in *"And Other Neighborly Names": Social Process and Cultural Image in Texas Folklore,* ed. Richard Bauman and Roger D. Abrahams (Austin: University of Texas Press, 1981), 44–75; Américo Paredes, *"With His Pistol in His Hand": A Border Ballad and Its Hero* (Austin: University of Texas Press, 1958); and José David Saldívar, "Chicano Border Narratives as Cultural Critique," in *Criticism in the Borderlands: Studies in Chicano Literature, Culture, and Ideology,* ed. Héctor Calderón and Saldívar (Durham: Duke University Press, 1991), 170–73.

19. Michel Foucault, ed., *I, Pierre Rivière, having slaughtered my mother, my sister, and my brother…* (Harmondsworth: Penguin, 1987), 206.

20. See Frank Luther Mott, *A History of American Magazines, 1850–1865* (Cambridge: Harvard University Press, 1938), 186–87, 325–37; Alan Nourie and Barbara Nourie, eds., *American Mass-Market Magazines* (Westport, Conn.: Greenwood, 1990), 284–91; and Gene Smith and Jayne Barry Smith, eds., *The Police Gazette* (New York: Simon and Schuster, 1972).

21. Nourie and Nourie, *American Mass-Market Magazines,* 285. See also Saxton, *Rise and Fall,* 207–9.

22. Mott, *A History of American Magazines,* 326.

23. See H.H. Bretnor, *The California Police Gazette, a brief description* (typescript in Bancroft Library, #88305, 1955); and *Joaquin Murieta, the Brigand Chief of California,* v.

24. *California Police Gazette,* 24 September, 8 October, and 15 October 1859.

25. Ibid., 24 September 1859.

26. Alonzo Delano, *Life on the Plains and among the Diggings,* 157, quoted in Winifred Storrs Hill, *Tarnished Gold: Prejudice during the California Gold Rush* (San Francisco: International Scholars Publications, 1995), 10.

27. See Pedro Castillo and Albert Camarillo, eds., *Furia y Muerte: Los Bandidos Chicanos* (Los Angeles: Aztlán Publications, UCLA, 1972); Daniel Cohen, *Pillars of Salt, Monuments of Grace: New England Crime Literature and the Origins of American Popular Culture, 1674–1860* (New York: Oxford University Press, 1993); Michel Foucault, *Discipline and Punish: The Birth of the*

Prison, trans. Alan Sheridan (New York: Vintage, 1979); Karen Halttunen, "Early American Murder Narratives: The Birth of Horror," in *The Power of Culture: Critical Essays in American History,* ed. Fox and Lears (Chicago: University of Chicago Press, 1993), 67–101; Eric Hobsbawm, *Bandits* (New York: Pantheon, 1969); Simon Joyce, "Resisting Arrest/Arresting Resistance: Crime Fiction, Cultural Studies, and the 'Turn to History,'" *Criticism* 37, no. 2 (spring 1995): 309–35; Peter Linebaugh, *The London Hanged: Crime and Civil Society in the Eighteenth Century* (Cambridge: Cambridge University Press, 1992); and Américo Paredes, *Folklore and Culture on the Texas-Mexican Border,* ed. Richard Bauman (Austin: CMAS, 1993), 129–41.

28. James Varley, *The Legend of Joaquín Murrieta: California's Gold Rush Bandit* (Twin Falls, Idaho: Big Lost River, 1995), 48–65.

29. Ibid.

30. Ibid., 75–76. See also Johnson, *Roaring Camp,* 38.

31. Varley, *The Legend of Joaquín Murrieta,* 138.

32. Johnson also notes that Ridge's novel "owed a debt to the genre of cheap fiction" about banditry. See *Roaring Camp,* 48.

33. James Parins, *John Rollin Ridge: His Life and Works* (Lincoln: University of Nebraska Press, 1991), 107.

34. Ibid.

35. See Cheryl Walker, *Indian Nation: Native American Literature and Nineteenth-Century Nationalisms* (Durham: Duke University Press, 1997), 111. According to Walker, although Ridge was of Cherokee descent, he was "a metropolitan, acculturated Indian who migrated from Indian territory to California and upheld views repugnant to those who wished to maintain traditional Indian cultural practices" (111). Nonetheless, Walker suggests that Ridge "speaks as much as an Indian as he does as a voice of white culture" (112). See also John Carlos Rowe, *Literary Culture and U.S. Imperialism: From the Revolution to World War II* (New York: Oxford University Press, 2000), 97–119.

36. On Cherokee Removal, see William Anderson, ed., *Cherokee Removal: Before and After* (Athens: University of Georgia Press, 1991); Lucy Maddox, *Removals: Nineteenth-Century American Literature and the Politics of Indian Affairs* (New York: Oxford University Press, 1991), 15–28; and Priscilla Wald, *Constituting Americans: Cultural Anxiety and Narrative Form* (Durham: Duke University Press, 1995), 23–47. See also Walker, *Indian Nation,* 112–19.

37. Parins, *John Rollin Ridge,* 55.

38. Ibid., 103.

39. Karl Kroeber, "American Indian Persistence and Resurgence," *boundary 2* 19, no. 3 (fall 1992): 6.

40. Peter Christensen, "Minority Interaction in John Rollin Ridge's *The Life and Adventures of Joaquin Murieta,*" *MELUS* 17, no. 2 (summer 1991–1992): 63.

41. On James Fenimore Cooper's distinctions between "good" and "bad" Indians, see Saxton, *Rise and Fall,* 191.

42. Christensen, "Minority Interaction," 62.

43. Parins, *John Rollin Ridge,* 126.

44. Ibid., 129.

45. Rosaura Sánchez, *Telling Identities: The Californio Testimonios* (Minneapolis: University of Minnesota Press, 1995), 275–79.

46. Hill, *Tarnished Gold*, 40. See also Donald C. Biggs, *Conquer and Colonize* (San Rafael, Calif.: Presidio, 1977), 202–6.

47. Almaguer, *Racial Fault Lines*, 9 and throughout.

48. Leonard Pitt, *The Decline of the Californios: A Social History of the Spanish-Speaking Californians, 1846–1890* (Berkeley: University of California Press, 1970), 53. See also Almaguer, *Racial Fault Lines*, 55; and Ramón Gutiérrez, "Unraveling America's Hispanic Past: Internal Stratification and Class Boundaries," *Aztlán* 17, no. 1 (spring 1986): 89.

49. Sister Mary Colette Standart, "The Sonoran Migration to California, 1848–1856: A Study in Prejudice," in *Between Two Worlds: Mexican Immigrants in the United States*, ed. David G. Gutiérrez (Wilmington, Del.: Scholarly Resources, 1996), 3–21.

50. Douglas Monroy, *Thrown among Strangers: The Making of Mexican Culture in Frontier California* (Berkeley: University of California Press, 1990), 206. For the figure on Sonoran migration, see David Gutiérrez, *Walls and Mirrors: Mexican Americans, Mexican Immigrants, and the Politics of Ethnicity* (Berkeley: University of California Press, 1995), 19.

51. Pitt, *The Decline of the Californios*, 52. See also Monaghan, *Chile, Peru, and the California Gold Rush of 1849* (Berkeley: University of California Press, 1973).

52. Cited in Monaghan, *Chile, Peru, and the California Gold Rush*, 114. See also Pitt, *The Decline of the Californios*, 55–56.

53. See Pitt, *The Decline of the Californios*, 56; and Standart, "The Sonoran Migration to California," 7.

54. Josiah Royce, *California From the Conquest of 1846 to the Second Vigilance Committee in San Francisco* (Boston: Houghton-Mifflin, 1886), 361.

55. See Pitt, *The Decline of the Californios*, 53; Royce, *California*, 277; Standart, "The Sonoran Migration to California," 10; and Johnson, *Roaring Camp*, 38.

56. David Gutiérrez, "Introduction," in *Between Two Worlds*, 10.

57. Royce, *California*, 364.

58. Michael Omi and Howard Winant, *Racial Formation in the United States: From the 1960s to the 1990s*, 2d ed. (New York: Routledge, 1994), 56, 79.

59. Omi and Winant define racial formation "as the sociohistorical process by which racial categories are created, inhabited, transformed, and destroyed" (55).

60. Almaguer, *Racial Fault Lines*, 57.

61. Ibid., 65–68.

62. In *Roaring Camp*, Johnson suggests that "the rangers seemed soldiers engaged in a rearguard action designed to shore up the gains of the late expansionist war" (37).

63. I borrow the term "national fantasy" from Lauren Berlant, *The Anatomy of National Fantasy: Hawthorne, Utopia, and Everyday Life* (Chicago: University of Chicago Press, 1992).

64. For more on Gonzales's "I am Joaquín—Yo Soy Joaquín" and the Murrieta bandit narrative, see Johnson, *Roaring Camp*, 50.

65. On the limitations of Chicano responses to displacement and loss that codify "machismo as a concept around which to ground cultural affiliation," see Gutiérrez-Jones, *Rethinking the Borderlands,* 123–62.

66. See Richard Rodriguez, *Days of Obligation: An Argument with My Mexican Father* (New York: Viking, 1992), 140. Thanks are due to Barbara Brinson-Curiel for telling me about this essay. See also Rosaura Sánchez, "Calculated Musings: Richard Rodriguez's Metaphysics of Difference," in *The Ethnic Canon: Histories, Institutions, and Interventions,* ed. David Palumbo-Liu (Minneapolis: University of Minnesota Press, 1995), 153–73.

67. See Ramón Saldívar, *Chicano Narrative: The Dialectics of Difference* (Madison: University of Wisconsin Press, 1990), 32, 36; and McDowell, "The Corrido of Greater Mexico as Discourse, Music, and Event," 45–46.

68. Limón, *Mexican Ballads, Chicano Poems,* 34.

69. Leal, "El Corrido de Joaquín Murrieta," 1–23.

70. Liner notes, "Joaquín Murrieta," *Corridos & Tragedias de la Frontera,* 37.

71. Avery Gordon, *Ghostly Matters: Haunting and the Sociological Imagination* (Minneapolis: University of Minnesota Press, 1997), 66.

72. Gutiérrez, *Walls and Mirrors,* 40.

73. Ibid., 45.

74. Francisco Balderrama and Raymond Rodriguez, *Decade of Betrayal: Mexican Repatriation in the 1930's* (Albuquerque: University of New Mexico Press, 1995), 53.

75. Ibid., 55.

76. George Sánchez, *Becoming Mexican American: Ethnicity, Culture and Identity in Chicano Los Angeles, 1900–1945* (New York: Oxford University Press, 1993), 211.

77. Camille Guerin-Gonzales, *Mexican Workers, American Dreams: Immigration, Repatriation, and California Farm Labor, 1900–1939* (New Brunswick, N.J.: Rutgers University Press, 1994), 78.

78. Walter Noble Burns, *The Robin Hood of El Dorado: The Saga of Joaquin Murrieta, Famous Outlaw of California's Age of Gold* [1932] (Albuquerque: University of New Mexico Press, 1999). Hereafter citations will appear in text.

79. See Thomas Doherty, *Pre-Code Hollywood: Sex, Immorality, and Insurrection in American Cinema, 1930–1934* (New York: Columbia University Press, 1999), 319–72. This book includes three appendixes that contain the text of the Production Code as well as related documents.

80. Cited in ibid., 351, 352–53, 356, 362, 364.

81. Helen Delpar, *The Enormous Vogue of Things Mexican: Cultural Relations between the United States and Mexico, 1920–1935* (Tuscaloosa: University of Alabama Press, 1992), 169, 170.

82. Alfred Charles Richard, Jr., *Censorship and Hollywood's Hispanic Image: An Interpretive Filmography, 1936–1955* (Westport, Conn.: Greenwood, 1993), 22.

83. C. L. R. James, *American Civilization,* ed. Anna Grimshaw and Keith Hart (Cambridge: Blackwell, 1993), 121.

84. *New York Times,* 14 March 1936.

85. Chris Strachwitz, "The Singers," in *Mexican-American Border Music.* Vols. 6 and 7: *Corridos & Tragedias de la Frontera,* Arhoolie Records, 1994, 16, 18. See also Sánchez, *Becoming Mexican American,* 183.

86. Sánchez, *Becoming Mexican American,* 184. According to Sánchez, District Attorney Burton Fitts, who "believed that only English should be heard on the radio and that only American citizens should have the right to broadcast" (184), was responsible for the arrest.

87. See ibid., 178, 183–85; and Gutiérrez-Jones, *Rethinking the Borderlands,* 2–3, 50–56. I agree with the latter that González's example shows how "the stereotypical ascription of 'criminality' to Chicanos must be read in the context of larger U.S. institutional aims, including the maintenance of Chicanos and Mexicanos as a malleable, productive underclass" (3).

88. Paredes, *Folklore and Culture,* 135.

89. María Herrera-Sobek, *Northward Bound: The Mexican Immigrant Experience in Ballad and Song* (Bloomington and Indianapolis: Indiana University Press, 1993), xxiii.

90. Paredes, *Folklore and Culture,* 9. According to Paredes's logic, a "nationalist sentiment" would first be strongly articulated in Texas because of the battles there in the 1830s. In general, nationalist feeling was weak in the borderlands areas after Mexican independence in 1821, especially in California, which was so far removed from greater Mexico. See also Gutiérrez, *Walls and Mirrors,* 30. According to Gutiérrez, "[In] the quarter century before annexation, many, if not most, Spanish-speaking residents of Mexico's northern provinces did not even identify themselves as Mexicans and instead probably thought of themselves first as Nuevomexicanos, Tejanos, or Californios" (30).

91. My understanding of hybridity has been influenced by Lisa Lowe's discussion of this concept in the Asian American context in *Immigrant Acts: On Asian American Cultural Politics* (Durham: Duke University Press, 1996). Lowe suggests: "Hybridization is not the 'free' oscillation between or among chosen identities. It is the uneven process through which immigrant communities encounter the violences of the U.S. state, and the capital imperatives served by the United States and by the Asian states from which they come, and the process by which they survive those violences by living, inventing, and reproducing different cultural alternatives" (82).

92. See Paredes, *Folklore and Culture,* 137–38, for information about *décimas, corridos,* and the Mexican broadside press.

93. See Sánchez, *Becoming Mexican-American,* 21–22.

94. James Clifford, "Traveling Cultures," in *Cultural Studies,* ed. Lawrence Grossberg, Cary Nelson, and Paula Treichler (New York: Routledge, 1992), 96–112.

95. Herrera-Sobek, *Northward Bound,* 34–63, esp. 41–43.

96. Paul Gilroy, *The Black Atlantic: Modernity and Double Consciousness* (Cambridge: Harvard University Press, 1993), 40.

97. Cited in Anne McClintock, " 'No Longer in a Future Heaven': Nationalism, Gender, and Race," in *Becoming National: A Reader,* ed. Geoff Eley and Ronald Suny (New York: Oxford University Press, 1996), 260.

98. Johnson, *Roaring Camp,* 33. See also 35 for a compelling analysis of how ideas about manhood figure in the Murrieta story.

99. For an excellent discussion of violence in working-class forms of popular culture in the 1930s, see C. L. R. James, *American Civilization,* ed. Anna Grimshaw and Keith Hart (Cambridge: Blackwell, 1993), 118–48.

100. Julie Skurski, "The Ambiguities of Authenticity in Latin America: *Doña Bárbara* and the Construction of National Identity," in *Becoming National,* ed. Eky and Suny, 371–40.

101. In Spanish, the lines are as follows: "No soy chileno ni extraño/en este suelo que piso./De México es California,/porque Díos así lo quizo."

102. Citing Fichte, Balibar suggests that for nationalism to take hold of subjectivities, "the 'external frontiers' of the state have to become 'internal frontiers' or—what amounts to the same thing—external frontiers have to be imagined constantly as a projection and protection of an internal collective personality, which each of us carries within ourselves and enables us to inhabit the space of the state as a place where we have always been—and will always be—'at home.'" See Balibar and Wallerstein, *Race, Nation, Class.* Hence the *unheimlich* qualities of the *corridos,* which haunt the U.S. home and make its borders unfamiliar.

103. Balibar and Wallerstein, *Race, Nation, Class,* 95.

104. Liner notes, "Joaquín Murrieta," *Corridos & Tragedias de la Frontera,* 37.

105. All Bush quotations are from the georgewbush.com website.

106. All Gore quotations are from the gorelieberman.com website.

107. All Buchanan quotations are from the buchananreform.com website.

108. *ColorLines,* 30 April 2001, 6.

109. *Los Angeles Sentinel,* 29 November 2000. See also the *Chicago Defender,* 11 November 2000, 1.

110. *Miami Times,* 23 January 2001, 1A.

Bibliography

MANUSCRIPTS AND ARCHIVAL COLLECTIONS

Bancroft Collection of Western Americana and Latin Americana and Rare Book Collection. Berkeley: Bancroft Library, University of California.

Bretnor, H. H. *The California Police Gazette, a brief description*. Typescript #88305. Berkeley: Bancroft Library, University of California, 1955.

Daly, Charles Patrick, Papers. Scrapbook Volume G. New York: New York Public Library.

Dime Novels and Penny Dreadfuls Collection. Palo Alto, Calif.: Department of Special Collections, Green Library, Stanford University.

Library. New York: New-York Historical Society.

Lippard, George, Papers. Philadelphia: Historical Society of Pennsylvania.

Mayer, Brantz. *Mexican Miscellanies; A Collection of Pamphlets, 1837–1848*. Vol. 11, no. 14. Berkeley: Bancroft Library, University of California, 1837–1848.

Newspapers and Periodicals and Printed Books and Pamphlets Collections. Worcester, Mass.: American Antiquarian Society.

O'Brien, Frank P., Dime Novel Collection. New York: Rare Books Division, New York Public Library.

Rare Book and Special Collections. Washington, D.C.: Library of Congress.

Rare Books Division. Pasadena, Calif.: Huntington Library.

GOVERNMENT DOCUMENTS AND REPORTS

Browne, J. Ross, ed. *Report on the Debates in the Convention of California on the Formation of the State Constitution, in September and October 1849*. Washington, D.C.: John T. Towers, 1850.

Congressional Globe

"Treaty of Guadalupe Hidalgo" [1848]. In *U.S.-Mexico Borderlands: Historical and Contemporary Perspectives,* edited by Oscar J. Martinez, 20–37. Wilmington, Del.: Scholarly Resources, 1996.

U.S. Congress, House, *Difficulties on the Southwestern Frontier,* H. Exec. Doc. 52, 36th Congress, 1st Session, 2 April 1860. In *U.S.-Mexico Borderlands,* 75–76.

NEWSPAPERS AND STORY PAPERS

California Police Gazette
Democratic Review
Flag of Our Union
Flag of the Free
Frank Leslie's Illustrated Newspaper
Massachusetts Quarterly Review
Ned Buntline's Own
Nineteenth Century
North Star
People's Rights and Working Man's Advocate
Quaker City
Radical
Republic
Star Spangled Banner
Subterranean
Uncle Sam
Voice of Industry
Working Man's Advocate
Young America

SELECTED NOVELS, SOLDIERS' NARRATIVES, AND OTHER PRIMARY LITERATURE

Alcaraz, Ramon, et al. *The Other Side; or, Notes for the History of the War Between Mexico and the United States* [1850]. Translated by Albert C. Ramsey. New York: Burt Franklin, 1970.

Alcott, Louisa May. "Pauline's Passion and Punishment" [1863]. In *Louisa May Alcott Unmasked: Collected Thrillers,* edited by Madeleine Stern, 3–31. Boston: Northeastern University Press, 1995.

Anderson, Gary, and Alan Woolworth, eds. *Through Dakota Eyes: Narrative Accounts of the Minnesota Indian War of 1862.* St. Paul: Minnesota Historical Society Press, 1988.

Armstrong, Arthur. *The Mariner of the Mines; or, The Maid of the Monastery.* Boston: F. Gleason, n.d.

Averill, Charles. *The Corsair King: or, The Blue Water Rovers. A Romance of the Piratical Empire.* Boston: F. Gleason, 1847.

———. *Kit Carson, the Prince of the Gold Hunters; or, The Adventures of the Sacramento. A Tale of the New El Dorado, Founded on Actual Facts.* Boston: G.H. Williams, 1849.

———. *Life in California; or, The Treasure Seeker's Expedition. A Sequel to Kit Carson, the Prince of the Gold Hunters*. Boston: G. H. Williams, 1849.

———. *The Mexican Ranchero: or, The Maid of the Chapparal. A Romance of the Mexican War*. Boston: F. Gleason, 1847.

———. *The Secret Service Ship, or, The Fall of San Juan D'Ulloa. A Thrilling Tale of the Mexican War*. Boston: F. Gleason, 1848.

———. *The Secrets of the Twin Cities, or, The Great Metropolis Unmasked: A Startling Story of City Scenes in Boston and New York*. Boston: G. H. Williams, 1849.

Aztec Revelations; or, Leaves from the Life of the Fate-Doomed. An Autobiography of an Early Adventurer in Mexico. Oquawka, Ill.: J. B. and E. H. N. Patterson, 1849.

Badger, Joseph, Jr. *Black Panther, the Half Blood; or, The Slaves of the Silver Mines. A Tale of Old Arizona*. New York: Beadle and Adams, 1872.

———. *The Black Princess; or, The Border Refugees*. New York: Beadle, 1871.

———. *Joaquin, the Saddle King: A Romance of Murieta's First Fight*. New York: Beadle and Adams, 1881.

———. *Joaquin, the Terrible. The True History of the Three Bitter Blows that Changed an Honest Man to a Merciless Demon. Beadle's New York Dime Library* 13, no. 165 (1881).

———. *The Pirate of the Placers; or, Joaquin's Death Hunt*. New York: Beadle and Adams, 1882.

Ballentine, George. *Autobiography of an English Soldier in the United States Army*. New York: Stringer and Townsend, 1853.

Ballou, Maturin Murray. *The Adventurer, or, The Wreck on the Indian Ocean. A Tale of Land and Sea*. Boston: F. Gleason, 1848.

———. *Aztec Land*. New York: Houghton Mifflin, 1890.

———. *Fanny Campbell, the Female Pirate Captain. A Tale of the Revolution*. Boston: F. Gleason, 1845.

———. *History of Cuba; or, Notes of a Traveller in the Tropics*. Boston: Phillips, Sampson, and Co, 1854.

———. *Red Rupert, the American Bucanier [sic]. A Tale of the Spanish Indies*. Boston: F. Gleason, 1845.

———. *The Spanish Musketeer. A Tale of Military Life*. Boston: F. Gleason, 1847.

Barker, Colin. *The Golden Belt: or, The Carib's Pledge*. New York: Beadle, 1860.

Broom, Jacob. *An Address Delivered at Castle Garden, Feb. 22, 1854, Before the Order of United Americans on the Occasion of their Celebration of the One Hundred & Twenty-Second Anniversary of the Birthday of Washington*. New York: W. B. Weiss, 1854.

Buchanan, James, J. Y. Mason, and Pierre Soule. "The Ostend Manifesto" [1854]. In *What Happened in Cuba?* edited by Robert Smith, 64–67. New York: Twayne Publishers, 1963.

Buntline, Ned [E. Z. C. Judson]. *The B'hoys of New York: A Sequel to the Mysteries and Miseries of New York*. New York: Dick and Fitzgerald, n.d.

———. *The Black Avenger of the Spanish Main: or, The Fiend of Blood. A Thrilling Story of Buccaneer Times*. Boston: Flag of Our Union, 1847.

———. *Buffalo Bill, and his Adventures in the West* [1886]. New York: Arno, 1974. Reprint of *Buffalo Bill, the King of Border Men*, serialized in *New York Weekly* beginning 23 December 1869.

———. *The Convict: or, The Conspirator's Victim: A Novel Written in Prison* [1851]. New York: Dick and Fitzgerald, 1863.

———. *Cruisings, Afloat and Ashore, From the Private Log of Ned Buntline.* New York: Robert Craighead, 1848.

———. *The G'hals of New York: A Novel.* New York: DeWitt and Davenport, 1850.

———. *Hillaire Henderson: or, the Secret Revealed. An Antecedent to 'The Death Mystery.'* New York: Frederick A. Brady, 1861.

———. *The King of the Sea: A Tale of the Fearless and Free.* Boston: Flag of Our Union, 1847.

———. *The Last Days of Callao: or, The Doomed City of Sin! A Historical Romance of Peru.* Boston: Star Spangled Banner, 1847.

———. *Magdalena, the Beautiful Mexican Maid: A Story of Buena Vista.* New York: Williams Brothers, 1846.

———. *Matanzas; or, A Brother's Revenge. A Tale of Florida.* Boston: George H. Williams, 1848.

———. *The Mysteries and Miseries of New Orleans.* New York: Akarman and Ormsby, 1851.

———. *The Mysteries and Miseries of New York: A Story of Real Life.* New York: Berford and Co., 1848.

———. *Our Mess; or, The Pirate Hunters of the Gulf. A Tale of Naval Heroism and Wild Adventure in the Tropics.* New York: Frederick A. Brady, 1859.

———. *The Queen of the Sea; or, Our Lady of the Ocean. A Tale of Love, Strife, and Chivalry.* Boston: Flag of Our Union, 1848.

———. *The Red Revenger, or, The Pirate King of the Floridas. A Romance of the Gulf and its Islands.* Boston: Flag of Our Union, 1848.

———. *Three Years After; A Sequel to the Mysteries and Miseries of New York.* New York: W. F. Burgess, 1849.

———. *The Virgin of the Sun: A Historical Romance of the Last Revolution in Peru.* Boston: Hotchkiss and Co., 1847.

———. *The Volunteer: or, The Maid of Monterey. A Tale of the Mexican War.* Boston: F. Gleason, 1847.

———. *The White Wizard; or, The Great Prophet of the Seminoles. A Tale of Strange Mystery in the South and North.* New York: Frederick A. Brady, 1858.

Burns, Walter Noble. *The Robin Hood of El Dorado: The Saga of Joaquin Murrieta, Famous Outlaw of California's Age of Gold* [1932]. Albuquerque: University of New Mexico Press, 1999.

Calderón de la Barca, Frances. *Life in Mexico* [1843]. Berkeley: University of California Press, 1982.

Cazneau, Jane [Cora Montgomery]. *Eagle Pass; or, Life on the Border.* New York: Putnam, 1852.

Chamberlain, Samuel. *My Confession.* New York: Harper and Brothers, 1956.

Cleveland, Alice. *Lucy Morley: or, The Young Officer.* Boston: F. Gleason, 1846.

Coolidge, Dane. *Gringo Gold: A Story of Joaquin Murieta the Bandit.* New York: E. P. Dutton, 1939.

Corridos & Tragedias de la Frontera. Mexican-American Border Music. Vols. 6 and 7, Arhoolie Records 7019/720, 1994.

The Crisis! An Appeal to our Countrymen, on the Subject of Foreign Influence in the United States! New York: American Republican Party, 1844.

Curtis, Newton. *The Hunted Chief: or, The Female Ranchero.* New York: Williams Brothers, 1847.

———. *The Matricide's Daughter: A Tale of Life in the Great Metropolis.* New York: Williams Brothers, 1847.

———. *The Prairie Guide: or, The Rose of the Rio Grande.* New York: Williams Brothers, 1847.

———. *The Vidette, a Tale of the Mexican War.* New York: Williams Brothers, 1848.

Davis, George. *Autobiography of the Late Col. Geo. T. M. Davis.* New York: Published by his legal representatives, 1891.

Denison, Mary. *Captain Molly; or, The Fight at Trenton, Christmas 1776: A Story of the Revolution.* New York: Beadle, 1856.

———. *Chip: The Cave-Child.* New York: Beadle, 1860.

———. *Edna Etheril, the Boston Seamstress, A Narative [sic] of Facts.* New York: Burgess, Stringer, and Co., 1847.

———. *Florida; or, The Iron Will. A Story of Today.* New York: Beadle, 1861.

———. *Gracie Amber.* Chicago: S. G. Griggs, 1857.

———. *The Mad Hunter; or, The Downfall of the LeForests.* New York: Beadle, 1863.

———. *Old Hepsy.* New York: A. B. Burdick, 1858.

———. *The Prisoner of La Vintresse; or, The Fortunes of a Cuban Heiress.* New York: Irwin P. Beadle and Co., 1860.

———. *Ruth Margerie: A Romance of the Revolt of 1689.* New York: Beadle, 1862.

———. *Tim Bumble's Charge.* New York: Beadle, 1862.

Duganne, A. J. H. *Art's True Mission in America.* New York: Geo. S. Appleton, 1853.

———. *Camps and Prisons: Twenty Months in the Department of the Gulf.* New York: J. P. Robens, 1865.

———. *The Daguerreotype Miniature; or, Life in the Empire City.* Philadelphia: G. B. Zieber, 1846.

———. *Emily Harper, or, The Coquette's Destiny. A Tale of the Strange Things of Real Existence.* Worcester: Thomas Drew, Jr., 1846.

———. *Eustace Barcourt; or, The Illegitimate. A Story of Conflict Between Good and Evil.* Philadelphia: G. B. Zieber, 1848.

———. *The Fighting Quakers; A True Story of the War for Our Union.* New York: J. P. Robens, 1866.

———. *The King's Man: A Tale of South Carolina in Revolutionary Times.* New York: Beadle, 1860.

———. *The Knights of the Seal; or, The Mysteries of the Three Cities. A Romance of Men's Hearts and Habits.* Philadelphia: Colon and Adriance, 1845.

———. *Massasoit's Daughter; or, The French Captives*. New York: Beadle, 1861.

———. *The Peon Prince; or, The Yankee Knight-Errant. A Tale of Modern Mexico*. New York: Beadle, 1861.

———. *The Poetical Works of Augustine Duganne*. Philadelphia: Parry and McMillan, 1855.

———. *Putnam Pomfret's Ward; or, A Vermonter's Adventures in Mexico*. New York: Beadle, 1861.

———. *Utterances*. New York: R. M. DeWitt, 1865.

Ellis, Edward. *The Hunter's Escape: A Tale of the North West in 1862*. New York: Beadle, 1864.

———. *Indian Jim: A Tale of the Minnesota Massacre*. New York: Beadle, 1864.

———. "Seth Jones; or, the Captives of the Frontier" [1860]. In *Reading the West: An Anthology of Dime Westerns*, edited by Bill Brown, 165–268. Boston: Bedford Books, 1997.

Emerald, John. *Cortina, the Scourge; or, The Lost Diamond*. New York: Beadle and Adams, 1872.

———. *The Crested Serpent; or, The White Tiger of the Tropics*. New York: Beadle and Adams, 1874.

Emerson, Ralph Waldo. *Miscellaneous Notebooks of Ralph Waldo Emerson*. Vol. 9 (1843–1847). Edited by Ralph Orth and Alfred Ferguson. Cambridge: Harvard University Press, 1971.

The Female Marine and Related Works: Narratives of Cross-Dressing and Urban Vice in America's Early Republic. Edited by Daniel Cohen. Amherst: University of Massachusetts Press, 1997.

Frost, John. *Pictorial History of Mexico and the Mexican War*. Philadelphia: Thomas, Cowperthwait and Co., 1849.

Giddings, Luther. *Sketches of the Campaign in Northern Mexico in Eighteen Hundred Forty-Six and Seven by an Officer of the First Regiment of Ohio Volunteers*. New York: George P. Putnam and Co., 1853.

Gleason, George. *Tippy, the Texan; or, The Young Champion. A Story of the Siege of Monterey*. New York: Beadle and Adams, 1874.

Greeley, Robert F. *Arthur Woodleigh; A Romance of the Battle Field in Mexico*. New York: William B. Smith and Co., 1847.

Greenwood, Grace [Sara J. Clarke]. *Greenwood Leaves: A Collection of Sketches and Letters*. Boston: Ticknor, Reed, and Fields, 1850.

———. *Greenwood Leaves: A Collection of Sketches and Letters*. 2d ser. Boston: Ticknor, Reed, and Fields, 1852.

Hall, William Jared. *The Slave Sculptor; or, The Prophetess of the Secret Chambers. A Tale of Mexico at the Period of the Conquest*. Vols. 1 and 2. New York: Beadle, 1860.

Halyard, Harry. *The Chieftain of Churubusco, or, The Spectre of the Cathedral*. Boston: F. Gleason, 1848.

———. *The Heroine of Tampico: or, Wildfire the Wanderer. A Tale of the Mexican War*. Boston: F. Gleason, 1847.

———. *The Mexican Spy: or, The Bride of Buena Vista*. Boston: F. Gleason, 1848.

———. *The Ocean Monarch: or, The Ranger of the Gulf.* Boston: F. Gleason, 1848.

———. *The Peruvian Nun; or, The Empress of the Ocean. A Maritime Romance.* Boston: F. Gleason, 1848.

Hamilton, W. J. [C. Dunning Clark]. *The Quadroon Spy; or, The Ranger's Bride.* New York: Beadle, 1870.

Hazel, Harry [Justin Jones]. *Inez, the Beautiful: or, Love on the Rio Grande. A Mexican Military Romance.* Boston: Justin Jones, 1846.

———. *The Light Dragoon: or, The Rancheros of the Poisoned Lance. A Tale of the Battlefields of Mexico.* Boston: Star Spangled Banner, 1848.

———. *The Rival Chieftains; or, The Brigands of Mexico. A Tale of Santa Anna and His Times.* Boston: F. Gleason, 1845.

Hazleton, Lieut.-Col. [Henry Hazelton]. *The Silver Bugle; or, The Indian Maiden of St. Croix.* New York: Beadle, 1864.

Henderson, J. Stanley [Edward Willett]. *The Blue Band; or, The Mystery of the Silver Star. A Romance of the Texan Border.* New York: Beadle and Adams, 1872.

———. *Karaibo; or, The Outlaw's Fate.* New York: Beadle, 1886.

The 'High Private,' with a Full and Exciting History of the New-York Volunteers, and the 'Mysteries and Miseries' of the Mexican War. By "Corporal of the Guard." New York: Printed for the Publisher, 1848.

Ingraham, J. H. *Montezuma, the Serf, or The Revolt of the Mexitili: A Tale of the Last Days of the Aztec Dynasty.* Boston: H. L. Williams, 1845.

———. *The Texan Ranger: or, The Maid of Matamoras. A Tale of the Mexican War.* New York: Williams Brothers, 1847.

Ingraham, Prentiss. *Adventures of Buffalo Bill from Boyhood to Manhood: Deeds of Daring and Romantic Incidents in the Life of Wm. F. Cody, the Monarch of Bordermen.* New York: Beadle and Adams, 1881.

———. *The Cuban Conspirator; or, The Island League. A Romance of Cuba and Cuban Waters.* New York: Beadle and Adams, 1874.

Iron, N. C. *The Two Guards.* New York: Beadle, 1863.

Isabel Mortimer; or, The Southerner's Revenge. An Autobiography. Cincinnati: H. M. Rulison, 1858.

Joaquin, the Claude Duval of California; or, The Marauder of the Mines. A Romance on Truth. New York: Robert DeWitt, 1865.

Joaquin Murieta, the Brigand Chief of California [1932]. Fresno, Calif.: Valley Publishers, 1969. Reprint of 1859 *California Police Gazette* edition of *The Life of Joaquin Murieta, the Brigand Chief of California.*

Kenly, John. *Memoirs of a Maryland Volunteer.* Philadelphia: J. B. Lippincott, 1873.

Klette, Ernest. *The Crimson Trail of Joaquin Murieta.* Los Angeles: Wetzel Publishing Co., 1928.

Life and Adventure of Charles Anderson Chester, the Notorious Leader of the Philadelphia 'Killers.' Philadelphia: Yates and Smith, 1850.

Life of Joaquin Murieta, the Brigand Chief of California, The. San Francisco: Published at the Office of the 'California Police Gazette,' 1859.

Lippard, George. *'Bel of Prairie Eden: A Romance of Mexico.* Boston: Hotchkiss and Co., 1848.

————. *The Empire City; or, New York By Night and Day. Its Aristocracy and Its Dollars* [1850]. Philadelphia: T. B. Peterson, 1864.

————. *The Killers. A Narrative of Real Life in Philadelphia.* By a Member of the Philadelphia Bar. Philadelphia: Hankinson and Bartholomew, 1850.

————. *Legends of Mexico.* Philadelphia: T. B. Peterson, 1847.

————. *The Nazarene; or, The Last of the Washingtons. A Revelation of Philadelphia, New York, and Washington in the Year 1844* [1846]. Philadelphia: T. B. Peterson, 1854.

————. *New York: Its Upper Ten and Lower Million* [1853]. Upper Saddle River, N.J.: Literature House/Gregg Press, 1970.

————. *The Quaker City; or, The Monks of Monk Hall* [1845]. Edited by David Reynolds. Amherst: University of Massachusetts Press, 1995.

————. "Valedictory of the Industrial Congress." *Nineteenth Century* 2 (1848): 186–89.

————. *Washington and His Generals: or, Legends of the Revolution.* Philadelphia: G. B. Zieber, 1847.

————. *The White Banner.* Philadelphia: George Lippard, 1851.

Livermore, Abiel Abbot. *The War With Mexico Reviewed.* Boston: Wm. Crosby and H. P. Nichols, 1850.

Lowell, Robert Russell. *The Biglow Papers.* London: Savill, Edwards, and Co., n.d.

Luff, Lorry. *Antonita, the Female Contrabandista. A Mexican Tale of Land and Water.* New York: Williams Brothers, 1848.

Maturin, Edward. *Montezuma; The Last of the Aztecs. A Romance.* Vols. 1 and 2. New York: Paine and Burgess, 1845.

McCarty, William, ed. *National Songs, Ballads, and Other Patriotic Poetry, Chiefly Relating to the War of 1846.* Philadelphia: William McCarty, 1846.

McSherry, Richard. *El Puchero: or, A Mixed Dish from Mexico.* Philadelphia: Lippincott, Grambo, 1850.

Moody, Loring. *Facts for the People: Showing the Relations of the United States Government to Slavery, Embracing a History of the Mexican War.* Boston: Dow and Jackson's Anti-Slavery Press, 1847.

National Reform Almanac for 1849. New York: Young America, 1849.

Paine, Thomas. *The Life and Writings of Thomas Paine.* Vol. 3. Edited by Daniel Edwin Wheeler. New York: Vincente Parke and Company, 1908.

Parker, Theodore. *Sermons on War* [1863]. Edited by Frances P. Cobbe. New York: Garland Publishing, 1973.

Paterson, Thomas. *The Private Life, Public Career, and Real Character of that Odious Rascal NED BUNTLINE!!* New York: Thomas Paterson, 1849.

Prescott, William H. *History of the Conquest of Mexico* [1843]. New York: Modern Library, 1998.

The Prisoner of Perote: A Tale of American Valor and Mexican Love. Boston: F. Gleason, 1848.

"Republican National Platform, 1856." In *What Happened in Cuba? A Documentary History,* edited by Robert Smith. New York: Twayne Publishers, 1963.

Ridge, John Rollin. *The Life and Adventures of Joaquín Murieta, the Celebrated California Bandit* [1854]. Norman: University of Oklahoma Press, 1955.

Robinson, Faye. *Mexico and her Military Chieftains, From the Revolution of Hidalgo to the Present Time.* Philadelphia: E. H. Butler and Co., 1847.

The Rough and Ready Annual and Military Souvenir. New York: Appleton, 1848.

Royce, Josiah. *California From the Conquest of 1846 to the Second Vigilance Committee in San Francisco.* Boston: Houghton-Mifflin, 1886.

Scribner, Benjamin. *Camp Life of a Volunteer.* Philadelphia: Grigg, 1847.

Sealsfield, Charles. *The Cabin Book; or, Sketches of Life in Texas.* Translated by C. F. Mersch. New York: J. Winchester, 1844.

Semmes, Raphael. *Service Afloat and Ashore During the Mexican War.* Cincinnati: W. H. Moore, 1851.

Smith, S. Compton. *Chile Con Carne; or, The Camp and the Field.* New York: Miller and Curtis, 1857.

Stephens, Ann. *Ahmo's Plot; or, The Governor's Indian Child.* New York: Beadle, 1863.

———. *Esther: A Story of the Oregon Trail.* New York: Beadle, 1862.

———. *The Indian Queen.* New York: Beadle, 1864.

———. *Mahaska: The Indian Princess.* New York: Beadle, 1863.

———. "Malaeska; The Indian Wife of the White Hunter" [1860]. In *Reading the West,* edited by Bill Brown, 53–164.

———. *Myra: The Child of Adoption. A Romance of Real Life.* New York: Beadle, 1860.

———. *Sybil Chase; or, The Valley Ranche. A Tale of California Life.* New York: Beadle, 1861.

Thomas, Henry. *The Wrong Man. A Tale of the Early Settlements.* New York: Beadle, 1862.

Thorpe, Thomas Bangs. *Our Army at Monterey.* Philadelphia: Carey and Hart, 1847.

———. *Our Army on the Rio Grande.* Philadelphia: Carey and Hart, 1846.

———. *The Taylor Anecdote Book: Anecdotes and Letters of Zachary Taylor.* New York: D. Appleton and Company, 1848.

Ullmann, Daniel. "The Course of Empire: An Oration Delivered Before the Order of United Americans." New York: William B. Weiss, 1856.

Victor, Frances Fuller Barritt. *Alicia Newcome, or, The Land Claim: A Tale of the Upper Missouri.* New York: Beadle, 1862.

———. *Anizetta, the Guajira; or, The Creole of Cuba. A Romance of the Spanish Isle.* Boston: "Star Spangled Banner" Office, 1848.

———. *East and West; or, The Beauty of Willard's Mill.* New York: Beadle, 1862.

Victor, Metta. *Alice Wilde: The Raftsman's Daughter. A Forest Romance.* New York: Beadle, 1860.

———. *The Backwoods' Bride. A Romance of Squatter Life.* New York: Beadle, 1860.

———. *Jo Daviess' Client; or, 'Courting' in Kentucky.* New York: Beadle, 1863.

———. *Maum Guinea and Her Plantation 'Children': A Story of Christmas Week with the American Slaves.* London: Beadle, 1861.

———. *The Two Hunters; or, The Cañon Camp. A Romance of the Santa Fé Trail.* New York: Beadle, 1865.

————. *The Unionist's Daughter: A Tale of the Rebellion in Tennessee.* New York: Beadle, 1862.

Walker, William. *The War in Nicaragua.* Mobile, Ala.: S.H. Goetzel and Co., 1860.

Walsh, Michael. *Sketches of the Speeches and Writings of Michael Walsh.* New York: Thomas McSpedon, 1843.

Warner, John S. *Isabel de Cordova; or, The Brethren of the Coast. A Tale of Sea and Land.* New York: Beadle, 1861.

Whittaker, Frederick. *The Black Wizard. A Tale of the Fatal Circle of Invisible Fire.* New York: Beadle, 1871.

————. *The Grizzly-Hunters: or, The Navahoe [sic] Captives. A Tale of the Lost City of the Sierras.* New York: Beadle, 1871.

————. *The Jaguar Queen; or, The Outlaws of the Sierra Madre.* New York: Beadle and Adams, 1872.

————. *The Mustang-Hunters, or, The Beautiful Amazon of the Hidden Valley. A Tale of the Staked Plains.* New York: Beadle, 1871.

————. *The Red Prince; or, The Last of the Aztecs. A Romance of the Lost Palace.* New York: Beadle and Company, 1871.

Whittier, John Greenleaf. *The Poetical Works of John Greenleaf Whittier.* Vol. 1. New York: AMS Press, 1969.

Willett, Edward [J. Stanley Henderson]. *The Man in Green: or, The Siege of Bexar.* New York: Beadle, 1881.

————. *The Twin Trailers: or, The Gamecock of El Paso. A Tale of the Texan Frontier.* New York: Beadle and Adams, 1872.

Zeh, Frederick. *An Immigrant Soldier in the Mexican War.* Edited by William J. Orr and Robert Ryal Miller. Translated by Orr. College Station: Texas A&M University Press, 1995.

SECONDARY SOURCES

Acuña, Rodolfo. *Occupied America: A History of Chicanos,* 4th ed. [1972]. New York: Longman, 2000.

Adelman, Jeremy, and Stephen Aron. "From Borderlands to Borders: Empires, Nation-States, and the Peoples in Between in North American History." *American Historical Review* 86, no. 1 (June 1999): 814–41.

Admari, Ralph. "Ballou, the Father of the Dime Novel." *American Book Collector* 4, no. 34 (September–October 1933): 121–29.

Albion, Robert. *The Rise of New York Port, 1815–1860.* Hamden, Conn.: Archon, 1961.

Allen, Theodore. *The Invention of the White Race: The Origin of Racial Oppression in Anglo-America.* Vol. 2. London and New York: Verso: 1997.

————. *The Invention of the White Race: Racial Oppression and Social Control.* Vol. 1. London and New York: Verso, 1994.

Almaguer, Tomás. "Ideological Distortions and Recent Chicano Historiography: The Internal Colonialism Model and Chicano Historical Interpretation." *Aztlán* 18, no. 1 (spring 1987): 7–28.

————. *Racial Fault Lines: The Historical Origins of White Supremacy in California.* Berkeley: University of California Press, 1994.

Alonso, Ana Maria. *Thread of Blood: Colonialism, Revolution, and Gender on Mexico's Northern Frontier.* Tucson: University of Arizona Press, 1997.

Anderson, Benedict. *Imagined Communities: Reflections on the Origin and Spread of Nationalism.* London: Verso, 1991.

Anderson, John Q. "Emerson on Texas and the Mexican War." *Western Humanities Review* 13, no. 2 (spring 1959): 191–99.

Anderson, William, ed. *Cherokee Removal: Before and After.* Athens: University of Georgia Press, 1991.

Aquila, Richard, ed. *Wanted Dead or Alive: The American West in Popular Culture.* Champaign: University of Illinois Press, 1996.

Arrom, Silvia Marina. *The Women of Mexico City, 1790–1857.* Stanford: Stanford University Press, 1985.

Ashwill, Gary. "The Mysteries of Capitalism in George Lippard's City Novels." *ESQ* 40, no. 4 (1994): 293–317.

"Augustine Joseph Hickey Duganne." In *Dictionary of American Biography.* Vol. 3, edited by Allen Johnson and Dumas Malone, 492. New York: Scribner's, 1937.

Baker, Jean. *Affairs of Party: The Political Culture of Northern Democrats in the Mid–Nineteenth Century.* Ithaca: Cornell University Press, 1983.

Baker, Shannon L. "'A Thread of Brittle Texture': Ann Chase and Manifest Destiny." In *Papers of the Second Palo Alto Conference,* edited by H. Joseph, A. Knopp, and D. Murphy, 23–28. Brownsville, Tex.: U.S. Department of the Interior, 1997.

Balderrama, Francisco, and Raymond Rodriguez. *Decade of Betrayal: Mexican Repatriation in the 1930's.* Albuquerque: University of New Mexico Press, 1995.

Balibar, Etienne, and Immanuel Wallerstein. *Race, Nation, Class: Ambiguous Identities.* Translated by Chris Turner. London and New York: Verso, 1991.

Barker-Benfield, G. J. *The Horrors of the Half-Known Life: Male Attitudes Toward Women and Sexuality in Nineteenth-Century America.* New York: Harper and Row, 1976.

Barnes, Elizabeth. *States of Sympathy: Seduction and Democracy in the American Novel.* New York: Columbia University Press, 1997.

Barrera, Mario. *Race and Class in the Southwest: A Theory of Racial Inequality.* Notre Dame: University of Notre Dame Press, 1979.

Barrera, Mario, Carlos Muñoz, and Charlie Ornelas. "The Barrio as Internal Colony." In *People and Politics in Urban Society,* edited by Harlan Hahn, 465–98. Beverly Hills, Calif.: Sage, 1972.

Basch, Norma. *In the Eyes of the Law: Women, Marriage, and Property in Nineteenth-Century New York.* Ithaca: Cornell University Press, 1982.

Bauer, Arnold J. "Rural Workers in Spanish America: Problems of Peonage and Oppression." *Hispanic American Historical Review* 59, no. 1 (1979): 34–63.

Baym, Nina. *Novels, Readers, and Reviewers: Responses to Fiction in Antebellum America.* Ithaca: Cornell University Press, 1984.

———. *Woman's Fiction: A Guide to Novels by and about Women in America, 1820–1870.* Ithaca: Cornell University Press, 1978.

Bazant, Jan. "From Independence to the Liberal Republic, 1821–1867." In *Mexico since Independence,* edited by Leslie Bethell, 1–48. New York: Cambridge University Press, 1991.

Bederman, Gail. *Manliness and Civilization: A Cultural History of Gender and Race in the United States, 1880–1917*. Chicago: University of Chicago Press, 1995.

Bennett, David H. *The Party of Fear: From Nativist Movements to the New Right in American History*. Chapel Hill: University of North Carolina Press, 1988.

Benson, Peter. "Maturin Murray Ballou" and "Gleason's Publishing Hall." In *Publishers for Mass Entertainment in Nineteenth-Century America*, edited by Madeleine Stern, 27–35, 137–45. Boston: G.K. Hall, 1980.

Bercovitch, Sacvan. *The American Jeremiad*. Madison: University of Wisconsin Press, 1978.

———. *The Puritan Origins of the American Self*. New Haven: Yale University Press, 1975.

———. *Rites of Assent: Transformations in the Symbolic Construction of America*. New York: Routledge, 1993.

Bergquist, Charles. *Labor and the Course of American Democracy: U.S. History in Latin American Perspective*. London and New York: Verso, 1996.

Berlant, Lauren. *The Anatomy of National Fantasy: Hawthorne, Utopia, and Everyday Life*. Chicago: University of Chicago Press, 1992.

———. "National Brands/National Body: Imitation of Life." In *Comparative American Identities: Race, Sex, and Nationality in the Modern Text*, edited by Hortense Spillers, 110–40. New York: Routledge, 1991.

———. "Pax Americana: The Case of Show Boat." In *Cultural Institutions of the Novel*, edited by D. Lynch and W. Warner, 399–422. Durham: Duke University Press, 1996.

———. "Poor Eliza." *American Literature* 70, no. 3 (September 1998): 635–68.

———. "The Subject of True Feeling: Pain, Privacy, and Politics." In *Cultural Pluralism, Identity Politics, and the Law*, edited by A. Sarat and T. Kearns, 49–84. Ann Arbor: University of Michigan Press, 1999.

Bernstein, Michael. "Northern Labor Finds a Southern Champion: A Note on the Radical Democracy, 1833–1849." In *New York and the Rise of American Capitalism: Economic Development and the Social and Political History of an American State, 1780–1870*, edited by William Pencak and Conrad Wright, 147–67. New York: New York Historical Society, 1989.

Berwanger, Eugene H. *The Frontier against Slavery: Western Anti-Negro Prejudice and the Slavery Extension Controversy*. Urbana: University of Illinois Press, 1967.

Beverley, John. *Against Literature*. Minneapolis: University of Minnesota Press, 1993.

———. *Subalternity and Representation: Arguments in Cultural Theory*. Durham: Duke University Press, 1999.

Biggs, Donald C. *Conquer and Colonize*. San Rafael, Calif.: Presidio, 1977.

Billington, Ray Allen. *The Protestant Crusade, 1800–1860: A Study of the Origins of American Nativism*. Chicago: Quadrangle, 1964.

Bold, Christine. "Malaeska's Revenge; or, The Dime Novel Tradition in Popular Fiction." In *Wanted Dead or Alive: The American West in Popular Culture*, edited by Richard Aquila, 21–42. Urbana: University of Illinois Press, 1996.

————. *Selling the Wild West: Popular Western Fiction, 1860–1960.* Blooming-ton: Indiana University Press, 1987.

Bourdieu, Pierre. *The Field of Cultural Production.* Edited by Randal Johnson. New York: Columbia University Press, 1993.

Bowser, Frederick. "Colonial Spanish America." In *Neither Slave nor Free: The Freedmen of African Descent in the Slave Societies of the New World,* edited by David Cohen and Jack Greene, 19–58. Baltimore: Johns Hopkins University Press, 1972.

Brack, Gene. *Mexico Views Manifest Destiny, 1821–1846: An Essay on the Origins of the Mexican War.* Albuquerque: University of New Mexico Press, 1975.

Brading, D. A. *Haciendas and Ranchos in the Mexican Bajio, León 1780–1860.* Cambridge: Cambridge University Press, 1978.

Brantlinger, Patrick. "What is 'Sensational' about the 'Sensation Novel'?" *Nineteenth-Century Fiction* 37, no. 1 (1982): 1–28.

Bridges, Amy. "Becoming American: The Working Classes of the United States before the Civil War." In *Working-Class Formation: Nineteenth-Century Patterns in Western Europe and the United States,* edited by I. Katznelson and A. Zolberg, 157–96. Princeton: Princeton University Press, 1986.

————. *A City in the Republic: Antebellum New York and the Origins of Machine Politics.* Cambridge: Cambridge University Press, 1994.

Brodhead, Richard. *Cultures of Letters: Scenes of Reading and Writing in Nineteenth-Century America.* Chicago: University of Chicago Press, 1993.

Bronstein, Jamie. *Land Reform and Working-Class Experience in Britain and the United States, 1800–1862.* Stanford: Stanford University Press, 1999.

Brooks, Peter. *Reading for the Plot: Design and Intention in Narrative.* New York: Vintage, 1985.

Brown, Bill. *The Material Unconscious: American Amusement, Stephen Crane, and the Economies of Play.* Cambridge: Harvard University Press, 1996.

————. *Reading the West: An Anthology of Dime Westerns.* Boston: Bedford, 1997.

Brown, Charles. *Agents of Manifest Destiny: The Lives and Times of the Filibusters.* Chapel Hill: University of North Carolina Press, 1980.

Brown, Dee. *Bury My Heart at Wounded Knee: An Indian History of the American West.* New York: Henry Holt, 1970.

Browne, Nick. "Race: The Political Unconscious of American Film." *East-West Film Journal* 6, no. 1 (1992): 5–16.

Buckley, Peter. "The Case against Ned Buntline: The 'Words, Signs, and Gestures' of Popular Authorship." *Prospects* 13 (1988): 249–72.

————. "To the Opera House: Culture and Society in New York City, 1820–1860." Doctoral dissertation. Stony Brook: State University of New York, 1984.

Buck-Morss, Susan. *The Dialectics of Seeing: Walter Benjamin and the Arcades Projects.* Cambridge: MIT Press, 1989.

Burgett, Bruce. *Sentimental Bodies: Sex, Gender, and Citizenship in the Early Republic.* Princeton: Princeton University Press, 1998.

Caplan, Caren, Norma Alarcón, and Minoo Moallem, eds. *Between Women and Nation: Nationalisms, Transnational Feminisms, and the State.* Durham: Duke University Press, 1999.

Castañeda, Antonia. "Engendering the History of Alta California, 1769–1848: Gender, Sexuality, and the Family." In *Contested Eden: California before the Gold Rush,* edited by Ramón Gutiérrez and Richard Orsi, 230–59. Berkeley: University of California Press, 1998.

———. "The Political Economy of Nineteenth Century Stereotypes of Californianas." In *Between Borders: Essays on Mexicana/Chicana History,* edited by Adelaida del Castillo, 213–36. Encino, Calif.: Floricanto Press, 1990.

———. "Women of Color and the Rewriting of Western History: The Discourse, Politics, and Decolonization of History." *Pacific Historical Review* 61, no. 4 (1992): 501–33.

Castillo, Pedro, and Albert Camarillo, eds. *Furia y Muerte: Los Bandidos Chicanos.* Los Angeles: Aztlán Publications, UCLA, 1972.

Chabram-Dernersesian, Angie. "I Throw Punches for My Race, but I Don't Want to Be a Man: Writing Us—Chica-nos (Girl, Us)/Chicanas—into the Movement Script." In *Cultural Studies,* edited by Lawrence Grossberg, Cary Nelson, and Paula Treichler, 81–95. New York: Routledge, 1992.

Chaffin, Tom. *Fatal Glory: Narciso Lopez and the First Clandestine U.S. War against Cuba.* Charlottesville: University Press of Virginia, 1996.

Chapman, Mary, and Glenn Hendler, eds. *Sentimental Men: Masculinity and the Politics of Affect in American Culture.* Berkeley: University of California Press, 1999.

Chauncey, George, Jr. "From Sexual Inversion to Homosexuality: Medicine and the Changing Conceptualization of Female Deviance." *Salmagundi,* nos. 58–59 (fall 1982–winter 1983): 114–46.

Chávez, John R. *The Lost Land: The Chicano Image of the Southwest.* Albuquerque: University of New Mexico Press, 1984.

Cherniavsky, Eva. "Subaltern Studies in a U.S. Frame." *boundary 2* 23, no. 2 (1996): 85–110.

Chevalier, Francois. "The North Mexican Hacienda: Eighteenth and Nineteenth Centuries." In *The New World Looks at Its History,* edited by Archibald Lewis and Thomas McGann, 95–107. Austin: University of Texas Press, 1963.

Chevigny, Bell Gale, and Gari LaGuardia, eds. *Reinventing the Americas: Comparative Studies of Literature of the United States and Spanish America.* Cambridge: Cambridge University Press, 1986.

Chomsky, Carol. "The United States–Dakota War Trials: A Study in Military Injustice." *Stanford Law Review* 43, no. 1 (November 1990): 13–98.

Christensen, Peter. "Minority Interaction in John Rollin Ridge's *The Life and Adventures of Joaquin Murieta.*" *MELUS* 17, no. 2 (summer 1991–92): 61–72.

Clifford, James. "Traveling Cultures." In *Cultural Studies,* edited by Lawrence Grossberg, Cary Nelson, and Paula Treichler, 96–112. New York: Routledge, 1992.

Cline, Howard. *Regionalism and Society in Yucatán, 1825–1847.* Related Studies in Early Nineteenth Century Yucatecan Social History. Part 3. Chicago: University of Chicago Press, 1958.

Cohen, Daniel. *Pillars of Salt, Monuments of Grace: New England Crime Literature and the Origins of American Popular Culture, 1674–1860*. New York: Oxford University Press, 1993.

———, ed. *The Female Marine and Related Works: Narratives of Cross-Dressing and Urban Vice in America's Early Republic*. Amherst: University of Massachusetts Press, 1997.

Cox, J. Randolph. *The Dime Novel Companion: A Source Book*. Westport, Conn.: Greenwood Press, 2000.

Cross, Harry. "Living Standards in Rural Nineteenth-Century Mexico: Zacatecas, 1820–1880." *Journal of Latin American Studies* 10 (1978): 1–19.

Curti, Merle. "Dime Novels and the American Tradition." *Yale Review* 26 (June 1937): 761–78.

Cvetkovich, Ann. *Mixed Feelings: Feminism, Mass Culture, and Victorian Sensationalism*. New Brunswick, N.J.: Rutgers University Press, 1992.

Davidson, Cathy. *Revolution and the Word: The Rise of the Novel in America*. New York: Oxford University Press, 1986.

Day, Mark. *The San Patricios: The Tragic Story of the St. Patrick's Battalion*. Vista, Calif.: San Patricio Productions, 1996.

Deaton, Dawn Fogle. "The Decade of Revolt: Peasant Rebellion in Jalisco, Mexico, 1855–1864." In *Liberals, the Church, and Indian Peasants: Corporate Lands and the Challenge of Reform in Nineteenth-Century Spanish America*, edited by Robert Jackson, 37–64. Albuquerque: University of New Mexico Press, 1997.

Delpar, Helen. *The Enormous Vogue of Things Mexican: Cultural Relations between the United States and Mexico, 1920–1935*. Tuscaloosa: University of Alabama Press, 1992.

D'Emilio, John, and Estelle B. Freedmen. *Intimate Matters: A History of Sexuality in America*, 2d. ed. Chicago: University of Chicago Press, 1997.

Denning, Michael. *The Cultural Front: The Laboring of American Culture in the Twentieth Century*. London and New York: Verso, 1996.

———. *Mechanic Accents: Dime Novels and Working-Class Culture in America*. Rev. ed. [1987]. London and New York: Verso, 1998.

Depalo, William. *The Mexican National Army, 1822–1852*. College Station: Texas A&M University Press, 1997.

Deverell, William F. "To Loosen the Safety Valve: Eastern Workers and Western Lands." *Western Historical Quarterly* 19 (August 1988): 269–85.

Dime Novels: Escape Fiction of the Nineteenth Century. Ann Arbor, Mich.: University Microfilms International, 1980.

Dimock, Wai Chee, and Michael Gilmore, eds. *Rethinking Class: Literary Studies and Social Formations*. New York: Columbia University Press, 1994.

Dippie, Brian. *The Vanishing American: White Attitudes and U.S. Indian Policy*. Middletown, Conn.: Wesleyan University Press, 1982.

Di Tella, Torcuato S. "The Dangerous Classes in Early Nineteenth Century Mexico." *Journal of Latin American Studies* 5 (1973): 79–105.

Dobson, Joanne. "The Hidden Hand: Subversion of Cultural Ideology in Three Mid-Nineteenth Century Women's Novels." *American Quarterly* 38, no. 2 (1986): 223–42.

Doherty, Robert. *The Hicksite Separation: A Sociological Analysis of Religious Schism in Early Nineteenth Century America.* New Brunswick, N.J.: Rutgers University Press, 1967.

Doherty, Thomas. *Pre-Code Hollywood: Sex, Immorality, and Insurrection in American Cinema, 1930–1934.* New York: Columbia University Press, 1999.

Douglas, Ann. *The Feminization of American Culture* [1977]. New York: Anchor-Doubleday 1988.

Drinnon, Richard. *Facing West: The Metaphysics of Indian-Hating and Empire Building.* New York: NAL, 1980.

Du Bois, W. E. B. *Black Reconstruction in America, 1860–1880.* New York: Russell and Russell, 1935.

Ducey, Michael. "Liberal Theory and Peasant Practice: Land and Power in Northern Veracruz, Mexico, 1826–1900." In *Liberals, the Church, and Indian Peasants: Corporate Lands and the Challenge of Reform in Nineteenth-Century Spanish America,* edited by Robert Jackson, 65–93. Albuquerque: University of New Mexico Press, 1997.

Dugaw, Dianne. *Warrior Women and Popular Balladry, 1650–1850.* Chicago: University of Chicago Press, 1989.

Durham, Philip. "Introduction." In *Seth Jones and Deadwood Dick on Deck,* edited by Durham, x–xiv. New York: Odyssey Press, 1966.

Ehrlich, Heyward. "The 'Mysteries' of Philadelphia: Lippard's Quaker City and 'Urban' Gothic," *ESQ* 18, no. 1 (1972): 50–65.

Elliot, J. H. "Spain and Its Empire in the Sixteenth and Seventeenth Centuries." In *Early Maryland in a Wider World,* edited by David Quinn, 58–83. Detroit: Wayne State University Press, 1982.

Elmer, Jonathan. *Reading at the Social Limit: Affect, Mass Culture, Edgar Allan Poe.* Stanford: Stanford University Press, 1995.

Emmons, David M. "Constructed Province: History and the Making of the Last American West." *Western Historical Quarterly* 25, no. 4 (winter 1994): 437–59.

Enloe, Cynthia. *Bananas, Beaches, and Bases: Making Feminist Sense of International Politics.* Berkeley: University of California Press, 1990.

Ernst, Robert. "Economic Nativism in New York City during the 1840s." *New York History* 29, no. 2 (1958): 170–86.

———. *Immigrant Life in New York City, 1825–1863* [1949]. Port Washington, N.Y.: Ira Friedman, 1965.

———. "The One and Only Mike Walsh." *New-York Historical Society Quarterly* 26, no. 1 (1952): 43–65.

Feldberg, Michael. *The Philadelphia Riots of 1844: A Study of Ethnic Conflict.* Westport, Conn.: Greenwood, 1975.

Fernández Retamar, Roberto. *Caliban and Other Essays.* Translated by Edward Baker. Minneapolis: University of Minnesota Press, 1989.

Fiedler, Leslie. "Introduction" to *The Monks of Monk Hall* by George Lippard. New York: Odyssey, 1970.

———. *Love and Death in the American Novel.* New York: Stein and Day, 1966.

Fields, Barbara Jeanne. "The Nineteenth-Century American South: History and Theory." *Plantation Society* 2, no. 1 (1983): 7–27.

Fisher, Phil. *Hard Facts: Setting and Form in the American Novel.* New York: Oxford University Press, 1985.

Foley, Neil. *The White Scourge: Mexicans, Blacks, and Poor Whites in Texas Cotton Culture.* Berkeley: University of California Press, 1997.

Foner, Eric. *Free Soil, Free Labor, Free Men: The Ideology of the Republican Party before the Civil War* [1970]. New York: Oxford University Press, 1995.

———. *Politics and Ideology in the Age of the Civil War.* New York: Oxford University Press, 1980.

———. *Reconstruction: America's Unfinished Revolution, 1863–1877.* New York: Harper and Row, 1988.

———. *Tom Paine and Revolutionary America.* New York: Oxford University Press, 1976.

———. "The Wilmot Proviso Revisited." *Journal of American History* 56 (1969): 262–79.

Foner, Philip. *The Anti-Imperialist Reader: A Documentary History of Anti-Imperialism in the United States.* 2 vols. New York: Holmes and Meier, 1984.

———. *A History of Cuba and Its Relations with the United States.* Vol. 2. New York: International Publishers, 1963.

———. *History of the Labor Movement in the United States.* Vol. 1. New York: International Publishers, 1947.

Forbush, Bliss. *Elias Hicks: Quaker Liberal.* New York: Columbia University Press, 1956.

Formisano, Ronald. "The Invention of the Ethnocultural Interpretation." *American Historical Review* (April 1994): 453–77.

———. *The Transformation of Political Culture: Massachusetts Parties, 1790s–1840s.* New York: Oxford University Press, 1983.

Foster, Morris W. *Being Comanche: A Social History of the American Indian Community.* Tucson: University of Arizona Press, 1991.

Foucault, Michel. *Discipline and Punish: The Birth of the Prison.* Translated by Alan Sheridan. New York: Vintage, 1979.

———. *The History of Sexuality: An Introduction.* Vol. 1. Translated by Robert Hurley. New York: Vintage, 1990.

Foucault, Michel, ed. *I, Pierre Rivière, having slaughtered my mother, my sister, and my brother . . .* Harmondsworth: Penguin, 1987.

Franchot, Jenny. *Roads to Rome: The Antebellum Protestant Encounter with Catholicism.* Berkeley: University of California Press, 1994.

Frederickson, George. *The Black Image in the White Mind: The Debate on Afro-American Character and Destiny, 1817–1914.* New York: Harper and Row, 1971.

———. *The Inner Civil War: Northern Intellectuals and the Crisis of the Union.* New York: Harper and Row, 1965.

Fregoso, Rosa Linda, and Angie Chabram. "Chicana/o Cultural Representations: Reframing Alternative Critical Discourses." *Cultural Studies* 4, no. 3 (October 1990): 203–12.

Fuller, John. *The Movement for the Acquisition of All Mexico, 1846–1848.* Baltimore: Johns Hopkins University Press, 1936.

Garber, Marjorie. *Vested Interests: Cross-Dressing and Cultural Anxiety.* New York: Routledge, 1992.

García Canclini, Néstor. *Hybrid Cultures: Strategies for Entering and Leaving Modernity.* Translated by Christopher L. Chiappari and Silvia L. López. Minneapolis: University of Minnesota Press, 1995.

———. *Transforming Modernity: Popular Culture in Mexico.* Translated by Lidia Lozano. Austin: University of Texas Press, 1993.

Gemme, Paola. "Legacy Profile: Ann Sophia Winterbotham Stephens." *Legacy* 12, no. 1 (1995): 47–55.

———. "Rewriting the Indian Tale: Science, Politics, and the Evolution of Ann S. Stephens's Indian Romances." *Prospects* 19 (1994): 376–87.

George, Rosemary. *Burning Down the House: Recycling Domesticity.* Boulder: Westview, 1998.

georgewbush.com website.

Gibson, Charles. *The Aztecs under Spanish Rule: A History of the Indians of the Valley of Mexico, 1519–1810.* Stanford: Stanford University Press, 1964.

Gibson, Charles, ed. *The Black Legend: Anti-Spanish Attitudes in the Old World and the New.* New York: Alfred A. Knopf, 1971.

Gilfoyle, Timothy. *City of Eros: New York City, Prostitution, and the Commercialization of Sex, 1790–1920.* New York: W. W. Norton, 1992.

Gillman, Susan. "The Mulatto, Tragic or Triumphant? The Nineteenth-Century American Race Melodrama." In *The Culture of Sentiment,* edited by Shirley Samuels, 221–43. New York: Oxford University Press, 1992.

Gilroy, Paul. *The Black Atlantic: Modernity and Double Consciousness.* Cambridge: Harvard University Press, 1993.

Glickstein, Jonathan. *Concepts of Free Labor in Antebellum America.* New Haven: Yale University Press, 1991.

Goddu, Teresa. *Gothic America: Narrative, History, and Nation.* New York: Columbia University Press, 1997.

Goldberg, Barry. "Slavery, Race, and the Languages of Class: 'Wage Slaves' and White 'Niggers.'" *New Politics* 3, no. 1 (summer 1991): 65–83.

Gordon, Avery. *Ghostly Matters: Haunting and the Sociological Imagination.* Minneapolis: University of Minnesota Press, 1997.

gorelieberman.com website.

Gorn, Elliot. "'Good-Bye Boys, I Die a True American': Homicide, Nativism, and Working-Class Culture in Antebellum New York City." *Journal of American History* 74, no. 2 (1987): 388–410.

Gossett, Thomas. *Race: The History of an Idea in America.* New York: Schocken, 1963.

Grimsted, David. *American Mobbing, 1828–1861: Toward Civil War.* New York: Oxford University Press, 1998.

———. *Melodrama Unveiled: American Theater and Culture, 1800–1850.* Chicago: University of Chicago Press, 1968.

Gruesz, Kirsten Silva. *Ambassadors of Culture: The Transamerican Origins of Latino Writing.* Princeton: Princeton University Press, 2001.

Guerin-Gonzales, Camille. *Mexican Workers, American Dreams: Immigration, Repatriation, and California Farm Labor, 1900–1939.* New Brunswick, N.J.: Rutgers University Press, 1994.

Gunning, Tom. "An Aesthetic of Astonishment: Early Film and the (In)Credulous Spectator." In *Viewing Positions: Ways of Seeing Film,* edited by Linda Williams, 114–33. New Brunswick, N.J.: Rutgers University Press, 1995.

———. "The Horror of Opacity: The Melodrama of Sensation in the Plays of André de Lorde." In *Melodrama: Stage, Picture, Screen,* edited by Jacky Bratton, Jim Cook, and Christine Gledhill, 50–61. London: British Film Institute, 1994.

Gutiérrez, David. "Significant to Whom? Mexican Americans and the History of the American West." In *A New Significance: Re-Envisioning the History of the American West,* edited by Clyde A. Milner II, 67–89. New York: Oxford University Press, 1996.

———. *Walls and Mirrors: Mexican Americans, Mexican Immigrants, and the Politics of Ethnicity.* Berkeley: University of California Press, 1995.

Gutiérrez, Ramón. "Unraveling America's Hispanic Past: Internal Stratification and Class Boundaries." *Aztlán* 17, no. 1 (spring 1986): 79–102.

———. *When Jesus Came, the Corn Mothers Went Away: Marriage, Sexuality, and Power in New Mexico, 1500–1846.* Stanford: Stanford University Press, 1991.

Gutiérrez-Jones, Carl. *Rethinking the Borderlands: Between Chicano Culture and Legal Discourse.* Berkeley: University of California Press, 1995.

Haas, Lisbeth. *Conquests and Historical Identities in California, 1769–1936.* Berkeley: University of California Press, 1995.

Halberstam, Judith. *Female Masculinity.* Durham: Duke University Press, 1998.

———. *Skin Shows: Gothic Horror and the Technology of Monsters.* Durham: Duke University Press, 1995.

Hale, Charles A. *Mexican Liberalism in the Age of Mora, 1821–1853.* New Haven: Yale University Press, 1968.

Hall, Stuart. "Notes on Deconstructing 'the Popular.'" In *People's History and Socialist Theory,* edited by Raphael Samuel, 227–40. London: Routledge and Kegan Paul, 1981.

———. "What Is This Black in Black Popular Culture?" In *Black Popular Culture,* edited by Gina Dent, 24–33. Seattle: Bay Press, 1992.

Hall, Thomas. "The Transformation of the Mexican Northwest into the American Southwest: Three Paths of Internal Development." In *Rethinking the Nineteenth Century,* edited by Francisco Ramirez, 21–42. Westport, Conn.: Greenwood, 1988.

Halttunen, Karen. *Confidence Men and Painted Women: A Study of Middle-Class Culture in America, 1830–1870.* New Haven: Yale University Press, 1982.

———. "The Domestic Drama of Louisa May Alcott." *Feminist Studies* 10, no. 2 (1984): 233–54.

———. "Early American Narratives: The Birth of Horror." In *The Power of Culture: Critical Essays in American History,* edited by R. W. Fox and T. J. Lears, 67–101. Chicago: University of Chicago Press, 1993.

———. *Murder Most Foul: The Killer and the American Gothic Imagination.* Cambridge: Harvard University Press, 2000.

Hamm, Thomas D. *The Transformation of American Quakerism: Orthodox Friends, 1800–1907.* Bloomington: Indiana University Press, 1988.

Hamnett, Brian. *Juárez*. London: Longman, 1994.

Handlin, Oscar. *Boston's Immigrants: A Study in Acculturation*. Cambridge: Harvard University Press, 1959.

Harris, Cheryl. "Whiteness as Property." *Harvard Law Review* 106, no. 8 (June 1993): 1709–71.

Hart, James. *The Popular Book: A History of America's Literary Taste*. New York: Oxford University Press, 1950.

Hart, John M. "The 1840s Southwestern Mexico Peasants' War: Conflict in a Transitional Society." In *Riot, Rebellion, and Revolution: Rural Social Conflict in Mexico*, edited by Friedrich Katz, 249–68. Princeton: Princeton University Press, 1988.

Hartman, Saidiya. *Scenes of Subjection: Terror, Slavery, and Self-Making in Nineteenth Century America*. New York: Oxford University Press, 1997.

Hartz, Louis. *The Liberal Tradition in America: An Interpretation of American Political Thought since the Revolution* [1955]. New York: Harcourt, Brace, Jovanovich, 1983.

Harvey, Charles. "The Dime Novel in American Life." *Atlantic Monthly* 100 (July 1907): 37–45.

Henkin, David. *City Reading: Written Words and Public Spaces in Antebellum New York*. New York: Columbia University Press, 1998.

Herrera-Sobek, María. *The Mexican Corrido: A Feminist Analysis*. Bloomington: Indiana University Press, 1990.

———. *Northward Bound: The Mexican Immigrant Experience in Ballad and Song*. Bloomington and Indianapolis: Indiana University Press, 1993.

Hietala, Thomas. *Manifest Design: Anxious Aggrandizement in Late Jacksonian America*. Ithaca: Cornell University Press, 1985.

Higgonet, Margaret. "Civil Wars and Sexual Territories." In *Arms and the Woman: War, Gender, and Literary Representation*, edited by Helen M. Cooper et al., 80–96. Chapel Hill: University of North Carolina Press, 1989.

Higham, John. *Strangers in the Land: Patterns of American Nativism, 1860–1925*. New Brunswick, N.J.: Rutgers University Press, 1955.

Hill, Winifred Storrs. *Tarnished Gold: Prejudice during the California Gold Rush*. San Francisco: International Scholars Publications, 1995.

Hirsch, Susan. *Roots of the American Working Class: The Industrialization of Crafts in Newark, 1800–1860*. Philadelphia: University of Pennsylvania Press, 1978.

Hobsbawm, Eric. *The Age of Empire, 1875–1914*. New York: Pantheon, 1987.

———. *Bandits*. New York: Pantheon, 1969.

———. *Primitive Rebels: Studies of Archaic Forms of Social Movement in the Nineteenth and Twentieth Centuries*. New York: Norton, 1959.

Hodge, Francis. *Yankee Theatre: The Image of America on the Stage, 1825–1850*. Austin: University of Texas Press, 1964.

Hogan, Michael. *The Irish Soldiers of Mexico*. Guadalajara: Fondo Editorial Universitario, 1997.

Holt, Michael. *The Political Crisis of the 1850's*. New York: John Wiley and Sons, 1978.

———. *The Rise and Fall of the American Whig Party: Jacksonian Politics and the Onset of the Civil War.* New York: Oxford University Press, 1999.

———. "Winding Roads to Recovery: The Whig Party from 1844 to 1848." In *Essays on Antebellum American Politics, 1840–1860,* edited by Stephen Maizlish and John Kushma, 122–65. College Station: Texas A&M, 1982.

Horkheimer, Max, and Theodor Adorno. *Dialectic of Enlightenment.* Newport, Conn.: Seabury, 1972.

Horsman, Reginald. *Race and Manifest Destiny: The Origins of American Racial Anglo-Saxonism.* Cambridge: Harvard University Press, 1981.

Howard, June. "What Is Sentimentality?" *American Literary History* 11, no. 1 (spring 1999): 63–81.

Howe, Daniel. *The Political Culture of the American Whigs.* Chicago: University of Chicago Press, 1979.

Hu-DeHart, Evelyn. *Yaqui Resistance and Survival: The Struggle for Land and Autonomy, 1821–1920.* Madison: University of Wisconsin Press, 1984.

Hugins, Walter. *Jacksonian Democracy and the Working Class: A Study of the New York Workingmen's Movement, 1829–1837.* Stanford: Stanford University Press, 1960.

Hunt, Michael. *Ideology and U.S. Foreign Policy.* New Haven: Yale University Press, 1987.

Huyssen, Andreas. *After the Great Divide: Modernism, Mass Culture, Postmodernism.* Bloomington: University of Indiana Press, 1986.

Ignatiev, Noel. *How the Irish Became White.* New York: Routledge, 1995.

Ingle, H. Larry. *Quakers in Conflict: The Hicksite Reformation.* Knoxville: University of Tennessee Press, 1986.

Jacobson, Matthew Frye. *Special Sorrows: The Diasporic Imagination of Irish, Polish, and Jewish Immigrants in the United States.* Cambridge: Harvard University Press, 1995.

———. *Whiteness of a Different Color: European Immigrants and the Alchemy of Race.* Cambridge: Harvard University Press, 1998.

James, C. L. R. *American Civilization.* Edited by Anna Grimshaw and Keith Hart. Cambridge: Blackwell, 1993.

Jameson, Fredric. *The Political Unconscious: Narrative as a Socially Symbolic Act.* Ithaca: Cornell University Press, 1981.

———. "Reification and Utopia in Mass Culture." *Social Text* 1 (1979): 130–48.

Jentz, John. "Artisans, Evangelicals, and the City: A Social History of Abolition and Land Reform in Jacksonian New York." Unpublished doctoral dissertation. City University of New York, 1977.

Johannsen, Albert. *The House of Beadle and Adams and Its Dime and Nickel Novels: The Story of a Vanished Literature.* 2 vols. Norman: University of Oklahoma Press, 1950.

Johannsen, Robert. *To the Halls of the Montezumas: The Mexican War in the American Imagination.* New York: Oxford University Press, 1985.

Johnson, Susan Lee. "'A Memory Sweet to Soldiers': The Significance of Gender." In *A New Significance: Re-Envisioning the History of the American West,* edited by Clyde A. Milner II, 255–78. New York: Oxford University Press, 1996.

———. *Roaring Camp: The Social World of the California Gold Rush.* New York: W. W. Norton and Company, 2000.

Jones, Daryl. *The Dime Novel Western.* Bowling Green, Ohio: Popular Press, 1978.

Jordan, Terry G. *German Seed in Texas Soil: Immigrant Farmers in Nineteenth-Century Texas.* Austin: University of Texas Press, 1966.

Joseph, Gilbert. "From Caste War to Class War: The Historiography of Modern Yucatán." *Hispanic American Historical Review* 65, no. 1 (1985): 111–34.

———. "On the Trail of Latin American Bandits: A Reexamination of Peasant Resistance." *Latin American Research Review* 25, no. 3 (1990): 7–53.

———. *Revolution from Without: Yucatán, Mexico, and the United States, 1880–1924.* Cambridge: Cambridge University Press, 1982.

———. "The United States, Feuding Elites, and Rural Revolt in Yucatán, 1836–1915." In *Rural Revolt in Mexico: U.S. Intervention and the Domain of Subaltern Politics,* edited by Daniel Nugent, 173–206. Durham: Duke University Press, 1998.

Joseph, Gilbert, Catherine Legrand, and Ricardo Salvatore. *Close Encounters of Empire: Writing the Cultural History of U.S.–Latin American Relations.* Durham: Duke University Press, 1998.

Joyce, Simon. "Resisting Arrest/Arresting Resistance: Crime Fiction, Cultural Studies, and the 'Turn to History.'" *Criticism* 37, no. 2 (spring 1995): 309–35.

Kaplan, Amy. "Commentary: Domesticating Foreign Policy." *Diplomatic History* 18, no. 1 (winter 1994): 97–105.

———. "'Left Alone with America': The Absence of Empire in the Study of American Culture." In *Cultures of United States Imperialism,* edited by Amy Kaplan and Donald Pease, 3–21. Durham: Duke University Press, 1993.

———. "Manifest Domesticity." *American Literature* 70, no. 3 (September 1998): 581–606.

———. "Romancing the Empire: The Embodiment of American Masculinity in the Popular Historical Novel of the 1890s." *American Literary History* 2, no. 4 (winter 1990): 659–90.

———. "The Spectacle of War in Crane's Revision of History." In *New Essays on the Red Badge of Courage,* edited by Lee Clark Mitchell, 77–108. New York: Cambridge University Press, 1986.

Kaplan, Amy, and Donald Pease, eds. *Cultures of United States Imperialism.* Durham: Duke University Press, 1993.

Kasson, Jay. *Buffalo Bill's Wild West: Celebrity, Memory, and Popular History.* New York: Hill and Wang, 2000.

Katz, Jonathan. "'Homosexuality' and 'Heterosexuality': Questioning the Terms," and "Coming to Terms: Conceptualizing Men's Erotic and Affectional Relations with Men in the United States, 1820–1892." In *A Queer World: The Center for Lesbian and Gay Studies Reader,* edited by Martin Duberman, 177–80, 216–35. New York: New York University Press, 1997.

———. "The Invention of Heterosexuality." *Socialist Review* 20 (1990): 17–34.

Kawaguchi, Lesley. "Diverging Political Affiliations and Ethnic Perspectives: Philadelphia Germans and Antebellum Politics." *Journal of American Ethnic History* 13 (winter 1994): 3–29.

Kelly, Mary. *Private Woman, Public Stage: Literary Domesticity in Nineteenth-Century America.* New York: Oxford University Press, 1984.

Kerber, Linda. "May All Our Citizens Be Soldiers and All Our Soldiers Citizens: The Ambiguities of Female Citizenship in the New Nation." In *Women, Militarism, and War: Essays in History, Politics, and Social Theory*, edited by Jean Elshtain and Sheila Tobias, 89–103. Savage, Md.: Rowman and Littlefield, 1990.

Kicza, John. *The Indian in Latin American History: Resistance, Resilience, and Acculturation.* Wilmington, Del.: Scholarly Resources, 1993.

Knight, Alan. "Mexican Peonage: What Was It and Why Was It?" *Journal of Latin American Studies* 18 (May 1986): 41–72.

Knobel, Dale. *"America for the Americans": The Nativist Movement in the United States.* New York: Twayne Publishers, 1996.

———. *Paddy and the Republic: Ethnicity and Nationality in Antebellum America.* Middletown, Conn.: Wesleyan University Press, 1986.

Kolodny, Annette. *The Land before Her: Fantasy and Experience of the American Frontiers, 1630–1860.* Chapel Hill: University of North Carolina Press, 1984.

———. *The Lay of the Land: Metaphor as Experience and History in American Life and Letters.* Chapel Hill: University of North Carolina Press, 1975.

Koscielski, Frank F. "Encountering the Other: American Soldiers in the Mexican-American War, 1846–1848." In *Papers of the Second Palo Alto Conference*, edited by H. Joseph, A. Knopp, and D. Murphy, 37–42. Brownsville, Tex.: U.S. Department of the Interior, 1997.

Kroeber, Karl. "American Indian Persistence and Resurgence." *boundary 2* 19, no. 3 (fall 1992): 1–25.

Krupat, Arnold. "Postcoloniality and Native American Literature." *Yale Journal of Criticism* 7, no. 1 (1994): 163–80.

LaFeber, Walter. *The Cambridge History of Foreign Relations: The American Search for Opportunity, 1865–1913.* Vol. 2. New York: Cambridge University Press, 1993.

———. *The New Empire: An Interpretation of American Expansion, 1860–1898* [1963]. Ithaca: Cornell University Press, 1998.

Lamar, Howard. "From Bondage to Contract: Ethnic Labor in the American West." In *The Countryside in the Age of Capitalist Transformation: Essays in the Social History of Rural America*, edited by Steven Hahn and Jonathan Prude, 293–326. Chapel Hill: University of North Carolina Press, 1985.

Larralde, Carlos. "Josiah Turner, Juan Cortina, and Carlos Esparza: Veterans of the Mexican War along the Lower Rio Grande." In *Papers of the Second Palo Alto Conference*, edited by H. Joseph, A. Knopp, and D. Murphy, 119–27. Brownsville, Tex.: U.S. Department of the Interior, 1997.

Latta, Frank. *Joaquín Murrieta and His Horse Gangs.* Santa Cruz, Calif.: Bear State Books, 1980.

Laurie, Bruce. *Artisans into Workers: Labor in Nineteenth-Century America.* New York: Noonday, 1989.

———. *Working People of Philadelphia, 1800–1850.* Philadelphia: Temple University Press, 1980.

Leal, Luis. "El Corrido de Joaquín Murrieta: Origen y diffusion." *Mexican Studies/Estudios Mexicanos* 11, no. 1 (winter 1995): 1–23.

———. "Introduccíon." In *Vida Y Aventuras del Más Célebre Bandido Sonorense Joaquín Murrieta,* by Ireneo Paz, 1–95. Houston: Arte Público, 1999.

Leverenz, David. *Manhood and the American Renaissance.* Ithaca: Cornell University Press, 1989.

Levin, David. *History as Romantic Art.* New York: Harcourt, Brace, and Jovanovich, 1959.

Levine, Bruce. *Half Slave and Half Free: The Roots of Civil War.* New York: Hill and Wang, 1992.

———. *The Spirit of 1848: German Immigrants, Labor Conflict, and the Coming of the Civil War.* Urbana: University of Illinois Press, 1992.

Levine, Lawrence. *Highbrow/Lowbrow: The Emergence of Cultural Hierarchy in America.* Cambridge: Harvard University Press, 1988.

Levine, Robert S. *Martin Delany, Frederick Douglass, and the Politics of Representative Identity.* Chapel Hill: University of North Carolina Press, 1997.

Limón, José. *American Encounters: Greater Mexico, the United States, and the Erotics of Culture.* Boston: Beacon Press, 1998.

———. *Mexican Ballads, Chicano Poems: History and Influence in Mexican-American Social Poetry.* Berkeley: University of California Press, 1992.

Linebaugh, Peter. *The London Hanged: Crime and Civil Society in the Eighteenth Century.* Cambridge: Cambridge University Press, 1992.

Lipsitz, George. *The Possessive Investment in Whiteness: How White People Profit from Identity Politics.* Philadelphia: Temple University Press, 1998.

———. " 'Sent for You Yesterday, Here You Come Today': American Studies Scholarship and the New Social Movements." *Cultural Critique* 40 (1998): 203–25.

———. *Time Passages: Collective Memory and American Popular Culture.* Minneapolis: University of Minnesota Press, 1990.

Looby, Christopher. " 'As Thoroughly Black as the Most Faithful Philanthropist Could Desire': Erotics of Race in Higginson's *Army Life in a Black Regiment.*" In *Race and the Subject of Masculinities,* edited by Harry Stecopoulos and Michael Uebel, 71–115. Durham: Duke University Press, 1997.

Lott, Eric. *Love and Theft: Blackface Minstrelsy and the American Working Class.* New York: Oxford University Press, 1993.

Lowe, Lisa. *Immigrant Acts: On Asian American Cultural Politics.* Durham: Duke University Press, 1996.

Maddox, Lucy. *Removals: Nineteenth-Century American Literature and the Politics of Indian Affairs.* New York: Oxford University Press, 1991.

Maizlish, Stephen. "The Meaning of Nativism and the Crisis of the Union: The Know-Nothing Movement in the Antebellum North." In *Essays on Antebellum American Politics, 1840–1860,* edited by Stephen Maizlish and John Kushma, 166–98. College Station: Texas A&M, 1982.

Mallon, Florencia. "Exploring the Origins of Democratic Patriarchy in Mexico: Gender and Popular Resistance in the Puebla Highlands, 1850–1876." In *Women of the Mexican Countryside, 1850–1990: Creating Spaces, Shaping*

Transitions, edited by Heather Fowler-Salamini and Mary Kay Vaughan, 3–26. Tucson: University of Arizona Press, 1994.

———. *Peasant and Nation: The Making of Postcolonial Mexico and Peru.* Berkeley: University of California Press, 1995.

Mandel, Bernard. *Labor, Free and Slave: Workingmen and the Antislavery Movement in the United States.* New York: Associated Authors, 1955.

Marez, Curtis. "Signifying Spain, Becoming Comanche, Making Mexicans: Indian Captivity and the History of Chicana/o Popular Performance." *American Quarterly* 53, no. 2 (2001): 267–307.

Mariscal, George. *Aztlán in Vietnam: Chicano and Chicana Experiences of the War.* Berkeley: University of California Press, 1999.

———. "The Role of Spain in Contemporary Race Theory." *Arizona Journal of Hispanic Cultural Studies* 2 (1998): 7–22.

Martinez, Oscar J., ed. *U.S.-Mexico Borderlands: Historical and Contemporary Perspectives.* Wilmington, Del.: Scholarly Resources, 1996.

Martínez-Fernández, Luis. *Torn between Empires: Economy, Society, and Patterns of Political Thought in the Hispanic Caribbean, 1840–1878.* Athens: University of Georgia Press, 1994.

May, Robert E. *The Southern Dream of a Caribbean Empire, 1854–1861.* Baton Rouge: Louisiana State University Press, 1973.

———. "Young American Males and Filibustering in the Age of Manifest Destiny: The United States Army as a Cultural Mirror." *Journal of American History* 78, no. 3 (December 1991): 857–86.

McCaffrey, James. *Army of Manifest Destiny: The American Soldier in the Mexican War, 1846–1848.* New York: New York University Press, 1992.

McClintock, Anne. *Imperial Leather: Race, Gender, and Sexuality in the Colonial Text.* New York: Routledge, 1995.

———. " 'No Longer in a Future Heaven': Nationalism, Gender, and Race." In *Becoming National: A Reader,* edited by Geoff Eley and Ronald Suny, 260–84. New York: Oxford University Press, 1996.

McConachie, Bruce. *Melodramatic Formations: American Theater and Society.* Iowa City: University of Iowa Press, 1992.

———. "The 'Theatre of the Mob': Apocalyptic Melodrama and Preindustrial Riots in Antebellum New York." In *Theatre for Working-Class Audiences in the United States,* edited by Bruce McConachie and Daniel Friedman, 17–46. Westport, Conn.: Greenwood, 1985.

McDowell, John. "The Corrido of Greater Mexico as Discourse, Music, and Event." In *"And Other Neighborly Names": Social Process and Cultural Image in Texas Folklore,* edited by Richard Bauman and Roger D. Abrahams, 44–75. Austin: University of Texas Press, 1981.

McEniry, Sister Blanche Marie. *American Catholics in the War with Mexico.* Washington, D.C.: Catholic University of America, 1937.

McWilliams, Carey. *North from Mexico: The Spanish Speaking People of the United States.* New York: Greenwood, 1968.

McWilliams, John P. *The American Epic: Transforming a Genre, 1770–1860.* Cambridge: Cambridge University Press, 1989.

Merk, Frederick. *Manifest Destiny and Mission in American History.* Cambridge: Harvard University Press, 1963.

Merriman, John. *The Agony of the Republic: The Repression of the Left in Revolutionary France, 1848–1851.* New Haven: Yale University Press, 1978.

Meyer, Roy W. *History of the Santee Sioux: United States Indian Policy on Trial.* Rev. ed. Lincoln: University of Nebraska Press, 1993.

Michaels, Walter Benn. "Anti-Imperial Americanism." In *Cultures of United States Imperialism,* edited by Kaplan and Pease, 365–91. Durham: Duke University Press, 1993.

———. *Our America: Nativism, Modernism, and Pluralism.* Durham: Duke University Press, 1995.

Miller, Angela. *The Empire of the Eye: Landscape Representation and American Cultural Politics, 1825–1875.* Ithaca: Cornell University Press, 1993.

Miller, D. A. *The Novel and the Police.* Berkeley: University of California Press, 1988.

Miller, Kerby. *Emigrants and Exiles: Ireland and the Irish Exodus to North America.* New York: Oxford University Press, 1985.

Miller, Perry. *Nature's Nation.* Cambridge: Harvard University Press, 1967.

———. *The Raven and the Whale: The War of Words and Wits in the Era of Poe and Melville.* New York: Harcourt, Brace and World, 1956.

Miller, Robert Ryal. *Shamrock and Sword: The Saint Patrick's Battalion in the U.S.-Mexican War.* Norman: University of Oklahoma Press, 1989.

Milner, Clyde A., II, ed. *A New Significance: Re-Envisioning the History of the American West.* New York: Oxford University Press, 1996.

Monaghan, Jay. *Chile, Peru, and the California Gold Rush of 1849.* Berkeley: University of California Press, 1973.

———. *The Great Rascal: The Life and Adventures of Ned Buntline.* New York: Bonanza, 1951.

Monroy, Douglas. *Thrown among Strangers: The Making of Mexican Culture in Frontier California.* Berkeley: University of California Press, 1990.

Monsiváis, Carlos. *Mexican Postcards.* Edited and translated by John Kraniauskas. London and New York: Verso, 1997.

Montejano, David. *Anglos and Mexicans in the Making of Texas, 1836–1986.* Austin: University of Texas Press, 1987.

Montgomery, David. *Beyond Equality: Labor and the Radical Republicans, 1862–1872.* New York: Alfred E. Knopf, 1967.

———. *Citizen Worker: The Experiences of Workers in the United States with Democracy and the Free Market during the Nineteenth Century.* New York: Cambridge University Press, 1993.

———. "The Shuttle and the Cross: Weavers and Artisans in the Kensington Riots of 1844." In *Workers in the Industrial Revolution,* edited by Peter Stearns and David Walkowitz, 44–74. New Brunswick, N.J.: Transaction, 1984.

Moody, Eric. *The Astor Place Riot.* Bloomington: Indiana University Press, 1958.

Morner, Magnus. "The Spanish American Hacienda: A Survey of Recent Research and Debate." *Hispanic American Historical Review* 53, no. 2 (May 1973): 183–216.

Mott, Frank Luther. *Golden Multitudes: The Story of Best Sellers in the United States.* New York: Macmillan, 1947.

———. *A History of American Magazines, 1850–1865.* Cambridge: Harvard University Press, 1938.

Nadel, Stanley. "From the Barricades of Paris to the Sidewalks of New York: German Artisans and the European Roots of American Labor Radicalism." *Labor History* 30, no. 1 (winter 1989): 47–75.

Nash, Gary. *Forging Freedom: The Formation of Philadelphia's Black Community, 1720–1840.* Cambridge: Harvard University Press, 1988.

Nelson, Dana D. *National Manhood: Capitalist Citizenship and the Imagined Fraternity of White Men.* Durham: Duke University Press, 1998.

———. *The Word in Black and White: Reading 'Race' in American Literature, 1638–1867.* New York: Oxford University Press, 1992.

Nerlich, Michael. *Ideology of Adventure: Studies in Modern Consciousness, 1100–1750.* Vol. 1. Translated by Ruth Crowley. Minneapolis: University of Minnesota Press, 1987.

Newfield, Christopher. *The Emerson Effect: Individualism and Submission in America.* Chicago: University of Chicago Press, 1996.

Nichols, David. *Lincoln and the Indians: Civil War Policy and Politics.* Columbia: University of Missouri Press, 1978.

Noble, David W. *The End of American History: Democracy, Capitalism, and the Metaphor of Two Worlds in Anglo-American Historical Writing, 1880–1990.* Minneapolis: University of Minnesota Press, 1995.

Noel, Mary. *Villains Galore: The Heyday of the Popular Story Weekly.* New York: Macmillan, 1954.

Norton, Anne. *Alternative Americas: A Reading of Antebellum Political Culture.* Chicago: University of Chicago Press, 1986.

Nourie, Alan and Barbara Nourie, eds. *American Mass-Market Magazines.* Westport, Conn.: Greenwood, 1990.

Omi, Michael, and Howard Winant. *Racial Formation in the United States: From the 1960s to the 1990s.* 2d. ed. New York: Routledge, 1994.

Osofsky, Gilbert. "Abolitionists, Irish Immigrants, and the Dilemma of Romantic Nationalism." *American Historical Review* 80, no. 4 (1975): 889–912.

Pagden, Anthony. *Spanish Imperialism and the Political Imagination.* New Haven: Yale University Press, 1990.

Paredes, Américo. *Folklore and Culture on the Texas-Mexican Border.* Edited by Richard Bauman. Austin: CMAS, 1993.

———. *"With His Pistol in His Hand": A Border Ballad and Its Hero.* Austin: University of Texas Press, 1958.

Paredes, Raymund. "The Origins of Anti-Mexican Sentiment in the United States." In *New Directions in Chicano Scholarship,* edited by Ricardo Romo and Raymund Paredes, 139–65. La Jolla: University of California, San Diego, 1978.

Parins, James. *John Rollin Ridge: His Life and Works.* Lincoln: University of Nebraska Press, 1991.

Parry, J. H. "The Spaniards in Eastern North America." In *Early Maryland in a Wider World,* edited by David Quinn, 84–102. Detroit: Wayne State University Press, 1982.

Pascoe, Peggy. "Miscegenation Law, Court Cases, and Ideologies of 'Race' in Twentieth-Century America." *Journal of American History* 83, no. 1 (June 1996): 44–69.

Patch, Robert W. "Decolonization, the Agrarian Problem, and the Origins of the Caste War, 1812–1857." In *Land, Labor, and Capital in Modern Yucatan: Essays in Regional History and Political Economy,* edited by Jeffrey Brannon and Gilbert Joseph, 51–82. Tuscaloosa: University of Alabama Press, 1991.

Pateman, Carole. *The Disorder of Women: Democracy, Feminism, and Political Theory.* Stanford: Stanford University Press, 1989.

Pavletich, JoAnn, and Margot Gayle Backus. "With His Pistol in *Her* Hand: Rearticulating the Corrido Narrative in Helena María Viramontes' 'Neighbors.'" *Cultural Critique* 27 (spring 1994): 127–52.

Pease, Donald. "Introduction: National Narratives, Postnational Narration." *Modern Fiction Studies* 43, no. 1 (spring 1997): 1–23.

Perry, Laurens. *Juárez and Diaz: Machine Politics in Mexico.* DeKalb: Northern Illinois University Press, 1978.

Pessen, Edward. *Most Uncommon Jacksonians: Radical Leaders of the Early Labor Movement.* Albany: State University of New York Press, 1967.

Pettit, Arthur. *Images of the Mexican American in Fiction and Film.* College Station: Texas A&M University Press, 1980.

Pitt, Leonard. *The Decline of the Californios: A Social History of the Spanish-Speaking Californians, 1846–1890.* Berkeley: University of California Press, 1970.

Pocock, J.G.A. *The Machiavellian Moment: Florentine Political Thought and the Atlantic Republican Tradition.* Princeton: Princeton University Press, 1975.

Potter, David. *The Impending Crisis, 1848–1861.* New York: Harper and Row, 1976.

Poyo, Gerald. *"With All and For the Good of All": The Emergence of Popular Nationalism in the Cuban Communities of the United States, 1848–1898.* Durham: Duke University Press, 1989.

Pred, Allan. *Urban Growth and City-Systems in the United States, 1840–1860.* Cambridge: Harvard University Press, 1980.

Price, Roger, ed. *Revolution and Reaction: 1848 and the Second French Republic.* London: Croom Helm, 1975.

Ramirez, Francisco, ed. *Rethinking the Nineteenth Century.* Westport, Conn.: Greenwood, 1988.

Reed, Nelson. *The Caste War of Yucatan.* Stanford: Stanford University Press, 1964.

Reina, Leticia. "The Sierra Gorda Peasant Rebellion, 1847–1850." In *Riot, Rebellion, and Revolution: Rural Social Conflict in Mexico,* edited by Friedrich Katz, 269–94. Princeton: Princeton University Press, 1988.

Reséndez, Andrés. "National Identity on a Shifting Border: Texas and New Mexico in the Age of Transition, 1821–1848." *Journal of American History* 86, no. 2 (September 1999): 668–88.

Reynolds, David. *Beneath the American Renaissance: The Subversive Imagination in the Age of Emerson and Melville.* Cambridge: Harvard University Press, 1988.

———. *Faith in Fiction: The Emergence of Religious Literature in America.* Cambridge: Harvard University Press, 1981.

———. *George Lippard, Prophet of Protest: Writings of an American Radical, 1822–1854.* New York: Peter Lang, 1986.

———. "Introduction." In *The Quaker City; or, The Monks of Monk Hall,* by George Lippard, vii–xliv. Amherst: University of Massachusetts Press, 1995.

Reynolds, Larry J. *European Revolutions and the American Literary Renaissance.* New Haven: Yale University Press, 1988.

Richard, Alfred Charles, Jr. *Censorship and Hollywood's Hispanic Image: An Interpretive Filmography, 1936–1955.* Westport, Conn.: Greenwood, 1993.

Ridgely, J. V. "George Lippard's *The Quaker City:* The World of the American Porno-Gothic." *Studies in the Literary Imagination* 7, no. 1 (spring 1974): 77–94.

Roach, Joseph. *Cities of the Dead: Circum-Atlantic Performance.* New York: Columbia University Press, 1996.

Robinson, Cecil. *The View from Chapultepec: Mexican Writers on the Mexican-American War.* Edited and translated by Cecil Robinson. Tucson: University of Arizona Press, 1989.

Rodríguez, Richard. *Days of Obligation: An Argument with My Mexican Father.* New York: Viking, 1992.

Roediger, David. *Towards the Abolition of Whiteness: Essays on Race, Politics, and Working-Class History.* London and New York: Verso, 1994.

———. *The Wages of Whiteness: Race and the Making of the American Working Class.* London and New York: Verso, 1991.

Rogin, Michael Paul. *Blackface, White Noise: Jewish Immigrants in the Hollywood Melting Pot.* Berkeley: University of California Press, 1996.

———. *Fathers and Children: Andrew Jackson and the Subjugation of the American Indian.* New York: Knopf, 1975.

———. *Ronald Reagan, the Movie and Other Episodes in Political Demonology.* Berkeley: University of California Press, 1987.

———. *Subversive Genealogy: The Politics and Art of Herman Melville.* New York: Knopf, 1983.

Rohrbough, Malcolm. *Days of Gold: The California Gold Rush and the American Nation.* Berkeley: University of California Press, 1997.

Romero, Lora. *Home Fronts: Domesticity and Its Critics in the Antebellum United States.* Durham: Duke University Press, 1997.

Rosenberg, Charles. "Sexuality, Class and Role in 19th-Century America." *American Quarterly* 25, no. 2 (May 1973): 131–53.

Ross, Steven. *Workers on the Edge: Work, Leisure and Politics in Industrializing Cincinnati, 1788–1890.* New York: Columbia University Press, 1985.

Roth, Michael. "War Correspondents on the Rio Grande: The Press and America's First Foreign War." In *Papers of the Second Palo Alto Conference,* edited by H. Joseph, A. Knopp, and D. Murphy, 43–49. Brownsville, Tex.: U.S. Department of the Interior, 1997.

Rotundo, E. Anthony. *American Manhood: Transformations in Masculinity from the Revolution to the Modern Era.* New York: Basic, 1993.

Rowe, John Carlos. *Literary Culture and U.S. Imperialism: From the Revolution to World War II*. New York: Oxford University Press, 2000.

Russell, Don. *The Lives and Legends of Buffalo Bill*. Norman: University of Oklahoma Press, 1960.

Said, Edward. *Culture and Imperialism*. New York: Knopf, 1993.

Salas, Elizabeth. *Soldaderas in the Mexican Military: Myth and History*. Austin: University of Texas Press, 1990.

Saldívar, José David. *Border Matters: Remapping American Cultural Studies*. Berkeley: University of California Press, 1997.

———. "Chicano Border Narratives as Cultural Critique." In *Criticism in the Borderlands: Studies in Chicano Literature, Culture, and Ideology*, edited by Héctor Calderón and Saldívar, 167–80. Durham: Duke University Press, 1991.

———. *The Dialectics of Our America: Genealogy, Cultural Critique, and Literary History*. Durham: Duke University Press, 1991.

Saldívar, Ramón. *Chicano Narrative: The Dialectics of Difference*. Madison: University of Wisconsin Press, 1990.

Samuels, Shirley. "Introduction." In *The Culture of Sentiment: Race, Gender, and Sentimentality in Nineteenth-Century America*, edited by Samuels, 3–8. New York: Oxford University Press, 1992.

———. *Romances of the Republic: Women, the Family, and Violence in the Literature of the Early American Nation*. New York: Oxford University Press, 1996.

Samuels, Shirley, ed. *The Culture of Sentiment: Race, Gender, and Sentimentality in Nineteenth-Century America*. New York: Oxford University Press, 1992.

Sánchez, George. *Becoming Mexican-American: Ethnicity, Culture and Identity in Chicano Los Angeles, 1900–1945*. New York: Oxford University Press, 1993.

Sánchez, Rosaura. "Calculated Musings: Richard Rodríguez's Metaphysics of Difference." In *The Ethnic Canon: Histories, Institutions, and Interventions*, edited by David Palumbo-Liu, 153–73. Minneapolis: University of Minnesota Press, 1995.

———. *Telling Identities: The Californio Testimonios*. Minneapolis: University of Minnesota Press, 1995.

Sanchez-Eppler, Karen. *Touching Liberty: Abolition, Feminism, and the Politics of the Body*. Berkeley: University of California Press, 1993.

Sandweiss, Martha, Rick Stewart, and Ben Huseman. *Eyewitness to War: Prints and Daguerreotypes of the Mexican War, 1846–1848*. Washington, D.C.: Smithsonian Institution Press, 1989.

Santoni, Pedro. *Mexicans at Arms: Puro Federalists and the Politics of War, 1845–1848*. Fort Worth: Texas Christian University Press, 1996.

Saxton, Alexander. "Blackface Minstrelsy, Vernacular Comics, and the Politics of Slavery in the North." In *The Meaning of Slavery in the North*, edited by David Roediger and Martin Blatt, 157–75. New York: Garland, 1998.

———. *The Indispensable Enemy: Labor and the Anti-Chinese Movement in California* [1971]. Berkeley: University of California Press, 1995.

———. "Problems of Class and Race in the Origins of the Mass Circulation Press." *American Quarterly* 36, no. 2 (1984): 211–34.

―――. "Race and the House of Labor." In *The Great Fear: Race in the Mind of America,* edited by Gary B. Nash and Richard Weiss, 98–120. New York: Holt, Rinehart, and Winston, 1970.

―――. *The Rise and Fall of the White Republic: Class Politics and Mass Culture in Nineteenth-Century America.* London and New York: Verso, 1990.

Schiller, Dan. *Objectivity and the News: The Public and the Rise of Commercial Journalism.* Philadelphia: University of Pennsylvania Press, 1981.

Schroeder, Albert. "Shifting for Survival in the Spanish Southwest." *New Mexico Historical Review* 43, no. 4 (October 1968): 291–310.

Schroeder, John H. *Mr. Polk's War: American Opposition and Dissent, 1846–1848.* Madison: University of Wisconsin Press, 1973.

Schudson, Michael. *Discovering the News: A Social History of American Newspapers.* New York: Basic, 1978.

Schulte-Sasse, Jochen. "Can the Disempowered Read Mass-Produced Narratives in Their Own Voice?" *Cultural Critique* 10 (fall 1988): 171–99.

Scisco, Louis. *Political Nativism in New York State.* New York: Columbia University Press, 1901.

Scott, Joan. "Gender: A Useful Category for Historical Analysis." *American Historical Review* 91 (1986): 1053–75.

Scott, Rebecca. "Defining the Boundaries of Freedom in the World of Cane: Cuba, Brazil, and Louisiana after Emancipation." *American Historical Review* 99, no. 1 (February 1994): 70–102.

Scroggs, William. *Filibusters and Financiers: The Story of William Walker and His Associates.* New York: Macmillan, 1918.

Sedgwick, Eve Kosofsky. *Between Men: English Literature and Male Homosocial Desire.* New York: Columbia University Press, 1985.

―――. *Epistemology of the Closet.* Berkeley: University of California Press, 1990.

Sellers, Charles. *The Market Revolution: Jacksonian America, 1815–1846.* New York: Oxford University Press, 1991.

Shannon, Fred A. "A Post Mortem on the Labor Safety-Valve Theory." *Agricultural History* 19 (January 1945): 31–37.

Sharpe, Jenny. "Is the United States Postcolonial? Transnationalism, Immigration, and Race." *Diaspora* 4, no. 2 (1995): 181–99.

Siegel, Adrienne. *The Image of the American City in Popular Literature, 1820–1870.* Port Washington, N.Y.: Kennikat, 1981.

Simmons, Merle. *The Mexican Corrido as a Source for Interpretive Study of Modern Mexico (1870–1950).* Bloomington: Indiana University Press, 1957.

Sinkin, Richard. *The Mexican Reform, 1855–1876: A Study in Liberal Nation-Building.* Austin: Institute of Latin American Studies, 1979.

Skurski, Julie. "The Ambiguities of Authenticity in Latin America: *Doña Bárbara* and the Construction of National Identity." In *Becoming National: A Reader,* edited by Geoff Eley and Ronald Suny, 371–402. New York: Oxford University Press, 1996.

Slotkin, Richard. *The Fatal Environment: The Myth of the Frontier in the Age of Industrialization, 1800–1890.* Middletown, Conn.: Wesleyan University Press, 1985.

———. *Gunfighter Nation: The Myth of the Frontier in Twentieth-Century America.* Norman: University of Oklahoma Press, 1998.

———. *Regeneration through Violence: The Mythology of the American Frontier, 1600–1860.* Middletown, Conn.: Wesleyan University Press, 1973.

Smith, Gene, and Jayne Barry Smith, eds. *The Police Gazette.* New York: Simon and Schuster, 1972.

Smith, Henry Nash. *Virgin Land: The American West as Symbol and Myth.* New York: Vintage, 1950.

Smith, Norman D. "Mexican Stereotypes on Fictional Battlefields: or Dime Novels of the Mexican War." *Journal of Popular Culture* 13 (spring 1980): 526–40.

Smith-Rosenberg, Carroll. *Disorderly Conduct: Visions of Gender in Victorian America.* New York: Knopf, 1985.

Somerville, Siobhan. *Queering the Color Line: Race and the Invention of Homosexuality in American Culture.* Durham: Duke University Press, 2000.

Sommer, Doris. *Foundational Fictions: The National Romances of Latin America.* Berkeley: University of California Press, 1991.

Spicer, Jack. *Cycles of Conquest: The Impact of Spain, Mexico, and the United States on the Indians of the Southwest, 1533–1960.* Tucson: University of Arizona Press, 1962.

Standart, Sister Mary Colette. "The Sonoran Migration to California, 1848–1856: A Study in Prejudice." In *Between Two Worlds: Mexican Immigrants in the United States,* edited by David G. Gutiérrez, 3–21. Wilmington, Del.: Scholarly Resources, 1996.

Stanley, Amy Dru. *From Bondage to Contract: Wage Labor, Marriage, and the Market in the Age of Slave Emancipation.* Cambridge: Cambridge University Press, 1998.

Stansell, Christine. *City of Women: Sex and Class in New York, 1789–1860.* Urbana: University of Illinois Press, 1987.

Stanton, William. *The Leopard's Spots: Scientific Attitudes toward Race in America, 1815–1859.* Chicago: University of Chicago Press, 1960.

Steinbeck, John. *The Harvest Gypsies: On the Road to the Grapes of Wrath* [1936]. Berkeley: Heyday, 1988.

Steinhauer, Dale. "The Immigrant Soldier in the Regular Army during the Mexican War." In *Papers of the Second Palo Alto Conference,* edited by H. Joseph, A. Knopp, and D. Murphy, 57–68. Brownsville, Tex.: U.S. Department of the Interior, 1997.

Stephanson, Anders. *Manifest Destiny: American Expansion and the Empire of Right.* New York: Hill and Wang, 1995.

Stern, Julia. *The Plight of Feeling: Sympathy and Dissent in the Early American Novel.* Chicago: University of Chicago Press, 1998.

Stern, Madeleine, ed. *Publishers for Mass Entertainment in Nineteenth-Century America.* Boston: G.K. Hall, 1980.

———. *We the Women: Career Firsts of Nineteenth-Century America.* New York: Schulte Publishing Company, 1963.

Stoler, Ann Laura. "Carnal Knowledge and Imperial Power: Gender, Race, and Morality in Colonial Asia." In *Feminism and History,* edited by Joan Wallach Scott, 209–66. New York: Oxford University Press, 1996.

———. *Race and the Education of Desire: Foucault's History of Sexuality and the Colonial Order of Things.* Durham: Duke University Press, 1995.

Stoler, Ann Laura, and Frederick Cooper. "Between Metropole and Colony: Rethinking a Research Agenda." In *Tensions of Empire: Colonial Cultures in a Bourgeois World,* edited by Frederick Cooper and Ann Laura Stoler, 1–56. Berkeley: University of California Press, 1997.

Stott, Richard. *Workers in the Metropolis: Class, Ethnicity, and Youth in Antebellum New York City.* Ithaca: Cornell University Press, 1990.

Stout, Janis. *Sodoms in Eden: The City in American Fiction before 1860.* Westport, Conn.: Greenwood, 1976.

Strachwitz, Chris. "The Singers." In *Mexican-American Border Music.* Vols. 6 and 7. *Corridos and Tragedias de la Frontera.* El Cerrito: Arhoolie Records, 1994.

Streeby, Shelley. "Haunted Houses: George Lippard, Nathaniel Hawthorne, and Middle-Class America." *Criticism* 38, no. 3 (1996): 443–72.

Sundquist, Eric. "The Literature of Expansion and Race." In *The Cambridge History of American Literature.* Vol. 2. Edited by Sacvan Bercovitch, 125–328. Cambridge: Cambridge University Press, 1995.

Thelen, David. "Rethinking History and the Nation-State: Mexico and the United States." *Journal of American History* 86, no. 2 (September 1999): 439–52.

Theweleit, Klaus. *Male Fantasies. Vol. 2: Male Bodies: Psychoanalyzing the White Terror.* Translated by Erica Carter and Chris Turner. Minneapolis: University of Minnesota Press, 1989.

Tomich, Dale. "The 'Second Slavery': Bonded Labor and the Transformation of the Nineteenth-Century World Economy." In *Rethinking the Nineteenth Century,* edited by Francisco Ramirez, 103–17. Westport, Conn.: Greenwood, 1988.

Tompkins, Jane. *Sensational Designs: The Cultural Work of American Fiction.* New York: Oxford University Press, 1985.

———. *West of Everything: The Inner Life of Westerns.* New York: Oxford University Press, 1992.

Tonkovich, Nicole. "Guardian Angels and Missing Mothers: Race and Domesticity in *Winona* and *Deadwood Dick on Deck.*" *Western American Literature* 32, no. 3 (fall 1997): 240–64.

Trachtenberg, Alan. *Reading American Photographs: Images as History, Matthew Brady to Walker Evans.* New York: Hill and Wang, 1989.

Turner, Frederick Jackson. *Rereading Frederick Jackson Turner: 'The Significance of the Frontier in American History' and Other Essays.* Edited by John Mack Faragher. New York: Holt, 1994.

Tutino, John. *From Insurrection to Revolution in Mexico: Social Bases of Agrarian Violence.* Princeton: Princeton University Press, 1986.

———. "Life and Labor on North Mexican Haciendas: The Querétaro–San Luis Potosí Region, 1775–1810." In *El Trabajo y los Trabajadores en la História de México,* edited by Elsa Frost, Michael Meyer, and Josefina Vázquez, 339–78. Tucson: University of Arizona Press, 1979.

Tuveson, Ernest. *Redeemer Nation: The Idea of America's Millennial Role.* Chicago: University of Chicago Press, 1968.

Tyler, Ronnie C. "Historic Reportage and Artistic License: Prints and Paintings of the Mexican War." In *Picturing History: American Painting, 1770–1830*, edited by William Ayres, 101–15. New York: Rizzoli, 1993.

———. *The Mexican War: A Lithographic Record*. Austin: Texas State Historical Society, 1973.

Valdés-Ugalde, Francisco. "Janus and the Northern Colossus: Perceptions of the United States in the Building of the Mexican Nation." *Journal of American History* 86, no. 2 (September 1999): 568–600.

Van Alstyne, Richard. *The Rising American Empire*. New York: W. W. Norton, 1960.

Vance, Linda. "Women and the Mexican War." In *Papers of the Second Palo Alto Conference*, edited by H. Joseph, A. Knopp, and D. Murphy, 51–56. Brownsville, Tex.: U.S. Department of the Interior, 1997.

Vanderwood, Paul. *Disorder and Progress: Bandits, Police, and Mexican Development*. Wilmington, Del.: Scholarly Resources, 1992.

Van Young, Eric. *Hacienda and Market in Eighteenth-Century Mexico: The Rural Economy of the Guadalajara Region, 1675–1820*. Berkeley: University of California Press, 1981.

Varley, James. *The Legend of Joaquin Murrieta: California's Gold Rush Bandit*. Twin Falls, Idaho: Big Lost River, 1995.

Vevier, Charles. "American Continentalism: An Idea of Expansion, 1845–1910." *American Historical Review* 65, no. 2 (1960): 323–35.

Viliesid, Lorena Careaga. " 'Ho! For Yucatan!': Los Voluntarios Norteamericanos Despues de la Guerra Con Mexico." In *Papers of the Second Palo Alto Conference*, edited by H. Joseph, A. Knopp, and D. Murphy, 110–18. Brownsville, Tex.: U.S. Department of the Interior, 1997.

Wald, Priscilla. *Constituting Americans: Cultural Anxiety and Narrative Form*. Durham: Duke University Press, 1995.

Walker, Cheryl. *Indian Nation: Native American Literature and Nineteenth-Century Nationalisms*. Durham: Duke University Press, 1997.

Wallerstein, Immanuel. *The Capitalist World-Economy*. Cambridge: Cambridge University Press, 1979.

———. "Should We Unthink the Nineteenth Century?" In *Rethinking the Nineteenth Century*, edited by Francisco Ramirez, 185–91. Westport, Conn.: Greenwood, 1988.

Warner, Michael. "The Mass Public and the Mass Subject." In *Habermas and the Public Sphere*, edited by Craig Calhoun, 377–401. Cambridge: MIT Press, 1992.

Weber, David J. *The Mexican Frontier, 1821–1846: The American Southwest under Mexico*. Albuquerque: University of New Mexico Press, 1982.

———. *The Spanish Frontier in North America*. New Haven: Yale University Press, 1992.

Weinberg, Albert. *Manifest Destiny: A Study of Nationalist Expansionism in American History*. Gloucester, Mass.: Peter Smith, 1948.

Wells, Allen. "Yucatán: Violence and Social Control on Henequen Plantations." In *Other Mexicos: Essays on Regional Mexican History*, edited by T. Benjamin and W. McNellie, 213–41. Albuquerque: University of New Mexico Press, 1984.

Wertheimer, Eric. *Imagined Empires: Incas, Aztecs, and the New World of American Literature, 1771–1876.* Cambridge: Cambridge University Press, 1999.

Wexler, Laura. "Tender Violence: Literary Eavesdropping, Domestic Fiction, and Educational Reform." In *The Culture of Sentiment: Race, Gender, and Sentimentality in Nineteenth-Century America,* edited by Shirley Samuels, 9–38. New York: Oxford University Press, 1992.

Wheelwright, Julie. *Amazons and Military Maids: Women Who Dressed as Men in Pursuit of Life, Liberty, and Happiness.* London: Pandora, 1989.

Widmer, Edward. *Young America: The Flowering of Democracy in New York City.* New York: Oxford University Press, 1999.

Wilentz, Sean. *Chants Democratic: New York City and the Rise of the American Working Class, 1788–1850.* New York: Oxford University Press, 1984.

Williams, Linda. "Melodrama Revised." In *Refiguring American Film Genres: History and Theory,* edited by Nick Browne, 43–87. Berkeley: University of California Press, 1998.

Williams, Raymond. *Culture and Society, 1780–1950.* New York: Columbia University Press, 1983.

———. *Marxism and Literature.* New York: Oxford University Press, 1977.

Winders, Richard. *Mr. Polk's Army: The American Military Experience in the Mexican War.* College Station: Texas A&M University Press, 1997.

Wynn, Dennis. *The San Patricio Soldiers: Mexico's Foreign Legion.* El Paso: Texas Western Press, 1984.

Young, Elizabeth. *Disarming the Nation: Women's Writing and the American Civil War.* Chicago: University of Chicago Press, 1999.

Young, Robert J. C. *Colonial Desire: Hybridity in Theory, Culture and Race.* New York: Routledge, 1995.

Yoval-Davis, Nira, and Floya Anthias. *Woman-Nation-State.* New York: St. Martin's, 1989.

Zahler, Helene. *Eastern Workingmen and National Land Policy, 1829–1862.* New York: Columbia University Press, 1941.

Zboray, Ronald. "Antebellum Reading and the Ironies of Technological Innovation." In *Reading in America: Literature and Social History,* edited by Cathy N. Davidson, 182–91. Baltimore: Johns Hopkins University Press, 1989.

———. *A Fictive People: Antebellum Economic Development and the American Reading Public.* New York: Oxford University Press, 1993.

Ziff, Larzer. *Literary Democracy: The Declaration of Cultural Independence in America.* New York: Viking, 1981.

Index

Text: 10/13 Sabon
Display: Sabon
Compositor: Impressions Book and Journal Services, Inc.
Printer/binder: Sheridan Books, Inc.